# HENRI LANGLOIS

First Citizen of Cinema

# TWAYNE'S FILMMAKERS SERIES

# HENRI LANGLOIS

First Citizen of Cinema

**Glenn Myrent and Georges P. Langlois**

**Translated from the French by Lisa Nesselson**
**Preface by Akira Kurosawa**

TWAYNE PUBLISHERS
AN IMPRINT OF SIMON & SCHUSTER MACMILLAN
NEW YORK

PRENTICE HALL INTERNATIONAL
LONDON • MEXICO CITY • NEW DEHLI • SINGAPORE • SYDNEY • TORONTO

Twayne's Filmmakers Series

*Henri Langlois: First Citizen of Cinema*
Glenn Myrent and Georges P. Langlois

Twayne Publishers
An Imprint of Simon & Schuster Macmillan
866 Third Avenue
New York, New York 10022

Library of Congress Cataloging-in-Publication Data

Langlois, Georges Patrick.
   [Henri Langlois, premier citoyen du cinéma. English]
   Henri Langlois, first citizen of cinema / by Glenn Myrent & Georges Langlois ; translated from the French by Lisa Nesselson.
   Translation of: Henri Langlois, premier citoyen du cinéma / Georges Patrick Langlois, Glenn Myrent.
      p.   cm.—(Twayne's filmmakers series)
   Includes bibliographical references and index.
   ISBN 0–8057–4522–X. — ISBN 0–8057–4521–1 (pbk.)
   1. Langlois, Henri, 1914–1977. 2. Cinémathèque française. 3. Motion pictures—Collectors and collecting—France—Biography.
   I. Myrent, Glenn. II. Title. III. Series.
PN1998.3.L38L3613 1994
026'.79143'092—dc20
[B]                                                                                  94–27336
                                                                                          CIP

The paper used in this publication meets the minimum requirements of American National Standard for Information Sciences—Permanence of Paper for Printed Library Materials. ANSI Z3948–1984. ∞™

10 9 8 7 6 5 4 3 2 1 (hc)
10 9 8 7 6 5 4 3 2 1 (pb)

Printed in the United States of America

In memory of Annie Langlois, who made
Henri's life and that of the Cinémathèque Française a reality,
and
for Lisa Nesselson, who has twice made this book a reality, first as
the inspiration for the French edition and now as the translator for
this English-language edition

# CONTENTS

# FOREWORD

## REMEMBERING LANGLOIS

I have at my house on the wall of my office a large photo of Henri Langlois. It was given to me by Mary Meerson. It's a color photo in which we see him reclining on a bench, in what seems to be a park, his head resting on his arm.

This nonchalant pose is so much *him* that at any given moment it reminds me of the Henri Langlois that I knew so well, who was alive and full of fire.

When I look at this photo I can't believe he is dead. On the contrary, I see his imposing silhouette tirelessly running through the rooms of the Cinema Museum at the Cinémathèque in the Palais de Chaillot.

In reality, Henri Langlois still lives on in my heart.

By way of illustration, I have one unforgettable memory: It was Langlois who passionately urged me to make color films. I objected because, on the one hand, not all of the technical problems had been solved regarding the quality of the color film stock and, on the other hand, I just didn't feel prepared, technically, to make a film in color. Langlois then dragged me into the Cinémathèque's screening room and showed me the scenes in color from *Ivan the Terrible*.

"What do you say to that? Eisenstein knew how to use color—and that was dozens of years ago!"

It was because of this that I made my decision to shoot in color and as a first experiment, I shot *Dodescaden*. After making *Dersou Ouzala*, I was finally able in *Kagemusha* to reach the level where I freely used color in my own way.

But when *Kagemusha* was selected for Cannes, Henri Langlois was no longer of this earth—and yet he was still the one person to whom I most yearned to show my film.

During the premiere of *Kagemusha* in Japan, a number of filmmakers and actors came from the United States and I told them of my wish. That was when William Wyler's wife said these kind and unforgettable words:

"You know Kurosawa-san, Henri Langlois will surely be at Cannes to see your film."*

Even more so than for *Kagemusha*, I would have liked for Henri Langlois to see *Ran*.

So, I believe he was there in the vast audience that came to see *Ran* when it was projected outdoors in front of the Pompidou Center in Paris.

Akira Kurosawa

* Upon receiving the palme d'or best prize at Cannes for *Kagemusha* in 1980, Akira Kurosawa dedicated the film to Henri Langlois and at the press conference said that he came to the Festival to show his film to H.L.

# ACKNOWLEDGMENTS

People often ask how I ended up in France. "I took an airplane, flew towards England, and turned right" is my usual smart-aleck reply.

I had never been out of the United States before 4 September 1975, when I landed in Paris to study French film for one year. I met Henri Langlois a week later, and the following yearlong exposure to life at the Cinémathèque Française changed my life, as it had for so many young men and women before. I fell in love once again with the movies.

Henri Langlois fascinated me to such an extent that I wanted to make a documentary about him, the Cinémathèque, and film preservation. With the help of a videotape production company called Video in Paris, I shot an interview with Langlois in his museum in March 1976. The project eventually fell apart for lack of funds and lost its star upon Langlois's death in January 1977. I was told later by François Truffaut, among others, that a film glorifying Langlois did not interest him. He recommended, however, that if I wanted to write a biography, he would grant an interview and share all he knew.

As with any investigative research, the more people I talked to, the more people I felt I needed to talk to. I thus crossed paths with Georges Langlois, who revealed after a few meetings that he, too, had a project for a book on his brother; he suggested that by combining our efforts, a much better volume would result. Having been the Cinémathèque's lawyer, Georges Langlois brought to the work mountains of legal documents and personal papers connected with the Cinémathèque's history; more important, he illuminated his brother's life with many firsthand memories.

Photographer Hugues Langlois, Georges's son, devoted entire days to tracking down some 100 photographs and helped to shape the French edition, which was published in September 1986. Without Hugues Langlois's dedication, the French edition would not exist, and without him, there is a good chance that Henri Langlois's museum would be presently in crates looking for a home.

We would like to thank the following people, who participated at one moment or another in Henri Langlois's life, for their generous time and effort in reconstructing the story:

Jocelyne Abbondante, Walter Alberti, Nestor Almendros, Kenneth Anger, Hubert Astier, Janine Bazin, Yannick Bellon, Suzanne Bidault, Agnes Bleier-Brody, Sonika Bo, Pierre Bracquemond, Florian Brody, James Broughton, Freddy Buache, James Card, Alberto Cavalcanti, Henri Colpi, Gianni Comencini, Costa-Gavras, Simone Cottance, Ralph Culpepper, Thomas Quinn Curtiss, Anatole Dauman, Marianne de Fleury, Hugues de Kerret, Sybille de Luze, Yvonne Dornès, Max Douy, Jean Dréville, Robert Edmonds, Pierre Eggimann, Lotte Eisner, Marie Epstein, Paul Falkenberg, Jacques Flaud, Charles Ford, Eve Francis, Georges Franju;

Alain Gabet, Farrokh Gaffary, Louis-Emile Galey, Philippe Garrel, Jean Gonnet, Maurice Gras, Frederick Gronich, Yilmaz Guney, Jean Guyard, Curtis Harrington, Charles Heimberger, André Holleaux, Claude Jaeger, Françoise Jaubert, Tom Johnston, Slavka Jovanovic, Pierre Kast, Kashiko Kawakita, Henri Klarsfeld, Arthur Knight, Akira Kurosawa, Ado Kyrou, André Laporte, Henri Lartigue, Jean-Paul Le Chanois, Guy Lemaitre, Jay Leyda, Marcel L'Herbier, Lucie Lichtig, Renée Lichtig, Serge Losique, Madeleine Malthête-Méliès, Alain Marchand, Bernard Martinand, Mary Meerson, Marion Michelle, Jean Mitry, Jack Moseley;

Geneviève Novik, William Novik, David Overbey, Jean Painlevé, Vlada Petric, Francine Pilato, Pierre Prévert, James Quinn, Jean Raine, Alain Resnais, Jean Riboud, Pierre Riedinger, André Rieupeyrout, Michel Rittener, Jacques Rivette, Raymond Rohauer, Frédéric Rossif, Jean Rouch, Edgar Roulleau, Georges Roulleau, Ken Russell, Jacques Saada, Volker Schlöndorff, Werner Schroeter, Noël Simsolo, Eugene Stavis, Henri Storck, Virginia Storck, Jean-Charles Tacchella, André Thirifays, Jerzy Toeplitz, Alexandre Trauner, François Truffaut, Denise Tual, Jack Valenti, Orson Welles, and Basil Wright.

We would like to express our gratitude to the former president of the Cinémathèque Française, Costa-Gavras, for recommending the manuscript to the French publisher Denoël; to Akira Kurosawa for meeting with us in Paris and for writing the foreword, and to Catherine Cadou for translating it into French; and to Serge Losique, president of the Montreal Film Festival, for some wonderful images of Henri, including the title for this book.

Noëlle Giret, former director of the Cinémathèque's library and museum, and Marianne de Fleury deserve praise for sharing with us documents found at the Cinémathèque, as does the Cinémathèque Française's library staff: Nadine Tenèze, Valdo Kneubuhler, and Michel Boule; the IDHEC library staff: Jacqueline Vairel, Marion Cress, Marie-Christine de Jabrun, and Hervé Regignano; the Cinémathèque Photothèque staff: Catherine Ficat and Marie Borel; the photo lab staff of the Cinémathèque: Daniel Keryzaouen and Jean-Pierre Jolly; and the Henri Langlois Cinema Museum staff: Alain Gabet, Danielle Kenzey, and Bruno Colomb.

François Truffaut merits a special note of thanks. He asked me one day in September 1979 if I wondered why he was helping me so much by answering my questions, opening his files, photocopying anything I asked for, and, especially, introducing me to Jean Riboud, Pierre Kast, and Janine Bazin. He proceeded to explain that he loved books and wanted to read a biography of Langlois. Life came in third place for François Truffaut, after movies and books.

Our thanks also to Geneviève and William Novik, Krishna Riboud, Pierre Cardin, and Mary Meerson, in memory of some exceptional evenings evoking the memory of Henri Langlois; to Dudley Andrew, Wendy Dozoretz, John Kuiper, Jean-Louis Langlois, Antoine de la Morinerie, Henri and Virginia Storck, Brigitte van der Elst, and François Laffort, for general information and introductions; to Marcel and Christiane Couvreur, for loaning a place to write; to Richard Abel, Robert Edmonds, Eve Ettighoffer, Farrakh Gaffary, Marvin Israel, Claudine Kaufmann, Gerald Mead, Jack Moseley, Elizabeth Saintesprit, and Madeleine Weiller, for reading passages of the book in progress and offering advice; and to Véronique Boscher and Paul Linhardt, for Apple computer information.

For the English-language edition, a word of thanks to Professor Frank Beaver of the University of Michigan for recommending Twayne Publishers; to Roberta Winston for copyediting at Twayne; and to Mark Zadrozny, Twayne senior editor, for his continued devotion to the project.

Thank you, Pepe Diniz and William Klein, for your masterful photos.

And for having put up with us all these years: Georges and Eva Adamczyk, Geneviève Blanc, Bonbon, Andy Borson, Mark and Susan Butterman, Luce Carel, Dominique Couvreur, Jean-François Couvreur, Geneviève Duchâteau, Abder Gharbi, Marc and Christine Guillier, Jill Kaplan, Karen Kaplan, Mitou, Debra Myrent, Kari Nesselson, Isobel and Gene Nesselson, Edward Noeltner, Piblette, Stan Pressner, Jeanne Quillard, Patrick and Chantal Quillart, Steve Rivele, James Ruebsamen, Squishem, Valérie Stark, Tippa, Akiko Tsuda, and Melanie Weiss.

Thanks to Suzanne Langlois for her hospitality and support.

For the English-language edition, *un grand merci* à David Roth for the flip-book. Please show it to Vortek Bijndt.

Finally, to Sylvia and Carl Myrent: Now you'll have a better idea why I've spent all these years in France.

# chapter 1

## THE TIME MACHINE

I was born on 13 November 1914, in Smyrna.

My parents were French but we lived in Turkey, which gave me the chance to be about a century behind the times.

My mother's grandfather, who was a doctor in the Imperial Court, immigrated to Smyrna in 1815. My mother, who was American on her father's side, belonged to a Bostonian family noted for its many artists. Her first cousin was ambassador to the United States.

My father, a journalist, was from Angers. One of my uncles was director of the Spanish branch of the Phoenix Insurance Company, another uncle was director of the Nationale Insurance Company in Egypt, and the last of my uncles was a senator.

I am the black sheep of the family. I loved the cinema too much.

Henri Langlois

Henri Langlois believed in the irrational, in the invisible, and in miracles. Born on Friday the thirteenth—a day of luck, according to his personal system of numerology—he would also die on the thirteenth, 62 years later, in January 1977, in Paris. His life was inseparable from that of his creation, the Cinémathèque Française. For the Cinémathèque was more than an archive, a museum, a haven for all things filmic—it was his flesh and blood, his child, his family, his home. Henri Langlois loved the cinema too much . . .

August 1914: War had broken out in Europe. Leaving his wife, six months pregnant, in Smyrna, Gustave Langlois returned to France to rejoin his regiment. From Toulon, he started back across the Mediterranean Sea, this time for the Gallipoli campaign. The end of the war did not mean an immediate return to Smyrna for Gustave, who had been wounded and decorated, then promoted to the Intelligence Bureau. After the Armistice he was assigned to the French consulate in Geneva, where certain conditions pertaining to the division of the Ottoman Empire were to be discussed at length. Therefore, it was not until April 1919 (the same time that Greek troops once again took control of the city, temporarily making it part of Greece) that Gustave returned home. His son Henri was already almost five years old.

Gustave Langlois was devoted to his family but failed to recognize anything of himself in Henri, an inveterate dreamer who seemed perpetually intrigued by some distant and glorious vision that he alone could see. Henri's eyes were like one-way mirrors, behind which something was happening that Gustave could not understand.

Father-son conflict continued until the mid-1930s, creating friction between a father who wished only for his son's scholastic success and a son who dreamed only about the movies. Henri's exceptional personality already seemed to single him out for a destiny so unconventional that Gustave Langlois couldn't help but wonder from what distant ancestor his son might herald.

Gustave was determined not to leave this world without having arrived at some plausible explanation for Henri's bent of character. One icy evening during the German Occupation and shortly before his death, Gustave gathered up all the Langlois family documents and, extending the dining room table with all three leaves for the occasion, spread them out in search of a clue to the enigma. A long sheet of brown wrapping paper filled with notes, speculations, and possible clues lay before him. Mary Meerson, Henri's companion, sidekick, sounding board, and all-purpose soulmate, came upon Gustave lost in his thoughts:

> "What's all this?" asked Mary. "Are you studying geography?"
>
> "No," answered Gustave. "Genealogy."
>
> Mary caught on immediately.
>
> "So you're trying to make sense of Henri, huh? Then don't bother with the Langlois side of the family—just take a look on your wife's side of the family tree. Look at the maternal branches: the Cros, Braggiotti, and Delanda families. That's where you'll find Henri's true ancestors—the dukes, the archbishops, the Venetian captains. As for me, I'll tell you this much: Your son is the explorer of a new age, the Age of the Image! Keep working your way back and you'll find the man you're looking for. Henri is none other than Marco Polo!"

Whether one chose to humor Mary or take her at her word about the strength of Mr. Polo's hereditary contribution to a twentieth-century descendant, Henri's ancestors were definitely an interesting bunch. Take Dr. Gaspard-François Cros, Henri's maternal great-grandfather, who was born in Montpellier in 1758. By the time he moved to Paris, he had earned degrees in medicine and was a master surgeon. His professional knowledge and skill allowed him to pass through the Revolution unscathed, before becoming one of young General Bonaparte's personal physicians.

Some choice bit of information to which Cros was privy proved important enough to change the course of his life. What was Dr. Cros's deep dark secret? We shall never know. The Langlois family tradition tells us only that one day Joséphine threw herself at the doctor's feet, begging him to reveal nothing to her husband. But Napoléon had his redoubtable secret police, and Dr. Gaspard Cros, increasingly uneasy with the burden of professional secrecy, decided to go into exile rather than risk Napoléon's wrath.

He boarded a boat in Marseilles for a long voyage with no particular destination. Having tired of Genoa, hesitated at Venice, stopped over in Athens, and rejected the Greek Isles as too rustic, Cros eventually arrived at the gulf of Smyrna. A glimpse of the harbor—one of the most magnificent and most secure in all Asia Minor—immediately told the doctor his wanderings were at an end. He was charmed by the cloudless sky and the cobalt blue sea, features that while predating the invention of photography and therefore of photo-bearing postcards, provided a postcard-perfect backdrop to the majestic city itself. Smyrna was built along the side of Mount Pagus, and the evocative ruins of a Byzantine fort dominated the skyline.

Gaspard Cros decided to make his new home in Smyrna, where highly favorable treaty conditions enabled the French to settle, circulate, set up shop, and enjoy the privilege of jurisdiction. The doctor founded the French Hospital as well as a family, and died respected and lamented by all at the age of 83. He carried the Empress Joséphine's secret to his grave.

His granddaughter, Marie Cros, known to friends and family as Maraya, would become Henri Langlois's maternal grandmother. The artful photos Henri took of her as an elderly woman show her dressed in gray or black with her white hair in a chignon and her bifocals perched on her nose. Maraya was the family's oral historian and delighted Henri and his brother Georges with peerless stories plucked from her memories.

She had acquired American citizenship by her marriage to George Braggiotti, a native of Charleston, South Carolina. Her grandsons especially loved to hear her descriptions of huge southern plantations. Henri took pride in reminding others that he was one-fourth American.

"Look on your wife's side of the family tree," had been Mary Meerson's advice to Gustave Langlois. Some exceptional women certainly did figure among Henri's ancestors. His other grandmother, Catherine, for example, who was sister to a young diplomat by the name of Count Delenda.

The story of the Delenda family was perfect to stoke young Henri's daydreams of chivalry and grandeur. After the fall of Jerusalem in 1099, Catalonian warriors fought Frankish knights over Greece and its islands. Emerging triumphant, the Catalonians inaugurated the new duchy of Athens and Néopatras. Thus had Francisco Delenda, belonging to a ducal family, come to settle in Thebes, before his descendants received in fief the island of Naxos, then capital of the Cyclades.

Henri often thought back on this family whose illustrious name resembled a battle cry, shouted forth in the thick of combat to provoke one's adversaries. The Latin expression *Delenda est!* (must be destroyed) became Henri's personal battle cry, flung at his dumbfounded classmates to express his unconditional determination to realize his ideas, which others did not understand.

Henri-Ferdinand Langlois, Henri's grandfather, met Catherine Delenda in Port Said at a masked ball given in honor of the Empress Eugénie, who had come to help inaugurate the Suez Canal.

Although Henri-Ferdinand had come to Egypt on temporary assignment as a journalist, he could not bring himself to return to France once his mission was over, for he had fallen in love with the beautiful Miss Delenda. They were not wed until 1879, after Henri-Ferdinand had become a merchant in order to assure himself of more stable employment. He was, however, soon bitten anew by demon journalism and decided to move to Smyrna in order to found the Agence nationale française, which gathered world news reports and disseminated them to Smyrna's large European community and to Europeans throughout the Middle East. And it was in Smyrna that Henri-Ferdinand and Catherine's son, Gustave, would meet and marry Annie Braggiotti.

Henri Langlois's personality was firmly grounded in his beloved birthplace and the events he experienced there as a boy. The attachment ran deep, for in his eyes, Smyrna was a prime example of a lost masterpiece that no one had been able to save. He would one day discover that there were other masterpieces, already lost for the most part or threatened with imminent destruction. Whatever genius they held was not chiseled in stone or hammered in metal but lay instead in the lit and shadowed gradations of emulsion clinging to a fragile strip of nitrocellulose or celluloid. And these reels of film were, like Smyrna at the brink of the 1920s, poised to perish in flames.

Who still remembers the Smyrna of Henri's boyhood? Rebuilt under the name of Izmir, this new city of modern Turkey with its palaces and skyscrapers has little in common with its predecessor, save an admirable location. But until 1922, the city—whose founder, Tantale, king of Lydia, named it for the Amazon Smyrna, mother of Adonis—had lost nothing of its legends or its history.

Smyrna was part of the Greek Empire when, in 1084, Tzachas the Turk overran it. Thirteen years later, the Greek admiral Jean Ducas wrested back the city, which, through the centuries, was to remain a much-sought-after prize. The Turks would reclaim it, only to be bested by the Christians. Tamerlane razed the city and, using an architectural technique that has thankfully fallen into disuse, mixed the heads of 1,000 prisoners into the mortar of a stone tower raised in recognition of the conqueror. After many a battle, the city became Turkish once again in 1424 and would remain, its Hellenism intact, attached to the Ottoman Empire until 1922. Smyrna had been the object of a seesaw battle of such intensity that the Turks nick-named the city "Smyrna, the Unfaithful One."

On 13 November 1914, the day Henri was born, there was no longer a French consulate in Smyrna. Turkey had allied itself with Germany and entered the war on 29 October. France had quickly pulled out its diplo-matic representatives, and the Langlois family found itself under the protec-tion of the United States. When Etienne Cros, an uncle of the newborn, presented himself at the American consulate to declare Annie and Gustave Langlois's firstborn, the consul general, George Harton, welcomed him with open arms. Representing a still neutral country and proud to find himself in charge of French interests, the consul personally made sure that everything was in order. So it was that an inscription in the registry entrusted to the American consulate established "the birth on 13 November 1914, at one o'clock in the afternoon, of Henri Georges Gustave Marie Langlois, son of Annie Braggiotti and her husband Gustave Langlois, resident of Smyrna and at present a soldier in the 112th Infantry Regiment."

If the war had separated Henri's parents, it did not modify daily life for the European community in Smyrna. The city seemed to enjoy a privileged fate. The sultan's authority remained far removed, and the Turkish army was mostly concentrated along the banks of the Bosporus or along the Caucasus border. Visitors who weighed anchor in this city of 240,000 inhabitants were struck by the diversity of its different quarters. In addition to the strong European colony, 100,000 Greeks lived in pleasant homes with chalk white walls and bright blue metal shutters. Followers of Christianity, with some 55 churches in which to worship, were in the majority.

Hundreds of yards' worth of lofty poplars cut through the town, forming a long straight hedge. This natural barrier did double duty as a rampart against the western wind and as a friendly border astride the Turkish quarter, which stretched upward along the flank of Mount Pagus. This part of the city was a cluster of picturesque brown roofs, stone walls, and secret enclosures. For the time being, only 60,000 Turkish Muslims lived there, following their own customs, frequenting their mosques, and maintaining their cemeteries.

Between these two worlds stood the central market, another city within the city. There the Europeans—French, English, and Italian, for the most part—rubbed elbows with a cornucopia of humanity that included Greeks, Albanians, Turks, Persians, Bulgarians, and Syrians. The Armenians were 15,000 strong, and there was Karatasch, the Jewish quarter near the sea, with its superb view. This array of cultures served to make Smyrna the most cos-mopolitan city imaginable. Everyone was welcome; everyone contributed to the astonishing blend of sensibilities and customs.

Until the age of five, Henri, nicknamed "Riri," was surrounded exclusively by women: his Greek nanny Pagona, his two grandmothers, and especially his mother, who, in her husband's absence, directed all her love toward her son. A fervent Catholic, Annie Langlois often took Henri to Ephesus in the countryside beyond Smyrna. There they visited Panaya Kapouli, where Mary, mother of Christ, had died. Annie told her son to pray to the Virgin Saint so that his father would return from the war safe and sound. Thus, the first years of Henri's life were steeped in an atmosphere of mysticism and faith.

Henri's mother was a gifted painter and an even more accomplished pianist. She never lost the singsong accent peculiar to those French accustomed to speaking Greek. Greek was spoken with the household servants, and Greek, quite naturally, became Henri's second language.

Annie Langlois took her son to the movies just as soon as the first French films arrived in Smyrna after the Armistice. Henri remembered and wrote of the shock he experienced when, at age four, he saw the first version of *Joan of Arc*:

> As a boy in Smyrna, I lived, like all children, in the present, and therefore had no conception of time. One day Mother took me to the cinema to see *Joan of Arc*—it wasn't De Mille's version, but I can place this memory around 1918 because I remember another film I saw at the same time, *Le Comte de Monte Cristo* [*The Count of Monte Cristo*, a Henri Pouctal serial, from 1917 to 1918]—and I realized that this Paris where people walked around in costume was not the Paris where my father, then still in the army, was stationed. So this Paris I was being shown was not the present. Consequently, the cinema became closely linked in my mind to this revelation of space persisting through time.
>
> As a kid this was a substantial emotional shock. Later, when I arrived in France and began to go to school, I discovered history and via history, time. But I never forgot that the cinema revealed time and space to me . . . Besides, even today, time for me is a space.

Henri had stumbled onto a powerful metaphysical revelation at a tender age. His movie-fueled memories of these imaginary voyages through the fourth dimension would serve as a theme for the fantastic stories and poems that were later to fill the pages of his school notebooks.

Henri's younger brother Georges was born on 20 February 1920 and became the center of attention in the family. Pagona, the servant, doted on the new arrival. Henri, now six years old, was considered big enough to run through the city in complete freedom. Each promenade was a treat. He strolled about the quays that welcomed new boats from faraway lands. There one could find on display all the products that made Smyrna famous: grapes and raisins, succulent figs, opium, cotton, tobacco, rugs, and more. Henri met young men with giant plates of sweets balanced on their heads. He saw an Orthodox priest with a majestic black beard hiding from the sun under a parasol. On his way back home to the "Frank" quarter, Henri moved through a colorful crowd where fezzes, turbans, skullcaps, boaters, and the large veiled hats worn by Westerners all mixed together. Never had the city seemed more beautiful or bewitching to his eyes. How could the child suspect the major upheavals to come?

The Allies had promised Smyrna's return to Greek hands in exchange for Greece's help during the war. In 1920 the Sèvres Treaty therefore allocated to Greece the city of Smyrna, along with all of eastern Thrace. The Turkish national reaction, carried out under the command of Mustapha Kemal, was swift and terrible.

On 7 September 1922, flames appeared above the roofs toward the outer quarters of Smyrna. Europeans climbed to their terraces for a better look at what was happening. They were reassured, since the burning homes were still few and far away, and in any case European battleships stood guard in the port. But hundreds of thousands of refugees—Greeks, Armenians, and Jews—had begun swarming into the city, fleeing for their lives before the advancing Turks. They installed themselves wherever there was room—camping on the sidewalks, overrunning the gardens—and they were laden with packages and had children and mules in tow. Servants from the Langlois household left to bring the refugees drinks and blankets, and when they returned, Henri picked up from their conversation the tragic details of the latest events.

That day, lunch was still being served according to custom, and Pagona brought the family coffee. Truth be told, the master of the house was quite pale and in need of any restorative available. En route to withdraw his savings from the bank, Gustave had come across a porter of his acquaintance who was holding on to a block of boundary stone. "What the devil are you doing there?" Gustave inquired. When he touched the porter lightly, the poor man's head tumbled neatly from his shoulders and fell into Gustave's arms.

That afternoon, tea was served as usual. The family chatted and passed around binoculars to get a better view of the approaching fire. By evening, entire quarters had been transformed into an immense inferno. Gustave made his decision to flee before it became too late. He assigned tasks. Annie and Pagona were to look out for Georges and for Grandmother Braggiotti. As for Henri, he was old enough to prepare himself alone. His father had too much to do. Gustave crammed into a large suitcase all of the family's precious jewelry, gold and silver that Dr. Cros had brought from France a century before. After hasty and franctic preparations, the head of the family gave the signal to depart. They had to make their way to the consulate. Henri appeared all set to go. Conscious of the gravity of the moment, he had dressed up in his best outfit, a sailor suit.

In those areas not yet devastated by the fire roved troops of savage cavalry who carved up anyone who got in their way, along with some of those who didn't. The sky was crisscrossed with sparks on their menacing trajectories toward the rooftops. From afar rose the rumbling of the crowd's cries, mixed with the thundering fire. Carrying Georges in her arms, Annie Langlois left the house with her husband, Henri, her mother Maraya Braggiotti, and their Greek servants, who feared that if they stayed behind, they risked having their throats cut. All of them headed for the French consulate a few blocks away.

As they approached the consulate, a virtual human tide lay siege to the large iron gates as thousands of Greeks sought refuge within. The Langlois family had to reach the front of the mob at all cost. At the height of the crush, and about to faint, Annie felt young Georges slipping from her arms. Gustave, a tall man, towered over the crowd and managed to lift his hands to wave for help. The cordon of combat-ready marine officers who were blocking the entrance to the consulate suddenly gave way. An officer had understood Gustave's gesture. With their bayonnets fixed, the marines charged forward and made a space for the Langlois family, pushing them toward the half-opened gates. Barely inside the courtyard, Gustave screamed as the gates slammed shut—the precious suitcase had remained outside! He had let go of it at the moment when his gesture had saved his family, but their entire fortune had now disappeared.

The family soon found themselves evacuated to the safety of the French battleship *Edgar Quinet*, which was going to take them back to France. From the ship's bridge they looked out at a panorama of the entire city—or what was left of it. Whole sectors were consumed in flames. While each passenger reflected upon his or her personal loss, Henri, whose sailor suit was frazzled and torn, tugged on the coat of an officer and begged him repeatedly, "Hey, mister! Take photos; take some photos!" Henri, at seven going on eight, had gotten it into his head that something tangible, a photographic record of all this, absolutely had to remain.

With two hands clenched to the ship's bulwark and his chin resting on the guardrail, Henri sank into contemplation of his native city. As the boat moved away into the Aegean Sea, the houses became smaller and smaller. The docks disappeared first. Henri saw Smyrna slowly slip away as if engulfed by the waves. Mount Pagus still seemed to float for a few seconds, but soon all that remained was a cloud of smoke rising above the burning city. Then everything toppled over behind the horizon. Smyrna, like another Atlantis, had disappeared before his eyes.

For Annie Langlois, the catastrophe of Smryna was offset by the euphoric prospect of finally discovering Paris. Her sadness had given way to genuine enthusiasm during the train trip from Toulon. Paris, in her eyes, was the only authentic capital of the arts. In fact, in that autumn of 1922 James

Joyce's *Ulysses* had just been published, as had François Mauriac's *Le Baiser au lépreux*, Jean Giraudoux's *Siegfried et le Limousin*, and the first of Roger Martin du Gard's *Thibault* series.

The coincidental sweep of history had made Annie's dearest wishes come true. She finally had a new world of museums, concerts, theaters, and cinemas within her grasp. Charles Dullin was creating smash after smash at the old Montmartre Theater. A young actor named Pierre Fresnay was making a splash at the Comédie-Française. Bourdelle showed his paintings at the Salon d'automne, as the Colonne concerts and Pasdeloup fought among themselves over Richard Wagner's works. The movie houses were showing *L'Auberge rouge* by Jean Epstein, *La Souriante Madame Beudet* by Germaine Dulac, and, the following year, *La Roue* by Abel Gance. "The Wheel," indeed. The future was off to a rolling start, and 15 years down the road, these very filmmakers would become a part of Henri Langlois's life.

The year 1922 also marked the introduction of Pierre-Victor Continsouza's invention, the Pathé-Baby. This small projector, which used a 9.5-millimeter film stock with centered sprocket holes, would become a runaway success. A noble ancestor to the Super 8 format of the 1960s and the household videotape recorders of today, the Pathé-Baby allowed home screenings of Charlie Chaplin films, Felix the Cat cartoons, Feuillade's serials, and eventually even Abel Gance's *Napoléon*. These crowd-pleasing titles were distributed by the Pathé Company under the direction of the renowned former film director Ferdinand Zecca. A Pathé-Baby in the house was a surefire indicator of parental prosperity and distinguished one's upper-class children from their classmates. The Langlois family was not yet able to afford such a luxury.

Henri found himself suddenly transplanted from the sun and the magic of the Orient to the drizzly gray of Paris and from a parochial school in Smyrna to the Condorcet public school on the rue d'Amsterdam. The beginning of this new school year was made particularly difficult for him by his still prominent Smyrnan accent. Henri was treated as a curiosity and had to contend with being "different," a difference he chalked up to the ignorance of certain Parisians. When each subsequent school year began, he dreaded the moment when it came time for the pupils each to fill out the form stating their nationality and the date and place of their birth, for inevitably the teacher, nose crinkled in distaste, would comment before the entire class, "You were born in Turkey? Then state your nationality or the date of naturalization by your parents." Henri's fellow students amused themselves by calling him a Turk. Henri blinked back his tears and kept his mouth shut. How could he explain to them that he was every bit as French as they were? No doubt Henri Langlois's later magnanimity and compassion for all minorities stemmed largely from his early firsthand experiences as an "outsider."

This was also a difficult period for Henri's father to embark on a new career. Gustave Langlois was 43. It would not be easy at his age to stake out a high rung on the career ladder. Having tried his hand at various jobs, Gustave finally obtained an interesting position as a salesman in Paris for the Fonderie moderne strasbourgeoise, which manufactured railroad equipment. Gustave Langlois was especially interested in a remarkable device called the "*purgeur*," or drain-cock, which ingeniously heated an entire train from locomotive to caboose by capturing and recycling the heating properties of steam vapor. The drain-cock became Mr. Langlois's abiding passion. He eventually succeeded in patenting a variation on the system, an achievement that brought in comfortable royalties. Thus was the family able to move into a large apartment in the ninth arrondissement at 14 rue Laferrière.

The extended Langlois family, having grown accustomed to their spacious house in Smyrna, sought a spacious apartment to replace it. Such apartments were rare and expensive. The rue Laferrière, however, a half-circle departing from and later rejoining the rue Saint-Georges, had its advantages, for if one-half of the half-circle housed respectable bourgeois families, the other was home to discreet enclaves where gentlemen callers might mingle with fallen women. Because the Langlois family's apartment was located in a building midway between the upstanding and lay-downing realms, Gustave was able to secure a lease at highly favorable terms.

Located several steps from the Notre-Dame-de-Lorette church, the building was also close to Oriental food shops where Pagona found grape leaves, dates, pistachios, raisins, and rose jam—all the indispensable things to satisfy Henri's already bottomless appetite for sweets.

The Langlois house in Smyrna had miraculously escaped the flames, and when the family was finally able to import its most precious furniture into France, the interior of the Langlois apartment took on a new elegance. The profusion of Oriental rugs was such that each outdid the next in a luxurious sparkle of colors.

A magnificent silver samovar and Annie Langlois's Pleyel piano dominated the salon where film enthusiasts would later gather together. To young Henri's delight, the apartment contained all sorts of bizarre partitions, which in his imagination took on the allure of secret passageways between the rooms.

Henri turned his bedroom into a hideout where his childhood fantasies reigned supreme. Rather than buy tin soldiers, he created a collection of buildings intricately fashioned from paper. Entire palaces unfurled their elaborate architecture from one end of the room to the other. He drew, painted, and cut out cardboard constructions that represented not only the facades but lavish interiors as well, each room decorated down to the slightest detail. Henri made believe that inside his constructs an entire world of figurine men and women lived, loved, and did battle. Some evenings he summoned his younger brother Georges and sat him down as a spectator. Henri proceeded to place a small lamp between the four legs of a stool, which he then covered with a white tablecloth. When he turned on the lamp, it created a tiny

Chinese shadow theater, and the phantasmagoric spectacle could begin. He brought the shadows of the famous back to life and conducted matter-of-fact conversations with the likes of Louis XIV, Robespierre, and Napoléon.

Henri sought a noble title as a sort of calling card, the better to stroll through the past in his imagination. Since he could be neither Cagliostro nor Monte-Cristo, he appropriated the identity of the Duke of Cigala, a character he'd come across in the family's archives.

His cardboard palace also served as a time machine. He needed only to open one of the many doors of his own design and to glide a figurine across its threshold in order to find himself transported through space and time to the period he had chosen to visit.

Many years after Henri had stopped playing with his paper soldiers, it would be these memories of imaginary trips through the fourth dimension that would inspire the offbeat stories and poems he wrote for relaxation. His mother saved many of those rough drafts, collecting them in a folder called "Phantoms":

If you want to travel through centuries in comfort, if you want have at your disposal a perfect espionage center without attracting the twentieth century's attention, do as I do.

Ask Le Corbusier for the ideal plan for a private house, complete with swimming pool, museum pieces, park, working fountains, winter garden, library, movie house, etc., and profit from a visit to the Middle Ages to buy a good lot at a low price. And then build where you please in the vicinity of Paris during Charles V's reign—in the village of Chaillot, for example. Then wrap walled towers made from good freestones around it so it will resist assault during the Hundred Years' War and the religious wars, after which you will be able to demolish it and then surround it with plaster and decorate it successively—at a fair price—in the styles of Louis XIII, Louis XIV, Louis XV, and Louis XVI.

Tear it down around 1830 to avoid its being classified as a historical monument (the Louis Philippe style will not yet be greatly prized), and take advantage of Paris's expansion to hide everything behind a wall of buildings, where you will live in the courtyard around 1880, at a time when the police and the state were not yet systematically organized enough to inspect imaginary households where phantoms dwell and whose altogether nonexistent offspring will do nicely as an excuse to set up housekeeping for the imaginary grandchildren you'll later install there, between 1910 and 1918.

Then you need only tear down the fake plaster set to reveal the true face of your modern house, which will have traversed through centuries with its bathrooms, central heating, telephones, private electrical generator, and all the marvels of modern comfort, with the exception of air conditioning, which you will have turned down in the architect's original proposal.

And that is how you'll be able to spend your weekends, as you choose, in the Paris that pleases you. Obviously, this will require several additional expenditures, since you'll need to keep a Rolls or two, cabs and baby carriages, phaetons, stately coaches, and a carriage on tap in the underground passageway so as to circulate at will, without calling undue attention to yourself, throughout the ages.

The advantages of this house are severalfold, since it allows you not only to be transported from Lebrun to Robespierre but to drop in on, as you please, from one room to the next, Charles V, Philippe Auguste, or Loubet, which should afford you considerable insight into those secret footnotes of history as yet unelucidated.

When Henri told such stories, he held his listeners spellbound. Many are those who remember how, during a walk with Henri in the Tuileries Gardens or at Versailles, he succeeded in giving them the impression that Madame Pompadour was just around the bend.

The day finally came when Henri's makeshift projections by lamplight, sheet, and four-legged stool were modernized, thanks to a Christmas gift: a much-hoped-for Pathé-Baby and a certain number of films. The showstopper of each projection was without a doubt *L'Assassinat du duc de Guise*. Henri particularly appreciated the historical detail of its costumes. The film was very short. Yet each projection lasted much longer than the official running time, since after each of the most dramatic moments Henri turned the handle of the projector backward.

The Duke de Guise, mortally wounded from the stabs of knives and swords, had just fallen when, thanks to the miracle of reverse motion, the audience saw him defy the laws of gravity and medical science to stand up again. As the daggers were slowly removed from his body, the assassins' hands drew back and the Duke de Guise was fully resuscitated before his bowing henchmen. How many times did the Langlois brothers thus murder then resurrect their dear Duke de Guise for the benefit of their dumbfounded schoolmates? It was certainly during the projection of this film, morning, noon, and night after night, that Henri Langlois fell madly in love with the cinema.

But the Pathé-Baby did not make Henri forget the real movie houses. The Langlois family apartment on rue Laferrière was conviently situated between Pigalle and the *grands boulevards* where one found a heavy concentration of cinemas. From the age of 12 on, Henri spent every Thursday and Sunday afternoon at the movies. His mother gave him the few francs required, but his possibilities were somewhat limited: "My parents, being neither rich nor poor," explained Henri, "had the means to offer me a movie but not at the Gaumont Palace. By this omission in admission, whereby I frequented the Pathé movie houses instead of those run by Gaumont, I missed out on all of the American releases prior to 1930. On the other hand, I saw the German, French, and Italian cinema."

At 13, Henri packed up his paper castles and characters for good. Space was at a premium, for he was about to transform his room into a first tiny cinema museum. He decorated the walls with images of his favorite stars—Brigitte Helm, Greta Garbo, Catherine Hessling, Musidora—and posters from his favorite films.

Above his "cozy-corner," where he kept his complete set of "Nelson" books, Henri placed an old movie camera and several film reels. He used a bookcase to store the film magazines he had faithfully collected, such as *Ciné pour tous*, *Cinémonde*, and *Pour vous*. In one of his school notebooks he began a running list, embellished with his own commentaries, of credits for films he'd seen.

Henri was a junior in high school when Denise Tual, one of the film editors of Jean Renoir's *La Chienne*, discovered his gray-clad figure for the first time. He appeared in the editing rooms as a thin mysterious character with a crewcut, as he threaded his way from one room to the next, picking through the outtakes discarded in the editing bins. "This gentle maniac," Tual recalls, "was ever so discreetly going about his business, collecting the images we were throwing out, in order, he said, to one day create a movie museum."

Henri's other major source of cinemabilia was the flea market. As soon as he returned home to the sanctuary of his room, he'd place his latest discoveries on the rug, after which no one else had the right to touch them. It was during these moments that Henri realized he possessed a sort of channeling power within himself. After he had stared at his beloved objects for many hours, they seemed to take on lives of their own and, as though in a dream, would "tell" him where in the room they preferred to be placed. It was this feeling, the magic of a harnessed daydream, that Langlois would summon up much later and seek to transmit through his exhibitions and in his museum.

José Corti's surrealist bookstore was located on rue Blanche. As so many of us do, Henri encountered surrealism on his way to high school, but in his case it was the genuine article: "The first contemporary authors I read were thus surrealists. Besides, Rimbaud and Lautréamont were my bibles. I still remember the enthusiasm that I felt reading the [*Surrealist*] *Manifesto* and my immense disappointment when I read *Nadja* after that. I couldn't understand how such a *Manifesto* could result in that. But when I saw *Un Chien andalou*, I couldn't contain my excitement."

Henri Langlois at age 17 was a true *cinéphage*, and a passionate reader with a soft spot for surrealism. He loved modern art and music and had a pronounced preference for Picasso, Auric, Honegger, and Debussy.

Henri was incapable of being a rank-and-file high school student. Gustave Langlois never understood how his son, who excelled in history and literature, could return home one day with a zero—the most unequivocal failing grade possible—in French composition. Far from feeling guilty, Henri rejoiced in his zero: It merely indicated his teacher's incapacity to broaden his own cultural horizons. The assigned subject was "The Comic and

Comedy." Henri Langlois had quite simply attempted to make his teacher fully aware of the work of Charlie Chaplin.

It was a horrible scene—the more his father screamed, the more firmly Henri held his ground. Lightning was welcome to strike him down, but he would not be criticized. To Gustave's proclamation that it mattered little who was right and who was wrong, that what really counted was to have his *baccalauréat*—the French high school diploma awarded after a grueling comprehensive exam in one or more specialized subjects—Henri made this counterproclamation: "I tell you, the history of the cinema will be taught at the finest universities one day. But since that is not yet the case, of what possible use would my *baccaulauréat* be? What I want to do is make movies!"

In June 1933 Henri Langlois finished his last year of high school. On his report card his French teacher wrote this evaluation: "Inquiring mind, with an already original bent. Will do very well if certain stylistic weaknesses don't detract too much from the content."

Henri could easily have earned his *baccalauréat* in literature if only he had wanted to. But he had decided otherwise. "*Bac*" in hand, he would have been under constant pressure at home to go right on succeeding in accordance with his father's wishes. Next thing he knew, his father would have demanded that he begin law studies. Henri decided to dash his father's hopes once and for all. He handed in a blank sheet of paper on exam day, and spent the rest of the day at the movies watching *Nosferatu, the Vampire*.

It was a pointed gesture—and Henri might just as well have driven a stake through his father's heart. All hell broke loose at the Langlois home. To understand the extent to which Gustave Langlois was affected by his son's attitude, one need only read the following letter from his cousin Laumonnier: "My dear Gustave, I'm returning from a seven-week trip to Africa, where, for the second time, I was asked to preside over the *baccalauréat* exams. Three thousand kilometers through Senegal, Sudan, Upper Volta, and the Ivory Coast. You don't mention a single word about your son Henri. Did he fail his test? If so, I share your worry and send my condolences."

If Gustave Langlois needed comforting, Henri stuck to his guns. He knew exactly what he was doing. The "black sheep" of the family loved the cinema too much to make concessions, and his success in life would not be measured by conventional degrees of social progress. It was at this time that he wrote in his notebook:

> I know what I am, what I want to become.
> A block of dynamite that will burst through time.
> But I don't know yet how to make the most of myself.
> I've got one trump card at my disposal: the Movies!
> The cinema comes naturally to me. I'll use it as my weapon.
> I was made to build things.

Today I leave in search of liberty and become the judge of my own life.

If that beautiful legend of Atlantis is true, it is by the cinema that we will enter into direct communication with nature. Movies will give us back the third eye.

In the meantime, Gustave too had reached a decision: "Since he failed his *bac*, he has only to go and find a job! In fact, I've found him a place in a printer's shop." Gustave felt certain that a good dose of workaday reality would dampen his son's imaginative fervor, but no sooner had Henri arrived at work than he created a stir in the company grapevine. His revelation was so fantastic that one of the employees would write about it to his brother: "I work in a printing house. There I met a guy who claims he's the Duke of Cigala. He's crazy, but you'll like him a lot. He talks only about movies. You should meet him."

The letter was sent to Georges Franju, with whom Langlois would eventually found the Cinémathèque. Franju and his twin brother, Jacques, born on 12 April 1912, were sons of a building contractor in Fougères, Brittany, where they lived for 15 years before moving to a Paris suburb. Georges Franju wanted to make a career in the theater as a set designer, and at first found some work at the Folies Bergère. But the Great Depression forced him, along with millions of other people around the world, to spend most of his time unemployed. In 1933 he was sketching his ideas for film posters in the hope of being hired to design the real thing. But he did not have a single connection, and he desperately needed money. So when his brother told him that he was planning to quit his job, Georges quickly took his place at the printing press. And thus did Georges Franju meet Henri Langlois.

Franju and the Duke became best friends. They made an odd pair. Langlois was a tall thin beanpole, topped by short hair with a stubborn cowlick; his face seemed to be nothing more than a staging area for his prominent saucer eyes. Franju was short and stocky, with a handsomely sculptured profile and curly black hair. Their personalities were as different as their physical characteristics: "Langlois had been placed in the printing house by his father to learn how to be tidy," Franju recalled. "That had always been the obsession of the Langlois family: to be tidy. So, since he didn't know the first thing about being tidy, we admirably complemented each other in the printing house. Langlois made a mess, and I cleaned it up. And this little setup lasted until we created the Cercle du Cinéma in 1935. Henri Langlois was very nice, very funny, and very skinny. He was my best friend, and I was his. It's thanks to him that I really learned about the silent era of cinema."

From this point on, and for more than 10 years, they would be inseparable, carried away in the same whirlwind of passion for the cinema. The Langlois hospitality would become legendary, but the first to be welcomed as an auxiliary member of the household was Georges Franju. The family, gathered together in the dining room, would pay him compliments on his poster illustrations, most of which were devoted to *The Cabinet of Dr. Caligari* or *M* and belied his attraction to the German expressionist cinema.

Langlois always loved to expound on his ideas to others, and in Georges he had found the perfect audience. Although Franju was two years his senior, it was Henri who seemed to take charge. He told Georges his peculiar stories, recited poems, and talked his ear off about the movies, dragging him along to countless films. In Franju Henri had found a true companion, an enthusiastic supporter to share his most farfetched dreams. Inevitably, the two friends were struck by a desire to make a film of their own. The subject? Henri found it under their feet: the Paris Métro, which they rode each day on their way to the movie houses.

Theirs was hardly the most professional assortment of equipment ever assembled. The budding geniuses used a borrowed camera with a fixed-focus lens, and three rolls of reversible 16-millimeter film stock, the cost of which was underwritten by first-time "producer" Annie Langlois.

According to Franju, "It was truly a film by amateurs—the most amateur there were. Langlois at the time was so timid—not reserved, exactly, but intimidated—that he could never touch the camera without reciting some incantations or going through some superstitious rigamarole. His superstitions would lead him to predict that each shot was going to be botched—out of focus or something." Langlois was so inexperienced that each time he held the camera, he would implore the heavens to watch over the next shot.

Once the film was finished, Henri told Georges, "Listen, let's show it to a young woman I know who works at the magazine *La Cinématographie française*." The woman in question was Dominique Johansen, who would later become Georges Franju's wife.

*Le Métro*, as it was called, was long presumed lost. In the mid-1980s, however, it turned up unexpectedly in the Cinémathèque's own archives. *Le Métro* begins with a panoramic view of Paris, followed by a shot of the Métro map. A subway train emerges from the depths of a tunnel. Then our attention moves to pedestrians going downstairs into the station. A reverse-angle shot evokes Eisenstein's Odessa steps sequence in *Potemkin*, as we see people's bodies from the waist down as they move down the steps. Having neither floodlights nor film stock sufficiently sensitive to shoot underground in the Métro itself, the two young film enthusiasts, shooting outdoors and by natural light, still succeed in creating an ambience proper to the Parisian subway.

Yet the difficulties encountered in making *Le Métro* put a damper on Langlois's desire to make other films. Although Mrs. Langlois's loan had covered film stock and laboratory fees, it did not guarantee audience acceptance or, least of all, a distributor. So, like many young filmmakers' first works, *Le Métro* was chalked up to experience and relegated to a closet. When asked, years later, if after making one film he still had aspirations to become a filmmaker, Henri Langlois let out a long laugh and replied, "Nooo. . . . All young people want to make films. The problem is that at that time it was difficult to make films in France. I discovered that anybody who wants to make films becomes a slave—and I don't like being a slave!"

Crazy about the cinema, but also a free man much enamored of his freedom, Henri Langlois was to find another way to live out his passion. His readings, his interest in the Italian theorist Ricciotto Canudo's work, his enthusiasm for Louis Delluc and the ciné-club movement—these would soon bind him up with Georges Franju in a great adventure. They were about to create the Cercle du Cinéma and the Cinémathèque Française.

## chapter 2

# BIRTH OF THE CINÉMATHÈQUE FRANÇAISE

Between me and the silent cinema is above all a great love. Try to imagine yourself in the mind of a young man who adored the cinema and who suddenly found himself transplanted from the films of Lang, Feyder, and Lubitsch into such French horrors as *Les Gaités de l'Escadron* or *La Tendresse*. It was awful. People accustomed to watching a certain kind of cinema were tortured by the arrival of sound.

Henri Langlois

It is the way of history for the new to clobber, then supplant the old. For those taken with the cinema, 1927 was the year a new clobberfest took hold: In one corner of the ring was the Silent, and opposite it, the hot new contender, the Talkie. Bets were fast and furious in both camps, but the new kid, still struggling to go the all-talking distance, was the favorite and gaining fast.

One year later, the three leading Russian directors, Alexandroff, Eisenstein, and Pudovkin, wrote their "Declaration on the Talking Film." They recognized that the silent film was handicapped in its way, but these masters of the silent form did not hide their fears: The addition of sound, particularly in light of the technical restrictions imposed by synchronous recording, posed a serious threat to the art of directing.

The battle was lost in advance. The first all-talking feature-length film, *Lights of New York*, made its debut in 1929 in the United States. From that point on, nothing could stop the evolution of talk, talk, talk.

Paris prided itself on keeping abreast of whatever trends it hadn't actually originated. Dr. Guillotin's celebrated blade could not have cut off the market for silent films with greater dispatch. By autumn of 1934, not a theater remained where one could readily see silent films. Practically overnight, the silent cinema had gone from being the entertainment of millions to serving as the outmoded amusement of lingering "hobbyists" who remained inexplicably old-fashioned in the face of progress. These backward souls gathered together in associations called ciné-clubs, and these were now the only setting in which one could see films made before the advent of sound.

Henri, who assiduously frequented the clubs, held a point of view rare at that time. He firmly believed that the cinema is an art in the same way that painting and music are—an art, furthermore, whose history remained largely unknown and, more serious by far, whose vestiges and artifacts were in danger of disappearing. Each period of history produces an art form born of the technology of the moment. Henri was convinced that the silent repertory constituted a veritable chanson de geste of the cinema, but unlike the cycles of Old French epic poems celebrating the deeds of heroes, this latter-day heritage stood a very good chance of becoming lost forever.

This prescient state of mind was far removed from that of the so-called cultivated classes, for whom the cinema remained an object of scorn, best suited to the easily satisfied masses.

Yet it was in 1911 that the Italian poet and critic Ricciotto Canudo had exclaimed, "The cinema is the seventh art!" Canudo, who had once served as a captain under Garibaldi, settled in Paris in 1902 and attracted to his circle—as Langlois would later do—painters, writers, musicians and poets. He founded a club called "the Friends of the Seventh Art," and personalities as diverse as Picasso, Léger, Cendrars, Carco, and Ravel were guests at his dinner parties.

It was not until the first American masterpieces by D. W. Griffith, Thomas Ince, and Mack Sennett appeared in France after the Great War that intellectuals had an inkling that the cinema could be more than a pleasant diversion. It should be noted that, prior to World War I, France was the world's leading producer of motion pictures; the United States was an isolated country whose films were rarely seen outside North America. Henri Langlois, in an unpublished essay entitled "The History of Cinema as Seen from France," described the shock waves produced by the discovery of this new breed of American films:

Up until then, Cendrars, Apollinaire, Léger, and de la Fresnaye liked to go to the movies in the same way one went to the banks of the Marne or to visit the annual Spice Cake Fair. One liked it as one "liked" postcards or popular posters, the way one liked certain brands of absinthe, the way one liked *Fantomas*, *Buffalo Bill*, and the *Pieds Nickelés* comedies. One went to the picture show out of romanticism and love of life, to relax, as one would by taking a stroll, but it did not occur to anyone to expect more than that from the cinema.

Art, with a capital A, was elsewhere. It could be found coupled with genius hanging on the walls of the Salon des Indépendants, on stage with the Ballets Russes, in the manuscripts of poets, in a staging of Jarry. So it was that, quite the contrary of the current situation, when one took one's seat in a movie theater in 1914 or 1915, one was ready for anything, but foremost, to be entertained. In those days, there was such a gap between the cinema and the art of the time that the old school—which had always believed in moving pictures as a means to record history and which has bequeathed us such a great variety of filmed documents on the life of the day—recorded Coquelin but ignored Nijinsky, left us the face of Saint-Saëns but forgot Debussy.

If you picture a Spitfire landing among a group of 1914 monoplanes or a modern high-speed automobile racing through a 1906 Bois de Boulogne, you'll have some idea of the effect produced upon the Paris of the period by the Triangle Company's masterpieces . . . Even today, these films continue to fill us with enthusiasm.

And as in the case of the Renaissance, the avant-garde to be born of this shock would be born in Paris, whence it swept Europe and the rest of the world. But why in Paris and not Rome? Why not London? Because it was in Paris, between 1900 and 1915, that modern art took form. Because Cézanne was French. Because Picasso, Chagall, and De Chirico met each other there.

Paris could hardly wait to discover that the cinema was no longer the cinema, but Art—and that triggered a great explosion.

It was the mainstream press—not the trade press, not the avant-garde publications, but the great daily newspapers—that bore witness to the birth of a critic who would appoint himself the spokesman, article by article, for this enthusiasm that was going to create the cinematic avant-garde, and with it, the renaissance of French cinema.

You'd be surprised by some of the bylines on some of the articles: Cocteau, Colette, Breton, Aragon. But Louis Delluc epitomized them all. He was truly the guide, the Moses who led the French cinema toward its new promised land. Each of his articles was a victory dispatch, marking, film after film, the steps in the discovery of and initiation into the rules of the new art.

Delluc, a young theater-critic-turned-*cinéphile*, was in favor of establishing an independent line of aesthetic evaluation to be applied to the cinema. He too had a knack for coining slogans and conjured up "We've got the touring club—we need the ciné-club." Such clubs, in his opinion, should concentrate on showing old films, as well as those French and foreign movies that didn't immediately lend themselves to commercial distribution. In 1920 he became the first to organize programs of animated shorts by Emile Cohl; a year later, Delluc was behind the Paris premiere of *The Cabinet of Dr. Caligari*. It was only a matter of time before the trailblazing critic-promoter put his expertise to the test. As a director, Delluc led the way, establishing a new tradition in French cinema—*l'avant-garde*. His finest works would be *Fièvre* and *La Femme de nulle part*.

In 1923 Léon Moussinac, a regular at the Friends of the Seventh Art screenings, in turn founded *le club français du cinéma*, with support from Feyder, Delluc, Poirier, and several others.

These forerunners played a fundamental role. The first clubs recruited their members mostly among confirmed *cinéphiles*, but were also in search of a wider audience. With a certain snobbery on their side, they managed to convince the elite of Parisian society that a select screening would be a suitable detour. The clubs most often met in small theaters and rented a projector. With the opening of the first permanent *salles d'art et d'essai* (art houses), the ciné-club audiences increased.

In November 1924 Jean Tedesco converted the Théâtre du Vieux-Colombier into a movie theater. He showed works by Jean Epstein and Man Ray and, eventually, Russian films. Two years later, the Studio des Ursulines opened its doors with an inaugural projection of *The Joyless Street* by Pabst.

But it was Studio 28 in Montmartre that would be the most famous *salle d'art et d'essai* of the late 1920s. Opened by Jean Mauclaire on 2 February of its namesake year, Studio 28 was devoted exclusively to experimental works and the discovery of films from far and wide, to be presented subtitled but never dubbed. Studio 28 would welcome the precursor of Cinerama, Abel Gance's triptych-screen finale to *Napoléon*, and would project *Pu-Chi's Rose*, the first Chinese film ever to be shown in France, as well as one of the earliest Russian films, *Bed and Sofa* by Alexander Room.

Today Studio 28 is the oldest continuously operating art house in Paris. On the occasion of the theater's fiftieth anniversary, critics Gilles Gressard and Michèle Levieux looked back on the early theater's atmosphere:

> Musicians such as Ravel, Jean Wiener, Georges Auric, and Darius Milhaud composed as they accompanied the films. All went well until the day Mauclaire displayed both the courage and good taste to welcome Buñuel back. *L'Age d'or* was a major event, as those spectators present still vividly recall. During one of the projections early on in the run, the theater—including its screen and surrealist paintings on display by Dali and Max Ernst—was demolished by right-wing extremists allegedly there to defend sancrosanct moral principles. This marked the last time *L'Age d'or* was shown, a serious setback for both Studio 28 and Jean Mauclaire.

The ruckus was so legendary and the film's perceived anticlerical attitude so potent that the film remained banned from theatrical release until 1982.

For some, the cinema was already an overtly political form. Before moving on to a career as a scriptwriter and director, Jean-Paul Le Chanois belonged to the Groupe octobre. He took an active part in screenings sponsored by the

Friends of Spartacus, a club devoted exclusively to showing Soviet films, which, at the time, were banned in France: "Thanks to the Friends of Spartacus, I was able to see the beginning of *Battleship Potemkin*. But just as the sailors were being herded under the tarp, the police burst in and impounded the film. For years after that, I had no way of knowing how the movie ended."

Movies from mother Russia were heady stuff in the 1920s and quickly caught on in intellectual circles. The room was always packed when the Friends of Spartacus Ciné-Club got its hands on *Mother, The Fall of Saint-Petersburg,* and *October,* in all their cinematic glory.

The undeniable triumph of talking pictures and the corresponding necessity of saving silent masterpieces inspired the ciné-clubs to band together. The first French Federation of Ciné-Clubs was formed in 1929, with Germaine Dulac as president and Jean Mitry as secretary.

In 1956 Henri Langlois, whose love of the silent cinema remained fierce, wrote his view of the situation as it stood between 1930 and 1934:

> All good intentions came to naught as talking pictures continued to gain ground and seduce the public. Efforts to support the silent cinema became increasingly sporadic, and all hope of maintaining a repertory theater—at the very least in Paris—appeared to be in vain.
>
> So ended a brief two-year period of transition. The silents were utterly obliterated by the time the worldwide depression hit France, two years late.
>
> By 1932, audiences who in 1930 still believed that the acceptable attitude consisted of a preference for silent over talkie would have been insulted by the very notion of going to see a silent film, as surely as women of the time would have considered their honor impugned by the very idea of wearing a short skirt once *la haute couture* had declared a return to long skirts.
>
> All was lost when La Salle des Agriculteurs—the last repertory house in France, perhaps the world, where Chaplin's *Woman of Paris,* Langdon's *Three's a Crowd,* and Howard Hawk's *A Girl in Every Port* were still shown—recovered its prestige as well as its box office with the triumphant debut of its first talking feature, *Scarface.*
>
> So ended an era whose standard had been borne by Louis Delluc—the flourishing of *Cinéma-ciné pour tous,* the valiant battles waged by the Seventh Art at the Ciné-Club de France and at the Vieux-Colombier. So ended the era of the first avant-garde.
>
> And the Vieux-Colombier, formerly one of the most brilliant film houses in Paris, went back to being a legitimate theater.
>
> The talkies had taken over for good. Silent films had lost all trace of commercial appeal and were destined to vanish entirely or to end up relegated to traveling carnival sideshows.
>
> The silent era came to an end as it had begun. Two forgotten theaters remained on the *grands boulevards*, squeaking by thanks to their low prices

and the opportunity they afforded certain women to rest awhile without altogether eliminating the prospects of finding a customer.

It was there and there alone that in Paris, up until 1934, one could still see the great films of Charlie Chaplin, Buster Keaton, the marvelous United Artists pictures with Douglas Fairbanks, and the last works of Griffith. . . .

Finally, these theaters too installed sound equipment, finding talkies more advantageous.

And then only the nursemaids, children, and fishermen, seated for a few pennies on the benches of the traveling theaters of the Vendée and of Brittany, still wept at the gestures of Lillian Gish.

The Langlois apartment on rue Laferrière was only three blocks away from place Pigalle. The quarter boasted so many movie houses in the 1930s that they stood virtually cheek by jowl along the boulevard all the way to place Clichy, where the Gaumont Palace reigned supreme. Its 6,000 seats, superb organ, and colossal stage set it apart as the largest cinema in Europe. Young Henri, finances willing, had more than enough theaters to choose from. He could devote entire days to repeated viewings of the latest French and American films.

Come nightfall, Henri and his accomplice, Georges Franju, set out for the programs sponsored by various ciné-clubs in the cozy 50-seat France International Films (FIF) screening room at 33 avenue des Champs-Elysées. There the two friends savored silent masterpieces such as Fritz Lang's *Destiny* or Max Linder's *Seven Years of Bad Luck*. Often the program featured talking pictures that remained on the fringes of commercial distribution: *Zéro de conduite* by Jean Vigo, Jean Cocteau's *Blood of a Poet*, or even "recent classics" from René Clair or Jean Renoir. Needless to say, on those occasions when Henri and Georges weren't glued to some screen, they were talking each other's ears off about what they'd seen.

Every Sunday afternoon at 3:00 P.M., the FIF theater was a livelier, more magical setting than usual, for each week at that time an attractive young woman named Sonika Bo hosted her brainchild, the Cinderella ciné-club, designed especially for children.

Sonika Bo, born in 1907, left Russia with her parents just before the Revolution. By the time she was 18, her father had died and her mother had become paralyzed. Sonika was obliged to go to work and earned her living modeling. A daughter was born to her in 1927, and not long afterward the young mother realized that films specifically suited to young audiences were rare. She put together programs featuring Chaplin shorts, Buster Keaton films, movies about animals, and early Disney efforts.

Among her regular customers, Sonika Bo remembers a family named Bouchara with 12 children and a tall, shy young man who didn't say a word: "One Sunday this young man came to the club accompanied by an elegantly dressed lady with a singsong accent. She introduced herself as Annie

Langlois, Riri's mother. We became friends, and Madame Langlois invited me over for tea, which was served with delicious Oriental pastries. During my early visits, Henri was still timid, and it was his mother who told me about how her son wanted to start his own ciné-club. She was bursting with enthusiasm for Henri's projects."

Henri, at age 20, was a prodigious cinema specialist with projects to spare. His knowledge of his chosen field was, in a word, encyclopedic.

Henri was determined to revive the films he loved most and was utterly indifferent to being branded a dreamer—or, worse still, a "prune pit," the phrase a classmate had coined to let Henri know his cinema fixation would never lead anywhere.

And then there was Gustave Langlois to contend with. In early 1935, Henri resolved to show his father that what appeared to be senseless stagnation was actually a period of rich creative gestation. He decided to give Gustave a proposal for an article entitled "Classics of the Silent Screen."

Skeptical but curious, Gustave agreed to look it over:

> The introduction of talking pictures having put an end to the production of silent films, this form of cinema can no longer evolve and belongs to the past. Therefore, the silent film escapes those passing fashions and infatuations that ordinarily skew critical observation. This results in a privileged state of affairs, permitting us to judge works of the past as if they were contemporary and therefore restore perspective.
>
> In some circles, film preservation is arousing growing interest. The creation of cinémathèques is likely. We have thus deemed it worthwhile to review a large number of silent films in order to see if, in the course of such a study, "screen classics" emerge. By this we mean those works that display a life of their own, whose value as spectacle emerges intact whatever the era, for the film stands independent of time.
>
> We have been able to observe that, yet again, the passing of time has led to a change in values. Certain famous films of incontestable historical importance—*J'accuse, La Fête espagnole, Eldorado, Fièvre, La Passion de Jeanne d'Arc*—are altogether invisible today. Others, however, that had far less illustrious careers—some little known, even unknown: *Ménilmontant, Brumes d'automne, Contes cruels, Les Mystères de la Tour Eiffel*—hold up beautifully for modern audiences.
>
> This state of affairs is sufficient to demonstrate the usefulness of this article, for if it holds us to an unexpectedly rigorous standard, it will in no way detract from these works or from the men who made them, whose reputations will stand them in good stead and whose legendary status will protect them.
>
> We've gotten into the habit of considering films from before the war as being devoid of artistic interest. We are wrong. Not only was Méliès a genius in his own time, but even today his remains the most original mind ever to have expressed itself with a camera in France, and this is not an isolated case.

Gustave Langlois was struck by his son's ardent conviction and his already evident talent for journalism. What if Henri had inherited something of his grandfather's gift? After all, Henri-Ferdinand had created the Agence national français in Smyrna.

The article, which went on to firmly and clearly expound upon the importance of Zecca, Feyder, Epstein, and René Clair, impressed Gustave: Unlikely as it seemed, perhaps Riri would amount to something.

Gustave Langlois, aware of the lunatic streak that ran through the film community, felt that certain precautions should be taken and so consulted his cousin, a senator from the Oise region.

The noble senator made inquiries in search of a film publication of serious tone and was able to recommend *La Cinématographie française*, a trade weekly that sold for three francs and featured translations of certain articles into Spanish, English, and German. For the times, it was the equivalent of today's *Variety* or *Le Film français*. The editor in chief, according to the cousin, was one Paul-Auguste Harlé.

Henri dared not present himself in person and opted instead for a submission by mail. Before the week was out, a letter arrived bearing the emblem of *La Cinématographie française*. Henri ripped open the envelope and began to read. His obvious excitement brought the entire family running, and Henri read to them aloud: Monsieur Harlé had found the article convincing and interesting and hoped to publish it before long!

Gustave Langlois beamed. He was flattered that Paul-Auguste Harlé not only liked his son's submission but also, as the man's deferential tone made clear, obviously believed he was writing to a man of age and experience. Harlé had apparently concluded that anyone who had seen so many silent films and who displayed such thorough and astonishing familiarity with film history must of necessity be well on in years.

The editor suggested that they meet at Henri's earliest convenience and was plainly shocked to see an enthusiastic young man enter his office. Harlé had expected to see someone at least as old as the Lumière brothers' first camera.

Henri's maiden article appeared in *La Cinématographie française* on 24 August 1935. From then on, he had a soapbox from which to launch his crusade. He took up the cause once again, in the next issue, and with practiced assurance made reference to the writings of the well-known and respected journalist René Bizet, who in his articles wondered what had become of the great silent films and put forth the idea that young French filmmakers might learn valuable lessons from them. "It is with considerable pleasure that we read our fine colleague René Bizet's article in *Le Jour*," Henri wrote. "May his wish to see that the conservation of old films is ensured be heeded and followed."

The campaign was under way. Langlois had created a platform; and others scrambled to hop aboard. Jean George Auriol, editor in chief of *Pour vous* and founder of *La Revue du cinéma*, was caught off guard and wondered who this heretofore-unheard-of colleague spouting such presumptious judgments could be. On 12 September Auriol in turn began a series of articles entitled "In Search of Classic Films." He agreed with Langlois that films must be saved, but he did take the liberty of inquiring by what means his "fine colleague" had arrived at his personal artistic hierarchy:

> By what right, for example, does he condemn to oblivion *J'accuse, Fièvre, Eldorado, La Passion de Jeanne d'Arc*? Why have these films become "altogether invisible" nowadays?
>
> Why, on the other hand, is *Paris qui dort* [*The Crazy Ray*] the culminating achievement of French cinema? All this may well be true, but it is better to back up such affirmations with solid arguments rather than to swear that the matter is closed.

Jean George Auriol's point was well taken. Henri, filled with youthful enthusiasm, had been so determined to set his personal favorites well apart from the overall cinematic output that he'd imposed his own rigid scale for assessing artistic value. With Auriol's advice in mind, Langlois soon turned his back on the very idea of hierarchical judgments in film research. With the same premonitory flair, Langlois established *Save Everything* as a fundamental principle. Everything must be saved, without regard for current taste or style, because the day might come when, for diverse and even contradictory reasons, "everything" might just turn out to be of inestimable value.

In October 1935 Henri and his inseparable friend Georges Franju met film historian Jean Mitry at the Ciné-Club de la Femme. Mitry, then 35, was impressed by these two young men who haunted the ciné-club circuit and often proffered intelligent remarks during postfilm debates. What's more, unlike many participants, Henri and Georges never spoke up for the sole purpose of calling attention to themselves. One day Langlois and Franju shared their objective with Mitry. They wanted to start a ciné-club devoted to silent films. Their club would be special, Henri explained: "What we mean to do, first and foremost, is to show films and not to talk about them afterward. Debates are useless. To make this difference clear, let's call ourselves the Cercle du Cinéma."

Jean Mitry warmly encouraged the two young men. That December, the first Cercle du Cinéma projection was held at the FIF screening room. The three classic films on the program—*The Cabinet of Dr. Caligari, The Cat and the Canary,* and *The Fall of the House of Usher*—proved so popular that it became necessary to schedule four repeat screenings that month.

Langlois had to pay rent to use the theater. In view of the Cercle's success with the public, the admission fees covered the rental. But the Cercle could not have gotten its start without the loan graciously made by one of Henri's "uncles"—in reality, Annie Langlois, who advanced the necessary funds to her son without her husband's knowledge.

In order to show old movies, Henri first had to find them, and this was no easy task. Mitry took him to Baudon Saint-Lô, Klein, Mueller, and Séfaire, resale merchants who still supplied such films to country fairgrounds. The original negatives were long gone, but there were still prints in good condition to be had. Henri made his first film purchases with money from his "uncle."

Each Cercle screening revolved around a specific theme, such as fantasy, psychology, or expressionism. Henri still felt too shy to introduce his programming choice himself, and so it was Jean Mitry who briefly told the audience when and how the film had been made.

In order to attend screenings, one had to join the Cercle by paying an annual membership fee in addition to individual admissions. The Langlois family volunteered to keep the Cercle running smoothly. The profits had to underwrite the acquisition of films. Annie sold tickets and handled the bookkeeping. Georges Langlois tore tickets and showed people to their seats. Everyone pitched in to transport film cans from the Langlois household to the projection site.

The atmosphere was always lively. Once the show was over, groups of spectators formed, spilling out onto the Champs-Elysées in heated discussion. More often than not, conversation extended well into the night at the nearest smoke-filled café. After a few short months, the Cercle began to attract professional attention. Jacques and Pierre Prévert, Alberto Cavalcanti, Jacques Becker, Jacques Brunius, Marcel Carné, Jean Paul Le Chanois, and Lotte Eisner were soon in attendance. The Cercle was a catalyst for countless other projects, including books, films, and magazines.

Annie Langlois boosted the reigning aura of friendship and creativity by inviting certain spectators to come over for tea. Thanks to Annie's hospitality, the Langloises' apartment became a sort of down-home artists' salon where young film buffs could meet their elders. Henri's passion won out over his timidity, and he ended up voicing his opinions, analyzing and debating with those present—without neglecting to sample the Oriental pastries his mother thoughtfully provided.

As in the days when recitation was the only way to pass down the exploits and lessons of history, so was the history of cinema transmitted orally by those who had experienced its early days firsthand. Jean George Auriol, Jean Benoît Lévy, Jean Painlevé, and other privileged witnesses were right there in the Langlois family living room. Certain film historians owe a great deal to these get-togethers. Henri Langlois had sought out and supported this kind of informal exchange, but some 40 years later, thinking back on the role filmgoing plays for the general public, he observed, "I think that the fact that filmmakers came to Cercle du Cinéma screenings and even, later on, Cinémathèque screenings is not in itself the most important thing. The most important problem is managing to show films. To know or not know the 'author' personally holds less importance. Nobody met Shakespeare, but everybody can read his work. Naturally, it's very nice to meet people and speak with them, but the real question is this, Is it better to meet the men who made the films or to see the films they made?"

All the same, thanks to the Cercle du Cinéma, Henri fulfilled one of his dreams: that of meeting Georges Méliès, the genius whose vision had meshed so well with Henri's own childhood fantasies. In Langlois's opinion, Méliès was still the symbol of absolute originality in *le septième art*. It was 1935—how to find the great man more than 30 years after his heyday? Henri knew only that, after having masterminded a flourishing film empire from 1896 to 1902, Méliès had wound up penniless. Méliès had made 503 films, which he wrote, shot, performed in, edited, and distributed. He had opened offices in New York, London, and Barcelona. The "Jules Verne of Cinema" was the father of special effects. And yet talent and imagination had not saved him from the perils of the unscrupulous marketplace.

Paul-Auguste Harlé supplied Henri with the lead he needed. For years, Georges Méliès had supported himself by selling toys and candy from a booth at the Montparnasse train station, but he was currently living in a home for aged film folk housed in the Orly Château. In fact, Monsieur Harlé managed the establishment in question.

Henri felt it wouldn't be good enough for two still obscure young men to visit Méliès—the occasion called for a bona fide respected director. René Clair fit the part and accepted with pleasure, and so it was that the three men set out for the château. Méliès's granddaughter, Madeleine Malthête-Méliès, who was only 12 at the time, was at the château and remembers the trio's arrival as though it were the emergence of the Three Wise Men from the desert:

> One Sunday morning, René Clair appeared at the château accompanied by two young men, age 20 or so: Henri Langlois and Georges Franju.
>
> Georges Franju, the smaller of the two, was handsome and curly-headed like a Greek patrician. Henri Langlois, tall and very skinny, had a tuft of frizzy hair sticking out atop his head. He was extremely shy and able only to mumble a few words.
>
> So it was Franju, who was more self-assured, who did the talking and explained to "Monsieur Méliès" what they wanted: They had recently founded the Cercle du Cinéma and wanted Méliès to come and present his *Trip to the Moon*.
>
> Naturally, "Monsieur Méliès" accepted. This was to be the start of a fast friendship between the elderly pioneer and these two young men who were wild about movies.

Through its programming choices, its absence of formal discussion, and its conviction that silence was indeed golden, the Cercle du Cinéma truly distinguished itself from other ciné-clubs. Twenty years later, Langlois would write:

> This repertory theater had finally come into being, and everyone was talking about it. It would be impossible to evoke the almost religious atmosphere that prevailed.
>
> Up until then, it had seemed inconceivable to show a film without musical accompaniment. The only exceptions to this rule had been the quasi-clandestine projections of Soviet films, announced by a tiny note tacked to the wall of the José-Corti bookshop on rue Blanche. In a huge theater in Belleville, the *Battleship Potemkin*, left to its own devices, fascinated, returned as it was to its inherent rhythm, which no sound ventured forth to disturb.
>
> Unaccompanied was always the manner of presentation at the Cercle du Cinéma, and whatever anyone says, this austerity corresponded to the very essence of the silent art.
>
> So it was that, week after week, month after month, the climate grew that would eventually make possible the creation of the Cinémathèque.

Early 1936 found Henri running around in search of feature films and short subjects shot between 1896 and 1930. His cowlick primed for battle, Henri made the rounds of brokers, production houses, flea markets, and fairgrounds. He carried in his head a list of films that had to be retrieved at all costs. These titles simply had to be seen, seen again, and shown to still others.

The major French studios—Pathé, Gaumont, and the Lumière Brothers—still had most of their silent films on hand. But there was no time to waste, for, having made the fortunes of their respective production companies, these films had become a storage burden for their owners. Thousands of films had been made, and dozens of prints had been struck from each negative. The studio archives in France, as elsewhere throughout the world, were full to bursting, and space was needed to store the new talking pictures, which were being cranked out at the rate of 100 to 200 a year. The old silents were no longer of any commercial interest to the production companies.

To his horror, Henri learned that the holocaust was already under way in the United States. Universal had destroyed its entire collection of silents, and RKO had opted to dump hundreds of old films into the East River rather than go to the trouble of collecting $30 for each reel sent to the foundry.

An entire industry had already sprung up around recycling the chemical components found in film negatives and prints. Salvage companies bought old films by the ton in order to extract their silver halide content, along with the low-viscosity byproducts used in the manufacture of cellulose varnish. Movies were being transformed into combs, toys, and—with the approach of war—explosives. Henri, as always, uncategorically stood his ground: The transmutation of masterpieces into their base components smacked of geno-cide.

Despite the encouragement lavished on his efforts, Henri was faced with the incomprehension and hatred of those whose routine he sought to disturb, for there were those who earned tips and commissions under the table each time they dispatched old films to the foundries—films in which others had invested millions of francs and months of effort to create. Henri redoubled his efforts and managed to acquire, with his limited means, a number of prints.

But as well he knew, at the same time that he was rescuing what he could, other films were disappearing for good. "Each day, while we struggle to swim upstream," he wrote, "works of art essential to our intellectual heritage are being destroyed, for these are works filmed not in barbaric countries but in the most civilized of nations. It will rate as one of the crimes of the twentieth century to have allowed the destruction of *Thérèse Raquin* by Feyder, *The Burning Earth* by Murnau, *The Aryan* by Thomas Ince, or *The Masked Amazon* with Francesca Bertini."

Although Louis Lumière's first public film projection at the Grand Café dated back to 1895 and one of his technicians, Boleslas Matuszewski, had suggested that films be safeguarded as early as 1898, no national *cinémathèque* had yet been established by the early 1930s. It was not until 1934 that Berlin and Moscow created their cinémathèques, to be followed, one year later, by cinémathèques in London and New York.

As late as 1936, France still had no such institution. Nonetheless, the nation's film legacy was protected, in part, by three very different establish-ments. First was the Army Cinema Archive, created in 1914, which stored footage of military news and maneuvers. Second was the Cinémathèque of the City of Paris, founded in 1925 by a teacher named Victor Perrot and devoted exclusively to educational films. The third institution, although named the Cinémathèque nationale, could hardly be said to deserve the title. Since its inauguration in January 1933, this cinémathèque had, curious-ly enough, amassed several thousand feet of film concerning World War I but not a single feature. Laure Albin-Guillot, a famous photographer, was put in charge of the Cinémathèque nationale. She had high hopes that one day the basement areas of the old Trocadéro might be converted into storage racks for countless films, as well as a laboratory and a screening room. Unfortunately, none of these ambitious plans would see the light of day— and not just because they were planned for underground. Despite fervent support from Jean Mistler of the Beaux-Arts Academy, the Cinémathèque nationale, in its seven years of existence, was never allotted even a tiny frac-tion of the funds it required to operate. It ran out of steam and died an unno-ticed death.

Several years earlier, Jean Mitry had also hoped to succeed in a film-preservation venture: "Jean Mauclaire and I had been to see a fair number of directors and critics, and we had the support of [influential critic] Moussinac at that time. We were planning to start up this cinémathèque with Mauclaire's money, since he was from a fairly rich family. But then he had a girlfriend with different ideas, and she said to him, 'Listen, a cinémathèque's nice, but it's a lot better to own a cinema.' He bought Studio 28, and our project fell apart."

As of 1932, Henri had already started collecting cinema magazines and found himself radically inspired by an article by Lucienne Escoube that appeared in *Pour vous*, entitled "Let's Save the Repertoire":

> What clairvoyant, generous man will take on the responsibility for this task?
>
> There is still time to save so much beauty. Here, then, is what we ask:
>
> First, the creation of an entity to seek out and buy all films of value, wherever they come from, whatever their propensity, whenever they were made.
>
> Second, the creation of a cinémathèque wherein will be kept the original film as well as two copies of each title. It would also be desirable for this library not only to collect films themselves but also to endeavor to assemble a comprehensive archive of cinematographic art: photos, articles, reviews, documents of all kinds.
>
> Third, the creation of a theater that will show only films from this repertoire, and will do so in a reasoned and intelligent way.
>
> Fourth, a provision for specialists and technicians to consult the archives of this cinémathèque and to screen, with special authorization, the original of the film under study.
>
> But if it is good to write, it is still better to act. Who will take charge of this movement? Time is terribly short. We must hurry if we do not wish to see everything destroyed and mutilated, if we want to save that which, contrary to today's "talkies," was a veritable plenitude of beauty and harmony, the cinema of yesteryear, a silent and magical art.

This clarion call had stuck in Henri's mind for four years. If someone had to "take on the responsibility" for this mission, then he would be the one. How many nights on end had he spent with his friend Franju talking of just such an enterprise? How many schemes had they conjured up together in the hope of finding the means to finance their grand project?

With Mitry's hearty encouragement and Franju's unwavering dedication to support him, Henri decided to charge forth into battle. He soon found the critical boost required in the person of Paul-Auguste Harlé, the same man who had given Henri his first big break as a journalist and who had steered him to his idol, Méliès. A gentleman given to rigor and caution in his own work, Harlé thought highly of Henri in particular and was drawn to the energetic faith of these enterprising young men. Henri's ambitious project delighted Harlé, who did not for a moment doubt that the tall, shy, stuttering kid who had entered his office when they first met was in reality the providential man that the film profession had been wishing and waiting for.

Better still, Harlé offered more than moral support: He contributed 10,000 francs so that the Cercle du Cinéma could continue to purchase films. Langlois and Franju rushed out to make use of this generous gift. From traveling fairs they bought a dozen 35-mm films, including Griffith's legendary Birth of a Nation.

Henri would never forget Paul-Auguste Harlé's beneficent gesture. He offered Harlé the presidency of the Cinémathèque Française he'd so concretely helped to create. After Harlé's death, in 1963, Langlois paid him a final tribute in La Cinématographie française:

> I am convinced that everything would have been different had it not been for the major and determinant personal intervention of Monsieur Harlé, whose vision anticipated the future and steered us to the manner of attack best suited to success. He was invaluable if only for having come up with the name Cinémathèque Française, about which he told me, "This title will enable the Cinémathèque to someday be the cinémathèque of all France." Then he threw me into the water equipped with one sole asset: the right to use his name. The weight and authority of that name, the affinities it awakened, were sufficent to transform the activities of two unknown young men, barely out of high school, into a course of action that, within months, made the Cinémathèque Française spring into form from nothingness.

Henri quickly caught on to the fact that Harlé's name opened many doors. Thanks to this powerful calling card, Henri was able to meet Alexandre Kamenka. Kamenka, the son of a wealthy Saint Petersburg banker, was the director of Albatros Films, the company that had produced a fine array of French classics in the 1920s, including films by Dulac, Epstein, Clair, L'Herbier, Renoir, and the talented white Russians of the école russe in exile in Paris.

When his heartfelt convictions took over, Henri forgot to be shy, and Kamenka, enticed by Henri's ardor, agreed to put his company's films on long-term deposit at the future Cinémathèque. This key gesture meant there could be no turning back.

The Cinémathèque was no longer a nebulous idea—its collection had begun to take form. Henri went on feverishly acquiring films, paying for them with profits from the Cercle and his mother's savings. He rescued treasures from places both likely and unlikely and hauled them back to the family apartment on rue Laferrière. The films came in rusty metal cans coated with dust and dirt. Since Annie Langlois feared for her handsome Oriental rugs, the first stop for the filthy containers was the apartment's only bathtub, where the cans could be scraped clean before being taken down to the basement.

Every rue Laferrière regular remembers that old tub with its ornate legs and its antique showerhead—an altogether plum bit of plumbing and deservedly famous, for it was, all things considered, the first depository of the Cinémathèque Française.

Gustave was not in the least amused by the onerous task of emptying the tub of its cursed film cans before he could take a bath, an effort made doubly aggravating by the certainty, born of experience, that the blasted objects would have made their way back by the following morning. Annie, however, employed her singsong voice, together with an indulgent helping of maternal logic, to calm her husband. "But Gustave," she'd say, "where do you *want* him to put them? He'll find someplace else eventually."

Henri's radiant glee in the presence of his newly acquired films also pleaded strongly in favor of their prolonged sojourn in the tub. Henri loved to hold them up to the light and revel in their transparent splendor as he ran the film stock between his fingers. This was to prove a lifelong pastime. All those who knew Henri knew that his fingers bore the indelible burn marks left by the nitrate stock he was forever handling. Like the vocation of the pioneer radiologists, Henri's passion was one that literally burned.

Encouraged by their early success, Langlois and Franju set off to win over Germaine Dulac, the famous director of 25 films, many of them feature length, spanning the entire period of the French avant-garde of the 1920s. Dulac was known to the public, respected and admired by her colleagues, and, most important, actively involved with the ciné-club movement, over whose federation she had presided since 1929.

That spring of 1936, she was in charge of the Gaumont Company's weekly magazine, *France actualités*. No sooner had she met Henri than she recognized in him the messianic gift she herself possessed for getting other people excited about a given project. She was won over immediately and put herself at Henri's disposal.

Dulac introduced Langlois to Jean Epstein, Jacques Feyder and Jean Renoir. Most of all, she arranged for him to be welcomed at Gaumont and Pathé, the two leading French production companies. She also gave Henri her unqualified friendship, and he became a frequent visitor to her apartment on the boulevard de Courcelles. Sonika Bo, who sometimes accompanied Henri, couldn't get over Dulac's expansive hospitality: "She showered us with little treats at all hours of the day or night. I'm not exaggerating when I say that she fell in love with Henri's plans."

Matters accelerated apace. Henri diligently continued meeting new personalities and building on the public support he had begun to muster. He published tributes to two pioneers he considered of fundamental importance: "Georges Méliès, Magician of the Cinema" and "Ferdinand Zecca: First Head of Production and Fabulous Director."

Starting in June, the first film deposits began to pour in, and words of encouragement arrived from far and wide. Henri couldn't have been happier. Everything was rolling along as if by magic, and the creation of the Cinémathèque was eagerly awaited by all.

Upon meeting in 1936 Englishwoman Iris Barry—director since its inception of the film collection at the New York Museum of Modern Art (MOMA)—and her well-to-do husband, John Abbott, Henri had taken one last decisive step toward his goal. With considerable cash on tap thanks to the Rockefeller Foundation, Iris Barry was conscientiously globe-trotting in search of lost films. While in London she had contacted the newly created British Film Institute and intended to make Paris her next destination; however, the American embassy formally advised her against crossing the Channel as "France is in the middle of a revolution."

In effect, the Popular Front had, since 11 May 1936, been an unpopular affront to would-be efficient travelers. A general strike paralyzed the country. But the atmosphere was debonair and joyous for most of the 100,000 workers who occupied their factories while picnicking to the ever-present strains of accordion music.

Revolution or no revolution, Iris Barry was not the sort of woman who gave up easily. She and her husband proceeded to board the ferry, then traveled to Paris on the elegant *Flèche d'or*. From the speeding train, Iris Barry noticed the hammers and sickles painted, in literally striking red, on factory walls.

In Paris, the telephones weren't working, the cafés and restaurants were closed, and taxis were as good as invisible. Pioneering director Jean Benoît-Lévy put himself at the newly arrived couple's disposal. René Clair treated them to a sumptuous feast, and Yves Chataigneau welcomed them at the Ministry of Foreign Affairs. At Chataigneau's suggestion, Iris Barry sponsored a press reception at the Hotel Crillon, an event that proved most constructive. Pathé and Gaumont promised her films; Man Ray and Fernand Léger handed theirs over. And it was there that the future director of the MOMA Film Library met the future secretary-general of the Cinémathèque Française: "Above all, this meeting gave us the opportunity to meet a very original young man, Henri Langlois, who the year before had succeeded in creating a French cinémathèque, an enterprise comparable to our own. We reached an immediate concordance of ideas and spontaneously agreed to engage in mutual cooperation through the exchange of films."

Iris Barry was wrong in thinking that the Cinémathèque had been created the year before, but in view of Henri Langlois's initial accomplishments, how could she imagine otherwise? She had correctly sized up the faith and determination of this "very original young man." Henri seized upon this occasion to ask Iris Barry and her husband to agree to an interview in the *Cinématographie française*'s office. By making a show, at least on paper, of the riches already held by the New York cinémathèque, he saw an opportunity to drive home his point to those as yet undecided. Henri's encounters and subsequent cogitations resulted in a forceful new article-cum-manifesto:

Cinémathèques are coming to life simultaneously the world over. This movement is united by the fact that these institutions are all the result of private initiatives sustained by enthusiasm. In general, it is the younger generations who take an active interest in the survival of films, who fight in behalf of the past and work with all their might to safeguard the cinema's masterworks.

Of all these cinémathèques, the richest and most active is the Film Library of the New York Museum of Modern Art. It has substantial means at its disposal, resulting in an effective edge over its cohorts. Apart from a Rockefeller grant enabling it to purchase whatever it wishes, the library is officially recognized and supported by the firms of Hollywood, which have made all of their negatives available to it in their original uncut form. Furthermore, Eastman Kodak donates laboratory services to the library, which will, once the product is perfected, be permitted to reap the benefits of Kodak's latest invention: indestructible film stock. As one can see, the Film Library leaves the German, English, and Russian cinémathèques far behind.

This tempting introduction was followed by a lengthy and appetizing enumeration of treasures held by the archive in New York. No fewer than 94 Méliès negatives had been discovered in Hollywood—and Moscow, it so happened, had just been found to possess a considerable number of prewar French films.

Henri instinctively knew how to get at the nation's pride. He went on, remarking with feigned innocence that just because there already existed upon the face of the earth an institution so utterly modern and fabulously important didn't mean other cinémathèques couldn't spring up and develop elsewhere on the planet. His conclusion emphasized the double purpose that a properly constituted archive must serve: that of collecting films *and* projecting the collection. Langlois ended his article with the later-to-be-famous slogan: "A cinémathèque must not be a cemetery!"

The message couldn't have been clearer. Unlike other cinémathèques, the Cinémathèque Française could not possibly be a mere storage depot crammed full of film cans. Stemming as it did from a thriving ciné-club, the Cinémathèque had a built-in obligation to show its films as often as possible to as many people as possible.

In Europe, the year 1936 was fraught with menace on every front. Henri, worried by the war in Spain, not to mention the rise of fascism in Germany and Italy, stepped up his efforts. That summer he fine-tuned the bylaws of the Cinémathèque with prodigious skill. All his life, Henri Langlois would delight in and excel at a special brand of administrative handicraft that earned him the admiration of diplomats . . . and the dismay of civil servants.

On 2 September 1936 the bylaws of a nonprofit organization, as defined in accordance with the French "Law of 1901" governing such associations, were filed with the Paris police headquarters. The Cinémathèque Française officially existed. Its headquarters was at 29 rue Marsoulan in the twelfth arrondissement, which was, unremarkably enough, the location of the *Cinématographie française* office. Paul-Auguste Harlé was the first president, Henri Langlois and Georges Franju were the secretaries-general, and Jean Mitry was the archivist.

The following people of note were designated founding members: Jean de Baroncelli, Jean Benoît-Lévy, Pierre Henry, Dominique Johansen, Alexandre Kamenka, Jean Kress, Henri Langlois, Fernand Léger, Man Ray, Marcel L'Herbier, Georges Loureau, Louis Lumière, Georges Méliès, Jacques Mathot, Jean Mitry, Léon Moussinac, Jean Painlevé, Pierre Prévert, Jean Renoir, Françoise Rosay, Georges Sadoul, Jean Tedesco, and Ferdinand Zecca. This impressive list reflected Henri's wish to honor not only the true founders of the Cinémathèque but also those who had donated their work or contributed moral support.

At the age of 21, Henri Langlois had become the "clairvoyant and generous man" Lucienne Escoube had hoped would ride into town before it was too late.

It was late 1936, and France had just witnessed the birth of its Cinémathèque. For Henri, the battle was just beginning.

chapter 3

# REMEMBRANCE OF FILMS PAST (I)

Before you can show an old film, it has to exist—that is, it has to have been "conserved" (in the archival sense). And in order to conserve it, first it has to have been "collected" (in the going-out-of-one's-way-to-rescue-and-save-what-others-discard sense).

Henri Langlois

If the Cinémathèque now legally existed, Henri still had to come up with the means to save films. A report from that time states that three months after its founding, the assocation had successfully obtained more than 1,000 films. And as of autumn 1936, Henri—true to his mother's patient prophecy—had also succeeded in obtaining several storage areas significantly larger than the Langlois family bathtub and basement.

Henri rented warehouse space from a production company called Central Union Cinema Films. Paul-Auguste Harlé soon arranged the loan of an abandoned blockhouse on the property of the Orly retirement home where Georges Méliès lived. Henri and Georges Franju had roamed around the château grounds and discovered the empty structure. After securing the necessary permission from municipal authorities, the cinema crusaders fixed the place up to accommodate a quantity of celluloid treasures. With the Kamenka collection firmly in place, the keys were solemnly presented to the most illustrious retiree on the premises. And so it was that Georges Méliès became the first official Cinémathèque Française conservator.

Henri's artfully cultivated connections to the workaday world of cinema professionals also paid off. André Laporte of the Pathé Company, who had already given Henri 5,000 francs to buy films, also lent him a company warehouse in which to store his acquisitions.

Laporte made use of his position at Pathé to do other favors for the Cinémathèque. For example, Pathé-Journal newsreels were systematically deposited with the Cinémathèque after their week-long run in the movie theaters. It was Laporte who, by calling Henri, enabled Langlois to rescue *Napoléon* from a second Waterloo. The Pathé Company had just decided to sell a truckload of film to a salvage firm that paid by the pound. The truck was ready to pull out for the foundry when Henri arrived, disheveled and breathless, to negotiate for its contents. Langlois discovered Abel Gance's masterpiece in what could have been a four-wheeled predecessor to Napoléon's Tomb: *The Movie*.

By the start of 1937, the Cinémathèque existed both on paper and as a tangible entity. Its ranks of donors included names as illustrious as Lumière, Kamenka, Pathé, and Gaumont, and its collection was far from negligible, even if Henri did occasionally inflate the figures concerning its holdings, the better to entice new donors.

In any event, Henri had enough films on tap early on to enable the Cinémathèque to institute an exchange policy with foreign cinémath- èques—with New York, of course, at the top of the list. But shipping was costly, and such exchanges presented a major financial obstacle. The two secretaries-general were stumped until Henri hit on a novel solution: "Let's say it's a problem in international relations. Then we can take it up with the Ministry of Foreign Affairs!"

The French State Department at Quai d'Orsay did in fact have a cinema department with an office to oversee French projects abroad. With unchar- acteristic nerve, Henri took Georges by the arm and dragged him off to see the minister. Without batting an eyelash, they asked to see someone high up in the administration, saying they had come in behalf of Henri's uncle, Minister Plenipotentiary Antoine Delenda. As a result, they were ushered into the office of the director himself, Yves Chataigneau.

Chataigneau did not conceal his surprise. How had these two rather bohemian-looking young men, now poised amid gilt paneling and ceremoni- al furnishings, managed to get this far without so much as an appointment? It mattered little; Chataigneau was an open-minded fellow, and so long as the youngsters were there, he heard them out. The more the two impassioned interlopers explained, the more the director was struck by the serious tone with which they spoke of the prestige and renown French culture command- ed abroad. He particularly picked up on the expression "*bibliothèque nationale* of cinema," which they coined straightaway to better describe the role of the Cinémathèque.

Once again, their passion proved contagious. Chataigneau assigned his assistant Suzanne Borel to help the cultural crusaders in their noble efforts to disseminate French excellence on a planetary scale. Henri and Georges were very much in luck, for Suzanne Borel was an exceptional woman to say the least. For starters, she had scored highest among all contenders on the

French civil service exam that was prerequisite to careers in diplomacy and in so doing had created quite a scandal in a realm where women did not yet have access to high administrative posts. Feelings on the matter ran so strong that the following year it was officially decreed that only individuals "in full possession of all their civic rights" could be considered. Women happened to be a category of "individuals" who did not yet have the right to vote.

Suzanne Borel proved a precious ally in more than one respect:

> We didn't have much to offer them in the way of financial help; the budget didn't include allocations to subsidize this sort of thing. So, I thought of two ways to help them.
>
> The first was to recommend them to our ambassadors and our institutions abroad to facilitate their search for films. It was on that occasion that I learned they'd been finding films in the most unexpected places—an American film in Istanbul, a French film in a garbage can in Tokyo, or a Japanese film in Australia!
>
> I ended up catching their enthusiasm. Whenever these films were discovered by Henri Langlois or one of his correspondents, the problem remained of getting them into France. I completely understood the financial worries of Langlois, who didn't have the money for costly shipping charges and who would run into all sorts of administrative difficulties and customs formalities. So, my second idea was to help the Cinémathèque by authorizing the use of the diplomatic pouch to transport films to the ministry, where Langlois would then come to get them.

This free circulation of films enabled the exchange program to expand rapidly. The first film exchange agreement to be drawn up was between Henri Langlois and Iris Barry, director of the MOMA Film Library. Henri negotiated that America bestow upon Georges Méliès a new print of his timeless gem, A Trip to the Moon. Prints of other works by the great film pioneer, including Le Docteur fin du siècle and Le Palais des mille et une nuits, would soon join the Cinémathèque's collection, to the immense joy of Méliès's most devoted fan.

The birth of the Cinémathèque had not meant an end to the Cercle du Cinéma. On the contrary, it was the Cinémathèque that permitted the Cercle to continue with the regularly scheduled programs that meant so much to Henri. He presented festivals devoted to Chaplin, Sjöström, and Fairbanks, and at the end of 1936 scheduled a special Méliès soirée attended by the great man himself.

One Cercle screening in February 1937 took on all the pomp of an international conference. Henri, who knew how to go through all the formal paces of "officialdom" when necessary, had invited not only the director of the Beaux-Arts but also the secretary-general of the prime minister's cabinet, a representative of the Hays Organization, and a wide array of journalists and filmmakers. In keeping with practiced ritual, Henri projected a selection of works by Lumière, Méliès, Cohl, Griffith, and Zecca for his distinguished audience. At the conclusion of the screening, he solemnly presented a representative of the MOMA Film Library with a number of American and European films long assumed lost.

Thunderous applause poured forth. The canny master of ceremonies was delighted—the Cinémathèque had become a veritable institution.

Despite the noncommercial nature of Cinémathèque screenings, attempting to project the work of others could be problematic. The Cinémathèque, in effect, owned copies of films produced by companies that had never ceded their rights to the material. So it was that when Franju, who had traveled to Brussels to show *The Pilgrim*, climbed up on the stage, full of pride at being able to present this Chaplin masterpiece, the proud showman was informed that bonded process servers had just come in the front door with instructions to impound the film: "I slipped out the back door and discreetly crossed the border, since we didn't have the authorization to show the film. The exclusive rights belonged to United Artists. Charlie Chaplin was always wary of bootlegging in the Old World, and at that time Belgium had a reputation as one of the major crossroads for contraband in Europe."

At that same time, Franju and Langlois found themselves seized anew with the urge to direct. Henri had gotten it into his head that he had to make a film called *Le Fantôme du Métro* (*The Phantom of the Métro*). Franju liked the idea. Their first stab at filmmaking, years earlier, had given them an inkling of the possibilities the Métro offered for those of imagination. The two friends came up with a wacky scenario and called upon Jacques Prévert to write the dialogue. They then marched off to ask Georges Méliès to draw the sets. Upon learning that the film reached its dramatic conclusion in the Père-Lachaise Cemetery, Méliès, who was game for nearly anything, found the story a bit too "funeral-parlorish" for his taste, but nonetheless went to work on some preliminary sketches. As Georges Franju recalls, "Méliès, carried away by his imagination, ended up quite a ways off the original track. He was already looking forward to the effect that the arms of the Chappe telegraph tower would create when, through trick photography, they reached out to the inventor's tomb or sent out joyous courtship signals to the giant bottle of Veuve Cliquot!"

Unfortunately, Méliès became seriously ill. Henri asked Dr. René Allendy, a Cercle du Cinéma regular, to admit the ailing auteur to the Léopold-Bellan Hospital, as an emergency patient. When Langlois and Franju went there to visit Méliès, he showed them a finished drawing. As Franju recalls, "The cork was popping out, and the champagne was bubbling over. And there, in his sunken, suffering face, his eyes laughed. He told us what the creator of cinematography-as-spectacle had told the audiences of the world: 'Laugh, my friends. Laugh with me, laugh for me, because I dream for you.'"

Méliès's death, in early 1938, deeply affected Henri, for Henri had learned to love the old wizard as much as he loved his films. The film project, dreamed up by a group of friends of which Méliès was an important member, was abandoned for good.

But Henri was not short on ideas. Langlois, always busy, forever in the throes of creative inspiration, convinced Franju to join him in yet another venture. Henri had not lost sight of the fact that his career as a journalist had begun with *La Cinématographie française*. What's more, had he not met his alter ego in a printing plant? What better preparation could two future publishers hope for? Georges and Henri ate, breathed, and slept cinema. They talked about their favorite films around the clock—and did so so diligently that they would, if necessary, have talked twice as fast just to recover that extra hour's worth of conversation when the clocks were switched ahead for Daylight Saving Time.

A new magazine in which to hold forth on film seemed to be in order. It would, of course, be absolutely different from all other publications devoted to the cinema, for it would be resolutely avant-garde, a wee bit libertarian, and, above all, financially independent.

The factor of financial independence was ensured by Georges Franju's mother, who advanced the budding press barons 2,000 francs. So far as the publishers-in-arms were concerned, their magazine could have only one title: *Cinématographe*, a name rendered even more alluring through a deliberate quirk in typesetting that boldly cut the word in two:

CINÉMA
tographe

The first issue came out in March 1937. The publication's young editor in chief had had no trouble filling its 16 pages with contributions from his friends. Dr. Allendy held forth on how the cinema fulfilled certain emotional needs, while Jacques Prévert had worked out a brillant pastiche of plots from Marcel L'Herbier films. Other contributors to the premiere issue included actor Brunius, producer/director Alberto Cavalcanti, and historian Lotte Eisner. As for the men atop the masthead, they had set aside the last pages for themselves. Langlois had written a review of Renoir's latest, *Les Bas fonds*, and Franju had prepared an article on Fritz Lang.

The magazine was a success. Of the print run of 2,000, only 200 copies remained unsold. And as Langlois—*indépendance oblige*—did not wish to entrust CINÉMA *tographe*'s distribution to the powerful Hachette conglomerate, it fell to the delivery crew for the newspaper *Le Soir* to graciously deliver the magazine to newstands.

The review soon boasted 150 subscribers, and Franju was thrilled when Fritz Lang himself wrote—all the way from Santa Monica, California—to thank Franju, with humor, for having revealed to him both his qualities and his faults.

The second issue appeared that May. Lotte Eisner penned a piece on Peter Lorre, and Claude Autant-Lara tackled the topic of censorship in America in an article entitled "Remaining Pure at the Risk of Remaining Stupid." Composer Jean Wiener wrote about movie music, and Langlois left himself only two paragraphs this time: one for a review of Zoltan Korda's *Elephant Boy*, and the other for *Black Legion* by Archie Mayo.

Sales were up by 30 percent, and the ever-increasing ranks of subscribers awaited issue number 3 with impatience. *CINÉMA tographe* was original, was the only magazine wherein true film fanatics could express themselves—and was about to go out of business. The two publishing kingpins were 500 francs short of the sum required to print and distribute the third issue. In the sacrosanct name of independence, they decided to cease publication and withdraw with dignity. The latter requirement meant they wouldn't be using Jacques Brunius's idea of bringing out an issue subtitled: "The Magazine That Appears without Warning."

Henri didn't waste a moment nursing his disappointment. Rescuing lost films and putting together his meaningfully eclectic programs at the Cercle kept him occupied. Henri's speciality was putting together films that complemented or contradicted each other. For example, on 23 April, he planned to show one of Hitler's anti-Soviet films followed by a Soviet anti-Hitler film.

Henri had scheduled an evening of German avant-garde films for 7 May. The spring program bulletin announced that the work of painter and filmmaker Hans Richter would be featured. Richter, known for his experiments with rhythmic montages of abstract objects in the 1920s, had fled the Nazis in Germany and currently lived in Switzerland, not far from Lugano.

Henri telephoned Richter to ask him which films he planned to present in Paris. Richter replied in a dejected voice that the bulk of his work, some 80 pounds' worth of negatives and prints, had been left behind in Bavaria with his parents, a Jewish couple now completely exposed to the first wave of persecution.

"Even if my parents escape what's brewing over there," said Richter, "my films are doomed. They're an extra risk for my family, and I'm going to have to ask them to destroy my work themselves, before the Nazis get their hands on it."

"Whatever you do, don't do that!" Henri exclaimed. "I'm going to find a way to get your films to France."

Now all Henri had to do was come up with a plan. While his mother corrected programs by hand, replacing "The German Avant-Garde" with "Charlie Chaplin Festival," Henri racked his brain—Richter's films *had* to be saved. Henri thought of using the diplomatic pouch that Suzanne Borel had put at his disposal. But he still had to figure out a way to get the films from the Richter household to the French embassy. Who could possibly undertake this rescue operation in Nazi territory?

Suddenly, the obvious answer came to him. One can well imagine his father's surprise when his good-for-nothing elder son took a sudden interest in his younger brother's grades at school.

"So, Dad," Henri solemnly began. "Georges will be taking his *baccalauréat* exam soon, and I couldn't help noticing that his grades in German are deplorable."

"True enough," Gustave replied. "But what can we do?"

"There's only one thing to be done," Henri declared with conviction. "He has to spend his summer vacation in Bavaria."

Gustave, no doubt wishing to encourage Henri's touching interest in his younger sibling's future, thought the idea wasn't half-bad. The matter was settled: Georges would spend the summer in Kempten at the home of a certain Frau Rinker.

In order to succeed in smuggling the films out of Germany, Henri had worked out a scenario worthy of a first-rate spy movie.

"It'll be easy," Henri told Georges. "To get to Kempten, you have to change trains at Ulm. When you get off there, you'll meet a member of the Richter family on the quay. This man will have two large sacks full of film, and he'll be looking for you. He knows you'll be wearing billowy golf trousers and a blue tie and carrying a plaid suitcase. The password is *Kunst*. You'll take the sacks and board the train for Kempten. Then all you have to do is get them to the French consulate in Munich as quickly as possible. Tell the consulate they're to be sent to the Ministry of Foreign Affairs at Quai d'Orsay via diplomatic pouch. And make sure you mention Uncle Antoine's and Mademoiselle Borel's names. Voilà! Any questions?"

And so, full of pride in his vital secret mission, Georges set off for Germany. There, however, as in every good espionage film, nothing went according to plan.

"The train was delayed at the border," Georges recalled, "and was so late that I missed my connection in Ulm. As for my Richter contact, he got scared when I didn't show up on time, panicked, and went straight to Kempten, where, in order to rid himself of the heavy sacks and their compromising contents, he left them sitting on Frau Rinker's doorstep. When I finally got there myself, 12 hours late, I learned she'd just taken the mysterious sacks to police headquarters!"

Georges put his German studies to the test in explaining that those bags were meant for him and he absolutely had to get them back. He and his hostess set off immediately for the police station, where Frau Rinker was obviously thought of highly. After all, her daughter was in the Hitler Youth and her nephew was a storm trooper. These familial credentials were good enough to convince two curious SS men that they needn't search through the bags before returning them.

"When we got back to her house," Georges remembereed, "Frau Rinker, with a conspiratorial air, showed me the way to the cellar. She'd figured out what was really going on. She put a finger to her lips and whispered 'Jude,' then went on to say, "You're lucky my husband is at work and my daughter's away at camp. You can leave your sacks here, but you'll have to get rid of them before my daughter gets back, because she'll denounce you.'"

Georges needed no further incentive to complete his appointed task and wasted no time in getting to the French consulate in Munich: "But when I explained to the consul that we had to save the films of a Jewish director, he blew up at me."

"It is out of the question that the diplomatic pouch be used to smuggle Jewish property!" he exclaimed. "That is not its purpose. I might add that such use would constitute an interference in the internal affairs of the Reich. I do not understand how a man such as Monsieur Delenda could possibly have led your brother to believe that I would commit an act so obviously contrary to regulations. As for Mademoiselle Borel, this doesn't surprise me, coming from her—she's a lunatic!"

But Georges was not about to give up, not when he'd gotten this far. "I stamped my feet and raised my voice," Georges said. "I was making such a racket that the consul summoned an aide to throw me out. At that moment, the door swung open, and who should walk in but the French ambassador, Monsieur François-Poncet himself!"

By sheer luck, the ambassador happened to be in Munich that day. At his request, Georges explained the situation. François-Poncet listened attentively, then, turning to his dumbstruck colleague, issued the following instructions: "You needn't concern yourself with whether these are Jewish films. As for the rest of the story, we didn't hear it. Let us simply say that Monsieur Delenda of the Quai d'Orsay would like for us to send him these parcels in care of Mademoiselle Borel. I see nothing wrong with that."

Monsieur François-Poncet had elegantly saved the day. In an ironic footnote to history, the French ambassador had come to Munich to attend the inauguration of an all-German museum of art, to be dedicated by the führer himself. Just a few hours later, François-Poncet must have silently congratulated himself as he, along with his fellow foreign ambassadors, listened to Hitler expound on the Nazi definition of art:

> Works of art that cannot be understood without having to resort to a pile of explanations in order to prove their right to exist and to affect those neurotics sensitive to this kind of stupidity and insolence can no longer openly affront the German people.
>
> Let no one be mistaken! National Socialism is determined to rid the Reich and our people of all influences that menace her existence and her character. The opening of this exhibition marks the end of insanity in art and, with it, the artistic pollution of our people.

Richter's "insolent" and "crazy" expermental films had escaped their otherwise inevitable fate just in the nick of time. This particular adventure was merely a hint of what Langlois would manage to do during the Occupation.

In June, Henri published a long article in *La Cinématographie française*. He wrote of the Cinémathèque's extensive holdings, including its latest acquisitions, and concluded by announcing the great exhibitions planned for the future. The article was followed by a long list of original manuscripts, drawings, and photographs.

Did Henri really have access to all he claimed? He had already assembled a great many precious documents, but probably not quite as many as he said he had. In any event, Henri was well aware that his lyrical albeit possibly exaggerated enumeration of holdings would serve as bait to attract still other treasures.

This article also marked the end of his brief journalism career. Paul-Auguste Harlé's magazine had served Langlois well as a platform from which to launch his crusade. He knew now that his message had gotten through, at least to *cinéphiles* and film professionals.

Now the time had come to conquer *le Tout-Paris*—French shorthand, then as now, for everybody who was anybody: the movers, the shakers, those who walked the earth to set or discard trends, to make or break the news. In the late 1930s, Paris was still the intellectual and artistic capital of the world; no movement or institution could truly exist without its blessing. Langlois had his work cut out for him. He knew that the cinema had to become fashionable in intellectual circles where, to date, it had been systematically scorned. This "pastime of the illiterate," as Georges Duhamel had written, had to be recognized as a legitimate art in its own right.

The perfect occasion to "seduce the enemy" presented itself when Langlois learned that the annual Congress of the International Federation of the Cinema-Related Press would be held in Paris in July. Henri arranged for the Cinémathèque, under the sponsorship of *Cinémonde* magazine, to organize the closing-night gala.

Langlois threw himself into his task with characteristic fervor. His days were consumed in screening films from which he would compose the program. At night he disappeared into his room, barely taking time out to eat. When his mother brought him a cup of coffee, she'd generally find him in bed, buried under a heap of phonebooks and directories. The carpet would be strewn with the lists he'd draw up and scatter. He'd cross things out, write things over, add a name here, and erase a name there, for Henri had also obtained the right to issue invitations in the Cinémathèque's own name. He had every intention of orchestrating the presence of those key members of the public most likely to contribute to the official recognition he sought. Henri added the names of writers and politicians to the basic list of journalists and conventioneers, in the hope that they would enjoy rubbing elbows with filmmakers and actors. For his own amusement, social register in hand, Henri selected three members of the nobility. Who could say? Maybe they'd actually come.

The gala took place on 6 July 1937, in the gardens of the International House at the Cité universitaire, the international student housing complex in southern Paris. The site was particularly apt, for it created a link between the cinema and youth. All along the central walkway, students struggled to get a closer look as the distinguished guests filed past the honor guard. They peeked around the Garde Républicaine and caught glimpses of all Paris had to offer in the way of celebrities and beautiful women. There were elegant actresses, such as Odette Joyeux, Françoise Rosay, and Anny Vernay. There were popular actors and singers, including Pierre Brasseur, Fernand Gravey, Jean Galland, Gilbert Gil, and José Noguero. There were men of letters, Pierre Benoit, Francis Caro, and Francis de Croisset among them. The Institute was represented by Firmin Roz. The American and Belgian ambassadors, as well as ministers from Canada and Germany, were present. The Italian movie director Freddi was on hand. The evening was a triumph. And to top it all off, even Prince Murat and the duchess of Clermont-Tonnere had accepted Henri's invitation.

Henri had put together a retrospective on a par with the scintillating audience. The first half of the soirée was devoted to pioneers of French cinema: Méliès, of course, along with Zecca and Cohl. After the intermission, Langlois showed excerpts from the work of Griffith, Lang, Eisenstein, and Chaplin. He concluded the evening with a reel of Leni Riefenstahl's coverage of the Berlin Olympics and the world premiere of Len Lye's color film about postal aviation.

The evening was a success. Upon reading the unanimously favorable press clips, Henri had no regrets about having donned a tux. *Cinémonde* ran the headline "*Le Tout Paris* Pays Its Respect to the Cinema of Yesteryear" and remarked, "This evening is unique, because even in America it is currently impossible to put together a retrospective of such value. It proves that the cinema is a complete art, possessed of its own masterpieces, and capable, like any other, of having a glorious past, rich with teachings."

In the autumn of 1937, Henri, encouraged by this first success, secured the patronage of *Pour vous* magazine in order to organize a new event at the Biarritz Cinema. Henri came up with the catchy title "le Gala des fantômes" (the Ghostly Gala). This time the public was invited to help the Cinémathèque find the funds needed to buy up films before they were destroyed.

Henri's carefully considered series of media events had produced results. This shy, 23-year-old young man had succeeded in convincing everyone that "his" Cinémathèque was an indispensable institution located in a modern and enlightened country. The general public was aware of and supported his struggle to save films. Even Laure Albin-Guillot, the director of the Cinémathèque nationale, was forced to give up. Not only did she acknowledge that Henri was in the process of succeeding where she had failed, but, in a move utterly uncharacteristic of those working for "rival" artistic institutions, she too was won over by Henri's exultation and unwavering faith.

In that signal year of 1937, Paris was dominated by the Exposition universelle, the most stylized and prescient world's fair to date. The old Trocadéro had been razed for the occasion, and the two massive wings of the new Palais de Chaillot had more than replaced it. The semicircular extensions framing a majestic esplanade pointed visitors toward a stunning view of the Eiffel Tower and Les Invalides beyond. For the run of the exhibition, two imposing examples of proud, ominous sculpture dominated the gardens, basins, and fountains at their feet. Face to immobile face stood an eagle perched atop a Maltese cross and a giant couple brandishing a hammer and a sickle. Langlois, more modestly, marked the Cinémathèque's presence at the exposition with a film program projected at the French Pavilion of Cinema and Technology.

The beginning of the following year was clouded by the deaths of two cinema pioneers, Emile Cohl and Georges Méliès. Emile Cohl, the first French creator of animated cartoons, was buried at Père-Lachaise Cemetery on 23 January. It was a freezing-cold Sunday, and Henri was doubly unhappy to see only a few people around the coffin, aside from the immediate family.

On 25 January the funeral of Georges Méliès attracted a considerable crowd. His fellow filmmakers and two film fanatics, mere boys who only a few days earlier had been hatching plans for the *Fantôme du Métro* sets with him, paid their last respects to the old wizard.

The Méliès family was faced with serious financial problems. The Léopold-Bellan Hospital was demanding payment, and Madame Méliès couldn't pay her late husband's medical bill. Once again, Henri set off on a mission. If *Le Fantôme du Métro* was never to be, the least he could do was scare up donations. Among others, Germaine Dulac contributed 200 francs, Françoise Rosay gave 500, and Henri managed to collect 319 francs from England for the right to publish photos and drawings pertaining to the late great Méliès. As a result, Méliès's family was rescued.

Henri hit upon the idea of hosting yet another theme evening to raise money for the families of the deceased film pioneers. This time it was to be "Le Gala des loufoques" (The Crackpots' Ball). The emotions stirred up by the words of remembrance and appreciation spoken by the dean of film critics, Georges Charensol, gave way to the laughter and surprise Méliès himself so loved to evoke. Langlois showed Pierre Prévert's *L'Affaire est dans le sac*, Mack Sennett's *Honeymoon Hardships*, *Entr'acte* by René Clair, and an assortment of American comic shorts. Then came a riotous you-had-to-be-there surprise. Langlois projected a campy old film called *Onésime le tzigane* (*Onésime the Gypsy*) and magnified its burlesque effect by playing a Tino Rossi record so that Rossi's famous voice, singing "Mena, ma sérénade s'élève dans le soir," fit perfectly in the gypsy's unsuspecting mouth. A rollicking time was had by all.

Widow Méliès expressed her thanks to Henri for his faithful friendship by donating to the Cinémathèque dozens of her late husband's original drawings and one priceless treasure: the famous camera Méliès himself had built. This lone and lovely device became the basis of Henri's entire collection of cameras.

When the Exposition universelle pulled up stakes, it left behind at least one magnificent building: the Palais de Chaillot. Henri, who looked upon the Palais as the perfect location for a major cinémathèque, and whose superstitious insights told him that this was the predestined spot for his success, already had his sights set on the site. To get destiny rolling, he moved the Cercle du Cinéma screenings to the movie theater of the new natural history museum, the Musée de l'homme, which was located on the second floor of the right-hand wing of the Palais.

Fantasy and enthusiasm were Henri's watchwords in the new setting. The programs were always a little off the deep end, and the audience adored the impromptu atmosphere. They came as friends, eager to see what new surprise Langlois had cooked up for them. Occasionally he took the liberty of announcing some famous film that was sure to draw crowds, only to pull a last-minute switch and substitute an unknown masterpiece. The audience was not terribly large, but it was extremely devoted. Ethnographic filmmaker Jean Rouch recalls the first time he attended a Cercle du Cinéma screening:

> We at Ponts et Chaussées [civil engineering school—literally, bridges and roadways] had received a flyer announcing that *Shoulder Arms* would be shown at the Musée de l'homme. So I went, and I saw a very skinny young man wearing a length of electrical wire in lieu of a belt. He told us, with a slight stammer, that the Chaplin film hadn't arrived and that he'd be showing *Enthusiasm* by Dziga Vertov instead.
>
> It was a fantastic shock for me. I remember that show, with its strange familial atmosphere. There were little girls playing right in the middle of the theater—[future filmmaker] Yannick Bellon and her sister [future playwright] Loleh Bellon, with Jacques Brunius's daughter. Brunius himself was there, of course, as were the Prévert brothers and a whole group of surrealist artists. There weren't the postwar crowds yet, but what struck me was the caliber of the participants. Many of them went on to become famous. You would've thought you were in an eighteenth-century salon rather than a simple ciné-club. The topics of discussion also brought us to current events, such as the Spanish Civil War or the Popular Front.
>
> Henri didn't need to talk—the films he chose spoke for themselves. He was already "directing" directors, putting them in the spotlight through his programming the way he'd later show his favorite films to their best advantage. This brilliant bric-a-brac was my first film school.

When Henri organized the Ghostly Gala at the Biarritz Cinema, soliciting a show of generosity from the general public, he had in mind a specific rescue operation. Two tons of films and negatives originally produced by the Eclair Studios were destined for the foundry if no one intervened to save them from a fiery death. The most notable components of the two-ton total included masterpieces by Germaine Dulac and Maurice Tourneur, along with the entire oeuvre of Jasset, who had made films featuring the famed theater troupes of directors Antoine and Gemier and who had made the very first police serial featuring debonair detective Nick Carter. Priceless footage of World War I was also at stake.

In Henri's opinion, one of the "liveliest and most important aspects of French cinema" hung in the balance. Henri was even more passionate than usual when it came to saving this particular batch of films, and it was a passion that would give him a few headaches at the time and a major nightmare some 20 years later.

In 1936 a Mr. Pellegrin, having acquired all the works of fiction produced by Eclair, promised Langlois he would deposit these films with the Cinémathèque Française just as soon as the Cinémathèque had a suitable blockhouse in which to store them. When, one year later, Henri could meet this condition, he phoned Pellegrin, only to discover that, despite his promise, Pellegrin had sold the entire collection to a manufacturer that specialized in salvaging the by-products of melted-down film stock. Worse still, when the films in question had changed hands, they'd been removed from their labeled film cans and thrown pell-mell into sacks.

Henri did some investigating, came up with the manufacturer's address, and hurried over to buy back the films. The manufacturer's asking price was 20,000 francs. Henri had his back to the wall: He was prepared to pay this amount but forced to admit that he didn't have it. The crafty businessman had figured out that Henri treasured these films and raised his price accordingly. He also threatened to destroy the films posthaste if Henri couldn't come up with the cash.

Langlois, desperate, made up his mind to beg New York's MOMA to display an interest in the imperiled films. It would be better to see them leave for the United States than to know they'd been turned into bombs! On 9 September 1937, Langlois sent Iris Barry a telegram: "All Eclair negatives 1909–1920 sold to explosives factory—Stop—Suggest Modern Art purchase 20,000 francs or selection 10,000 otherwise all films destroyed—Stop—Urgent."

Iris Barry was not interested and proved unsupportive to boot. She suggested that the Cinémathèque Française "figure out something." But having tried everything, Henri was fresh out of "somethings." He'd made public appeals and secured the support of *Pour vous* magazine. On 25 September he in turn replied with a certain aloofness:

> I received your telegram. How could you imagine that the
> Cinémathèque after one year of existence could possibly pass up the

chance to buy even Zigomar or Nick Carter by the pound? If we sent a telegram, it was because of this manufacturer's business savvy—he insisted upon all or nothing. Or, if need be, half, and still we couldn't get that. 20,000 francs for 2,000 kilos or else 15,000 for 500 kilos, or, as a last resort, 10,000 for 250 kilos: as usury goes, that's not bad. Monsieur Harlé wanted to drop the whole thing. I couldn't resign myself to that, and I did the right thing because I'll get those 15,000 francs. The press here is giving us wonderful support, and our appeals for money are not in vain.

Langlois and Franju thought they'd be able to buy smaller batches of 250 to 500 kilos at a time. They lost money by making down payments that the manufacturer simply kept when they couldn't pay the balance. This manufacturer was a versatile fellow—one day he'd threaten to incinerate the whole collection; the next, he'd say that insofar as his holdings were veritable treasures, it stood to reason that the purchase price would be considerable. In the long run, Langlois's patience, coupled with the threat of war, brought about a miracle: The owner agreed to deposit the whole kit and caboodle with the Cinémathèque. Henri was beside himself with joy; the films wouldn't be melted down after all. He had no idea what was in store for him.

The films had been removed from their cans, spooled off their individual reels, and tossed together like lettuce leaves. This celluloid hodgepodge had then been stuffed into sacks. Henri was faced with a two-ton brainteaser. And just to keep things challenging, there was another problem: The negatives of silent films did not correspond to the final prints, in that the title cards were shot on separate rolls and inserted later. It was like having the mixed-up galley proofs for a bunch of different books—only all the chapter headings had been removed and thrown into other containers at random, and there were no tables of contents from which to work.

Georges Franju, who was soon joined by another Langlois follower, Jean Kress, began the impossible task of sorting through the scrambled batches of film. Most of the strips were less than 30 feet long. It would take more than a lifetime to reassemble the footage correctly. But Henri had a nearly religious reverence for this collection, so lovingly snatched from the jaws of destruction. As he pored over the frames, he recognized well-known actors and scenes of tradespeople at work whose utility had been phased out in the march of progress. They had rescued evidence of the cultural life of an entire era. Even in fragmented form, these films were an inexhaustible source for montage films about France at the turn of the century. Langlois dreamed of making a magical compilation film along the lines of what Nicole Védrès would later do in *Paris 1900*.

Henri knew that the rescue and restitution of France's film heritage was closely linked to international cooperation, which meant the founding and proliferation of other cinémathèques. A film considered lost in France might just turn up abroad. The time had come to proselytize. Henri published ads under the "Miscellaneous" heading in La Cinématographie française, encouraging others to answer the call—there was a new vocation to be filled, and film saviors only need apply. Langlois concentrated on three directions: Brussels, Vienna, and Milan. He helped André Thirifays, who with Henri Storck had cofounded a ciné-club in Brussels, to create a Belgian cinémathèque. Langlois also made contacts in Vienna.

In Italy, however, the problem was more delicate. Cinéphiles beyond the Alps did not have the right to found an association unless it was part of the officially mandated fascist university groups. It was within these narrow limitations that film fanatics such as Luigi Comencini and Alberto Lattuada got together in Milan with Mario Ferrari to found the Cineteca Italiana. The first film exchanges were carried out secretly. The fascist administrators were not unaware of the fact that the Italian answer to French ciné-clubs were hotbeds of opposition to the regime, and so films had to cross the border hidden in suitcases that in turn were placed at the bottom of the third-class luggage compartment.

Henri sent films by René Clair and Marcel Carné—sterling examples of French artistry—to Milan, but also passed along works by Eisenstein and Pudovkin. The Italians also had the opportunity to discover recent masterpieces of French naturalism that would serve as models for the neorealist school after the war.

In return, Paris received Piero Fosco's marvelous Cabiria and was also able to see, for the first time, Italian stars of the 1910s and 1920s, such as Pina Menichelli, Lyda Borelli, and Francesca Bertini. Langlois fell in love with the images of these "fatal divas, these vampire women." These visions of beauty were Langlois's true loves until the day he succumbed to the more immediate charm of Jean Renoir's ex-wife, Catherine Hessling, who would eventually be supplanted for good in favor of Mary Meerson.

Alberto Cavalcanti served as the Cinémathèque's liaison with the British Film Institute (BFI). Cavalcanti, who was born in Rio in 1897, had studied law and architecture in Geneva, then gotten his start in the film industry doing set-design work for Marcel l'Herbier before going on to direct his own films. Jean Renoir introduced him to Henri in late 1936. Cavalcanti, who had worked in London, was well acquainted with the director of the BFI, Miss Olwen Vaughan. "She was an extraordinary woman," Cavalcanti recalls. "Sometimes she appeared rather disorganized, but beneath the apparent disorder, she, like Henri, had her own personal system for organizing things."

The films exchanged between France and England were not always of comparable interest, and Henri had to make a trip or two to London to put things in order. In any event, one thing was clear: The Cinémathèque Française was fully recognized by its two English-speaking counterparts, the

MOMA Film Library and the BFI archive. Henri felt the time had come to realize a project dear to his heart: He intended to organize an international federation of cinémathèques.

The opportunity to do just that presented itself in May 1938, when the exhibition "Three Centuries of American Art" opened at the Jeu de paume. Iris Barry and John Abbott had crossed the Atlantic anew in order to present part of their collection of films and photographs. Henri grabbed this perfect chance to bring New York, London, and Paris together.

In order to put those concerned in the proper mood, Henri organized another ball at the Cité universitaire. This 15 June soirée, which took on the atmosphere of a true political and diplomatic event, was even more successful than its predecessor. Leading filmmakers rubbed elbows with prominent publishers, scholars, writers, painters, and musicians. The American ambassador was there with his military attachés and the French ministers of foreign affairs, education, and the navy were also on hand.

Europe was on the brink of crisis. Hitler had just annexed Austria, and the growing menace had pushed France, England, and the United States closer together. Everyone had a feeling that war was inevitable, and Langlois's casually formal soirée took on the appearance of a summit conference. The newspapers would remark upon the tête-à-tête between the American ambassador, William Bullitt, and Monsieur Campinchi, the French naval minister.

In Berlin, there was consternation over the fact that so far as the federation of cinémathèques was concerned, Germany was being held at arm's length. One day Franju and Langlois were taken by surprise by a stranger who turned out to be none other than Frank Hensel, director of the Reichsfilmarchiv. Henri, needless to say, detested Nazism and was full of prejudices upon meeting Hensel. But as soon as the two men began talking, Henri realized that Hensel sincerely loved the cinema. If war was truly inevitable, wouldn't it be better if the cinémathèques remained at peace? Whoever emerged victorious and whoever suffered defeat, there would always be films to save in France as well as Germany. Berlin therefore joined the federation.

The formation of the Fédération internationale des archives du film (FIAF) was officially announced on 15 July 1938 in an article written by Franju. The FIAF united five nations: the Unites States, Great Britain, France, Germany, and Italy. Much to Langlois's delight, Paris was selected as FIAF headquarters.

As an international organization, FIAF was reasonably well financed with respect to the day-to-day funds needed for general operations and to remunerate administrative staff. The salaried position of executive secretary went to Georges Franju, for, unlike Henri, who still lived with his parents, Georges needed a salary to live on.

According to FIAF's principle of operation, as soon as any two cinémathèques exchanged films, copies were to be circulated among all the remaining member archives. Things were fine and dandy when it came to exchanges between London and Paris, but Berlin displayed some rather special interests. So it was that Hensel wrote to Langlois in February 1939 to announce that he was sending a print of Leni Riefenstahl's *Triumph of the Will*. In exchange, he requested *Double crime sur la ligne Maginot*, a political thriller that took place on France's first line of defense against the Germans, the Maginot Line. True, this film had been showing in theaters all over France for the past two years and could hardly be considered a military secret; however, just to be on the safe side, Henri decided to consult Yves Chataigneau, the open-minded gentleman whose initial support had led to the Cinémathèque's use of the diplomatic pouch and who now served in the prime minister's cabinet.

Henri also took the precaution of asking the film's director for his opinion on the matter. Félix Gandera hit the ceiling. His film, he screamed, was of genuine strategic importance! *Double crime sur la ligne Maginot* would never be sent to Berlin, but Henri did succeed in tricking Hensel by adding one condition to the transaction: "First send me *The Blue Angel*." Hensel complied, and so it was that Henri acquired the last copy of Joseph von Sternberg's famous film, the only print to survive in wartime Europe.

The New York World's Fair was set for June 1939, and Langlois shipped over a large number of films designed to introduce the French film to American film buffs. The first FIAF congress was also scheduled for New York, and Georges Franju was planning to represent Paris. But at the last minute, his ulcer acted up and he had to be hospitalized.

Henri ended up taking his place. His journey, which began as modestly as possible, with a third-class ticket aboard the *Ile-de-France*, would eventually take him to the uppermost reaches of high society, including the exclusive inner circle of Rockefeller himself.

In the interim, Henri wouldn't miss a single chance to mingle with the average citizen, getting in touch with the American people as he took the "grand tour" by bus.

When the film critic Arthur Knight invited Henri to dine in one of New York's most elegant restaurants, Henri turned him down. He wanted to go to an Automat and feed coins into the slots of automatic food dispensers, as he'd seen people do in American movies!

On another occasion, film-historian-to-be Jay Leyda had something of a shock when he dined at a typical American restaurant with "this guy who ate frog legs." Langlois took everything in stride and accepted each dish graciously. When it was time for dessert, he didn't skip a beat. Langlois ordered a bowl of vanilla ice cream—with ketchup on top.

At the MOMA Film Library, Langlois stunned his American colleagues with his ardent defense of a film they considered nothing more than a typical example of mediocre commercial filmmaking. The film in question was *Only Angels Have Wings* by Howard Hawks. "Make sure you get a copy at all costs," Langlois told them. "In 20 years, it'll be a classic."

Henri had begun keeping a travel diary not long before boarding the train for Le Havre. Its pages contain the novel observations of a young man of 25 as he discovered America:

*July 1939*

I take a taxi to go pick up my passport. The cab is going around the Arc de Triomphe. Along the sidewalk, there are buses with soldiers hanging out the windows.

The driver starts talking to me, and I find out that these are *bat d'af* [members of the Foreign Legion]. "Oh—guys who like war," I say. That breaks the ice. Big political and social conversation. He's not being taken in by Hitler's blackmail and says to me, after he sees how old I am, "You're young, but I'd say you're speaking from experience. I didn't see things as clearly as that at your age. Yes, yes, you're right. A year from now, I'll be wearing a uniform; so will you. And both of us will be goose-stepping to prove to Hitler that France is strong."

As for the *bat d'af*, I took a good look at them. However old they are, they're not men. They're children.

*14 July (Bastille Day)*

I have to see the parade. I feel I have to see it because I've never agreed to see it before. I'll watch from Catherine [Hessling]'s balcony. Lotte [Eisner] will be there too.

What a crowd! It's impossible to get to the rue Galilée. I have no idea if the Métro's working. Avenue Mac-Mahon: stuck behind the Horse Guards. Avenue de la Grande-Armée: completely blocked! I get in a taxi at Ternes and try to get around Etoile via the *bois*: It's blocked too! Oh well—too bad. I take the Métro. One hour down the drain. The taxi gets me to Catherine's in one piece.

There aren't many people in evidence on rue Galilée, just a few clusters of folks on balconies—friends of concierges, for the most part. Across the way, rue Lord-Byron is swaying like a wheatfield mottled with poppies—it's all people. Meanwhile, the parade continues. The mountaineering units. The artillery. The shouts, the hurrays, the applause grows frenetic: The Foreign Legion is in view. Followed by the Spahis [soldiers of the native cavalry corps in French North Africa] on white steeds.

Lotte is delighted. I bawl her out!

Am I to blame for this spectacle surging past me like some reminder of the old-fashioned illustrations I used to buy on the cheap on rue des Dames when I was low on cash? No, this parade is not of our time. I must admit, I feel like I'm stuck in the Second Empire: horses marking time with their hooves, colorful uniforms, the exultant crowd. But these are toy soldiers, off to fight the Mexican Army in 1869!

Catherine gives me a piece of her mind!

### That Night

So there I am with Catherine, [actress] Renée [Falconetti], a gentleman who works at the French embassy in Rome, and a horse-faced socialite afflicted with a nasty inflammation she's trying to cover up with a silver fox. We eat dinner at Georges's place, where I try mixing together caviar and raspberries. Not a bad combination!

Then it's off to see the fireworks. For the fun of it, we filled in foreign-sounding names on our invitations. There will be "half-breeds" in sad President Lebrun's reviewing stand. Catherine and I are "Monsieur and Madame Gogola." But it's impossible to reach our rightful spot at Trocadéro from any direction. We give up and watch from the Alma Bridge with the rest of the crowd. It's a soggy, halfhearted sort of display; something seems to be missing. Afterward, it's the crowds all over again, French and British soldiers in uniform, people laughing, an atmosphere of forced frivolity.

In all the time I've known Paris, I've never seen a Fourteenth of July like this. I know what a real Fourteenth of July is like, but here at Trocadéro, these flowers, all this pomp, these flags—it all smacks of jin-goistic officialdom, so uncharacteristic of this particular holiday. The public and these cars are also uncharacteristic. Cars on the Fourteenth of July! Why the devil are these ladies and gentlemen party to all this? I feel uneasy—my guts are all knotted up. I feel afraid and panicky, and I tell [Renée] Falconetti. She tells me she's feeling the same way. What anxiety!

This Bastille Day smells of war. I imagine this Bastille Day being like the one in 1918—same uniforms, same splendor, same exhilaration. But with one slight difference: No war has just ended. So this is like the Bastille Day of 1914. "Falco" feels so uncomfortable that we go home.

I have the strangest impression. The fellow from the French embassy in Rome who was with us—he didn't seem to know a thing about Italy. The product of a handful of elegant salons, he's never so much as looked into Italy. Heaven help French diplomacy!

### Departure

The boat sails for New York. The third-class passengers are horrible—no two ways about it. But even worse are the French from *La Revue des deux mondes* on their way to visit the world's fair. Where do these people *come* from? From what hole in the ground, what Jean-Paul Laurens painting? They walk around on deck in their slippers.

An astonishing surprise: They showed Chaplin films to the passengers traveling deluxe, first-, and second-class. There were children in the room—and nobody laughed. Absolutely nobody. Oh yeah—one person, next to me, did laugh. The usherette!

### Receptions

I've put July's warnings completely out of my head. This is New York. American snob hospitality. What a thin layer it is! And get this: Rockefeller wearing a suit in goose-shit brown, so ugly it makes you want to puke.

The poor head of the Italian delegation is no dope, but he's certainly knocking himself out trying to exonerate the Prince of Piedmont from the sin of pederasty!

Whitney seems like a nice fellow. There's also a clergyman—head censor for the League of Decency. A priest who gets around.

While I'm talking to Whitney, Mrs. Abbott rushes over to drag him away. What a joke! The place where I am is the most expensive spot in New York. To tell the truth, in all the world there's nothing more hideously snobbish than an American snob. It's the quintessence of snobbery. I adore the American people—they're a handsome species with a splendid way of going about their business. I feel like I'm back in the best eras history has to offer. The crowds in the streets are true enchantment.

### Hensel

The Germans plaster smiles on top of their smiles every time. They look my way. I don't think they realize just how insolent my attitude is.

Hensel comes in and says to me point-blank, all cordial-like, "To be a socialist when you're 20 years old shows that your heart's in the right place. But at 40, it means you're stupid or you should have your head examined." He starts in again the next day. He's certainly trying to tell me something.

### Skyscrapers

In New York they strike me as small, whereas in Chicago they produce the effect you expect. Is this just an optical illusion? No, because in New York they're taller; let's get our values straight.

In Chicago the skyscrapers are real skyscrapers, which is to say multistoried buildings. In New York they're towers, castle keeps. Most of them have no justification save vanity.

Corollary: In Chicago all the skyscrapers are grouped together downtown. In New York they stand in the middle of little houses, empty lots, and parking garages, and the most recent examples are inept, so they have no logical reason to exist.

They really are feudal dungeons. When your ship approaches the dock, the Statue of Liberty is a big fat gossip and nothing more. But what's marvelous is the movement—boats, ferries, bridges, the cars on the highways, the subway, the trains, the planes. Later on, I'm going to get to know the highway system, whose roads are splendor itself.

New York is the only city that can equal and make you forget Paris, just as Paris is, I think, the only city that can make you forget New York. Paris is the calm mobility of lakes; New York, the surging of waves.

A few days after my arrival, the skyscrapers looked to my eyes properly proportioned.

### Democracy

In Central Park or in Chicago, a man who sleeps on a bench at night is a man who sleeps on a bench. In France, as throughout Europe, he's a bum that some policeman has to wake up and shoo away.

### The Middle Ages

The United States takes me back to the Middle Ages. The social setup is the same. The feudal lords and their fiefs (the trusts and those who toil on their behalf). The clerics and scholars (at the universities). The people and royalty, the president mediator between the third estate and the noblemen (Washington).

Make no mistake, Washington occupies the same position as Capetian royalty. It's the buffer between the millionaires and the electorate. Whereas, *chez nous*, the bureaucracy delivers up a defenseless people to the new feudal lords who have recaptured power.

### Freedom

He who lives in the United States lives in freedom. Freedom means choice. And the American can certainly choose.

If he's a slave, if he lives in a vicious circle, if he gets to be like the Abbotts—loyal supporter, parasite, client to the great feudal lords—then he'll need money and always more money on top of that. I can only feel sorry for him. He's sacrificed his freedom for money. But outside this vicious circle, the American may live freely, for whereas in Europe meager earnings mean discomfort, ugliness, *Belleville*, Tino Rossi, and dubbed movies, an American who's not well-off can still get himself nice things for practically nothing: 3¢ buys Fats Waller or Louis Armstrong. In France the populace is stuck with wearing hideous skimpy suits, suspenders, detachable collars, and socks with garters.

The American dresses with an elegance, an assured casualness, an array of bright colors that the best among us would envy.

### Contempt

The average American doesn't give a second thought to millionaires. He knows where these guys' grandfathers came from, and he knows he could've struck it rich too. I might add that the origin of these respectable men's fortunes is not unknown to the man in the street. The millionaire, high atop his skyscraper, has forgotten his origins. He is descended directly from God, by the Good Lord's grace. Europe jumps when he says "Jump!" Republics pay him homage, and he receives messages from His Holiness the Pope. Why ever should you want him to lower his eyes toward the smallfry below as they scurry among the skyscrapers?

And that is how the American man can live in freedom and liberty, in the heart of Brooklyn. When you're in New York, you feel like Paris is a city whose days are numbered. Broadway at midnight: the bustle, the hubbub, the crowds! The day is just beginning! It's at night that you feel the vitality of a city.

Jazz clubs? I have the feeling I'm taking part in a bewitchment. When Count Basie plays, it's intoxicating.

Now and then, New York reminds me of southern Italy—the same magnificent populace, the same bric-a-brac. I say Italy, but I could just as easily say Barcelona or any other Mediterranean city. One can say the same thing for Chicago. Surprising, for Anglo-Saxons. Here, apart from the great comics like Chaplin and Sennett, I realize to just what extent the cinema of Hollywood falls short of its model. Hollywood, or, America Reduced to the Desiderata of the Daughters of the American Revolution. Even so, you'd swear that, pale copy or not, it's still better than what's available in Europe.

Re-release of *Hallelujah*. I honestly think this film is the pinnacle of American moviemaking. It's incredible—it hasn't aged one bit. Jacques Becker told me that [King] Vidor made this film out of contempt for Europe. Should I believe him? This film is a series of ups and downs for audiences here. They laugh at the great naive poetry I find so moving and fall suddenly silent during the magical singing. It's not that they're paying attention; they're just frightened, very frightened.

### The World's Fair

Finally—an international exposition that's more than a competition ground for architects and decorators! Finally—an exposition where you can actually learn something!

That it's ugly, I won't deny. But where have you ever seen an international exposition that was beautiful? My entry fee wasn't money down the drain; I'm learning things. Dali has really done a great job: His section is magnificent. What a beautiful wax museum! There aren't many people here, just a few young kids who spend hours glued to the display windows staring at the mermaid, their cameras at the ready.

Right next to it there's a woman with Magritte's dove cage for a head, asleep in a plush red bed. There's a young guy from Texas, a regular cowboy with a stentorian voice. He wants to know if the lady's made of wax. She's alive? He doesn't believe it. Then she moves, so he knocks real hard on the glass and shouts, "Get up! Come on with me!" Alongside, the others are still waiting for the mermaid. They were still there when we left.

All of a sudden, I spot Henry Fonda in the crowd. From the back, anyway, you'd swear it was Fonda. Leyda smiled and said, "No, it can't be. Fonda's not a guy who hangs out with the general public." Turns out they're just students.

*Diorama*

The trains run, the sun sets, the lights of the city go on, and the ferry goes by. In one minute you can take in the whole transit network around New York. Then you go back in time, locomotives from all the different eras go by and ladies in crinoline get off, and then Lincoln. The General Motors Pavilion is impossible to get into. Skydivers making high-pitched shrills land at the edge of the lake.

Billy Rose's *Old New York*: two statues that are worth a detour. Made of wood and wax, dressed and animated. They do the belly dance and there's nothing more thrilling. The City of the Future is the only grotesque thing in the whole exposition.

*On the Motorcoach*

The American countryside, wooden houses. Why this rush of tenderness? I suddenly have the feeling I'm back in touch with my childhood, Grandma, Gustépé. It's impossible to explain. Logic tells me I wasn't born in these white houses, and I never played in these gardens. And yet it's as if I'd been born here. The rocking chair that sits on every front porch, that house that turns back to its true color in the rain, that woman in the straw hat, those woodworkers, those people sitting on their doorsteps. It all seems so familiar to me that I'm overcome.

Who's the European who dared write that the American countryside is monotonous? The houses are unquestionably similar, but what grace, what architectural purity, what variety! The Greek temples too were built on one model, and who would dream of faulting them for it? What's more, the American countryside is D. W. Griffith and the McNeil family.

*Chicago*

In Chicago I saw an absolutely dazzling Van Gogh. I've never seen anything like it in my life. It gleams so, it has such depth, it makes you blink. The field glistens with dew and glows in the sunshine. I'm not kidding. It's a tactile effect—the physical impression is extraordinary, unbearable.

Since I'm not a photographer or a painter and I don't have the camera it would take, I give up on trying to describe the fairy-tale spectacle of the quays of Chicago. And that's without even talking about the ice cream and sundaes and other American marvels, or the touching celebrations at the university.

In Chicago, with the McNeil family, I got my introduction to puritan life. Should I admit how very much these people please me? Their hospitality, their surprising naïveté—perhaps it's all this that makes America so dear to me. Here I've rediscovered the pure flexible simplicity of my family in Smyrna. Apart from the McNeils, there are the blacks. Truth be told, they're the ones I look at most on the streetcar and in the shops. I want to know what they're all about, these blacks who don't come from Africa.

Need I say it? I'm struck dumb with admiration. Besides their incomparable physical beauty and noble bearing, they radiate a sort of gentleness, a divine goodness. I have to say, I understand the white man's fears. There are no two ways about it: Folklore, popular art, songs—it all comes from them. That's why, despite their "detachment," their great nobility, their deep sense of what really matters—which, even more than patience or fear, are the genuine reasons behind their extraordinary indulgence toward white behavior—the Negros are on their way up. Tomorrow America will be theirs.

### Departure

I still have the time to see *The Wizard of Oz* and to have the pleasure of discovering that Mickey Rooney is a creepy kid, a disgusting tyke, a budding fascist, and anything else you'd care to come up with along those lines. Don't ask me, "But what did you see him do?" All I had to do was see him on stage.

The next day, thanks to Burstyn, I didn't miss the boat—which I would have if we'd arrived five minutes later. We leave, America slips away.

### At Sea

The *Champlain* has better third-class accommodations than the *Ile-de-France*. There's a French musician on board, a guitarist who has to go back to serve in the military. German propaganda has caught on in the United States. All you have to do is listen to this guy. He keeps trotting out all the resentments Hollywood must be full of. According to him, America is being sucked dry by the Jews.

At noon the following day, when they pass out the ship's paper, I learn of what I take to be a German-Soviet military pact.

My chest constricts in apprehension.

I think of all the young men and women of America—what are they thinking? In any case, the news is terrifying, and all the more so since the ship's paper is short on details. I admit, however, that I don't believe there'll be war. I think that, more likely, there will be a second Munich Accord. Consternation is the reigning sentiment on board ship, and it increases overnight. For my part, I'm breathing easier: It isn't a military pact after all. But what does it mean? What to think? Everybody's talking about it. Meanwhile, you may not believe me but not a single Frenchman in third class blames Moscow. They all blame Munich. I listen and keep my mouth shut, because although I don't believe war will break out immediately, I do know the bell has begun to toll for the Western world. And yet I refuse to believe there will be a war. I reassure people, I work, I write.

I'd forgotten the warning signs of July.

As we draw closer to Europe, the news grows worse. Mobilizations, speeches on the radio, the whole feverish routine of September 1938. Yep—not the warning signs of July, not Hensel's hasty departure, and not the men's overcoats cut like those in 1914 manage to make me believe there will be a war. When we dock at Southhampton, there's a mad rush to get the papers. Too late—the passengers in first class bought up every copy in sight.

I'll wait until we reach Le Havre. I want to get my bearings. When we arrive, they ask for passports.

"Merci, mon brave," the inspector says to me. "My good courageous fellow" indeed! Hmmm. Now I get it. . . .

When I get my hands on *L'Oeuvre*, *Le Temps*, and *L'Humanité*, I'll get to the bottom of the mystery.

"*L'Humanité?*" says the woman at the newsstand. "But, my dear sir, it's been banned since yesterday."

"All right," I say. "Then give me *Ce Soir*." That's banned too. One musn't take this the wrong way. This woman personally finds nothing wrong with my choice of reading matter. To my considerable surprise, she goes on counting while I register shock. "Okay. Then let me have *Regard*." Which she does—but it's from last week. They're still patting each other on the back over the Franco-Soviet negotiations. Oh well, skip it. *L'Epoque*, *Le Figaro*, *L'Oeuvre*, and *Le Populaire* will set me straight.

The train leaves, and I start reading. Here they're mobilizing, making decrees and redecrees, but the whole thing appears to be less serious than I'd imagined. It's still at the blackmail stage. The Russians are paying back the Allies, but good. I don't see them going along all that much with the Germans. I feel calmed. It's September 1938 all over again. There's still time.

There are no porters when we arrive at Saint-Lazare Station. People are asking for them, and the conductors reply, "They're on the Maginot Line. Leave us alone!" I spot one all the same. I ask him a few questions to get an idea of what's really going on. He doesn't think there'll be a war either. Thanks be to the heavens, there are still taxis. When I get to rue Troyon, my mother's glad to see me—she was already picturing me sunk by a torpedo.

To think I left 100 phonograph records behind in New York and they didn't even open my bags at customs!

Henri's diary ends there, along with his trip. The good times were over. On 1 September, the day after Henri's return, Germany invaded Poland. World War II had begun.

## chapter 4

# WAR AND OCCUPATION

And these are the courageous ones, those who escape from the long columns
that the Germans are leading toward enormous camps.

Henri Amouroux, *Le Peuple du désastre*


Just as soon as he'd returned from America, Langlois rushed to
the Palais de Chaillot to check on his precious films—and was stunned to
discover that they'd disappeared.

He learned, on 2 September, that, in accordance with orders issued by a
Monsieur Huisman, director of Beaux-Arts, the entire film collection had
been evacuated the previous Monday. Such a measure was perfectly understandable in light of possible bombardments, but it had been carried out in
spectacular—and in all likelihood premature—haste. In direct contrast to
the brand of lethargy that would more or less envelop the nation until the
German offensive of May 1940, the first days of mobilization had been awash
with frantic activity. Matters concerning the cinema or photography were
being overseen by Monsieur Chataigneau, assisted by representatives from
the navy and the French equivalent of the FBI, as well as Mademoiselle
Suzanne Borel and Madame Claude Bacheville.

Finally, Henri learned that the films had been sent 100 miles from Paris to
the Château de Coucy in the Aisne region where, they were sure to be subjected to unacceptable levels of humidity. Horrified, Henri tried all sorts of
methods in an attempt to bring the films back to Paris before the Aisne was
declared a militarized zone. The Beaux-Arts administration displayed obvious ill will toward Henri, and so he pinned all his hopes on Suzanne Borel.
On 18 September 1939, he sent her the following brief letter:

Mademoiselle,

I dislike being obliged to bother you again when you have so much to do, but I beg you to see me, if only for a moment. My trip to Coucy was useless. It was impossible for me to withdraw our films, despite my presenting a written order to that effect. It seems that the letter Madame Albin-Guillot gave me was insufficient and did not conform to regulations!

In two days, Aisne will become part of the militarized zone. I must therefore be able to get back to Coucy before the twentieth. I now know which documents I must obtain from the Beaux-Arts administration, but I need them before tomorrow. That is why I implore you to see me for just a few minutes. I have an appointment with Madame Albin-Guillot later today.

Yours in devotion,

H. Langlois

The route the films would travel from the declaration of war until the Germans' decisive breakthrough at Sedan, and then during the lightning-swift campaign to follow, was a veritable free-form ballet, several steps removed from rhyme or reason. The Cinémathèque's most precious possessions were to be subjected to events of the most unpredictable nature.

One can easily picture the "paternal" anguish that clutched at Langlois's heart when he contemplated the fate that might await his defenseless films, far from home.

On 5 April 1940, a certain number of the films stored at Coucy began the trip back to the Palais de Chaillot, in the most roundabout way imaginable.

Just a few days later, however, Langlois received his mobilization order. As the Germans drew nearer to the capital, Henri could only send back instructions to his mother in Paris, asking her to make certain that the films immediately be taken to an address on the rue du Plateau, from which they would be evacuated by the Army Film Corps. After that, the political situation would worsen considerably, and he'd have no further means of knowing what had become of his beloved films.

Before being called to active duty, however, Henri had had the time to indulge in one last international peacetime adventure with his Italian friends at the Cineteca Milanese.

Langlois had just obtained from Mary Meerson, widow of the famous set designer Lazare Meerson, the loan of a selection of her late husband's set designs so that Henri might exhibit them at the Milan Triennial. Since Alexandre Trauner had worked with Meerson more closely than anyone else, Henri asked him to come along to help install the show.

At that time, Trauner still had a Hungarian passport. Yet Henri somehow managed to get him an exit and reentry visa. Langlois had been invited to stay with the Comencini family, and Trauner had booked a hotel room. Luigi Comencini met them at the train station. On the way to their respective accommodations, Henri stopped short in front of a Motta ice cream parlor. He marched right in and proceeded to taste every flavor the shop carried—25 in all!

In the middle of the night, Trauner was awakened by a frantic phone call from Signora Comencini: "Come over right away—Henri's in terrible shape!"

When Trauner arrived on the scene, he burst out laughing at the peculiar operation under way: Henri was stretched out on the kitchen table while Signora Comencini ironed his stomach. Her objective: to melt the ice cream! She went on ironing for 45 minutes or so, after which Henri felt much better (and possibly much flatter and wrinkle-free).

The following morning, on the way to see Ponti, the founding architect of the Milan Triennial, Langlois stopped at Motta and began ordering all over again. Trauner naturally expressed his surprise at this swift bout of recidivism, to which Langlois replied that this time he'd have the entire day to digest the stuff.

In view of the Triennial's importance, Langlois had planned a large exhibition, including all sorts of cameras, documents, posters, scale models, and costumes. There would also be a film series. And so it was thanks to Langlois that Renoir's *La Grande Illusion* was shown in Italy for the first time. Needless to say, the print had been smuggled in from Paris.

The audience at the screening was wildly enthusiastic. At the moment in the film when the French prisoners begin singing "La Marseillaise," the crowd stood and began to sing along in the darkness. But there were also some fascists in attendance who whistled and jeered before commencing to sing "Giovanezza." The lights went back on. Lattuada grabbed the microphone and implored the audience to consider this cinematic chef d'oeuvre from an aesthetic, rather than political, point of view. At that point, the police burst in, in search of those responsible. Luigi Comencini and Alberto Lattuada hid in the projection booth prior to escaping over the rooftops. This epic projection marked the end of the Cineteca Milanese. Italy would join the war before long and all film screenings of this kind were banned.

All the same, Comencini and Lattuada managed to hide the dozens of films Henri had brought, along with their own holdings, at a farm outside Milan. There they would remain throughout the war, safe from the bombardments and the searches carried out first by the fascists and later by the Germans. The farm in question was an ideal hiding place—so ideal that Henri would, with his Italian friends' loyal complicity, hide still other films there later on. "We were able to hide Jean Renoir's films," recalls Gianni Comencini, brother to Luigi and director of the cinémathèque in Milan.

"Henri feared that the Germans would seize his collections. Then he got the idea of also hiding the negatives of Jean Vigo's films in Milan, convinced that no one would ever dream that those films were here with us."

In France, military activity had been at a standstill throughout the last four months of 1939. After a short offensive in the Sarre, the French command ordered that all operations cease and that the troops return to the border. And so began what came to be called *la drôle de guerre* (the phony war). Five million men began to wonder why they'd been dragged away from their homes, their fields, and their factories just to hang around doing nothing, their guns unused at their feet. The Germans had launched a barrage of psychological warfare. Reams of newspapers and tracts, as well as hours of radio broadcasts, pelted the soldiers on the Maginot Line, asking them whether it could possibly be worthwhile to die for Gdansk or for the English. The troops went on stewing in their encampments. They were completely idle and took to drink to pass the time.

The Office of Information was so grossly incompetent that Suzanne Borel wrote to her mother, "If the army is as screwed up as the High Commission, France stands a real chance of losing the war." Mademoiselle Borel's lucidity was not to the liking of her superior, Jean Giradoux. She immediately found herself out of a job.

One anecdote perfectly illustrates the level of carelessness at work in the very heart of the Office of Information and its censorship division. The king of England had come to visit the French troops, and this visit had been filmed by the army's newsreel photographers. Pierre Descaves, director of the Comédie-Française, was himself unable to screen the resulting film and so appointed an infantry colonel to replace him. The colonel refused to approve the film from the word go—and he had what he thought was a very good reason.

"We see, standing beside the king, General de la Porte de Theil, commander of this army," the colonel explained. "The general has a large, distinctive mustache by which he may easily be recognized. The Germans will therefore know where the king is."

"But the king has already left," pointed out Roger Weil-Lorac, director of Pathé-Cinéma. "People will find this demonstration of Franco-British friendship very cheering. And besides, the Germans have certainly known for a long time where the king has gone to visit."

Shaken by these arguments, the colonel watched the film a second time but refused to give in. He may have had a fine grasp of infantry work, but his understanding of the nature of documentary footage left something to be desired. "Shave off the general's mustache," he qualified, "and you can distribute the film."

This was the general atmosphere in which the Cinémathèque Française set about organizing film programs for the troops and charity galas for the benefit of the Red Cross. These special shows lifted the soldiers out of their apathy and often led to demonstrations of patriotic fervor.

As for Henri, he was delighted to broaden his audience and, at the same time, give the Cinémathèque a role of genuine national importance.

Marguerite Bussot, a journalist at *Pour vous* magazine, tells in an article of how she went, in November, to a program of films organized by the gunners of the Fiftieth Group of the DCA, the antiaircraft artillery unit. She had first heard a short speech by Brigadier André Robert, who introduced the films from the Cinémathèque. The soldiers, she notes, had turned out in large number, and were attentive and interested. The high-ranking officers still considered it beneath them to attend, but the troops and lower-ranking officers took genuine pleasure in seeing *L'Illusion* by Méliès; *Léonce à la campagne* by Perret; an Italian version of *Julius Ceasar* from 1913; *Snooky the Chimpanzee*, an American offering from 1917; and Charlie Chaplin's *The Cure*. After an intermission, the soldiers were able to see Marcel Ichac's film *Mission de la France*.

The growing success of Cinémathèque projections would eventually result in the lifting of all objections from the censor. Better still, the various branches of the military would soon be joined in their unqualified approval by both civil and religious authorities, a victory that did not go unnoticed by the press.

Even if Langlois was soon to be mobilized, it mattered little, for everything was functioning smoothly. He had provided the Army Bureau of Film Services with those films needed to continue the program, and Henri trusted André Robert to carry on with it. Special galas were organized in several cities. Not only did the Cinémathèque itself not benefit from any sort of subsidy at the time, but in the space of just four soirées, its old films brought in no less than 45,000 francs for the army's own charity projects under the direction of Edouard Daladier. This far-from-negligible result was not one that anyone would dream of mentioning years later, when the Cinémathèque's reputation was being maligned.

Henri was called up for active duty at the beginning of April 1940 and assigned to DCA depot 409 in Tours, where it was quickly determined that he was not particularly gifted for handling firearms. But his excellent memory enabled him to make himself useful in the communications division, where he learned Morse code. He was a diligent student and during this brief training period managed to strike a pleasant balance between reading the magazines he asked his mother to send and learning the language of the telegraph, in which, once he could tap it out automatically, he discovered a sort of poetic rhythm.

On 25 April he joined the Fortieth Antiaircraft Artillery Regiment, where he used his new telegraphy talents to send transmissions. The Germans invaded two weeks later. Because of the nature of his work, Henri was one of the first to be aware of the orders and counterorders that came in at ever-increasing intervals. The leaders' false assurance turned to panic.

Less than one week after the start of operations, the situation was already judged to be so serious that the Quai d'Orsay in Paris was burning its archives. Events moved swiftly. By 17 May, Guderian had reached the Oise. The antiaircraft unit had to do battle with the Germans' Stukas. The soldiers were taken completely by surprise, and their artillery batteries were spread too far apart to prove effective. On 10 June the prime minister left the capital, and on 12 June Paris was declared an open city. The troops were still resisting, but a final blow was dealt them when, at noon on 17 June, Marshal Pétain announced over the radio that all combat must cease.

As was the case for countless others before it, it was Langlois's unit's turn to be captured. One final marching order set the place—behind Tours—where the men were to assemble to surrender to the Germans. Certain men rushed to get there as though they couldn't wait to get it over with. The majority imagined that the war was over and their liberation near.

Henri was utterly convinced that the opposite was true. As he walked through the Loire countryside with other defeated soldiers, he was not thinking, as they were, of the wife and children awaiting his return. He moved forward and with each step became more convinced that the fate of his films depended entirely upon him. Certainly, he had made all the necessary arrangements so that they might be evacuated along with those of the Army Bureau of Film Services. But where were they now? Had they reached a safe place? Had they been destroyed by bombardments or fallen into enemy hands?

Henri found no comfort in remembering gags from *Shoulder Arms*. This march toward captivity could easily mean the obliteration of all his past efforts, the irrevocable loss of his collections, the end of the Cinémathèque Française itself. No, it was not Chaplin but the final scenes of *Grand Illusion* that came back to him now, for they were surely closer to the reality that awaited him: He would never be able to escape from a prisoner-of-war camp somewhere in the wilds of Germany. And then, all of a sudden, what had been only a vague premonition became a full-fledged certainty. Right now, at this very moment, his films were in the greatest of peril. In a matter of hours, it would be too late. It was now or never that he had to make his escape!

He remembered a schoolboy trick that had enabled him to get into the movies without paying. Silly as it seemed, in order to sneak into the theater by slipping through the crowd on its way out from the previous show, all one had to do was—walk backward!

The decisive moment had come. He would first let those who were in a hurry pass him by. There was no reason to hurry; he could mark time at select intervals and—why not?—give his old sneaky recipe a try by walking backward. The gap had grown between two groups that were dragging their feet. The time was ripe: A small wooded area broke up the fields and ran alongside the road. Henri eyed the depth of the roadside ditch, leaped over it as best he could, and ducked quickly into the trees.

Henri's army buddies would spend the rest of the war in a camp. But his destiny lay elsewhere: in Paris, fighting for his creation.

One month later, in the family apartment on rue Troyon, Annie Langlois sadly set the table for dinner. There were only two places—one for her and one for her husband. She hadn't had news of her two children for many long weeks. The instant the radio had announced that the capital would no longer be defended, Georges had left Paris for the Southwest by bicycle, in the company of the Cinémathèque's secretary, Yvonne Cathala. As for Henri, his last message dated back to May: a hastily scribbled note written in search of assurance, for the umpteenth time, that his films would really and truly be evacuated to safety.

The doorbell rang at that moment—a series of short rings that Annie Langlois was sure she recognized. With her heart in her throat, she opened the door to see her disheveled-looking elder son wearing an unbelievably peculiar getup, that of an agricultural worker who had fallen on hard times and become a vagabond. It was a comic and jovial Henri who fell into his mother's arms with a loud sigh of relief.

"There were times when I thought I'd never make it," Henri admitted. "While I was out in the country, things were still all right, but as soon as I reached the suburbs, people began giving me the once-over. Fortunately, I had this idea—I picked up this vegetable cart loaded with food, thanks to which I got across Paris. Without papers and dressed like this, it was as good as a pass."

Following his now-or-never plunge into the woods, Henri had taken refuge on a farm where the elderly owner immediately agreed to hide him. Disguised as a farmhand, Henri had patiently awaited an opportunity to set off for Paris. "That was when," he added, "I saw the true nature of my situation: To the Germans, I'm an escaped prisoner, and Vichy might also consider me a deserter."

"But Riri," his mother implored, "tell me what happened—what got into you on that road?"

"Don't even try to understand. It can't be explained. I won't go so far as to say I heard voices, but . . . Let's just say that at that very instant I understood they were in danger."

"But *who* was in danger?"

"The films! The films the army was supposed to evacuate."

"But they were evacuated—I'm sure of it," his mother affirmed.

"Well, then, it's at that very moment that something bad befell them. Please, Mom, tell me what's happened to them."

Annie Langlois didn't have the slightest idea. All she knew was that the Army Bureau of Film Services had taken them as arranged, but she had no indication as to what direction the loading vans had gone.

Henri had complete confidence in Jean Rossignol, a devoted regular at Cercle screenings who had been mobilized into the Film Services headquartered at rue Plateau, under the direction of Colonel Calvet and Captain Watrin. It was to that address that—with the help of a good word from Henri Chaumette and from Jean Renoir—Henri had had most of the Cinémathèque's films sent.

He had no reason to doubt that Rossignol had diligently carried out his mission. But why, then, had he had that naggingly sinister premonition on the march toward Germany?

The facts seemed to bear out Henri's premonition, for he would soon learn that the films that had been spirited away in trucks and driven to the region of La Rochecorbon had subsequently been hidden in caves in that vicinity. But civilians had denounced these hiding places to the enemy, and the Germans wasted no time in impounding the entire collection—at more or less the same moment Henri suddenly felt he must escape and come to their aid.

In the meantime, Annie unburdened herself of a worry that had been tormenting her. It seems that 10 days before Henri showed up, she had received a surprising visit from a German officer in full uniform, a man of some years who announced, in perfectly accented English—that he was looking for Mr. Henri Langlois. Annie was very frightened.

"I didn't want to tell him anything—not even that you'd been drafted. I told him you didn't live here anymore and we hadn't heard from you. I don't know if he believed me. Anyway, I couldn't tell from his expression. He ended up saying, 'If you see him, give him my card.' I've got it here in the top drawer of the buffet."

There were two words imprinted on the card, in Gothic lettering: Major Hensel. An address in Vichy had been written in by hand. Henri stood there dreamily for a moment, then reassured his mother: "Don't worry about it. I have to think this through—but first, I have to get some sleep."

The next day, the last Sunday of August 1940, Henri sat turning the major's calling card over and over again between his fingers. He stared at the Germanic characters and couldn't make up his mind. He felt he knew Hensel, but the fact that he was now a major in the Occupation army posed a serious problem.

Henri had to face up to facts: The Cinémathèque Française no longer existed. It had lost most of its films and no longer had a meeting place to call its own. Its secretary, Yvonne Cathala, had joined the mass exodus out of town, and Georges Franju, Henri's faithful friend, was hiding somewhere out in the country. The decision, fraught with potential consequences of the unpleasant variety, was his alone to make.

FIAF headquarters was still located in Paris, but there were plans afoot to have it transferred to Berlin—at which point the federation would fall apart, since the British and the Americans would no longer want to have anything to do with it. Henri still remembered how reluctant Iris Barry and Olwen Vaughan had been about allowing the Reichsfilmarchiv to become a member in the first place.

Henri made up his mind that night. He was convinced that the stakes were too high to not take a chance, but decided to first take up the matter with Claude Bacheville. Madame Bacheville, who would go back to using her real name, Yvonne Dornès, after the war, was half-Jewish and thus in no danger of feeling sympathetic toward the Nazis.

Henri confided in her, outlining his plans: Resist through every available means, but never miss a trick in the battle to save films. To preserve her integrity, his young confidante had resigned from her position in the prime minister's office and taken over as director for the Office of Public Information, a bureau whose communications resources she would soon put at Henri's disposal in order to facilitate the clandestine transport of films, thereby helping him to get Cinémathèque cargo into the unoccupied zone where it could then be safely hidden, notably in the Béduer Château. For the time being, Henri asked her to travel to Vichy and sound out Hensel.

In the meantime, Henri exercised caution when he left the house, but he wasn't all that worried for himself. After all, he was so incredibly skinny that anyone would assume he'd been turned down as unfit for military service. Paris seemed practically vacant. Whereas before Henri had rarely known a day when he was not bubbling over with energy and enthusiasm, he now felt drained and hollow.

The fellow heading across the completely deserted place Saint-Augustin one late afternoon at the end of August 1940 was none other than Jean-Paul Le Chanois. He couldn't shake an "end of the world" feeling brought on by the complete absence of street activity and, looking back at the place he'd known to be so full of traffic and people, said to himself, "It's so empty it's frightening." He turned to continue on his way. The rue de la Boétie stretched out before him, also as still as could be. "Is there at least one other pedestrian somewhere in this ghost town?" he wondered. The answer appeared to be yes, for he began to make out a silhouette several hundred yards in the distance. The figure was still too far away to discern whether it was a man or a woman. The individual seemed to hesitate at the cross street, then opt to continue in the same direction and was finally drawing near enough to be seen more clearly. Le Chanois felt a sudden shock of recognition: "At that instant I realized that this lone pedestrian was a man and that the man was Henri. A wonderful stroke of luck!"

Their chance meeting was doubly providential, in that neither of the men had the slightest notion what had become of the other. They'd last seen each other a year earlier. Upon Langlois's return to France from New York, he went to see Le Chanois, wondering what his friend thought of the German-Soviet pact, since Le Chanois both hated the Nazis and held membership in the Communist party.

For Langlois, who had just then been thinking about Le Chanois, their meeting was "utterly fantastic." Le Chanois, more pragmatic, pronounced the event merely "wonderful." Henri, more excited than ever, got straight to the point: "So what are you up to now?"

"Be careful," Le Chanois replied. "Write down my address and come over for dinner. Then we can talk."

Henri was delighted at the invitation, and when he arrived at Le Chanois's place, he greeted him with "Whew! Well, here I am, all the way to Moscow to gather information."

The two friends certainly laughed, but this greeting in the form of a jest concealed Langlois's thirst for information and action. He had always admired Le Chanois, not only as a member of the Friends of Spartacus and a participant in the Groupe octobre, but also as a journalist and scriptwriter. Le Chanois, who was four years older than Henri, had already worked at nearly all the jobs the cinema had to offer: line producer, film editor, assistant to directors as skilled and well known as Duvivier, Korda, Ophuls, and Renoir. He knew tons of people, be they illustrious film directors or the lowliest technicians and stagehands.

Henri counted himself among those who couldn't accept defeat as a punishment France deserved. If he was there seated with his host, it was because he knew that Le Chanois must be up to something. He broached the subject again:

"So tell me, what are you doing these days?"

"Since I'm lucky enough to own a bicycle, I can get around. I make my living working for an electrician."

"That's not what I'm asking. Now, what *else* are you doing?"

Le Chanois turned serious. "I'm thinking of bringing together all the film people."

"In that case, sign me up and tell me what I'm supposed to do."

"Keep on doing what you've already done: Hide as many films as you can. And don't forget all the films that are still at the labs—they're at risk too, if someone decides they're not about the 'correct' subject matter."

In early September, Yvonne Dornès went to Vichy to secretly contact Hensel. Vichy, as of 12 July, was the administrative capital of a vanquished nation cut in two. Thanks to its extensive hotel accommodations, the central administration and many of the civil servants it employed had been reassembled there. The enemy's swift advance had caught the previous administration by surprise, and the selfsame people were working for the new regime. Some, like the head of the Film Service of the Ministry of Information, fell all over themselves to fulfill the wishes of the German delegations. But the majority of the old staff had held on to their critical faculties and their free-dom of opinion.

Yves Chataigneau and Suzanne Borel were also in Vichy. The former would soon go to London to join General de Gaulle; the latter was stuck with her position at the Ministry of Foreign Affairs. As she went about her business, working in the heart of the Censorship Committee, Borel contin-ued to speak her mind and refused to be made to toe the line. French film production was paralyzed for the moment, and German films were out of her control. That left British and American films on which to pass judgment. The Censorship Committee held its meetings around a large table in a room right next to the office of the *maréchal* himself, Pétain. The arguments were often so loud that one day, fed up with the noise, the elderly statesman was obliged to personally calm the members of the committee. On another occa-sion, the film on the block had the tale of a divorce as its theme. Several of Suzanne Borel's colleagues were shocked that such a subject could figure as a major element of a filmscript. She flew off the handle at their prim, narrow attitudes and said, "Why should we ban it? Divorce *is* legal in France."

To which a representative from the Ministry of Youth replied with com-punction, "It would not fit in with the *maréchal*'s general views."

Suzanne Borel leaped from her chair, unable to believe her ears. "Not fit in with his views? Why, if it weren't for divorce, the *maréchal* wouldn't even be married!"

A live hand grenade tossed out on the table couldn't have had a more devastating effect. Everyone knew that Pétain had married a divorcée, but no one would have dreamed of stating the fact out loud. In any event, Suzanne Borel's brave outburst had a beneficial outcome: The Censorship Committee decided to approve the film.

As for Yvonne Dornès, she met with Hensel and found him to be most understanding. He did not wish to betray his country, but in the higher interest of cinema, he was prepared to make certain concessions for the Cinémathèque Française.

When Yvonne Dornès returned to Paris to report to Henri on the results of her mission, the status of the cinema in the occupied zone was nothing short of catastrophic. Not only had French film production ground to a complete halt, but the authorities would permit only German films to be imported. The vast majority of films that arrived from other countries during the exodus were impounded at customs, and in Paris itself only those films that were already in release at the moment of capitulation remained in circu-lation. Among its demands, the German delegation to the Armistice Committee had insisted that all French films that dealt with war or espi-onage and might be considered an offense to the dignity of the Wehrmacht be pulled off the screen. This edict, which in the unoccupied zone meant simply that such films could not be projected, was interpreted much more severely in Paris and gave rise to thorough hunts conducted by the German SS, who were determined to get their hands on—and destroy—films like *Alerte en Méditerranée*, *Mata-Hari*, *Trois de Saint-Cyr*, and anything else with a suspicious title.

Henri's torment could only grow: The Germans were making the rounds of all the film labs, confiscating everything on hand in order to salvage the cellulose and silver salts lurking in the prints and their negatives. Langlois was haunted by the idea that these precious lengths of film would be transformed into incendiary bombs. In the wake of the Luftwaffe's bloody raid on Coventry, in November 1940, Langlois's sleep was long disturbed by the same vivid nightmare: As a city went up in flames, from the billowing smoke emerged the ghostly forms of characters from English films.

On 17 October the Germans took a decisive new step. All films made after 1939 were to be seized in accordance with an edict from the military commander that began with the no-nonsense phrase, "By virtue of the full powers granted to me by the führer."

Faced with a situation of this magnitude, Henri decided to make use of Major Hensel's kindly predisposition to the cause of film preservation. Hensel's assistance, which sometimes flirted along the edges of outright complicity, constitutes a rare phenomenon in the annals of collaboration, since, in this case, the occupier was collaborating for the benefit of the occupied. The single-minded passion of Franju and Langlois can also be credited with bringing about this small miracle.

It must be pointed out that Major Frank Hensel, an influential figure in Hitler's Germany and then in his early fifties, was no ordinary man. His mother was English, and he had remained an ardent Anglophile. Before the war, Hensel directed a railway company whose Paris offices were located near the Opera. A bon vivant and confirmed film buff, Hensel was more than satisfied that the FIAF gave him an excellent excuse for remaining in Paris throughout the Occupation—which was infinitely preferable to braving the rigors of the front. Hensel knew that he owed his FIAF presidency to Langlois and also knew how to show his gratitude. When Georges Franju returned to Paris, he was invited to once again take up his post as executive secretary.

Franju and Langlois succeeded in convincing Hensel that regardless of the war industry's needs, it was imperative that at least two prints and the negative of each film be preserved. The two friends were also able to obtain free access to and the use of the subbasements of the Palais de Chaillot. "On one condition," Hensel told them, as he handed over the keys to the subterranean storage area. "And that is that you deposit nothing here that could be considered damaging or compromising to Germany." For safety's sake, Langlois would keep this promise and stored at Chaillot only those films completely free of political overtones. All other works, those banned or sought by the Nazis, he managed to hide in secret caches where the Germans were certain never to find them. This "blockhouse" at Chaillot would prove to be a most useful locale, for, to top things off, a very official-looking sign forbid the military itself to enter the premises. Only Langlois and Franju had the keys.

Later on, Hensel would even go so far as to tip off Langlois to certain operations the Germans planned to carry out, thereby enabling Henri to avoid a multitude of dangers and to in turn warn his friends who were being hunted by the Gestapo. Hensel would have had to have been blind, for example, not to notice that Henri was sending money orders to Lotte Eisner under an assumed name. When the Allied forces landed in North Africa on 10 November 1942, and German troops were preparing to invade the unoccupied zone of France, it was again thanks to Hensel that Langlois could give advance warning to his friends in hiding there.

As a member of the Nazi party, Hensel should not be considered a resistance fighter, not by a long shot. Nonetheless, the fact remains that he could have done a great deal of damage had he so wished. Hensel never once betrayed Henri or any of Henri's friends. He knew, for example, through their acquaintance before the war, that Paul-Auguste Harlé was Jewish. How could he not have known that Langlois was in contact with Harlé when he traveled into the southern zone and that, as a result, Harlé was eventually able to avoid being deported?

When the tables turned and Hensel was obliged to head back to a Germany already shattered by bombardments, he found himself curious about one last thing: How exactly had Henri made use of the Palais de Chaillot's basement? He asked Georges Franju to take him there for a visit. The president of the Reichsfilmarchiv could not conceal his utter stupefaction when confronted with a seemingly endless mass of film cans, stacked one atop another from floor to ceiling as far as the eye could see. Ever the gentleman, he had only one understated remark to make: "You've done quite a nice job here, but you were right not to tell me everything."

A certain element of mystery remains in regard to Frank Hensel, as to why he chose to behave as he did. Whatever his reasons, his conduct toward the Cinémathèque was meritorious. Hensel, who died years later in West Germany, never ran into problems after the war, or indeed even felt the need to plan for such an eventuality by prevailing upon Langlois as a reference.

As Henri was leaving the dinner at Le Chanois's house, his newly refound friend advised him to quickly round up those films the Germans wanted that were still being stored at the labs where they'd been printed. This activity, while hardly negligible, didn't completely satisfy Henri. He wanted to be part of the Resistance, to create his own movement within it, if necessary. The first meeting was held at the Langlois's apartment on rue Troyon.

Set designer Max Douy remembers the occasion well:

> I met Henri Langlois when some of us got together to create a movement that we called the Resistance Organization against Nazism in France. We met in groups of three, four, or five at most to produce tracts, and organized meetings in the places where films were made, where we'd contact others who, like us, thought that things couldn't go on as they were. It was toward the end of 1941. I was with Le Chanois, and the meeting was at the Langlois place on rue Troyon. That was the beginning of the Resistance in the entertainment field, and things got organized very quickly with Jean-Paul Le Chanois, Louis Daquin, Zwaboda, and Langlois. Langlois was very worried about the films he'd already managed to accumulate. Then he invited me to become part of the Cinémathèque, since I was a set designer. Because I'd been assistant to Trauner and Meerson, Langlois knew he could count on me to have a certain measure of respect for the work he was carrying out. Langlois didn't flaunt his allegiences, but as far as I'm concerned, he was a member of the Resistance. He knew how to surround himself with the contacts he needed to carry on with what he'd begun—a massive project of preservation and discovery.

Langlois stayed in contact with Le Chanois throughout the early years of the Occupation. But their meetings, which were inevitably shrouded in a certain mystery, broke off in 1943. From that point on, Le Chanois pursued an increasingly difficult course of action, eventually becoming part of a nearly military structure. The dangers of underground activities, the time he spent in the Vercors maquis, where he grabbed shots on location for sequences in his film *Au coeur de l'orage*, made it necessary for him to take excessive precautions. He couldn't risk the slightest slip-up, and Henri, who at the time was stepping up his clandestine screenings, had him somewhat worried:

> Henri kept me posted on what he'd been able to rescue, and I told him "Bravo!" because when the Germans raided a blockhouse, they took everything that wasn't nailed down—it's just that, so far as a lot of these locations were concerned, Henri had gotten there first. My role required such security measures that I couldn't go on seeing Henri. He was an incredibly likable kid, but all the same, he could be dangerous at times. He wanted to rush into things too fast and would shout, "We've got to do something!" and I was the one who had to calm him down. It all started with the secret projections he, along with Max Douy, was holding at his house. There's no doubt about his wanting to do more, but I decided to put Henri on the "back burner" by telling him one last time and for good: "As for you, your job is to take care of the Cinémathèque—nothing more and nothing less. Save films and keep your nose out of other business."

Since Henri had deaf ears for the voice of reason, he thumbed his nose at the German authorities. The truth of the matter was that, forbidden or not, Henri could no more do without seeing and showing films than he could do without oxygen.

Throughout France, the winter of 1940–41 was one of terrible privation. It had crept up on a nation both unsuspecting and unprepared, and the black market and all the other clever little ways of getting around the system were not yet in operation. Henri, who was skinnier than ever, listened without batting an eyelash as Gustave Langlois announced to his family, on Christmas night, "We've just opened the last of our supplies. Pretty soon, we'll have nothing left to eat."

Gustave had been supporting his family on the proceeds from his patented invention for heating trains with the steam the locomotive itself produced. But he had not received a cent in royalties owed him by the Fonderie moderne strasbourgeoise since May 1940. All the commissions due him for the use of his invention over the prior year remained unpaid, since the Germans had, once again, annexed Alsace. Gustave had paid a personal visit to the great warehouses at Villeneuve-Saint-Georges, only to be told, "Oh! You know, mister, we've got other things to think about besides heating trains. If you're looking for orders, there are always the requisitions. You can take it up with the Germans."

Gustave Langlois had refused to "take it up with the Germans" and, as a result, had been living on his savings since September 1939. The family put their heads together. Annie Langlois and Gustave himself agreed that Henri's work was much too important to give up in exchange for a paying job. That left Georges to save the day. Handily enough, the Ministry of Agriculture and Provisions had just announced a recruitment exam. Georges applied and went straight to the head of the class. He was unable to continue attending his law school courses at the university, but that was not an insurmountable obstacle; one could still sit for the bar exam, after studying stenciled materials, without actually attending classes. Georges began working in February 1941 and was quickly promoted to head the general provisions detail in the Seine-et-Oise, northeast of Paris. His salary enabled him to support the family until 1943, when his full-time involvement with the Resistance obliged him to resign.

Freed of all worry about where his next meal was coming from, Henri was able to devote himself entirely to his various nonprofit activities. Foremost among these were the secret film screenings he put on with an old 35-millimeter projector, wherever he could and starting, of course, with his own home.

Fortunately, the living room and dining room were connected by a large opening that made it possible to sit a reasonable distance away from the makeshift screen. Come nightfall, with the shutters shut tight and the drapes drawn closed behind them, everyone pitched in to prepare for the screening. The table had to be removed from the dining room. Then someone would stand on a chair and mount the sheet that Annie Langlois had just ironed by pushing thumbtacks into the frame of the mirror over the mantlepiece. One screen ready for duty!

The atmosphere was always one of warmth and shared enthusiasm. Henri cast himself as a smiling and mysterious master of ceremonies. He slowly pried open the film cans, recited the selected title with a flourish, then threaded and started the projector. The audience fell silent and forgot the clackety-hum of the projector, caught up in moving images that—as the cinema has done so well since it first began—set them free. Simone Signoret was often present at Langlois's secret projections. It was at one such screening that she first saw *Potemkin*: "All the Russian films, the banned films of Renoir and those by Prévert, the only beautiful films I saw during that entire period were the ones Henri Langlois showed at his parents' place. He moved the films to and fro on the Métro, which sounds comic now, but posed a certain danger at the time."

The last Métro train left the end of the line at 11:00 P.M. Curfew went into effect at midnight. Henri had only to walk a few blocks from home whenever he wanted to devote his evening to visiting with Catherine Hessling. Jean Renoir's ex-wife, the actress who portrayed the title role in the 1926 version of *Nana*, lived in an apartment on whose walls were displayed several Auguste Renoir canvases, along with photos of Catherine in all her glory as a silent star, when she had worked with Cavalcanti, Pabst, and Chenal, among others. It was not uncommon for Henri to lose all track of time in Catherine's charming company, and he would have to run all the way home, dashing across the Champs-Elysées with his heart pounding lest a German patrol spot him.

On other occasions, the appointed hour took him by surprise while at the homes of still other friends who, naturally, invited him to stay the night. Henri couldn't have paid less attention to regular habits or regular hours— the bohemian life suited him. His friends would have sworn that he lived on a diet of film stock and preferred to sleep on the bare floor beside his films rather than be apart from them for even one night.

Among his most devoted friends, Henri could always count on Denise Tual, a producer and director whom he'd known since childhood. If Henri needed money, he turned to Denise, and he often entrusted her to keep a film or two for a few days, between official hiding places. One evening when Henri neglected to leave the Tual apartment before curfew, Madame Tual came upon him, in the middle of the night, rolled up in the living room rug like a giant crepe, with only his head sticking out. That selfsame head whose inner workings were so inexplicable to others lay sound asleep on a rock-hard film-can pillow. The dragon slept peacefully with its treasure. . . .

Henri soon grew dissatisfied with the technical limitations of the household projections. He wanted a real projection booth and the screen to match. Langlois would make use of a small professional screening room located on one of the upper floors of a building at 44, avenue des Champs-Elysées. Beginning in mid-1941, it was there that the clandestine screenings would be held as the war dragged on, with increasingly subversive films on the bill. In the months just prior to the Liberation, Henri would go so far as to show documentaries on the American war effort, including Frank Capra's still stirring *Why We Fight* series. It remains a complete mystery how Langlois was able to obtain such films, since they had been shown only in liberated North Africa or in Portugal.

Through the Occupation years, Langlois's primary concern was to keep up morale and to reward those who were helping him by offering them the pleasure of secretly seeing the American films the rest of the population was forced to do without. These secret events were organized not with cloak-and-dagger, but over the telephone. Henri picked up the phone, dialed one of the chosen few, and merrily asked, "How would you like to see an American comedy with Billie Burke?"

In general, the recipients of such calls wouldn't believe their ears, but would recognize Henri's voice and know that, with Henri, anything *was* truly possible.

"Seriously?"

"But of course! On the Champs-Elysées itself, no less."

Langlois knew exactly how to pick the trustworthy and deserving. Among those who came to his aboveground underground ciné-club were Marc Allégret, Druant, Gide's nephew, Marcel Duhamel, Henri Filipacchi, Pierre Prévert, Claude Jaeger, Denise Tual, and Michel Rittener. Henri issued invitations on a rotating basis, since both the size of the theater and basic security ruled out large audiences.

The consensus was that Henri was slightly nuts. But, crazy or not, people placed their trust in him—and besides, any occasion to put one over on the Germans was too good to pass up. Each participant managed to surmount his or her own apprehensions (we can trust the projectionist, can't we?), sure to emerge energized from a few magical hours before the forbidden screen.

It was a sustained miracle that this running gag never took a serious turn toward disaster. But there were close calls, such as the time everyone was assembled and eagerly waiting to see Joseph von Sternberg's *The Docks of New York*. Langlois was late, but no one was really worried because, after all, it took time to get the film from its secret hiding place. Suddenly, ominous footfalls sounded outside, headed toward the screening room. Two German police officers marched in, took a good look around the room, inspected the projection booth, and then left without saying a word. Everyone felt certain that Henri had been arrested. But no, he swept in shortly thereafter, out of breath, covered with sweat, and carrying a large stack of film cans. A power failure had held him up. Denise Tual was part of the audience that night:

> Before going ahead with the projection, one of us checked to make sure the Germans were really gone. That done, the film was threaded up and the lights went out. There on the screen, instead of Paramount's logo we saw the Gaumont Newsreel emblem, then the title "Monsieur Thorez's Trip to North Africa." We were stunned and stood up to motion to the projectionist to stop the film. If the risk Langlois was taking in running around with an American movie was already substantial, it became enormous in the case of a political film on the red-hot subject of communism."

Langlois was falling out of his chair, laughing uncontrollably. When he got hold of himself, he explained to his friends that, as a result of switching labels on film cans so that nobody else would be able to make sense of them, he'd ended up tricking himself!

On his way out, Michel Rittener, a young assistant director, stopped Langlois. "Tell me the truth—did you do that on purpose?" he asked.

"No," Langlois replied. "I honestly didn't know what was in the can."

We'll never know for sure. For Rittener, Langlois's innocence is less than certain. What was unquestionable was that Henri took enormous pleasure in his secret screenings and that they helped satisfy his innate taste for provocation. He was also able to collect a little bit of money, which he then gave to the Resistance.

Says Rittener, "For someone like me who was living sort of outside societal norms, Henri was completely off the scale."

Sometimes Henri laced his security precautions with a practical joke or two. One such caper had Rittener as its target. Langlois singled out the young assistant director and said, "As for you, I'm going to give you all the Communist films."

Rittener did, in fact, have a storage area in the basement that nobody knew about. It was a perfect setting, since Rittener's upstairs neighbor was a member of the Gestapo and the tenant below was a German who worked as a purchasing agent. When the two men met on the stairs, they'd exchange a gruff "Heil Hitler." They had reached the conclusion that their French neighbor was a negligible creature who did something related to the cinema. Rittener, a confirmed Communist, religiously placed some 500 film cans in his basement hideaway: "One fine day, I felt curious enough to go down there and take a better look at these Communist films I'd so proudly been hiding. I was very excited—which Russian films could they possibly be? By holding things up to the light here and there, I had to come to terms with the evidence: There was nothing there but films with Musidora, some Marcel L'Herbier . . . all sorts of old stuff. Henri had switched the containers once again. I discovered the switcheroo by unrolling a few reels, and in the end I found the whole thing very funny."

For Langlois, all films were equally precious, be they *Les Vampires* by Feuillade or *The Fall of Saint-Petersburg* by Pudovkin. He'd known just how to entice Michel Rittener but no doubt thought that it would be better, in case of a raid, that only politically innocuous films be discovered.

If the Germans knew nothing about Langlois's clandestine activities, they did end up noticing the preferred treatment the Cinémathèque received from Major Hensel. Apart from the internecine struggle between the Gestapo and the Abwehr, the military administration was divided into all sorts of separate divisions and services, all diligently spying on one another. Langlois sensed that problems were inevitable. He wasn't worried about the Film Inspection Service, where German technicians could barely conceal their admiration for Langlois's single-minded dedication. But rumor had it that the powerful officers at the Propaganda Staffel had it in for Henri and the Cinémathèque. It was vital that Henri find a way to diffuse their mounting displeasure. Friends suggested the cordial, civilized approach: Invite the enemy to dinner. As one fellow put it, "Weave some kind of spell over them or your proverbial goose is cooked!"

As he customarily did whenever a crisis arose, Henri began by consulting the cards. Annie Langlois, meanwhile, set off for the Saint-Ferdinand Church to light as many candles as it took to placate humorless guys wearing monocles and swastikas.

There was far too much at stake and the meeting was too compromising for Langlois to attend it alone. He required a witness. And what better choice than the president of the Cinémathèque, Marcel L'Herbier? L'Herbier had held the post on an interim basis since November 1940, when Paul-Auguste Harlé had been forced to take refuge in the unoccupied zone.

And so Henri and his "lightning rod," Marcel L'Herbier, set out toward the private dining rooms of the Cercle Gaillon on the Champs-Elysées, to which they had invited three important representatives of the Propaganda Staffel. The meeting got off to a poor start. The two Frenchmen found themselves blasted by accusations, all of which the Oberführer summed up as follows: "Your Cinémathèque is pro-American and pro-Jewish and is concealing poisoned treasures."

When in a tight spot, Langlois always fell back on his provocative bent. "The way things stand," he told himself, "the best way to get out of this bind is for me and L'Herbier to find out just how extensive their knowledge of the cinema really is."

And so a verbal pole vault began in which the two Frenchmen kept raising the bar of cinematic minutiae until the three proud officers were straining to match them, jump for jump. It was out of the question that they be shown up as less cultured than these Frenchmen. So, rather than allow matters to evolve to the point where they'd be forced to admit defeat, the

Germans took a tack straight out of the purest tradition of American film comedy. If their hosts were specialists in film trivia, then they would prove themselves to be toastmasters extraordinaire. L'Herbier recalls that the Germans changed their tune in the course of the meal—"so thoroughly, in fact, that by the end of dessert, there reigned a certain harmonious facade. The Oberführer had traded his fury for playfulness, going so far as to propose a toast to the Cinémathèque Française. Better yet—and here we nearly burst out laughing—his colleague hastened to add the finishing touch by loudly singing the praises of the American cinema, and particularly Charlie Chaplin, Jew among Jews [sic]! . . . We wouldn't have been surprised if, to top off this masquerade, we'd all ended up singing 'La Marseillaise.'"

　　　　Apart from the small sums the Ministry of Public Education had reimbursed for expenses incurred while on cultural missions abroad, Henri Langlois had not yet been able to secure any form of permanent subsidy for the Cinémathèque. France seemed to be locked into the rigors of the Occupation for some time to come, and Henri's financial problems could only become more pressing, since his scope of interest was no longer strictly limited to the Cinémathèque proper. He appointed himself crusader on an even more urgent mission, that of helping all those who were being menaced or persecuted, while not forgetting those old-timers who had worked in the field of cinema.

Among his "good works" in the latter category figured, among others, Nathalie Lissenko, a former acting partner of Ivan Mosjoukine who later showed her gratitude by donating all of her theatrical costumes to the Musée du Cinéma. Another beneficiary was Joë Hamman, a picturesque character whose cinema debut dated back to 1907. An actor as well as the director of several films, Hamman belonged to the league of multitalented performers who had come to the screen by way of first being a journalist, caricaturist, and screenwriter. What Henri found most fascinating about Hamman was that after having experienced the Old West firsthand (and learning to handle a mean lasso as part of Buffalo Bill's traveling Wild West Show), he had become the French cinema's most famous cowboy in a wonderful serial called *Arizona Bill*. Henri used the utmost of tact, for fear that Hamman would feel like a charity case. Then he hit upon a means of assistance that the former cowboy could not possibly find demeaning: Langlois paid him, in installments, advances against a volume of his memoirs—a volume that in fact did eventually appear, although not until 1961. This "delay" mattered little to Henri. His primary wish was to help Hamman over a rough patch—and besides, you couldn't put a price on the pleasure Langlois experienced listening to his friend recount his fabulous adventures.

Henri was, of course, equally concerned about the plight of several of his closest friends. He helped as best he could Paul-Auguste Harlé, Alexandre Trauner, and the composer Joseph Kosma, all of whom had managed to take refuge in the unoccupied zone of France. But the two most serious cases were those of two women he held particularly dear, Lotte Eisner and Sonika Bo. In order to help them, he needed real freedom to act.

If money was nice in peacetime, it was essential in time of war. If he meant to help his friends, he also had to find the money needed to finance the clandestine transport of films, including money for drivers and money for the fuel the trucks they drove ran on. The Cinémathèque would be miles ahead of the game if only Henri could arrange for it to receive some sort of government subsidy.

But the Vichy administration could not know how these allocations would actually be used. For this episode, Henri employed his finely tuned taste for conspiracy and mystery, to which he added a dose of what Denise Tual called his "convoluted mindset." Without detailing what he intended, Henri communicated the general idea that it would certainly be pleasant if some sort of official aid could be obtained for the Cinémathèque. Denise Tual advised Henri to contact Louis Emile Galey. Galey, who would become the first director of the Centre national du cinéma (CNC), had just come to Paris as a delegate of the government in Vichy. Since he was not cut out to collaborate, Galey had chosen to serve in connection with the cinema, an administrative domain he imagined to be free of problems insofar as there was no longer any cinema to speak of in France.

Henri had initial reservations about Galey. Didn't people say that he was a friend of Prime Minister Laval's son-in-law De Chambrun and that he personally enjoyed the prime minister's support? If Galey was that closely connected with the regime, wouldn't Henri be playing straight into their hands?

But another choice bit of information was nearly all the assurance he needed: Louis Emile Galey was also a close friend of Henri Jeanson. This was one of the best references imaginable. Jeanson was the famous screenwriter who had penned Arletty's immortal lines, in Carné's *Hotel du Nord*, "Atmosphere. Atmosphere. Est-ce que j'ai une gueule d'atmosphere?"—lines as resonant and familiar to every French-speaking filmgoer as are Rhett Butler's parting words to Scarlett O'Hara, for Americans. Jeanson, a former editor of the satiric newspaper *Le Canard enchaîné*, as well as a pacifist and idealist who had already been to prison on several occasions as a direct consequence of his independent thinking, could not be suspected of being a fascist sympathizer.

It was settled then. This time Jeanson would be Henri's lightning rod. Together they went to see Galey, having first cooked up a little scenario that was to the humorist's liking. Galey himself made the following account of the day Langlois entered his life:

> I had a friend named Henri Jeanson. He was a humorist, an author, a very talented dialogue writer, and also a very good friend. One day he showed up in my office with some guy I didn't know. It was Henri Langlois. I had never before seen anyone so peculiar. He immediately made me want to

laugh—and in those days, we rarely had occasion for laughter. And, of course, Jeanson wasn't exactly a fellow who inspired bouts of sadness! He was a joker, and here he was telling me—he lisped—"I've brought you a young man who has a declaration to make to you. . . ."

Whereupon the following exchange took place:

"What have you to say to me, sir?" Galey courteously inquired.

"Well, then," Langlois replied, "I have a very important declaration to make to you. I feel I must make certain you know about this. It has to do with a film that I arranged to be sent abroad. Bound as I am by professional secrecy, it is impossible for me to tell you to *which* country."

"Oh. But what film are we talking about?"

"I really can't possibly give you the title."

"Then at least tell me who made it."

"Impossible! I cannot reveal to you the director's name."

"Well, then," Galey exclaimed. "What *can* you tell me?"

"Nothing."

"Nothing?"

"Nothing. But I thought that you should know."

Louis Emile Galey didn't know whether he was coming or going. Of one thing he was certain: His visitor was grateful for this opportunity to be received and greatly appreciated Galey's having given his complete attention to what he didn't have to say. Jeanson was doubled over with laughter. He found this revelation that zero plus zero equals zero irresistibly funny.

As for Galey, this little interview with Henri was just the first in a series of absurd dialogues that would continue throughout the Occupation: "With Langlois, there was a game under way that I didn't understand a single thing about. He was always making succinct allusions to something that was a complete and utter mystery to me. 'I can say no more,' 'Follow my eyes,' 'You see what I mean to say.' And when I'd ask him to be more precise, 'No,' he'd say, 'because you're being watched.'"

Despite the stationary runaround Henri specialized in spouting, Galey grew fond of this exasperating character and arranged for the Cinémathèque to receive a modest subsidy of 2,000 francs.

On 1 June 1942 Louis Emile Galey was promoted to general director of cinema. But he no longer wished to be dependent on the Ministry of Information, which was too politicized for his taste. It was, in effect, the Ministry of Information that watched over the press and radio and subsidized the making of propaganda films. Thanks to his friend De Chambrun, Galey was able to report directly to the prime minister. "With Laval, who has never set foot in a cinema," Galey told himself, "I shouldn't have any problems."

In the autumn of 1942, the first Centre national du cinéma set up shop in a *hotel particulier* (mansion) at 7, avenue de Messine. Pierre Riedinger served as liaison between Galey and the minister of finances. It was Riedinger who drew up budget proposals, set movie admission prices, and organized a system of subsidies for filmmakers that prefigured the *avance sur recette* (advance against admissions) system in place today. And it was thanks to this arrangement that the CNC was able to help Carné make *Children of Paradise* and Bresson to make *Les Dames du Bois de Boulogne*.

Langlois contacted the CNC during the summer of 1942 and was able to obtain from Pierre Riedinger a subsidy far greater than the first one had been. The money changed hands without any real control imposed as to how it be spent, but those concerned trusted Henri to use it well. Galey met with Langlois once a month, ascertained that he was doing a million things at once, and was generally left with some new impenetrable secret transmitted in tones so hushed that only a lip-reader could have made heads or tails of it—and even then, probably only tails.

In early 1943, Galey offered Langlois two rooms at avenue de Messine in which to set up the Cinémathèque's offices. He also allowed Langlois to use the tiny screening room on the main floor for private projections.

Little by little, thanks to Galey's indulgence, the avenue de Messine would become a regular nest of Resistance activity. The head of the secretarial pool, Mademoiselle Mazac, received orders directly from the Secret Army. Also to be found in the office was a lovely, no-nonsense blond named Christine Gouze. The underground knew her as Renal. Christine Gouze-Renal would become a film producer, sister-in-law to François Mitterrand, and wife to actor Roger Hanin, in that order. To top things off, Pierre Riedinger belonged to another Resistance group, L'Organisation civile et militaire, whereas Jean Painlevé worked with the Communists.

All these conspirators for the good of the cinema and the glory of France required passes to carry out their clandestine activities. Each Saturday a laissez-passer line formed outside Galey's office. He had decided once and for all to cover for his co-workers without asking too many pointed questions about what possible use they could have for all these as-yet-unfilled-out official forms they so sweetly asked him to sign.

Thanks to these documents, which he made out to suit the occasion, Henri was able to cross the demarcation line at will and perform priceless services for his friends in hiding in the unoccupied zone. He was thus able to contact producer Jean Benoît-Lévy's assistant, Marie Epstein, to let her know that he had not only managed to save the films made by her brother, Jean Epstein, but also planned to show them in Paris.

"As our name indicates," Marie Epstein explained years later, "we're of Jewish origin, and it took plenty of courage to project my brother's films during the Occupation. . . . Langlois had succeeded in hiding the negatives and made sure they were well out of reach of the enemy. If one can still see *The Fall of the House of Usher* or *La Glace à trois faces* today, we owe it to Henri."

But of all Henri's acquaintances whom events had banished to the precarious safety of the South, it was surely Lotte Eisner who ran the greatest risk, for she was Jewish, German, vehemently anti-Nazi, and a political refugee.

As early as 1933, the National Socialist party newspaper had declared, "When heads begin to roll, that of Lotte Eisner shall roll first." On 23 March of that same year, the Reichstag "voted" the führer dictator of the Reich. On 31 March, Hitler dissolved the legislature throughout Germany. That same day, Lotte fled by train to Paris, where her sister and her French husband lived. When her brother-in-law came to meet her at the station, he wished her a pleasant vacation—to which Lotte replied, with a bitter smile, "It's going to be a long vacation."

When war was declared, Lotte, despite her status as a political refugee, found herself interned by the French authorities in the camp at Gurs. Langlois struggled through the steps necessary to have her released and assigned to a forced residence in Montpellier. In November 1942, the Germans crossed the line of demarcation, creating total panic. Henri, who had had some prior warning of events to come, rushed to the post office and fired off these few words in haste: "Lotte, leave immediately, but let me know where you are, as the Germans are going to cross the line."

Too late! Lotte had just come nose to nose with Wehrmacht soldiers while visiting the municipal bathhouse. Fortunately, their mission was limited, for the time being, to scrubbing themselves clean. But this double warning was good enough for Lotte. With her brother-in-law's help, she found a small village, near Rodez, where she could hide. A blank identity card was obtained, and on it she wrote "Escoffier," a name she'd found in *Carmen* by Prosper Mérimée. It was a choice of name that revealed something of her state of mind vis-à-vis the Nazis, for in Provençal it meant "to kill."

Just as soon as Henri knew where to find her, he rushed to Lotte's side. He found the region overrun with German soldiers and advised his friend to go to Nice instead. But Lotte did not want to end up in a big city. Henri suddenly hit upon a solution: "Not far from here, in Figéac, there's an entire batch of films that I took there in total haste. They need to be examined to see what sort of shape they're in. We need a list of their contents, and most of all they have to be hidden more thoroughly. I'll tell you what we'll do."

And Henri returned to Paris, where he made out an official document for one Louise Escoffier. With this pass in hand, Lotte went to the Béduer Château. It was unbearably cold, but that was where Lotte spent her days, surrounded by flammable films, not daring to light a fire in the huge medieval fireplaces.

Above her head, starving rats kept up a hellish racket, but despite the setting and soundtrack worthy of a horror film, Lotte applied herself to the job at hand with brave determination. She broke her nails prying off the lids from rusty film cans in order to ascertain the condition of the films they held. It took her a solid month to complete the inventory, after which she put Henri's last bit of advice into effect: Gathering her strength, she put the heavy cans in the castle dungeon and then carefully covered them over with hay. "The best possible hiding place," Langlois had told her. "Worthy of

Alexandre Dumas!" And there, where Lotte had stashed them, was where Henri would find them, safe and sound, after the Liberation.

Lotte then made herself out to be a cook so as to find a job in a girls' boarding school. Following Langlois's advice, she passed herself off as an Alsatian in order to explain her accent. But the headmistress found this employee, who received mysterious visits from the likes of Henri Langlois and Georges Sadoul, highly unsettling.

Luckily, Lotte met an admirable woman, Madame Guittard, who took her in without fear for the possible danger involved. Whenever anyone inquired as to who this mysterious Mademoiselle Escoffier might be, Madame Guittard replied, without batting an eyelash, "I knew her grandfather."

One day in May 1944, the SS swarmed into the town, which they regarded as a nest of Resistance fighters, and assembled some 840 people in the town square prior to deporting them to Bergen-Belsen. Lotte had hidden in her bedroom as soon as the SS appeared. They demanded to see her identity card, which they then deemed insufficent. Luckily, Henri had recently sent her a document attesting to her employment with the Cinémathèque Française. This attestation, drawn up by Henri himself, was written out on a sheet of letterhead from the Ministry of Information of Vichy and bore an authentic government stamp.

Impressed by these official papers, the SS finally left. Lotte found Madame Guittard, pale as a cadaver.

"I've had enough!" exclaimed Lotte. "I'm leaving to join the Resistance!"

"Most certainly not," retorted goodhearted Madame Guittard. "Not with your bronchitis, you aren't. If necessary, we'll just die together."

Madame Guittard would not meet Henri until after the Liberation, when he came to fetch Lotte and take her back to Paris. Even before she'd ever laid eyes on him, she had fallen in love with this mythic character Lotte had never stopped talking about.

Throughout this time, Henri had battered away at the bureaucratic treadmill separating him from those films captured by the Germans. In July 1942 Langlois had obtained from the German authorities the restitution of those films that had been seized in Ballan Miré at the beginning of the war. Diplomatic, crafty, and tireless, Langlois had never let up pestering the Film Inspection Service with increasingly vehement notes to the effect that, since the films whose return he sought belonged to a private collection, they did not fall under the jurisdiction of the armistice agreement. The Germans themselves ended up feeling a certain admiration for this obstinate Frenchman.

Far less happy was the fate of the Eclair collection, for which Henri had so tenaciously fought in 1938. These miles of early footage had remained at the Coucy Château, where theoretically they were safely stored in the dungeon. Unfortunately, the English bombardments had destroyed the castle, bringing tons of stones crashing in on the 1,200 to 2,000 precious negatives. When

Langlois, through repeated badgering, finally secured their return, the Germans could give him nothing more than a few scraps of mucky gelatin, gone gooey from humidity. Filled with despair to see so many masterpieces by Tourneur, Jasset, and Germaine Dulac gone forever, Henri could not foresee all the trouble these poor lost films were yet to cause him.

Now fearful of British bomdardments, Henri organized the move, in 1943, of an important collection of films from the Gaumont Company's basement storage depot in Les Lilas, outside Paris, to the basement of the Palais de Chaillot. This operation took a good month and a half, for it concerned more than 3,000 films. Knowing the Allies had strict orders to avoid bombing sites like Chaillot, Henri finally felt reassured: The films were safely tucked away where no harm could come to them. The only thing he'd forgotten to consider was that one day Hitler would give the order to blow up all the monuments in Paris.

The year 1943 marked an important turning point in the history of the Cinémathèque, because its subsidy had increased to the point where Langlois could afford to hire a small paid staff. The days of heroic volunteerism were over for Jean Mitry, whom Langlois snatched back from his obscure post as an accountant somewhere out in the countryside, and for Madeleine Méliès, whom Langlois hired as secretary.

But Henri had to face up to the power struggle brewing at the very heart of the Cinémathèque, for he was having a hard time getting along with Marcel L'Herbier. L'Herbier would soon turn 53, whereas Langlois was not yet 30. L'Herbier was an established figure in French cinema, having made a series of ambitious films that placed him among the most distinguished directors of silents. As for Henri, he was both founder and secretary-general of the association. As an association, the Cinémathèque was composed of members, most of whom had contributed a film or other tangible object to its collections, and each of whom held one vote when the General Assembly convened. The membership had complete confidence in Henri, and all considered Langlois to be the rightful final arbiter whenever a situation requiring a decision arose.

It was Henri, for example, who had decided—based on advice from Germaine Dulac and with the support of Harlé—that L'Herbier was the one to be put in charge at the outset of the Occupation, since he was capable of standing up to the Germans. But three years later, Henri had had it with reporting to L'Herbier. He had held back too long and could no longer tolerate the air of importance that the president of the Cinémathèque Française gave himself. With Galey's involuntary assistance, Henri would remove L'Herbier from office with one of the simple yet effective little ruses that came to him without apparent effort.

One day the director of the CNC sat back in his chair as Marcel L'Herbier entered his office, flanked by his skinny secretary-general, who, to Galey's great surprise, did not utter a word. L'Herbier, however, began to speak his piece: "*Monsieur le directeur*, we must ask that the most serious professional secrecy be applied to what we are about to divulge. We call upon your feelings of patriotism, sir. This secret is of capital importance to the Cinémathèque. You are aware, naturally, that a large number of people who have deposited materials at the Cinémathèque are Jewish, and that we consider them all members in good standing of the association."

"And so?" Galey said, slightly perturbed.

"So? The General Assembly will be held in one month, and Langlois here holds in his pocket 45 blank ballots that these Jewish members have given him by proxy. I want you to know that these are Jewish votes but that we consider them fully valid."

Galey's concern grew. He suspected that Langlois could easily have done without this particular declaration, but that L'Herbier had wanted everything to be conducted aboveboard. He could not officially condone this illegal operation. But because he had to say something, he said the following: "I won't tell you I'm agreed, because what you've explained runs counter to the law. But I will tell you this, speaking off the record: Go ahead and do it. Just don't bother me with it! Langlois can submit his ballots without signing specific names to each one, or else he can write in 'vote delegated by' and fill in whatever name you like."

A month went by, and Galey gave the matter no further thought. The day after the General Assembly, he received an urgent phone call from L'Herbier demanding to be seen immediately. Shortly thereafter, he swept into Galey's office and, in a furious tone, began: "Do you remember our little meeting the other day? Well, I don't want to be forced to denounce Langlois to the Gestapo, but after all, there are limits."

"What's going on?" Galey calmly inquired.

"What's going on? You want to know what's going on? With those 45 votes Langlois had in his pocket, he managed to get Grémillon elected to my job!"

Galey burst out laughing. "Listen, you're the one who came here asking for my permission. Now, if you ended up getting screwed by Langlois, what do you expect me to do about it? Tough luck for you."

As if by way of compensation, Galey would soon choose Marcel L'Herbier to direct a new film school: L'Institut des hautes études cinématographiques (IDHEC).

To Henri's way of thinking, the German defeat was merely a matter of months, so he had set out in search of someone who could represent the Cinémathèque on Liberation Day. He had to be a director, like L'Herbier, but also a man who had played an active part in the Resistance. Jean Grémillon had just made *Lumière d'été*, a film that had displeased Vichy considerably, and was preparing to shoot *Le Ciel est à vous*, which would be a work of hope and lyricism in praise of France and its virtues. In the course of lengthy and discreet conversations, the two men had been able to talk about their vision of the future.

Had Grémillon actually mentioned that someday he wanted to make a film about the long-awaited Allied landings, or had Henri had one of the psychic revelations he sometimes claimed to experience? Whatever the case, Henri had just pulled off one of his best coups, because to head the Cinémathèque, he had chosen the future director of *The Sixth of June at Dawn*.

chapter 5

# LOVE AND LIBERATION

Nothing of greatness is accomplished in this world without passion.

G. W. F. Hegel

In March 1943, Henri experienced the pain of losing his father. Although he resembled him not at all, Henri still knew how much Gustave had worried about the future of a boy who preferred the Cinémathèque to a more reasonable career. Over the past few years, the old patriot had begun to see his son in a new light and to take pride in what he saw. This debonair giant, who at one time weighed as much as 235 pounds, had shrunk more each day from undernourishment. At the age of 63, he was a frail echo of his former self. On the night of 7 March, Gustave, grown terribly weak, was stretched out beside his sleeping wife. She found herself awakened by the touch of his hand and the sound of her name. "Annie," he said softly, "hand me my shoes. It's time for me to go."

Not wanting to annoy him, Annie got up to do as Gustave asked. When she returned, he had departed, for good.

Gustave Langlois's funeral was well attended by friends of the Cinémathèque, for he had been known to all as a man whose door was always wide open to film enthusiasts. There were those in attendance who remembered the rue Laferrière apartment, famed for its bathtub, and those who saw in the clandestine projections at the rue Troyon a nice bit of vengeance for the humiliations of the Occupation. Henri, who had always paid less than no attention to his physical appearance, refusing to wear a hat or gloves as his father wished, was nearly unrecognizable that day. He was clean-shaven, every hair was in place, and he wore an impeccable dark suit, graced by a black armband on his sleeve and a black tie around his neck. This was Henri's way of pleasing his father one last time.

Henri would no longer live on rue Troyon on a regular basis. The change occured imperceptibly. Henri would come home to sleep for two or three nights and then disappear for three nights in a row. The Cinémathèque occupied both his nights and his days, but he had also begun to feel the need for womanly presences other than that of his mother, whom until then he had been unable to do without.

Henri, at age 28, bore no resemblance to a playboy. For starters, his hair would not behave any more than its owner would. Langlois's lanky frame and large eyes suggested a friendly alien more than they did a ladies' man.

He had not yet taken on the allure of the "dragon who watches over our treasures," as Jean Cocteau would later write of him. For the time being, Cocteau classified Henri in the rarefied category of the angelical. He had seen him appear as a poet who had sprung from the workaday, an escapee without a diploma or an honorable discharge to his name who nevertheless displayed the stuff of heroes and heroism:

> Gaze upon the furious angel
> who sweeps down from the sky
> like an eagle, the angel of Delacroix
> and the angels for which Greco was
> condemned by the Church—
> for not having painted regulation
> wings upon them.

Langlois radiated an indefinable and captivating charm. When Henri spoke—and spoke, and spoke—women were fascinated. Madeleine Méliès, who makes no attempt to hide the fact that she was in love with Henri at that time, says only, "He was adorable and had a heart of gold."

But it was not easy being Langlois's secretary! Henri looked upon work as a perpetual state of creation, quite immune to Sundays and vacations. Evenings, when he and Madeleine left the Cinémathèque's office on avenue de Messine, Henri would insist on walking her to her door, which was not far from Montmartre. Once there, he could not simply say goodnight—it was still early, and he had so much left to say, so many projects to entrust her with. So the two young people ended up retracing their steps as far as place Clichy, where "Mado" would point out, smiling, "Well, now you're not all that far from your house."

"Fine," he'd reply. "Then I'll go back a little ways with you." And sure enough, Langlois would go right on talking about the Cinémathèque, because it was his life and his reason for living. Mado hung on every word. Their understanding was perfect: passionate friendship, chaste but absolute.

Another event would bring great joy to Henri: his reunion with another of his ancient admirers, Sonika Bo, from whom he'd had no word since the mass exodus.

One fine day, the beautiful young woman with the Slavic features came knocking at his door. Henri couldn't believe his eyes. Sonika Bo, standing there in her torn clothes, looked just like the innocent damsel in distress of generic Western fame, a good woman whose frontier pluck had enabled her to escape from her evil pursuers. She had come to seek refuge at Henri's homestead.

Sonika told him of how, after ending up in Nice in 1940, with her paralyzed mother and 14-year-old daughter to feed, she had worked as a cab driver to support her family. How she had been arrested by an Italian patrol while trying to smuggle refugees across the border. How she had finally ended up in Cavalaire, where she joined the Resistance, using the code name Cinderella.

It was while in Cavalaire that she received the order to return to Paris. She had hesitated a great deal before boarding the train because she already had the feeling she was being hunted. She shared her train compartment with a young soldier wearing a French uniform, and he continually stared at her, admiring, no doubt, this strange and beautiful traveler. In midjourney the train ground to an abrupt stop. The brakes screeched to a halt, the hiss of steam died down with a distinct fading whoosh, and guttural shouts drifted up from the platform: The German police were conducting a surprise identity check. Young militiamen on the quay were motioning to the French soldier to bring his companion down off the train. Furious with despair, Sonika Bo began insulting her traveling companion, screaming at him that it was impossible that he'd take orders from the Germans while wearing a French uniform. And then, all at once, she blurted out, "I'm a refugee. I have a false passport. You must save me!"

"Grab me by the throat and pretend you're holding a knife to my back," the young man replied.

And so it was that Sonika, her arm locked around his throat, moved toward the compartment door. Just as they'd reached it, the train started up again. Through the half-open door, the young stranger shouted, "Don't do anything! She's got a knife to my back!" The authorities took chase, attempting in vain to board the moving train.

Had she had the strength to push him through the open door, or was it his courageous idea to jump? Whoever took the initiative, it had been a convincing performance and a crucial maneuver. Sonika herself was unable to explain how she'd hit upon the idea of hopping off the train just before it pulled into the station in Paris, only to repeatedly twist her ankle crossing row upon row of railway track, finally finding a way out without panicking. She had operated on pure instinct, with but one thought in mind: to walk and walk and walk some more, until she reached Langlois's house, where she could take shelter.

Up until that point, Henri had never really been in love with anyone except the divas of the Italian screen or the heroines of his private fantasies. This state of affairs (or state of nonaffairs) had not prevented him from writing beautiful poems dedicated to women either imagined or gone:

> I would have liked to see you in a photograph
> But that is not a possibility for us
> And so I went to museums
> To gather images that retrace our life together
> And then I went to the flea market
> Where I searched in vain for an object
> We both had loved.
>
> And I went to Versailles in the rain
> And I saw nothing but death
> And suddenly I remembered
> That there was a place
> Where we had left a mirror
> And I went there.
>
> And from the mirror I lifted
> Thousands of images
> That we had left there.
>
> And I saw you again
> And we loved one another.

It would take a woman as rare as a unicorn, whose charms rivaled those of Scheherazade and whose allure equaled that of Marlene Dietrich, to supplant the fantastic women who lived in Henri's imagination. He who so loved talking about his dreams would soon find a living, breathing ingredient to blend in with them perfectly. And so, sweet inexperienced Mado Méliès—who had successfully managed, all the same, to divert Henri's attention from a beautiful young Italian named Julia Veronese—could do nothing but melt into the woodwork: "I was aware of Henri's feelings for me. But how could I, a mere girl of tender years, have continued to exist for him after he had found a woman as superb as Mary Meerson, dazzling widow of the ever-so-famous Lazare Meerson!"

There was no widow more sincerely wracked with despair than she. Lazare Meerson, the finest set designer in the history of French cinema, the man who had brought his brilliance to bear on the films of

L'Herbier, René Clair, and Jacques Feyder, had died in London in 1938. Meerson, who had made backlot canals indistinguishable from the real thing for *Carnival in Flanders*, worked like a madman and, like Langlois, paid no attention whatever to his health. While hard at work on King Vidor's *The Citadel* for producer Alexander Korda, Meerson suddenly fell ill. His condition deteriorated so rapidly that Korda had him flown to a Swiss clinic. The doctors diagnosed meningitis. And shortly thereafter Meerson died, at age 40, at the height of his fame. Throughout his illness, Mary had never left his side.

Lazare Meerson had been born in Finland in 1897. His artistic aspirations brought him, by way of Berlin, to Paris, where he settled for good in the early 1920s. He began designing sets—those for *Carmen* and *The Italian Straw Hat*—and quickly developed a certain reputation. He frequented the crowd of Montparnasse painters who gathered at the Dôme and who regarded him as one of their bunch. According to Alexandre Trauner, who worked as Meerson's assistant, it was through his painter friends that Lazare met the mysterious and exceptionally beautiful Mary, "the most dazzling woman in all Paris." Most of the painters of the day were after Mary to pose for them, but she sat for only three: De Chirico, Kissling, and Oskar Kokoschka, who made a complete series of portraits of her.

It was against the rollicking backdrop of Montparnasse that the epic couple of Lazare and Mary joined forces in 1928.

Meerson's collaboration with René Clair would give rise to *Sous les toits de Paris*, *Le Million*, and *14 Juillet*. This was his "white period," during which, drawing inspiration from the walls of Paris, he sought to make use of this color in every possible gradation and shade. He also knew how to integrate realism with poetry. Through diligent research, he hit upon covering different objects with fine starched nets and veils of tulle, a technique that presented to the camera the poetic dimension sought by the directors with whom he worked.

Lazare and Mary lived at the Hotel Saint-Sulpice until prosperity knocked, enabling Meerson to acquire a magnificent artist's loft on rue Gazan. Light streamed into the apartment through a large bay window facing the Montsouris Park. Meerson, of course, decorated the place himself, making liberal use of his favorite color, white.

Lazare and Mary were madly in love with each other. Since each was possessed of a volcanic temperament, the violent passion that held them together was not without its corresponding eruptions. He, on the one hand, did not have much of a sense of humor, and his work had taught him the meaning and value of precision. Mary, on the other hand, was far more whimsical and kept track of time like a broken sundial. On those occasions when Mary had completely forgotten she'd invited friends over for dinner, she'd burst out laughing and remedy the situation by announcing, "My dears, I'm taking you all to Dominique, in Montparnasse. It's the only place that serves caviar and vodka good enough for you."

They lived an unbridled existence and their ever-increasing circle of friends and acquaintances seemed to mirror the expanding universe itself. One day Mary would know exactly how to put these connections to work for Langlois.

Mary, overcome by Lazare's death, had been living in London for more than a year, wrapped up in her grief. Robert Flaherty, touched by Mary's pain, had become a second father to her.

It so happened that in May 1939 Henri decided to organize a retrospective of Flaherty's films at the Cercle du Cinéma. Langlois had managed to interest the scholars at the Musée de L'homme in Flaherty's work by reminding them that he was above all a great explorer. Jean Renoir had been instructed to invite Flaherty to the inaugural screening. Flaherty, a tender-hearted man, saw in this trip an excellent opportunity to snatch Mary away from her dark musings and so invited her to join him, his wife, and their daughter on the excursion to Paris. Mary let herself be talked into making the trip, and in no time Renoir was introducing Langlois to Flaherty and his accompanying family.

This was a meeting of little or no importance for Mary, who all the same did register the presence of a young man so skinny she could have encircled his waist with just one hand. As for Henri, he was pleasantly disoriented as a result of the peculiarly charming way this woman was looking at him—a look that, however entrancing, any trained oculist would immediately recognize as an advanced case of myopia. Henri seated his guests and found it impossible to clear from his mind the thought of this toothsome young woman, who seemed to him as inaccessible as some far-off planet, most likely Venus.

Once the gala was over, Flaherty, who had thoroughly enjoyed himself but was in a hurry to get back to London, warmly thanked Henri before loading self and family into a limousine and speeding away. Henri, his heart already sinking, told himself he'd probably never again see the woman he'd taken to be Robert Flaherty's niece.

Some weeks later, Henri attended a party hosted by Alberto Cavalcanti. As soon as he walked in, Langlois was dumbfounded by the sight of the woman he'd assumed was back in London. There she was, calmly seated in a corner of the living room. Henri reeled backward, caught completely off guard by a wave of emotion.

Mary was minding her own business when she suddenly heard a colossal burst of laughter from the adjoining room. Cavalcanti was laughing so hard that Mary got up to see what could possibly be so funny. She came face to face with Henri, obviously troubled, whereas Alberto gaily explained, "Do you know what Langlois here just asked me? He wanted to know why Flaherty's niece didn't go back to London with him!"

A group had assembled to join in the hilarity. Poor Henri was utterly confused. Everyone, save he, knew who Mary was. Between two guffaws, Cavalcanti finally set the record straight.

"She's not Flaherty's niece—this is Mary. Mary Meer——..."

"You're Mary Meerson!" Henri interrupted, rushing over to the woman in question. "Why, I've been trying to get in touch with you for months. Destiny has finally brought us together. I simply must put on an exhibit of Lazare Meerson's designs, paintings, and sketches next February, for the Milan Triennial."

Mary tossed her magnificent hair as if to say "Hmph!" and replied, "Not so fast—we're going to be at war soon."

It would take more than the threat of pan-European conflict to discourage the creator of the Cinémathèque. Amused at first, then intrigued, Mary listened as Henri brought to life each detail of the exhibit as he'd imagined it. Struck by his admiration for Lazare, but determined not to be taken advantage of, Mary, thinking she could gain some time, agreed that Henri might telephone her and make an appointment to come over and discuss the matter more calmly.

As on every occasion when he wanted to obtain something, Henri assembled a regular delegation to accompany him. When he rang Mary's bell, she was surprised to see not only Henri, but Alberto Cavalcanti and Luigi Comencini, who had made the trip from Italy just for this meeting. So as to leave nothing to chance, Henri bore a letter written by Giorgio De Chirico, who happened to be a benefactor of the Triennial as well as a friend of Mary's. The letter, in tandem with Henri's overwhelming enthusiasm, had a magical effect: Mary's reticence dissolved. The works she loved more than anything else in the world and had never dreamed of letting out of her sight were soon nimbly packed and on their way to Milan.

The war had broken out, and Meerson's priceless sketches and watercolors vanished. Henri felt so terribly guilty that once he'd returned to Paris, he dared not show his face at Mary's, such was his fear of her wrath.

He had no way of knowing that the Meerson sketches would be found, five years later, by an insurance inspector from Lloyd's of London. In the meantime, there was every reason to believe that the saga of Henri and Mary had come to an irreversible impasse.

To those who knew the violent outbursts of which Mary was capable, the most astonishing thing was that she seemed to take this momentous loss in stride. One night in 1941, Henri went to visit Catherine Hessling and, once there, found himself face to face with Mary, whom he had sadly assumed he had forfeited the right ever to see again.

Henri and Mary were both born under the astrological sign of Scorpio, which, so the handbooks say, is the sign of the forces of nature, of passions unleashed and applied. What could possibly mitigate the shock of two headstrong Scorpios clashing in the night—or, for that matter, day? Any self-respecting charter of charts would say that in a couple such as this, one partner might end up dominating the other, whereupon a bitter power struggle would most likely ensue. And yet nothing of the sort came to pass—they fit together like mighty bookends that had agreed to support the same precious collection. Mary discharged her excess combative energy by bonding with the Cinémathèque. And the bond between Mary and Henri and Henri's brainchild only grew stronger in the face of adversity.

Mary's imagination soared to the same often stratospheric heights as Henri's. Having dissipated a lifetime's worth of sadness while mourning for Lazare, Mary was an expert at vanquishing melancholy and overcoming monotony. When the future looked darker than a subterranean screening room during a power failure, it was Mary who spoke of the triumphs to come. Henri could never be bored in her company; she spun wonderful tales laced with mystery.

Chief among these mysteries were certain of her own vital statistics. Mary made a point of leaving her past as vague as possible and refused to tell anyone her date of birth. It was known only that she had been born in Bulgaria, in Sofia, and that she had spent her childhood in Finland in the time of czarist Russia.

On those rare occasions when she let a sliver of her past slip through, it was only to speak of some childhood sensation or memory: waking up to a breakfast of tiny smoked fish that had swum up but one stream, laid side by side on a huge chunk of bread toasted over an open fire; running barefoot through the snow first thing in the morning; cold baths, her sweet little face smudged with crumbs of toasted bread. But heaven help the soul who tried to take advantage of some brief digression to ask a specific question, for the door to Mary's past would slam shut in an instant. It was a domain that belonged to her and her alone.

Among Mary's many talents was the gift of tongues. At Cinémathèque galas after the war, she would prove a constant source of amazement because of her linguistic showmanship when among visiting dignitaries from foreign lands. Mary handled English every bit as well as she did French, and enjoyed calibrating her accent according to whether her interlocutor hailed from New York or London. She was also completely at home speaking Italian, German, and Russian and sometimes even resorted to snatches of Yiddish, which Lazare had taught her. Whatever the importance of their post, be they ministers or high-ranking business executives, gentlemen would find themselves out of their depth in the face of her linguistic assurance. At official receptions, it was to Mary that the distinguished foreigners gravitated to express their respect and affection: Charlie Chaplin, Orson Welles, Rossellini, Fellini, and so on.

This, then, was the exceptional woman who would become the lifelong companion of Henri Langlois. Some have said that his life would surely have been calmer without her. None, however, would argue that it would have been considerably less exalted.

At the end of 1943, Henri's brother Georges resigned from his position overseeing the districtwide distribution of food and supplies in order to join the Resistance and open a law practice in his mother's apartment on rue Troyon. Since Georges required an office and a waiting room, Henri jumped at the chance: The apartment was now officially too small; therefore, he would relocate to rue Gazan and move in with Mary Meerson.

In November Henri received a strange letter from Robert Brasillach. Back in 1935, around the time he had been preparing the first edition of his *Histoire du cinéma*, Brasillach had been part of the group that met at rue Laferrière. Langlois was an inexhaustible source of documentation for the writer and film historian, and the two men were quite friendly. Then, with the passing of time, Brasillach developed a consuming interest in politics. During the Occupation, his increasingly vicious articles established him as being in the forefront of collaborationist writers. He and Langlois no longer saw eye to eye, or each other.

What had this belligerent polemicist been thinking of when he wrote to Henri? Had he taken pen in hand on an evening of depression, doubt, or, possibly, regret? An evening of nostalgia for the trouble-free days when he, as a poet and historian, had come to do research in the company of his friend, the living encyclopedia? Had he suddenly foreseen that his talent would soon be turned against him in retribution for having turned it against others, but not the right ones? In any event, Brasillach still thought of Henri as someone capable of accomplishing prodigious feats:

Cher Monsieur,

It has been a very long time since last we met, but I imagine you still remember me. I have an address for you, from the days when I was at the ministry's Cinema Department. I know not if my letter will reach you. But I take that chance, in memory of the era of the clubs.

You are perhaps aware that at the beginning of the year, Maurice Bardèche's and my *Histoire du cinéma* was republished, updated to 1940. I've had the outlandish and rather difficult idea of obtaining some information about the American cinema since 1940. Would you by any chance happen to have any pertinent reviews, magazines, or newspapers along those lines? It goes without saying that I shall return them. I realize how extravagant my request is, but I throw it out all the same, like a letter in a bottle.

Cordially yours,

Robert Brasillach

He had apparently thought that at the peak of the German Occupation, only Langlois would have material written about the American cinema since 1940. Does this mean that he actually knew that Henri was secretly projecting American films and was indeed stockpiling movie magazines smuggled in from across the ocean?

Henri was touched by this letter, which he saw as the cry of a man unencumbered by hope or illusions. Langlois handed the letter to his brother with the following words: "It's too bad about Brasillach, but it's too late for him now. Hang on to this, if you like. Maybe one day it will be of some use to him."

In 1945 Robert Brasillach was one of the first writers to be condemned to death and shot for the crime of collaborating. It would not have done any good to produce the letter at his trial, for if it demonstrates the sensitivity of one who, in contacting Langlois, was making the time-honored gesture of a drowning man, a love for the cinema did not count for much before a political tribunal. Brasillach was condemned in advance.

Brasillach was, of course, correct in his assumption that Henri, despite the Occupation, was working to save and protect American films. When Denise Tual asked exactly which American films he had saved during the war, Langlois replied, "Oh, you know, if you just mention them all, you can be certain not to make a mistake."

When Paris fell to the Germans, the United States was still a neutral country, meaning that those films belonging to American companies were protected under international law. The German military command had begun by prohibiting their projection in the occupied zone, but could not legally lay a hand on the films themselves. The Nazis considered the total output of the American film industry to be a dangerous product of Jewish minds. Most of the Europeans who headed branch offices of the major Hollywood Studios had fled when fleeing was the advisable thing to do, leaving the company's films behind in Paris warehouses. It was obviously difficult for the American directors of Columbia, Fox, MGM, Paramount, and United Artists to prevent their property from being impounded, even if such seizures were illegal. The entire situation was dependent on the devotion and initiative of their remaining representatives in Paris.

It must be noted that Henri Lartigue, who worked for MGM's Paris office, showed exceptional courage, for he suceeded in moving some 100 films to the unoccupied zone, a few at a time. He was arrested for his trouble in July 1942.

The situation being what it was, the field was wide open for Henri's rescue activities. Langlois benefited from the complicity of those at the bottom rungs of the career ladder, particularly the stockboys. Thanks to the information Henri obtained through his friends in the "entertainment" branch of the Resistance, he was able to work only with trustworthy accomplices. These people, certain that the United States would soon enter the war, were also doing a kind of Resistance work each time they handed over another batch of films that their recipient, the secretary-general of the Cinémathèque, subsequently removed to safety.

But the U.S. entry into the war on 8 December 1941 broke the fragile moral barrier still protecting the warehoused films. The German police and military police came to the Gestapo's assistance on its immediate mission to ambush and impound what they hoped would turn out to be a great many films.

A sinister and unscrupulous individual named Maertens popped up at the height of the hunt. Maertens, who had traded in his uniform for dashing civilian clothes, nonetheless behaved like a fanatic and arrogant Nazi. His raids were carried out briskly and methodically. He moved from one company to another, arresting employees and confiscating films and documents. At the end of each clean sweep, the offices were shut down and official seals were placed over the locks.

If Maertens had no way of determining that Langlois had reduced a given company's stock through selective withdrawals, the evidence of anti-enemy initiative was quite plain at MGM—there was practically nothing left. Since there were no films to take, Maertens helped himself to 12 million francs from the safe deposit boxes. By sheer luck, Henri Lartigue was off in another office. His accountant, however, soon denounced him to the authorities, whereupon Lartigue was arrested and taken to the prison at Fresnes, where he spent three months.

Upon his release, Lartigue was surprised to receive a summons asking him to report to the Hotel Intercontinental. There he met Alfred Greven, director of the Continental Film Company, who politely invited him to take a seat. No sooner had Lartigue been seated than he noticed, with even greater surprise, that Maertens was behind Greven, standing practically at attention and looking pale and defeated. Maertens was no longer dressed in his spiffy duds but instead wore the uniform of a simple German soldier. His misappropriations of funds—and no doubt several even more unpardonable crimes—had come to light. He would soon be shot by his own men. A still more remarkable detail was yet to come: Greven told Lartigue that he had recovered the stolen funds and would hold them in an account so as one day to restore them to MGM—which, in fact, he did, shortly before the Liberation.

Greven no doubt was looking out for the future. French filmgoers openly avoided films that were too obviously German. Continental Film, pretending to be a French company but operating on German capital, had found a way to use French actors and directors and had been quite successful. As a result of regular contact with his French co-workers, Greven had already distanced himself from the ideological concepts of the Third Reich—distanced himself so far, in fact, that he nearly lost his position. After the triumphant success of the company's *La Symphonie fantastique*, based on the life of the great

French composer Hector Berlioz, Greven thought the minister of propaganda would be pleased and so sent him a copy of the film in Berlin. But things worked out somewhat differently, since Goebbels, having screened the film, angrily wrote: "I am furious that our Paris office is showing the French how to portray nationalism in their films. I have issued clear directives so that the French produce only films that are lightweight, vacuous, and, if possible, idiotic."

What interested Langlois henceforth was not his "mole" work that had already saved so many films. He now wanted to concentrate on making sure that the American films that had fallen into German hands would not be evacuated to Germany. After the Allied landings in Normandy, this idea became a virtual obsession. Langlois gave the matter his constant consideration, hatching wild schemes and remaining on the lookout for a propitious moment in which to act.

As luck would have it, the apartment on rue Troyon where the Langlois family had lived since 1938 was almost directly across the street from the Columbia Pictures building, which happened to be where the Germans had installed their Film Inspection Service. Amazingly enough, it was also there that the film collection belonging to the Cinémathèque and seized in Ballon Miré had long been stored. And it was there too, right across the street, that the Germans would soon assemble all of the American films they had confiscated since the day the United States entered the war.

Although he now lived with Mary Meerson, Henri hardly ever failed to return to the rue Troyon apartment on a daily basis. As soon as he arrived, he'd go to the window, pull back the shade a tiny bit—so as to see without being seen—and then remain at his surveillance post for hours on end. Georges took up the relay, when Henri was not there, carefully observing the comings and goings of the Germans at Columbia headquarters. If he saw anything suggesting an imminent move of any kind, he had orders to notify Henri immediately.

Twelve days before the Paris insurrection, a bus pulled up to the Columbia building to pick up the soldiers, the German employees, and their belongings. As soon as he got word of this development, Henri rushed to his observation post. The street was calm once more. From time to time, a soldier could be seen standing guard. Henri, unable to bear the suspense, anounced, "I have to find out what's going on. I'm going to go down and talk to him!"

Two days later, André Laporte was working in his office at Pathé when Henri burst in and, without beating around the bush, asked him for 10,000 francs. "You're crazy," Laporte replied. "I don't have the right to give you that kind of money. And what do you need it for, anyway?"

"I can't tell you that," Langlois answered. "But believe me, it's indispensable and absolutely urgent."

"I'm sorry," the future treasurer of the Cinémathèque said curtly. "But I cannot give you the money without a valid reason."

"Oh, all right," Langlois conceded, as if Laporte were the one with the unreasonable request. "I'll tell you everything. Voilà: There's one guard left at the Film Control Depot. He's waiting for the trucks that are going to evacuate the American films to Germany. Everyone else is already gone. For two days, I've been trying to convince him that Germany's lost the war. It turns out he's in love with some French girl who lives in Orléans. He's agreed to give me the keys to the depot if I give him some money and a motorcycle. That's why I need the 10,000 francs right away."

Monsieur Laporte, convinced, handed over the money. Langlois took off at a gallop and concluded his business with the German, who obligingly disappeared. The moving operation was carried out at breakneck speed. Despite the curfew, that very night a goodly portion of the films had already been transferred to the vestibule of the Langlois's building.

At dawn, Henri, exhausted but triumphant, went off in search of a truck. Sonika Bo rushed over with other volunteers, and within the day the entire stock of American films had been safely transferred to the basement of the Palais de Chaillot, under the very eyes of the German sentries who, as usual, believed they had no jurisdiction over this area, since it was clearly marked "off limits" in German.

The operation had not been completed a moment too soon, for, as Georges Langlois vividly recalls, "48 hours later, I was keeping watch from the 'family observatory' when I saw two Wehrmacht trucks pull up to load and transport the films. The German soldiers' stupefaction was obvious. I heard all sorts of shouting and finally the sound of ignitions starting up: They left empty-handed."

When the war was over, Hollywood producers didn't know how to show Langlois their gratitude. Since the United States does not have an order of merit for noncitizen civilians comparable to the French Legion of Honor, the producers made the resolutely American gesture of offering him a check— which he, of course, refused. Still, if only because Langlois's antics belonged up on screen, Hollywood would never forget him.

Georges Langlois has another vivid memory from the tail end of the Occupation:

One fine day in August 1944, Henri phoned me to say, "Stay where you are—I'm at rue Gazan and I'm on my way!"

I was used to this. I knew how long it would take him to reach rue Troyon. When it was just about time for him to show up, I opened the window to watch for him. It was a magnificent sunny day, and I spotted Henri as he reached the sidewalk at the corner of the avenue Wagram.

In the time it took to turn my head and shout to my mother "Henri's here!" he had vanished. Yet he had to be just a few yards away on the side-walk opposite. At that very moment, two German military policemen, wearing helmets and black leather jackets with machine guns slung over their shoulders, stopped their motorcycles in front of our building. They pounded on the door, shouting for "Heinrich Langlois," then came in and examined every room in the apartment. They gave me a good looking over but decided I didn't fit the description. And then they left, just like that, without a word of explanation.

Fifteen minutes later, Henri turned up, all smiles. "Did you know that the hotel on the corner is a bordello? I was right in front of it when the guys on the motorcycles arrived. I went in and kept a lookout from one of the girl's rooms until they left."

And without giving our mother a chance to say how worried she'd been, Henri forged on.

"Okay, that's not all. I came to give Georges some written orders, along with this."

And from the packet of old newspapers he had under his arm, he unwrapped a machine gun.

"It's for you," he said, just like that.

The two orders he handed me said the same thing in two different lan-guages. Basically, they said that all French and Allied authorities were to aid and assist the bearer, whose responsibility it was to see that no one touched the films stored in the Palais de Chaillot. One of the documents had the stamp of the FFI [Forces françaises de l'intérieur, the name given in 1944 to a collection of Resistance military units in France] and was signed by Colonel Rol-Tanguy, and the other, with the message in English, was signed by an officer for the American intelligence services. Both orders said that in case of difficulty, they were to be referred to the FFI or the Allied high command.

"Your job is to guard the Palais de Chaillot," Henri told me. "The insur-rection's just broken out. The police are busy. Don't let anybody in. If the FFI shows up, or French soldiers, you show them the first document, and if they're American soldiers, the second."

"And if they're Germans?"

"Well, then you have your machine gun—and this FFI armband, which I almost forgot. Here, it's for you, along with the keys to the Chaillot base-ment."

And I did, in fact, spend the Liberation of Paris holed up in the base-ment of the Palais de Chaillot, monitoring the noises outside, with my machine gun at the ready, prepared to defend the treasures of the Cinémathèque. Fortunately, nothing happened. General von Choltitz didn't carry out Hitler's order to destroy the monuments of Paris—and me right along with them!

The first meeting of those who would be at the core of the Cinema Liberation Committee had been held, you will recall, at the Langloises' rue Troyon apartment toward the end of 1941. After his experiences with the underground in the Vercors, Jean-Paul Le Chanois patiently structured an organization that would be ready to film the battles for the Liberation of Paris while they were under way. Around Le Chanois, Marc Maurette and Max Douy had each formed a Resistance group made up of people in the entertainment field, including cameramen and film-lab technicians. On 20 August 1944, during a meeting held at the Pagode Cinema, the decision was made to occupy the Comité d'organisation de l'industrie cinématographique (COIC), the Vichy-controled cinema organization. The mission was carried out briskly, with military efficiency. At the appointed hour, the Resistance members charged the site, found Robert Buron on the premises, and put him under arrest. Buron protested violently, saying there'd been a mistake. There was much arguing and carrying on until someone had the bright idea of calling the CNC at avenue de Messine. Langlois picked up the phone at the other end and heard, "We've just arrested Robert Buron."

"You're out of your minds!" Langlois exclaimed. "He's in the Resistance— he represents de Gaulle!"

And it was thanks to this telephone call that Robert Buron, minister-to-be under General de Gaulle, was immediately freed.

The compartmentalization required for secrecy's sake sometimes meant that some groups within the Resistance had no idea what other groups were doing. Langlois wanted to get the jump on any uncontrollable factions that might have gotten it into their heads to capture the CNC. On the morning of 22 August, accompanied by a group of friends, Langlois took possession of the building and occupied the offices where the man who kept the Vichy Ministry of Information up-to-date had his desk. Langlois was determined to entrench and hang on to the premises for as long as it took, until the Liberation.

Alerted by all this hurly-burly, Riedinger, who belonged to yet another Resistance movement, the Organisation civil et militaire, immediately informed Louis Emile Galey.

"That's quite understandable," Galey sighed on the other end of the phone.

On the night of the twenty-fourth, all were at their posts, alert and ready for anything, when, at 11:00 P.M., the bells of Notre-Dame Cathedral began to ring, soon multiplying into an insistent chorus of ding-dong-dings as all the other churches of Paris joined in. The bells announced the long-awaited arrival of the first detachment from the Second Armored Division.

At CNC headquarters, everyone wanted to know what was happening, and soon a mass of people were elbowing for space and taking the steps four at a time. They climbed to the old servants quarters, and flung open the garret windows, the better to hear the rich, reverberating chimes as they sounded through the night air of Paris.

The exchange of power at CNC headquarters would take place in an honorable fashion and without violence. In occupying the Centre before the "competition," Henri, who thought very highly of Louis Emile Galey, had in mind that, if need be, he would be on hand to protect Galey—whose help in behalf of Langlois's efforts had been considerable—from charges of collaboration.

Jean Painlevé arrived at avenue de Messine and crisply introduced himself by his code name: Boulanger, government commissioner. Despite the gravity of the situation, Galey couldn't keep from smiling: *painlevé* meant "leavened bread"; whoever was handing out aliases in the underground could've come up with something better than *Boulanger*, which, of course, meant "baker."

Painlevé then announced that he would be relieving Monsieur Galey of his functions. Although technically Galey had served in a position ripe with possibilities for collaboration, he was not worried for his future. He would in fact be named to the new Ministry of Information:

> At the time I was removed from my post, there was nothing against me except a very nasty letter written by Marcel L'Herbier. Nasty, but ineffective and idiotic. Inspector General Crouzet, Teitgen's principal private secretary, presided over the purge committee. The first thing he told me was that he had nothing to reproach me about. The next day he summoned me to his office to announce, "I want to shake your hand. You are the sole person I've met in the course of my new duties whose hand I've shaken. Be that as it may, I greatly regret the fact that I am unable to let you keep your position—that, I'm afraid, is impossible."

Langlois showed Galey his gratitude by asking him to join the Cinémathèque's board of directors, a position he would hold for many years. As for the splendid building on avenue de Messine, the Ministry of Information soon moved on to greener pastures—or shinier parquet—leaving the entire structure to the Cinémathèque. For as long as the implicit lease could legally be renewed, that is where the association's headquarters would remain.

Oddly enough, Henri Langlois and Jean-Paul Le Chanois would not run into each other during the crazy, up-for-grabs days of the Liberation. Langlois had two specific objectives: to occupy the CNC's headquarters at avenue de Messine and to protect the films being stored under the Palais de Chaillot. As for Le Chanois, whose pseudonymn was Commandant Marceau, he was far too busy to take time out to direct the documentary he had hoped to make about the Liberation as it unfolded. Still, the clandestine film corps he had put together functioned admirably. Le Chanois had managed to set aside a quantity of unexposed film stock and had hand-picked a team of brave cameramen who, when the time came, covered all the key combat positions. As soon as the film was exposed, liaison officers transported it to the lab, where other Resistance workers were waiting to develop it. In this way, the documentation kept pace with events and was edited as the crews went along. The people of Paris were able to see the almost instant replay of their own history in record time—a filmed history including General de Gaulle's famous words, "Paris outraged; Paris broken, Paris martyred! But Paris is free! Having freed itself, freed by its people."

In the wake of these events, Le Chanois would not have the time to see Henri. He took off immediately for the Vercors, where he shot the final sequences of *Au coeur de l'orage*. As for Langlois, he set out to retrieve Lotte Eisner, his "dearest Lotte," who had stayed near Tulle, always a hair's breadth from danger.

Langlois and Le Chanois would not put their heads together for some time yet. But in 1968, when Henri would have need of all his friends, Le Chanois would be there at his side.

## chapter 6

# THIRST FOR CINEMA

Let us beware of legends and look instead at the results and at the films, for it's there and there alone that the truth is hidden.

Henri Langlois

As far as history books are concerned, Saturday, 26 August 1944, during daylight hours, gets top billing, because that is when General de Gaulle made his triumphant journey down the Champs-Elysées. But those who experienced the drunken delight of that magical endless night, once the late-summer sun had sunk on the freshly liberated horizon, will tell you that the night was more fun by far. For the first time since 3 September 1939— and for one night only—Paris shone once again, illuminated to its last bulb. All the restrictions on electricity consumption were lifted: no curfew, no blackout, no stubby candles, no dark corners, and no sad thoughts allowed. Subway cars filled to bursting discharged their jubilant passengers at Etoile, place de la Concorde, and Nôtre Dame. Up out of the Métro they spilled by the thousands to see the City of Light once more live up to its name.

And in this crowd were several hundred privileged individuals on their way not to some monument any tourist would know but to one particular address, an address Langlois had given them, along with an invitation to wind up the night celebrating the Liberation with him. As a line began to form along the sidewalk of rue Troyon, those summoned to the spot had to accept that, incredible as it seemed, this was not a joke. No, the Studio de l'Etoile Cinéma was very much open, and Langlois was waiting there to welcome them. He had promised his friends a major surprise, but would not so much as hint at what it might be. Not until the distinctive opening credits began to roll did his guests discover that they were lucky enough to be watching the European premiere of *Gone with the Wind*. The general public would have to wait a full year for the film's official release on Paris screens. Never had the film—from the burning of Atlanta to "Frankly, my dear, I don't give a damn"—given rise to more emotion than it did for the enthralled audience that saw it the very day after the Liberation.

Henri had set his heart on the Studio de l'Etoile. In the days and weeks to follow, the Cinémathèque Française and the Cinema Liberation Committee, working in perfect harmony, would project many other American films in private screenings for film professionals and their families. This would not seem all that exceptional unless one knew that nearly every movie theater in Paris was shut down and would remain that way until 13 October. Months prior to the Allied landings, however, the Propaganda Services of the U.S. Army had prepared a plan whereby films could be projected in towns as soon as they were liberated.

The Psychological War Department had seen to it that the most representative American, British, and Russian films were assembled in England, whence they were transferred to North Africa in order to follow the advancing troops. An entire program, tailored for the French, had been put together. The goal was not only to show the public the most recent mainstream entertainment of which it had been deprived but, more important, to bring the people, via the screen, information about the events of the war—events about which most of the population, apart from the happy few who attended Henri Langlois's last few clandestine screenings, had been ignorant during the four long Occupation years.

The entire program had been put together by Anglo-American specialists using the latest scientific methods. Specialists or not, as each town was liberated they had to face the fact that the prewar circuits for commercial distribution no longer existed.

After having set up special centers, as best as could be managed, in Cherbourg and in Rennes, Lacy Kastner, head of the Film Section of the Psychological War Department, concentrated entirely on Paris. His assistant was a resourceful French liaison officer dispatched from the Forces françaises libres. Together they managed to find a truck—an English truck that had been taken by the Germans in 1940, equipped to run on methanol. This fabulous specimen, discovered in a stable, was now part of the Film Section's modest booty. Still, it was thanks to this very vehicle that the films and the staff were able to reach Paris in advance of the Liberation. Kastner came to town on the twenty-fifth, and everything was in place and ready to go. There was one minor drawback, however: no electricity.

All the same, with the help of emergency generators three cinemas were able to project the film about the Liberation of Paris, along with the footage of the Allied landings, collected under the title *The Free World*.

Not just anyone would have been able to organize screenings at the Studio de l'Etoile in a situation such as this. Henri had both the films to show and the support of the Film Technicians Union needed to show them. Langlois turned over the box office receipts to this union.

These private screenings took place throughout September, October, and November 1944. But Henri was anxious to move on to a wider sphere of influence. He couldn't wait to show his treasures to larger audiences of film buffs. Langlois slated the reopening of the Cercle du Cinéma for 7 December 1944 at the Studio de l'Etoile. Even the mainstream press took note.

Thanks to Langlois, the younger spectators at the Cercle would finally get the chance to see the old movies that were at the core of film history, but that had literally dropped out of sight because of the Occupation.

This conspicuous void had been a source of frustration for William Novik and most of his classmates, who had completed their film studies at the School of Cinema on rue de Vaugirard between 1940 and 1942. They'd been able to get only a rough idea of these film classics from class lectures and from the descriptions in Bardèche and Brasillach's reference volume. As soon as the grand reopening of the Cercle was announced, Novik and friends were off and running to the Studio de l'Etoile. Remembers Novik:

> It was incredible—hundreds of people jostling each other at the entrance. The place held about 300, but when things first got under way again, as many as 1,000 would show up, waiting to see the films of Chaplin, Sennett, Lubitsch, Renoir, or Clair. Since the crowds came close to rioting more than once, Langlois and I had the idea of organizing a two-week-long contest in order to occupy the people who were waiting in line. We gave them a questionnaire to fill out; it was a sort of test of how much you knew about the cinema. At first, we did it almost as a joke. But people took the thing very seriously, and so we were obliged to make the questions increasingly difficult. Langlois awarded membership cards in the Cercle du Cinéma to those who came up with the best answers.

After four years of restrictions, the young were starved for movies. The Cinémathèque would not only jump right into the cultural gap and try to make up for lost time, but also expand its activities to give another of Langlois's special talents free reign. Henri would soon mount his first major exhibition on the cinema.

Right after the Liberation, Henri decided the time had come to display some of his film-related treasures to the outside world. It was precisely then that a journalist named Nicole Védrès came to ask Langlois for permission to look through the Cinémathèque's photo archives. She said she was looking for photographs with which to illustrate a book on the French Cinema. Henri immediately put both himself and the collection at her disposal. He showed her certain shots and helped her make her first selections. She left with packets of photographs tucked under her arms.

Langlois had made such a strong impression on Nicole Védrès that she had the feeling he was looking over her shoulder as she sorted through the material and was silently guiding her choices by remote control. In an article for *L'Ecran français*, she described Langlois and hinted at some Langloisian essence permeating her work: "Langlois is not a rationalist when it comes to classification. He knows that the state of distribution of the treasures of French cinema being what it is, it is better to rely on one's instincts than on catalogs. Nor is he a technician or a progagandizer of cinema—he's more like a *mahatma*: He gives us his blessing, adding, 'Take off and dive into the thick of the mystery; you'll see where you are when you get there.'"

Langlois started telling himself that it would be a double success if Nicole Védrès's book of photos and the exhibit he was planning could both appear at the same time and under the same title: "Images of the French Cinema."

Since he never conceived a cinema exposition without spectacular adornments, Langlois would be needing hangings and curtains and precious as well as preposterous pieces of furniture to set off and complement the objects he planned to display. Throughout December 1944, Henri made the rounds of antiques dealers and furniture shops, buying up—with his own money or else Mary Meerson's—all sorts of items that would later end up at the Cinémathèque.

Langlois had already begun to enchant journalists, who found him to be a surefire source of copy. One reporter, by the name of Charles Rochefort, accompanied Langlois on his peregrinations and caught him in the act of acquiring fanciful furnishings: "We were able to follow Monsieur Langlois into the very heart of his preparations, and we followed him as far as the furniture dealers, where he carried off with great panache the purchase of a cross section of turn-of-the-century consoles, incredible trestles, and other objects of a fantastic nature so as to fashion a suitable setting and supporting framework for the various pieces from the collection that are to be displayed."

Henri came and went, purchased and filed, and came face to face with myriad difficulties of a material nature. One day he went over to 92 avenue des Champs-Elysées, where the Cinema Committee of Liberation was still located. As was his custom, he greeted the janitor, Charles Heimberger, but on this occasion chatted more than usual with the young man. And when Henri chatted, there could be but one thrust to his chatter: the Cinémathèque.

"Ah," he sighed, "I'm very, very annoyed. The doors don't work back at avenue de Messine. There's no gas, and the electricity isn't working either. Everything's broken."

After listening to a succession of complaints, Heimberger, despite his essentially timid nature, managed to blurt out, "I can fix anything!"

"Now, that interests me," Langlois said, considering. "Would you like to work at the Cinémathèque Française? You're hired!"

They immediately consulted his present employer, who agreed, and that is how in January 1945, at age 25, Heimberger signed on for what would turn out to be a stay of 34 years. Charles was soon nicknamed "Charlot" (pronounced *Shar-low*)—the nickname by which Charlie Chaplin was known to the French-speaking world—and would show devotion above and beyond the call of duty.

From the moment Charlot set foot in the former mansion on avenue de Messine, he saw for himself that Langlois wasn't kidding about everything needing repairs. With the exception of a few offices, the vast building was altogether vacant and in deplorable shape. The water was cut off, and the plumbing was ancient. Heimberger had his work cut out for him and would serve as plumber, electrician, and handyman. But things were obviously too far gone for just one person, however skilled, to set them right. Langlois asked Charlot if he knew of anyone who could help.

Charlot did have just such a friend: Roger Tourret, an electrician who worked at the Billancourt Studios just outside Paris. Tourret accepted the offer and became half of a team that came to practically worship Langlois.

Each day, Henri presented them with a different problem. Langlois brought objects of considerable value to avenue de Messine—columns, Louis XIV balusters, doors that had once belonged to the Marquise de Pompidour—and asked his helpers to accomplish tasks that often struck them as bizarre. But Charlot and Roger quickly became accustomed to their boss's extravagances.

Henri went about organizing brilliant receptions to bring together the most touted segments of *Tout-Paris*. Langlois, displaying impeccable taste, decorated the salons with huge vases full of flowers. In those days, the central produce market, Les Halles, was the heart of Paris, and Henri thought nothing of arriving there at 5:00 A.M., with faithful Charlot in tow, in order to select the best-possible blossoms. Then it was back to headquarters, where Charlot would set the tables, clean the light fixtures, and do whatever else needed to be done to make the evening a success.

But the priority among priorities was to make certain that the exhibit "Images of the French Cinema" was ready in time. Langlois worked like a madman, chain-smoked without inhaling, and drank only water. Come dawn, Henri, utterly exhausted, would conk out right there on the floor, rolling himself up blintzlike in the nearest rug. Needless to say, he dreamed only of the exhibit.

As for Charlot and Roger, when they left for work in the morning neither could say what time he'd be home. But they had the feeling they were participating in the creation of a true work of art. In a way, they had become physical extensions of Langlois. Some can lay claim to being a right-hand man; Langlois had two right-hand men. Heimberger and Tourret respected Langlois's raging need to please, to seduce, to convince others, and to discharge as best he could his love for the cinema. They understood that in

Henri's case, the drive to organize exhibitions was every bit as much physical as it was intellectual. They said it themselves: Langlois's need to put on shows bordered on a sexual need.

Charlot and Roger stayed up with Langlois the night before the opening. Up to the last possible moment, the place looked like a construction site. And then suddenly, as if a particularly effective magic wand had swept through the rooms, everything fell into place a mere half-hour before the guests were due to arrive. Short on self-waving magic wands, they made one last manual tour with earthbound brooms before the dignitaries and the public came to call. Charlot and Roger were too weary to take another step, but not Langlois: He still had to inaugurate his exhibition!

All the loving preparation most definitely paid off. "Images of the French Cinema" was a rip-roaring success and a *Tout-Paris* triumph. Henri's sole regret was that the compilation of photos by Nicole Védrès was not ready for release at the same time the exhibit opened. The show began in January 1945; the book would be published by Editions du Chêne that summer.

In order to express his vision of cinematographic art, Langlois had mounted a show that was itself a work of art. Langlois hated the stodgy, the didactic, the pedagogical approach to anything. His juxtaposition of objects left as much to the imagination as it gave. His show illustrated the projections that accompanied it, enchanted the greatest poets of the day, and was the basis of Jean Cocteau's admiration for its auteur. It was undoubtedly all for the best that the exhibition preceded the volume of photographs by several months, for the exhibit inspired Paul Eluard to write this preface to the book:

> There was a swan so very curved that it spied black through Leda's rainbow. And for the journey there was a road of black and white, and upon this road seasonal shadows kicked up in turn clouds of dust, gusts of heat, stacks of laughter, tons of feathers, rivers of tears, and long, long dresses, most charming. There was a very beautiful Greek courtesan as well, who did not age, but *faded*, and faded out. . . .
>
> All the same, around nine in the evening, in a cinema as closed as could be, the swan did not pass up its chance. Around 10:00 P.M., the shadows slanting across the piano had a body, and they deserved it. And the beauty among beauties promised to be beautiful without promising to be.
>
> Between nine and midnight, between wakefulness and slumber, real images half-perceived fulfill our unreality. Halves, quarters, millionths of true imagery. Fruits bereft of pulp and pit bid us forget palaces, tongue, and teeth. Our eyes slip back into their shell, as does our gaze toward that which it dreamed of seeing.
>
> Suddenly, temptation clashes with desire. One must not desire; one must lay oneself open and submit.
>
> Obey without bending. Confusion undertakes its tyrannical spread across a piece of linen most clean. The dreamer, enchanted, decides to

make a break, without knowing exactly what with—to break off for the sake of breaking off.

Here, then, is the summing up of an experience. The fragments of moving images assembled here prove that the cinema has discovered a new world within the reach, like poetry, of every imagination. Even when it sought to imitate the ancient world, nature (or theater), it produced fantasies. In copying the earth, it showed us the star.

The specter of talking pictures would worry fine minds. But they were soon forced to admit that, in confronting *to see* and *to hear*, in blending with a moving vision those components of language that get lost or linger on, the talking picture could render full meaning to the beautiful alphabet of gesture and grimace that was the supreme cripple, the silent film.

Despite the general admiration aroused by the exhibition, some made it known that the exhibit would have been substantially improved by an accompanying catalog that explained to visitors what, exactly, they were seeing. These critics had fallen far afield of the overall meaning Henri had intended to impart. Langlois let his annoyance show and once and for all outlined his philosophy while delivering a lecture at the IDHEC film school:

The exhibition "Images of the French Cinema" is so closely linked to the book of the same name recently published by Editions du Chêne that it is useless to try to speak of one without the other.

Many a criticism could have been avoided if, as we had wished, this book had been released during the course of the exhibition.

The admirable preface that this work inspired Paul Eluard to write—one of the most beautiful pages ever written about the cinema—would have dispelled all equivocation and silenced a great many people. Should we mumble and groan about it?

I, for my part, regret it not one bit. As we leave a period wherein the cinema, gutted of all substance, made the general public yawn, nothing could be more agreeable than for us to hear those selfsame individuals who condemned realism in favor of I-don't-know-what-sort-of escapist moviemaking, educated and competent people who are pleased with themselves, pleased as can be with the lethal boredom of dime-store immortality, clamoring for subtitles and explanations of images whose poetry is completely obvious.

Can beauty be explained? Should it be explained? Is a painting a memory? Do those who visit an exhibition of Chinese art demand a full account of the Han Dynasty in order to appreciate the show? And what need is there for historical accounts of an art form where folklore and fantasy have converged for more than 20 years and where all the dreams and lost opportunities of humanity shall go right on converging?

Can an image as weighty and as mysterious as the one that brings Monca, Grétillat, and Robinne face to face in *La Proie* possibly support a commentary?

Does it not possess an inherent value all its own? Is it not a justification in itself? Is it less precious than a painting, a sketch, an angel from the Middle Ages, a child's drawing or the popular engravings cranked out at Epinal?

I am perfectly well aware of the fact that to have such faith in the taste of the reader as well as in that of the visitor, to regard them as one's equals, as capable of understanding, of appreciation, as possessed of faculties of taste and judgment, is a very shocking thing for those who in their own nearsighted eyes constitute the elite, in a time when stupidity, ignorance, and fascism conceal themselves with base demagoguery. And this is why both the exhibition and the book are seen as being antipopular.

The success of the exhibition, the welcome response it evoked from all those who love and are interested in the cinema, the number of people for whom one visit was not enough and who made the time to come back again, the cleaning women, the workers, the hairdressers, the clerks who signed up at the Cercle du Cinéma as a result, its popularity with school-age youngsters much to the deadly deception of pedants, these are the very best justifications imaginable.

Langlois's collaboration with Nicole Védrès would lead, two years later, to the making of a compilation film, *Paris 1900*, which would delight French audiences and win the Prix Louis-Delluc. *Paris 1900* was seen and reseen by an entire generation of audiences, and although its black-and-white frames were temporarily ignored for an interval after color films made their triumphant sweep, interest picked up again as soon as a new generation of viewers came along. The movie is made up of more than 600 snippets of film from the turn of the century, newsreel and documentary footage mixed in with fiction, all edited together with a subtle flair that brings *la belle époque* back to life. It is and shall remain a chef d'oeuvre.

When the exhibition closed, the Cercle du Cinéma left the Studio de l'Etoile for the Ingénieurs des Arts et Métiers Théâtre at 9 bis avenue d'Iéna. Henri Langlois inaugurated this new setting on 27 March 1945 with a festival of Eisenstein films. Screenings were held every Tuesday and Wednesday at 8:30 P.M. Langlois programmed mostly silent classics, with a new twist that was really an old twist: The films were accompanied by piano music, improvised in keeping with the action on the screen. Those in attendance have never forgotten these particular showings, because the pianist was none other than the composer Joseph Kosma. Kosma, who was already famous for his score for *Children of Paradise*—composed while he was in hiding from the Nazis—contributed his talents out of friendship for Henri and because it pleased him to do so. It often happened that he had not seen the film in advance and so would *truly* improvise while discovering, along with the audience, *Nosferatu* or *The Cabinet of Dr. Caligari*.

The new improved Cercle not only attracted film-starved youngsters, who were catching up at the rate of one or two films a day, but also appealed to a generation's worth of poets, writers, and artists who were delighted to be able to reexperience the classics they'd known before the war. The atmosphere at screenings was warm and enthusiastic, sometimes downright meditative. Should a laugh or giggle happen to issue forth during an old silent film, there was always a voice in the crowd to confound the irreverent ingrates: "If this doesn't appeal to you then go see something with Fernandel!"—which was akin to suggesting that they would find a Don Knotts double feature more in keeping with their level of maturity.

Iranian filmmaker Farrokh Gaffary, who was still a student at the time, clearly remembers that "from the very start, Henri's absolutely contradictory and fascinating character bedazzled us all. He'd introduce a film, give you all sorts of pertinent details about it, and run off immediately afterward. And then an entirely different film would be projected! Some people were surprised, of course, but I, along with others, had quickly gotten used to this sort of thing. And when Henri came back after the film was through and learned what had happened, he'd exclaim, 'Everything I told you in connection with the other film remains absolutely valid for the one you've just seen.' Nothing threw him."

Director-to-be Jean-Charles Tacchella, then 20, had come to Paris from Cherbourg to become a film critic. He attended nearly all the Cercle du Cinéma screenings and summed them up on a weekly basis for *L'Ecran français*. Years later, Tacchella would write:

> Those who did not live through that era will doubtless have trouble imagining just what it was like in the spring and summer of 1945. The war had ended, France was free, but most of all, when the Occupation was over, the established structure exploded. Whatever the domain, there was renewal, rebirth, and immense hope for a new society.
>
> Our big problem was to see films from the past—classics from the silent era and films from the beginning of talking pictures that we'd heard about but had never seen for ourselves. In less than two years, thanks to Henri Langlois and the Cinémathèque, as well as the ciné-clubs that began to take off around 1946, we were finally able to see them. Just about the same people came to most screenings: Bazin, Kast, Doniol-Valcroze, Thérond, Astruc, Colpi, Rossif, me, and a few others. Naturally, our discussions were endless.

Nazi Germany conceded defeat on 8 May 1945. In Paris, as in all the Allied capitals, jubilant crowds poured into the streets. Waves of humanity crashed up against the steps of the Opera and all up and down the major thoroughfares. That night, the Cinémathèque Française hosted a Cercle du

Cinéma screening devoted to Buñuel and Dali with *L'Age d'or*, *Un Chien andalou*, and *Terre sans pain*, accompanied by choice excerpts from the full range of the French avant-garde. Film-collector friends lent their prints to Langlois, and he obtained Buñuel's work directly from his "producer," the Count de Noailles. After being banned for 15 years, *L'Age d'or* proved a major emotional upheaval for audiences. Pierre Kast had never experienced anything quite like it: "Seeing *L'Age d'or* in 1945 was phenomenal! No one knew who Buñuel was. People didn't even know *where* he was. The Occupation had been a period of savage capitalism, and certain people were still expressing their contempt. But *L'Age d'or*—what in the world was this?"

When Pierre Kast looked back on the circumstances in which he first met Langlois, he liked to emphasize that, "for me, our meeting had nothing whatsoever to do with luck, because I don't believe in luck."

Kast had set out before the war to qualify for the *agrégation*, the highest competitive examination for teachers in France, granting instant tenure at the university level. But at the Liberation, after four years of guerrilla activities, he no longer felt like picking up his studies or pursuing a career in politics. What he wanted most could be summed up in one infinitive: to work. Kast too had been a film fanatic since his adolescence and often skipped classes to see one, two, or even three films in the same day.

When his friend, the writer Roger Vailland, started the weekly newspaper *Action*, Kast signed on immediately as film critic. One day he set out to locate an old document that he absolutely had to find. It occurred to him that there must be some sort of official something in charge of collecting and preserving films themselves and the relevant archival materials to go along with them. He took the telephone book in hand but found no such listing as "National Cinémathèque." He did, however, come across "Cinémathèque Française," which sounded promising. Kast picked up the phone, dialed, and encountered a voice, which wanted to know:

> "Who are you?"
> "I work with Roger Vailland at *Action*."
> "Then come right over."
> "Who should I ask for?"
> "Ask for me."
> "Well, who are you?"
> "My name is Henri Langlois."

Once he got to 7, avenue de Messine, the young critic found himself face to face with the man who would prove to be a permanent source of surprise. Kast, it so happened, had just taken the competitive entrance exam for admission to IDHEC and had tied for first place with Jean Prat, who would go on to have a major career in French television. Kast mentioned his latest accomplishment to Langlois, who responded, "Don't bother going to

IDHEC; it's not worth it. I'll take you on here." And from that moment on, Pierre Kast was assistant to Henri Langlois and, without knowing it, about to enter a magical realm:

> Thanks to him, I would get to know the major figures of Cinema with a capital C. I'd never set eyes on any of them until then, and right off the bat I was talking to Jean Grémillon for starters, and all of Langlois's close associates: Mary Meerson, Nicole Védrès, Lotte Eisner, Jean Mitry, and then another faithful group after them, notably Elie Lotar, the Prévert brothers, Max Douy, and Trauner.
>
> There were also surprising characters, such as Jean Castagnier, an anarchist painter who had made a few films and been assistant and scriptwriter for Jean Renoir. It was also in starting to work at the Cinémathèque that I met Renoir himself and Jacques Becker, whom I adored, because he was marvelous.

Pierre Kast had a tough life—his job at the Cinémathèque consisted of watching films all day long! In this way, over the course of over two years, he would see several thousand:

> The Cinémathèque didn't have a [motorized] Morritone film viewer at the time, so I had to watch everything on a hand-cranked gizmo. I remember it as a wonderful experience.
>
> There was something prodigious about working side by side with Langlois in those heroic years from 1945 to 1948. There was always wild activity when it came time to select the films he'd be showing for the next program. We'd get started around 9:30 or 10:00 in the morning, and we'd still be at it by 2:00 or 3:00 A.M. the next day. It was a time of total craziness and hyperactivity.
>
> From being in contact with Langlois, I came to realize that he was a much more important individual than any director, because it was his voice that gave expression to the eternal dialectic of the art of cinema and its history, for its past as well as its future.

Being Langlois's assistant meant seeing films, inspecting films, transporting films, and spending entire sleepless nights putting together exhibitions. This period of manic activity coincided with the start of the great era of Saint-Germain-des-Prés, when the cafés and clubs of the streets that lay in the shadow of or just a bit beyond the oldest church in Paris were the vortex of youth and talent, as Montparnasse and Montmartre had been before it. One night, Kast stopped into a bar for a drink and found himself beside a great beanpole. The two fresh acquaintances traded small talk and jokes for a while. Kast ended up telling his tall, thin new pal, "I work with Langlois," whereupon a lively discussion about the cinema ensued. Eventually, the fellow he'd been speaking to introduced himself—it was Boris Vian. Vian, the prolific, razor-sharp writer, poet, and musician who would die tragically at the age of 39, would be Kast's best friend for the next 10 years.

In March 1945, five ciné-clubs were in operation in Paris: the Cercle Technique de l'Écran, which stemmed from the Film Liberation Committee; the Cercle du Cinéma; the Cinderella Ciné-Club, the University Ciné-Club; and Ciné-Youth. They decided to band together to form the first Federation of Ciné-Clubs, with Jean Painlevé, director of the CNC, as president, and the critic and film historian Georges Sadoul as secretary-general.

During this period, Henri Langlois supported the ciné-clubs and literally held their hands. He gave the federation office space in the Cinémathèque's building and lent its members films throughout that first year.

The clubs had dedicated themselves to increasing the number of people interested in the cinema and intended to do so by increasing the number of places and the frequency with which films were shown. Every new member was a new devotee in the ranks, a new fanatic. The results exceeded everybody's wildest dreams and at the same time created a serious problem between the two nonprofit structures. In one year, the number of ciné-clubs multiplied from 5 to 90 and their membership skyrocketed from a few hundred to more than 10,000. For the Communist party, the flowering of new ciné-clubs indicated a vast cultural movement upon which it might exercise its influence. The clubs' continued development demanded intensive programming, and the Federation of Ciné-Clubs looked upon the Cinémathèque as an inexhaustible source of films.

But it soon became impossible for Langlois to keep up with the demands of nearly 100 ciné-clubs spread out all over the place, each clamoring for the rarest prints. The Cinémathèque did not have the means to print multiple copies and, more often than not, held one-of-a-kind originals that could stand up only to a limited number of projections.

As a result, war broke out between the ciné-clubs and the Cinémathèque. And when Langlois responded to their requests with "I'm showing that film at avenue de Messine—all you have to do is come here if you want to see it," the others, furious, accused him of competition and of deliberately wanting to undermine their efforts.

Langlois bore allegiance to no political party; his only party was the Cinémathèque. His sole concerns were to safeguard the longevity of the films with which he had been entrusted and to defend the best interests of those who owned the rights to said films. All of a sudden, Langlois and the Communists found themselves on the verge of blows. The matter proved especially awkward between Langlois and his friend Georges Sadoul.

In July 1948, the secretary-general of the French Federation of Ciné-Clubs sent a particularly virulent letter to the new CNC president, Monsieur Fourré-Cormeray, speaking of the underhanded and systematic opposition Henri Langlois was applying to the requests of the ciné-clubs. In addition to this, Sadoul set off a publicity campaign in the press. The Cinémathèque's board of directors unanimously consolidated behind Langlois and approved the decision of the Cinémathèque's president, Jean Grémillon, to resign from his position on the board of directors of the Federation of Ciné-Clubs. Whatever the attack, Langlois held his ground.

This war would last for nearly three years, until the day when Georges Sadoul, in the course of a meeting of the Cinémathèque's board of directors, threw in the towel. "You're too tough for me, Langlois," he said. "I'm not going to fight you anymore. It's over."

In short order, mutual respect and friendship were back where they belonged. Langlois would help Sadoul, facilitate his access to photos at the Cinémathèque's phototèque, and write the preface to his *History of World Cinema*. The affection these two men shared for each other would know no further setbacks.

Langlois, however, was forced to sacrifice the Cercle du Cinéma screenings lest the Cinémathèque be suspected of showing favoritism toward the ciné-club that it had, after all, sired. From now on, Langlois would project films in the name of the Cinémathèque alone.

With "Images of French Cinema," Henri Langlois had created an entirely new kind of exhibit and, at the same time, a prestigious "product" of sorts that could be exported—a neat trick, in view of the fact that France had been stripped bare and was thinking of little more than its own reconstruction.

The exhibition would soon be presented, with the same success, in London, Venice, Algiers, and Tunis. But first, Langlois needed the international stamp of approval. Henri chose the most propitious spot for such acclaim as a strategist would: with map in hand. He did not have the financial resources to travel too far from home and did not care to start with a country that had undergone the war. Therefore, he would go to Switzerland, and in order to easily transport his collections, he would require a city on the Paris-Brigue rail line. He circled Lausanne on the map.

His choice made, Langlois wrote to Michel Rittener, his old accomplice from the days of the clandestine screenings who, conveniently enough, was now in Switzerland, to let him know he should be there to meet him at the train station in Lausanne. As for Charlot, Langlois didn't think to inform him of the trip until the night before their departure: "Oh, by the way—I didn't tell you, but we're leaving tomorrow for Lausanne."

Michel Rittener was on time to meet them. Henri had not actually made any preliminary contact with the municipal authorities. Once again, he put his trust in his instincts, convinced that once he was there, he'd have no trouble persuading the necessary parties. The day after his arrival, Langlois proceeded to the Association des intérets of Lausanne, asked to see its president, and introduced himself as follows: "I am the Cinémathèque Française. I should like to offer you the exhibition that all Paris rushed to see."

The Swiss were thrilled. The exhibition would be held in September and October 1945 at the Rumine Palace. But everything remained to be done, since nothing was ready.

Rittener rented an apartment large enough for Charlot, Tourret, Henri, and himself. They would live together for two months, working more often than not as many as 15 hours a day.

Henri adored Charlot and Tourret, who, according to Rittener, represented to Henri the working classes. For the duration of their preparations for the exhibit, Henri's entire social sphere would consist of these two workers who were not proletarians but skilled film technicians.

Charlot had contracted scurvy from a lack of vitamins during the Occupation. While in Lausanne, he realized that he was on the brink of losing all his teeth. Rittener immediately took him to a doctor, who was horrified to see someone with such an advanced case of the illness who persisted in working. But Charlot refused to stop: "It was indispensable. I couldn't abandon Langlois. So the doctor treated me with a drastic remedy, prescribing that I paint my mouth with methylene blue. My teeth were all black, and my tongue was blue. To boost morale, I'd stick out my tongue—it was absolutely horrible to look at. But only one thing mattered to us: finishing the exhibition. We worked 50 hours in a row without rest. It was crazy. But we had to finish before the inauguration date. It nearly killed us, and Langlois did eventually become ill."

Just a few days before the show was to open, Langlois did in fact come down with the flu, accompanied by a high fever. Rittener wanted to call the doctor, but Henri categorically refused: "No, no, don't bother. I don't trust doctors. I'll just treat myself my own way."

Rittener finally gave in and left Langlois alone in the apartment. When Rittener came back a few hours later, he found Langlois wrapped up in newspapers and sleeping between two mattresses! Henri would remain that way, like a human sandwich, all night. Come morning, his fever was gone.

With just a quarter-hour left before the inauguration, Langlois, clad in a painter's smock encrusted with plaster, was still hammering nails into the wall. At the last possible moment, he slipped out of the Palais de Rumine and ran to buy a suitable shirt for the opening. He spotted one to his liking in a shop window, put it on in a hurry, and made his entrance into the Grand Salon of the Palace. Langlois's choice bore a large number on the back: it was a rugby player's shirt! Needless to say, Langlois's appearance amid the dignitaries of Lausanne did not go unremarked.

The exhibition had been well publicized, and many young people made a point of attending. One of the most assiduous of the bunch, Freddy Buache, then in his twenties, took a seat in the small salon where 16-millimeter films were being shown. He was utterly bedazzled by the sight of Ivan Mosjoukine's *Le Brasier ardent* and *Entr'acte* by René Clair.

And then I saw *Un Chien andalou,* and I staggered out of *that* completely dumbfounded. I immediately went to find out if there'd be other projections, and it turned out that the man I asked was Langlois. He had no doubt noticed that I looked a little odd and said, "You've got to come have a drink with me." And so, although I didn't know him from Adam, I found myself with him and a bunch of people who were drinking *fendant* and singing the praises of Swiss food. (They had just emerged from five years of rationing.) Langlois introduced them to me one after the other, saying, "You should come see this gentleman's film tonight." And it was Grémillon. Then he added, "And this gentleman will have the pleasure of accompanying it on the piano." And it was Kosma! Langlois then told me that other people had reacted as I had and that it would be good if we got to know one another better. Then he took off again."

No sooner had Langlois returned to Paris than he decided to mount an entirely different exhibition, to be held at avenue de Messine and to be devoted to animated cartoons and the Frenchman whose work prefigured them, Emile Reynaud. The you-are-there beginning of a radio program from that time gives us an idea of the curiosity the show aroused: "We are standing in front of number 7, avenue de Messine. Why number 7 in particular? For no crime has been committed here, no murder attempted. There is, quite simply, an exhibition on animation. I open the door. . . ."

The description published in *La Cinématographie française* on 23 February 1946 gives us all the details:

Starting with the entryway, we are greeted by all the familiar characters. Here are Popeye and Olive Oyl, life-size—if I dare to employ that term—striking a dramatic pose under the placid eye of a large fish who figures prominently in a charming Disney film, while meanwhile, in a corner, sullen Donald, he of the eternal bad luck, thinks hard upon his misfortune. On the left there's Mickey, Minnie, Goofy, Pinocchio, and Pluto in the form of graceful little statuettes, judiciously arranged on the squares of a checkerboard. To the right, some ancestors are on display in a glass case: *phénakisticope* disks and a magic lantern.

As we begin our visit, we see a board explaining the method by which animated cartoons are made. There are sketches made by Grimault in preparation for his next film, and photos of the workshops where tracing, inking, animation, and so on, are done straight through to the shooting process and the finished film. Above a display case containing Alexieff's pinboard rests one of Disney's original drawings for *Fantasia.*

The room devoted to Emile Cohl retraces the life and work of the forerunner of animated filmmaking who created every sort of animation: anecdotal designs, puppet films, Chinese shadows, abstract films, commercials, and educational films. This work is illustrated through numerous photos and drawings. We then enter the "Retrospectives" room, where photos taken from the most significant animated films since the form began are displayed: *Gertie the Dinosaur* by McCay (1908); *Felix the Cat* by Pat Sullivan (1913); *The Skeleton Dance*, made by Disney in 1929; *The Little Czar Doulandaï*, a Russian film from 1934; *Snow White* (1937); *Pinocchio* (1938); *Gulliver's Travels* (1939); *Fantasia* (1940); *Victory through Air Power* (1942); and so on. . . .

In an adjacent room, looking very much like a tableau in a wax museum, we see the great scene from Painlevé's *Bluebeard*, reenacted with the help of the marionettes from the film. . . .

Voilà! Films by Len Lye, emulator of Fischinger, photos of Alexieff, of Lotte Reiniger, and so forth.

But the centerpiece of this exhibition is the presentation by Jacques Damiot of the Starevitch marionettes, where we find the Fox, the Cicada and the Ant, the Frog, the Lion, and so forth, cleverly positioned and lifelike as can be.

Across the way is a board reserved for French animation: Arcady, Grimault, Image, and so on, with all the documents arranged in a jolly tricolored setting.

The part of the show devoted to Emile Reynaud is located on the second floor of the building and enables us to see the different inventions of the cinema's forerunners. In a highly nineteenth-century setting we find displayed the zoetrope, the thaumatrope, the phakinescope (a plagiarism of Reynaud), and above all, Reynaud's inventions: praxinoscope and *photo-scénographe*. But the loveliest piece on exhibit, bar none, is the hand-painted filmstrip *Pauvre Pierrot*, which was projected at the Maison de la Chimie on the occasion of its fiftieth anniversary. This is one of the most precious documents in existence from the early days of the *théatre optique*, and we are able to see it today thanks to the kindness of the Musée des Arts et Métiers. Other documents are on loan from the inventor's sons, Paul and André Reynaud.

Finally, as no exhibition on the cinema can be understood without the projection of films, one may view, in the Cinémathèque's small theater, a selection of animated works, including a *ciné-rythme* by Fischinger, a film by Paul Grimault, and two Mickey Mouse cartoons, of which one, *Building a Building*, is a little masterpiece of comicalness.

Langlois would continue to mount exhibitions at a runaway pace. From June through August, he put together "The Movie Poster from 1895 to 1946" and "Zecca and the Pathé Realist School in 1900." Foreign cultural attachés were eager to host these shows in their own countries. In 1947 the Cinémathèque's international prestige increased through a series of exhibitions combined with film programs, designed to demonstrate the historic role of the French pioneers in the earliest days of moviemaking. Such was the case with "The Birth of French Cinema," presented in Brussels.

Henri Langlois, at the suggestion of André Thirifays, was invited to mount this particular exhibition in conjunction with the World Film and Beaux-Arts Festival of Belgium. During one of his visits to Brussels, Henri was introduced by Thirifays to a young Belgian artist named Jean Raine. In his autobiographical volume *Autothanatographie*, Jean Raine recounts, "While still in short pants, I met Magritte, Scutenaire, and Lecomte from the Belgian surrealist group, and many others. Ghelderode fascinated me, and time flew. Soon I'd be 20. Capital encounter, that with Henri Langlois—I let myself be carried away by his charm. There I was caught and for a long time, in the narrow mesh of the magic net that is the Cinémathèque Française, which made me immigrate to Paris."

Jean Raine was a very cultured young man, and Langlois took an immediate liking to him. In no time at all, Henri was asking Raine, who was 13 years his junior, for his opinions about all sorts of things. As much as Langlois had delighted in meeting and learning from the "senior citizens" of cinema when he himself was barely out of his teens, he liked to surround himself with young assistants who, in his opinion, possessed an energy level not often found among the more chronologically adult. Young people were open-minded, receptive to the future, and refreshingly undogmatic. The Cinémathèque was in no danger of becoming a stodgy institution when there was so much young blood around.

In January 1947 Jean Raine became part of the Cinémathèque and discovered an amazing new world: "The Cinémathèque Française was a little bit like Versailles—say, the King's Court—and there I learned as much if not more than I had in my theoretical courses at the university. It was a marvelous era when the cinema was flirting with surrealism, with humor, and with *l'amour*, period."

The exhibition was held from Saturday, 14 June, through Friday, 20 June, in 1947. Langlois finished setting things up as usual: in a crisis-level burst of sleepless nights shot through with manic energy. And as the officials advanced through the exhibit on opening day, Langlois simply walked backward just ahead of them, kicking aside any stray objects still in evidence.

Entry to the exhibition was free, and it attracted enormous crowds but cost an equally enormous sum to create. Langlois dared not show his face before Monsieur Selliers de Moranville, the festival treasurer. This touchy duty fell to Jean Raine:

> I went over and saw the bill—300,000 or 400,000 francs, which was a considerable amount of money at the time. Thirifays covered for us completely, and that's what got him in trouble. He hadn't realized that bringing over 10 people and putting them up in ultrachic hotels like the Astoria would go way beyond all the cost estimates. The Bon Marché Cafeteria was so disgusting that we all took our meals at the Astoria. I have to admit, we did go a bit overboard—we'd have room service bring up lobster, some fine wines, and some bottles of whiskey, and pretty soon we had a circus on our hands!

Jean Raine had no qualms about discussing a more intimate aspect of his relationship with Langlois:

In my life, in addition to my two marriages, I've experienced two very profound homosexual relationships, one of which was with Langlois. It's common knowledge that Langlois was a homosexual. Everybody knows, but nobody dares talk about it. Our relationship was mostly sentimental, but it also went beyond that. Henri Langlois was a shy person, and we took incredible strides together. We complemented each other perfectly. Henri was capable of a wealth of tenderness, finesse and emotion. I can say it was something I've rarely seen between a man and a woman. There was a subtlety and an incredible joie de vivre about him. . . . He always knew how to surround himself with enough people who played along with the game. Mary was jealous of these relationships and at the same time found them a source of satisfaction because, in the end, she really did become the only woman in his life.

From Brussels, Langlois went to Warsaw to organize another exhibition, this one devoted to the theme "Forty Years of French Cinema."

These exhibitions that Langlois carted across Europe were a preliminary testing ground for an eventual museum of cinema, which he had dreamed of creating since his adolescence. When his museum took shape, he would finally be able to give free reign to the unique art form he excelled at: transforming ordinary walls and partitions into juxtaposed decors so powerful that each visitor would feel compelled to experience the space around him in the same way a director moves his camera through a studio set.

## chapter 7

# 7, AVENUE DE MESSINE: CRADLE OF THE NEW WAVE

For me, the Cinémathèque is a place that should be a kind of home away from home, where people come as they are and walk out different.

Henri Langlois

In the late 1940s, for most people the cinema meant actors and actresses like Gérard Philipe, Micheline Presle, Edwige Feuillère, maybe a director or two—say, Henri-Georges Clouzot or Jacques Becker—and, if you were over 30, lingering presences such as Mae West, Douglas Fairbanks, or Jean Vigo.

Wrong.

To Langlois's way of thinking, the cinema was brewing even before pioneering geniuses like Lumière or Edison came along. He contended that the movies went all the way back to the advent of Chinese shadow puppets, to the magic lanterns of the seventeenth or eighteenth centuries, with their hand-painted glass slides lit by candle flame, to an ingenious gadget like the praxinoscope.

Henri Langlois's first Museum of Cinema, which occupied three floors at 7, avenue de Messine, was inaugurated on 26 October 1948. Langlois had artfully installed all the relevant objects and documents he possessed. There was the original contract of partnership between photographers Niepce and Daguerre, dated 1829; there were magic lantern slides, Lumière's Kinora, and Marey's marvelous rifle for "shooting" motion studies, *le fusil chronophotographique*. These devices, hand-crafted witnesses to the prehistory of cinema, were bathed in a soft and noble light that sifted gently through the tinted, one-of-a-kind "filmstrips" drawn by Emile Reynaud.

Up by the ceiling a huge and menacing "Selenite" (one of the critters Méliès created), fashioned from red cardboard, greeted visitors, who were also welcome to try out the "man without a body" special effect set up in the corner, an item that had assisted the great magician Robert Houdin.

The press was dazzled by this poetic and well-thought-out history of cinema. But it was André Bazin's appreciation A *Museum of Shadows: White Magic, Black Magic* that best evoked the atmosphere of the museum:

Henri Langlois is a man who has figured out that the word *museum* contains *muse*, as in *amusement*. At first glance, the Cinémathèque Française, on avenue de Messine, doesn't look like anything special. As the carriage entrance does not appear to lead to heaven or to hell, you are entitled to expect to find a foyer paved with black-and-white marble, and comfortable rooms tastefully gilded as befits the beginning of a Third Republic still aware of the beauty it possessed during the Empire.

Perhaps you've already been a bit unnerved by that surprising black-and-white poster [for the exhibit] seen on walls around town, with a peculiar series of white batons strolling across it like the skeleton of a macabre bit of choreography. Well, that's nothing compared to the surprise that awaits you once you step inside. Right off the bat, the show grabs you more assuredly than those carnival attractions that claim to take you on a visit to Hell. A room hung entirely in black compels you to follow the labyrinth of its display windows and dim grottoes. You have to venture in, for the Minotaur here is the cinema. He won't gulp you down all at once when you wander off to look in a window—he has already begun to dissolve you, to digest you, to absorb you via the thousands of tiny images that surround you, like the facets of a praxinoscope eye. If the demonic master of the house has chosen black as a background, it is no doubt the better to help us understand that the cinema was born in color. In the imagination of the first inventors and above all in the naive paradise of Emile Reynaud, as prehistoric and useless as that of Adam and Eve, there is an extraordinarily prestigious luxury of dyes and tintings both bright and delicate. The inexpiable error, the original sin for which the cinema was driven out from the innocent world of colors, was the temptation for knowledge. The tree of photographic science. We see it well in the strange, ghostlike images of Marey, while meanwhile, hanging overhead on the end of an invisible string like white bats, hover the ectoplasm of seagulls deconstructed in flight by the *fusil chronophotographique*. In the display cases, the skeletons of the praxinoscope, phénakisticope, and zoetrope inform us about the paleontology of the cinema.

Entering into yet another circle via the spiral staircase, you discover the "magic" of "lanterns." Behold the glass slides in their primitive frames. Their colors are refreshingly naive, and the movement of a slide through the lantern is as basic as can be and yet altogether, astonishingly perfect. Slide, lantern, and light source are all that's needed to present a true spectacle that lacks nothing in the way of charm and surprise. I swear that you would trade in a forest full of Technicolor Bambis for the poetry of a deer who drinks. Pause for a moment in front of the severed head of Robert Houdin, before climbing still higher. The eighteenth-century automatons lie in their boxes, flayed and scratched by time, all their fibers exposed. The seventeenth-century Chinese shadows dance their backlit dance, chiseled like gemstones or jewelry. It is with them that you enter the last infernal circles of the cinema. There where the fantastic blends with movement and with appearances, in the shadow of the world. One more step and you'll bump your head against the wall of Plato's Cave.

You walk back up the avenue de Messine in daylight, your soul deliciously exhausted. What did you just go through? A museum? . . . Why, a museum of cinema! So why be surprised?

The extravagant setting of this nineteenth-century mansion held the necessary ingredients to excite Henri's imagination: a red carpet, green plants, an ornate staircase. It was a location where no sensible architect would have dreamed of putting a projection room. Yet there was one, installed in the large salon on the ground floor. Sixty or so spectators could be seated there, 100 if need be, provided they sat practically in each other's laps. In order to keep the waiting public happy and to entertain habitués while they waited in the foyer, Langlois installed a tiny screen atop a column draped with red velvet. This enabled him to run continuous projections, most likely old Westerns, followed perhaps by some vintage Disney cartoons.

In order to enter the screening room itself, one had to—well, at least one was supposed to—have a ticket and then hand it over to a robust fellow standing guard at the door. This hale and hearty individual was a Yugoslavian named Frédéric Rossif. He had been recommended to Henri by the Prévert brothers, and Langlois had hired him on the basis of a rather unusual contract: "Everybody wants to get in without paying," Henri explained to Rossif. "So, if you don't make sure that at least a minimum number of people actually pay, I won't have the money I need to pay you." This, of course, was incentive enough for Rossif to run after gate-crashers. But as soon as he turned his head to chastise one admission evader, a good 20 others grabbed the chance to sneak in.

"The room is full," Henri pointed out one evening with surprise, "and you have only 10 ticket stubs!"

Behind the screen there was a loudspeaker that did not always work. Charlot Heimberger was used to this and never became alarmed. He would go to the site of the problem and inevitably find three of the people who routinely wrangled their way in without paying, standing on the cable. Charlot would plug it back in, tell the offenders, "Now, watch what you're doing!" and return to the projection booth.

The young spectators who flocked to avenue de Messine wanted to see the films at all costs (the aforementioned exceptions excepted), even if it meant sitting right on top of the screen. This had become a custom, and if they really wanted to sit an inch away from the image, Langlois didn't have the heart to kick them out. Charlot would sometimes go so far as to let them watch the show from the projection booth: "They were students, and Henri was generous. 'It's no big deal,' he'd tell me. 'What difference does it make?'"

Among the youngsters who wormed their way in was a 17-year-old boy named François Truffaut: "Our goal was to see as many films as possible, and our problem was to try to see several in a row without paying each time. So, in the beginning, we weren't entirely aboveboard with the Cinémathèque. Next to the screen there was a hallway and the toilets. And that's where we'd go sometimes and lock ourselves in a stall, then come back in to see another film on the same ticket."

Truffaut didn't work up the nerve to talk to Langlois until 1950, when, before heading off to perform his obligatory military service, he offered the Cinémathèque his "personal archives," in exchange for a free pass to screenings, effective at his discharge. The "archives" were, in fact, no more than a bunch of press clippings and stolen photos from movie theaters, but Henri was moved by the symbolic gesture and began to look upon Truffaut as a spiritual son.

The screenings began at 6:30 P.M. but went on until very late. Many weren't over until the middle of the night, and the cramped quarters, rather than being a drawback, meant that everyone got to know everyone else. It was in this tiny room that Truffaut would meet Godard, Rivette, Rohmer, and Suzanne Schiffman. This band of friends always sat together in the front row.

The viewing public also included its share of weirdos, such as the young man who made a point of dressing like a picturebook Greek. He wore open-toed sandals laced up to his knees and very short shorts. His hair was long, and he came to each show proclaiming, "I am the existentialist of Nevers!" Then he would be quiet and sit through all the films, all the while coloring in file cards until they were solid black. This went on until the day he returned to Nevers-Nevers-land for good.

Even this fellow knew enough to keep his mouth shut when the projector was on. The atmosphere was very serious: No one was to even think of saying a word during the actual projection. If, by chance, some member of the audience pronounced even a mere handful of wayward syllables, the miscreant would be lucky to escape with his or her limbs intact.

The tiny auditorium soon became something of a cultural salon. Seated among the students one might spot Gide on one side of the room and Malraux on the other. Braque came fairly often, and Fernand Léger came all the time. Sartre and Simone de Beauvoir sometimes stopped by after a hard day of philosophizing or pontificating. There was a sort of snobbish appeal to frequenting the Cinémathèque, and many of the Saint-Germain-des-Prés crowd were in evidence.

The Cinémathèque had always catered to a social class that was rich not in terms of money, but in terms of culture. It had always been a privileged realm. Although anyone was welcome to attend, one could not really refer to the Cinémathèque audience as being popular. One had to possess serious cultural references to be interested in Langlois's programming: Depending on where he'd gotten his prints that night, he might end up showing a German film dubbed into Czech, or a Czechoslovakian film with German subtitles.

One day, before projecting a Swedish film, Langlois made the following announcement: "Unfortunately, there are no subtitles. But don't worry. I've arranged for someone to translate." And so he had. But regrettably, the "someone" was Chinese, and he was blithely translating the film into Mandarin! The audience may not have followed what was going on, but they had a great time.

In April 1948 the government began cracking down on films projected without the benefit of an official "visa," a registration number that linked each title to the Censorship Bureau and the fiscal authorities. A circular issued by the Ministry of the Interior announced that theaters would be inspected by the police, that tickets would be issued (the pay-up-or-go-to-jail variety, not the enjoy-the-show variety), and that unregistered films would be impounded. Any infraction was subject to fines ranging from 1,000 to 1 million francs. In order to avoid eventual harassment, Langlois decided that, from now on, the screenings would be an integral part of the museum. In order to see a film, one paid 100 old francs for admission to the exhibition and 1 symbolic franc for the film. Luckily, there were no government regulations prohibiting one from indulging a deep need to visit the same exhibition seven days a week.

At avenue de Messine, Henri began giving his first retrospectives in homage to great figures of the cinema. Insofar as possible, he ran these screenings with the director present, thereby promoting an attitude that was new at the time: the preeminent importance of the auteur. Most memorable among these evenings was undoubtedly the soirée devoted to the first retrospective of Erich von Stroheim's work. When thunderous applause followed the end of Foolish Wives, von Stroheim was silent with emotion and then suddenly burst into tears. For the public, the contrast between the individual he portrayed on the screen, the nature of his films, the legend he had built up around himself, and the sight of this same man overcome with emotion, was striking.

Never in the history of French cinema would regular attendance at a space so small produce such a large effect. In those days, there were only two ways to approach a filmmaking career: Either you got accepted at IDHEC or enrolled at the technical college on rue de Vaugirard, or else you became an apprentice and tried to work your way up through the studio hierarchy. The "New Wave" that would appear at the end of the 1950s sprang directly from those determined youngsters who assiduously watched films at the Cinémathèque until their eyes glazed over. It was while seated on the benches at avenue de Messine that "the children of the Cinémathèque" would learn what cinema is. They would first become critics, then turn to directing, unconsciously reviving the lost tradition begun by Louis Delluc, Jean Epstein, and Marcel L'Herbier.

In this way, *L'Ecran français* and trade papers such as *Le Film français* and *La Cinématographie française* would soon have new, independent publications for company. Titles included *La Gazette du cinéma*, *Saint cinéma des prés*, and, above all, starting in 1951–52, *Les Cahiers du cinéma* and *Positif*.

The Cinémathèque did not stop at showing old films. Langlois also liked to show recent works that had not been picked up for commercial distribution in France. Such was the case, for example, for de Sica's now-classic *The Bicycle Thief*. It was only after the film's triumphant screening at the Cinémathèque that it found a willing distributor.

The tiny theater was packed almost every night, and the spectators stayed put for several programs in a row, sometimes remaining until 2:00 in the morning. People would refuse to leave, and Rossif would have to give them a gentle push toward the door.

One night there were so many people waiting to get in that the line stretched down the sidewalk for at least 200 yards. Two police officers were needed to keep the crowd orderly. All of a sudden, muffled cries could be heard from within the building. They grew closer until they seemed deafening. One could make out a woman's voice shrieking, "You're killing me! You're killing me, Henri!" These words of endearment were issuing forth from the elevator cage. The door opened, and one saw two bodies embracing and slugging it out at the same time. It was just Henri and Mary making their entrance.

Between their own screaming and the noise of the folks outside shoving to get in, the scene was apocalyptic, grandiose—and typical. On such occasions, one might mistake the Cinémathèque for the Comédie-Française with a tragic melodrama on the bill: "Thou art killing me. You wisheth me dead!"

On another occasion, the audience heard a mysterious sound behind the screen. Viewers asked themselves what could possibly produce such a peculiar noise. Some people even poked around, trying to uncover its source. A government minister who happened to be in the audience finally exclaimed, "But what *is* that we're hearing?"

"It's the phantom of the Cinémathèque," replied Langlois, with such gravity that one would have to conclude he truly believed in what he was saying.

"But really—what's behind that screen?" insisted the minister, less than satisfied with the first explanation.

"Nothing whatever," replied Langlois. "That's the problem."

To Langlois's credit, he was never exclusive or narrow in his interest for certain styles and directors. He never said, "I like realistic movies, and I don't like poetic ones. I like Lubitsch, and I don't like Wyler." On the contrary, he accepted everything—without distinguishing among genres and without ever passing judgment—so long as it was cinema. Langlois's overriding passion was to hunt down works that had disappeared or to exhibit films that were completely original, as his attraction to surrealism and the avant-garde demonstrates.

His sixth sense enabled him to recognize as-yet-unrecognized talent as well as to attract it to him. By what farfetched, miraculous leap of faith did a young American who had begun making films at the age of 12 have the idea of striking up a correspondence with Langlois and of sending him, from Los Angeles, a copy of his latest short, *Fireworks*? He was 17 years old at the time, and his name was Kenneth Anger.

Henri, brimming with enthusiasm, immediately decided to show *Fireworks* at the Festival du film maudit (Accursed Film Festival) in Biarritz. The reception the film provoked convinced Langlois—as if he needed to be convinced!—that here was a fine discovery. Jean Cocteau, who happened to be a member of the jury, was apparently so emotionally overwhelmed by the images in *Fireworks* that he nearly passed out during the projection. Cocteau immediately wrote to Anger to express his boundless admiration. Apropos of *Fireworks*, Jean Boullet wrote in *Saint cinéma des prés*:

> The silence being maintained in connection with *Fireworks* is not to be believed—this is an evil we must do away with posthaste. Some of us believed that the cinematic limits of eroticism had been attained by *L'Age d'or*, *Un Chien andalou*, *Les Chasses du comte Zahroff*, and *The Isle of Dr. Moreau*. . . . We were badly mistaken, and a recent American film, *Fireworks*, presented until now in silence and with a measure of discretion bordering on the clandestine, has just, in one clean sweep, dispelled all the most established notions of the relationship between the cinema and sexuality. This extraordinary confession, this avowal laid out in broad daylight, shatters everything we've known up until now. The contribution of *Fireworks* to the cinematic domain is comparable to that of Jean Genet in the realm of contemporary literature.

In the case of both men, thieving and a propensity for seminal breakthroughs would seem to go hand in hand, for as Anger himself describes it, "I stole and sold my family's sterling flatware and solid-silver tea service, bought a Greyhound ticket and a ticket on the *De Grasse*, pride of the fabled French Line, and hightailed it to Paris. There I met a dictator, not of front offices or backlots, but of something more fabulous: Henri Langlois, Grand Pasha and Sultan of the Cinémathèque Française. I worked 10 years for the Terrible Turk, a consensual bondage, since Henri loved movies more, much more, than I ever could."

Anger docked in Le Havre in the spring of 1950. Cocteau had gone there personally to welcome him and was waiting with a full cortege of limousines to escort the new prodigy to the capital. But Anger preferred to avoid such pomp and ceremony and discreetly (if rudely) boarded a train for Paris, where Henri and Mary had a room set aside for him in their apartment on rue Gazan. Langlois also had an exceptional project set aside for his guest: Henri entrusted Anger with the precious footage to *Que Viva Mexico*, so that he might begin editing it together according to the notes left by Eisenstein, who had died two years earlier.

The appearance of this new "privileged child" at the Cinémathèque unleashed some "fireworks" all right. True to his moniker, Anger angered some key people. Paradoxically enough, Godard, Rivette, and Truffaut, as Truffaut told us, had a hard time accepting the new arrival: "We were all hostile toward him. We contemptuously called him an avant-gardist. For our part, we were against the avant-garde. We upheld a certain classic vision of cinema."

But as Langlois saw it, the Cinémathèque should be at the service of *all* means of cinematic expression. That is why he helped finance Anger's *Rabbit's Moon*, which he shot in four weeks at the Panthéon Studio, rented for him by Henri and Mary.

Anger would stay and work with Langlois for 10 years, feeling he was more appreciated at the Cinémathèque Française than in his native America. It took Frenchmen like Langlois and Cocteau to point out Anger's worth to his own compatriots. It was not until the 1960s and 1970s that MOMA and universities throughout the United States would take the hint and acknowledge the importance of Anger's films.

If Langlois was instrumental in bringing Anger to (relative) prominence, it would not be the last time he helped a filmmaker to attain renown. The process would be repeated from Ozu to Philippe Garrel, from Tay Garnett to Joseph Losey, from Akira Kurosawa to Yilmaz Guney.

The ricochet principle was in good working order, and Langlois himself ended up being "discovered" in the four corners of the globe. His reputation grew quickly. "Henri," says Kenneth Anger, "did for the history of cinema what Victor Hugo did for the history of France."

Soon another of Anger's countrymen heard the benign siren call of the Cinémathèque and journeyed to France. His name was Curtis Harrington. In thinking back to the time he spent at avenue de Messine, Harrington is at a loss to thank Henri and Mary for all they did: "Mary never needed to tell me, 'Make yourself at home here—you're *chez vous*,' because she did everything she could so that I'd just instinctively feel that way."

Harrington too believes that the fact that Langlois showed his films at the Cinémathèque helped him to acquire an international reputation that served him well upon his return to the United States. Harrington quickly became friendly with Jacques Doniol-Valcroze and André Bazin. Unlike Anger, Harrington got along well with everyone, from Jacques Rivette to the Greek filmmaker, critic, and surrealism specialist Ado Kyrou: "I remember that Ado

Kyrou organized a sort of homage to surrealism at the Cinémathèque. Certain specific scenes from *Shanghai Gesture* would be projected, and then the members of the audience were supposed to think up and write down their own version of scenes that could have come before or after. People really let their imaginations run wild. It was a lot of fun. It was marvelous. You were never at a loss for ideas around Mary and Henri."

Henri Langlois would also be the first to recognize the value of a brand-new French filmmaker who had taken off in the little-pursued direction of ethnological moviemaking. Jean Rouch talks about the first time he showed his work to Langlois:

> When I started making movies, it was really on a shoestring, in Africa with an old camera, and the first person to ask to see the results was Langlois. He was still over on avenue de Messine at the time. I know this sounds strange, but he made the same impression on me as when I met André Breton for the first time. I had the feeling I was face to face with a major personality. Langlois had just seen my films and I, with my heart pounding, was awaiting the verdict—his opinion meant everything to me! Langlois was very quiet, seemed to be thinking something over, and then said to me, "Would you mind if I took your films to Antibes? I'm organizing something down there, and I'll be showing Cocteau's films at the same time."
>
> I was filled with wonder. I said yes, and then all at once I understood that in a certain way I'd been accepted into the family. From that moment on, I spent all of my time at the Cinémathèque, and I discovered this absolutely indescribable world: a world of such overriding passion for the cinema that you have to wonder how such a thing could ever have existed. I never went to film school, so if I learned anything at all, it was by devouring the films that Langlois showed me and in showing him my own. It was a completely shared experience and absolutely irreplaceable.

Langlois always had big plans to help young people make their first films. Between 1948 and 1955, he gave raw film stock to nearly 100 people, film-makers-to-be or established celebrities such as Raymond Queneau, René Char, Jean-Paul Sartre, and Jean Genet. The result: *En passant* by Queneau, *Un Chant d'amour* by Genet, and a short documentary about Sartre were shown in 1950 at the Festival du film de demain (Festival of the Film of Tomorrow).

The oldest international film festival is the one held in Venice. Langlois and Franju had attended it before the war. But in 1946, Langlois wanted the Cinémathèque and the International Federation of Film Archives (FIAF) to make an entrance that would be noticed. There, where the latest works of filmmakers from all over the world aspired to a spot in the jury's heart, Langlois intended to point out that the cinema also has a past. Iris Barry, then serving as president of the FIAF, came from New York to join Henri in Paris. Langlois also had a plan for an international colloquium on films for children, to be run by Sonika Bo, as a fringe event to the festival proper.

The three associates decided to drive down to Venice together in the same car. Langlois stuffed the trunk full of films, and they were off. When they reached the Italian border, a customs inspector asked if they had anything to declare. "No," they chimed in unison. But the official was suspicious and asked for the keys to open the trunk.

"I don't have them," said Henri. "I gave them to Iris."

"No, you didn't," said Iris. "I don't have them. I gave them to Sonika."

"That's not true," said Sonika. "In any case, I don't have them either."

What started out as a joke turned to genuine embarrassment when the three merry pranksters discovered that they really had left the keys behind in Paris!

But Henri, through an inspired series of mimed expressions, managed to persuade the inspector to let them pass. "Henri missed his calling," Sonika Bo thought to herself, in admiration. "He would've made a marvelous actor." Her reaction was substantially less laudatory upon discovering that Henri had neglected to reserve a hotel room for her. Iris refused to let Sonika have a corner of her room, and so did Henri. So it was that Sonika Bo spent her first night in Venice huddled in a gondola.

If Henri wasn't a particularly gifted travel agent, he still managed to get around. The following year he attended the International Film Festival in Locarno, followed by the Knokke-le-Zoute Festival in Belgium, where, accompanied by Grémillon, Painlevé, and Kamenka, he showed an assortment of experimental films, including Cocteau's *The Blood of a Poet*, Buñuel's *Un Chien andalou*, and Fernand Léger's *Le Ballet Mécanique*.

The Cannes Film Festival was held for the first time in 1946. This new event, which would add to the prestige of France, was yet another opportunity for Langlois to meet people and exchange both ideas and films. He had gotten into the habit of organizing his own projections at a spot just a few miles away in the old port of Antibes. In 1950 the Cannes Film Festival was not held at all, thus giving Langlois the perfect excuse to put on a Cinémathèque festival in Antibes.

Showing unusual faith in the time-space continuum, Langlois chose the title: "Festival of the Film of Tomorrow." Without neglecting certain forerunners to the work of the day, Langlois sought to show films that, in his eyes, presented a vision of the film of the future. With this in mind, he assembled all sorts of scientific documentaries, giving special importance to Painlevé's work with microscopic and underwater organisms, Jacques Cousteau's documentaries pertaining to sea life, and—for the first time ever for general audiences—a selection of medical films.

Langlois also emphasized the art world, showing *The World of Paul Delvaux* by Henri Storck, *The Lascaux Grotto and Its Prehistoric Images* by an American named Chapman, *Matisse* by François Campaux, *Medieval Images* by William Novik, and *The New Realism*, which Bouchard had shot in the United States and which included footage of Fernand Léger demonstrating his painting technique. Langlois also presented work from the Orient and the Middle East: Hindu, Japanese, Chinese, and Egyptian films—a first for the general public.

The festival took place from 20 August to 20 September in 1950. Henri monopolized the entire town—its covered market and public squares, its stronghold and museum—in order to show films amid stones, water, and sky. Picasso was living in Saint-Paul-de-Vence, and the municipality of Antibes had given the great artist rooms in the Palais Grimaldi so that he might fill them with his paintings and drawings. Henri obtained the use of the remaining quarters as a setting for his collection of posters, sketches, and set designs. The two men were at work in the same museum and ran into one another on a daily basis. They paid each other lengthy visits, and their mutual admiration grew to friendship.

Since Henri was out to attract popular audiences, the majority of his projections were held in the open air. These shows were free and could be viewed by a large number of people. Langlois went out of his way to make certain that the films didn't arrive subtitled in a language other than French. When there was no other choice, as with the screening of Dovzhenko's *Zvenigora*, the Russian subtitles were translated aloud by Sonika Bo.

From the very start, the festival attracted such crowds that the summer residents of neighboring towns felt obliged to look down on the event. At the Casino in Cannes, as well as in the luxurious villas of Cap-d'Antibes, polite conversation reverberated with speculation about the sudden burst of activity sweeping Antibes: "Apparently it's a festival, but it must be a festival for the flea-ridden." But the news reports bouncing back from Paris soon informed the millionaires that the director of New York's Museum of Modern Art, Jacques Becker, Simone Signoret, Yves Montand, and other persons of note could be spotted in the crowds, apparently unconcerned by the potential for flea bites.

Langlois projected *Greed* under the stars to the accompaniment of the breeze off the Mediterranean. After a typical showing of rare prints, Langlois, Sonika Bo, Jacques and Pierre Prévert, Picasso, Chagall, and Cocteau would take over a few tables in one of the small restaurants, where, as noted by Freddy Buache, the waiters would impatiently wait for their guests to leave so that they might carefully rip off the portion of the paper napkin where Picasso had, with the tip of his finger, imaginatively extended a bit of spilled red wine. If the meal happened to be lunch, Picasso would then proceed to the beach to paint the knees or belly of some lucky sunbather—who would be proud to have been chosen, but also torn by thinking of the fortune she might collect if only basic hygiene didn't require that she shower eventually.

Henri was happy, for in a way he had rediscovered the sky over Smyrna and the sea along whose shores he had been born. Antibes still held all the charm of a genuine fishing village on the Côte d'Azur. The southern accent of its inhabitants and their volubility seemed like something straight out of a Pagnol film. The atmosphere was carefree and fun. It was very hot that summer. Henri, who had arrived from Paris in a winter-weight suit, now went everywhere clad in espadrilles, feeling right at home in a loose-fitting pair of white cotton trousers and a matching sort of jacket adorned with six buttons and large lapels. The festival goers and more illustrious visitors wondered where this unconventional costume had come from.

One day Henri spotted an extremely elegant gentleman coming toward him in the company of a small group of people. The man in question wore a flower in his lapel and was easily recognized, for, one way or another, the circumstances of his life had destined him for fame. It was the duke of Windsor. The duke inquired of Henri as to which projections might be most interesting and asked how he could obtain tickets for himself, his wife, and friends. Henri, with a noble flourish replied, "You are all my guests. As a matter of fact, the overall population is my guest, because none of the outdoor screenings require tickets and those are the most beautiful. All you need do is get some chairs and pick a spot."

The duke thanked Langlois and bid him good afternoon. But then, after a moment's hesitation, he retraced his steps. "I should like to ask you a somewhat indiscreet question, if I may," the duke began. "Could you possibly tell me in what tailoring establishment you had your suit made?"

And Henri, with a sweep of his arm, replied, "Your Highness, if you'll be so good as to turn around and look over there at the corner of this street, you can see the sign from here." There was indeed a sign, and it said, "Work Clothes—Uniforms for Bakers and Pastry Chefs."

The duke was delighted, and soon this very getup was de rigueur for the serious festival goer.

Each day, a massive game of musical chairs was played out through the streets of Antibes. Some screenings were held in the Musée Grimaldi; others were held outdoors, in the covered market, or at other settings around town. When it was time to move from one location to the next, the males present were asked to help transport the seats to their new destination.

No one dreamed of complaining. Consequently, one saw highly respectable gentlemen carrying chairs—in a dignified manner, of course—from venue to venue.

Several projections were truly exceptional, chief among them being *Mitchourine* by Dovzhenko and *The Land* by Robert Flaherty. Flaherty's film, which had been commissioned by the U.S. Department of Agriculture, was finished just after Pearl Harbor, by which time the government, otherwise engaged, had lost interest in distributing it. For this special occasion, Langlois had somehow secured a copy of this documentary about land abuse and rural unemployment.

A journalist named José Zendel described perfectly the impression lent to each screening by the majestic settings Henri had chosen: "They are breathtaking, whether it's the Bastion Saint-André where the screen overlooks the sea and seems suddenly endowed with a whole new dimension, or the covered market, with its somber mass of viewers, above whom stretches the only bright spot in the room—the screen—or this rectangle of canvas, pitched like a sail at sea before the people crowded together along the quays."

Erecting a screen beside the sea was Henri's grand idea. This enterprise seemed completely crazy—or at least colossal—but Langlois was able to pull it off thanks to the enthusiastic help marshaled from the local workers and fishermen.

First they had to solve an enormous problem, that of electrical power. Henri requisitioned three street-sweeping trucks from the city of Antibes. These vehicles ran on electrical systems and were equipped with powerful storage batteries. Roger Tourret hit upon the idea of linking them up in sequence, and thanks to this brilliant piece of handiwork, the projectors ran smoothly and the bulbs burned bright, even for a film as lengthy as Abel Gance's *Napoléon*.

Thousands of spectators, massed along the quay, experienced this unique spectacle. At the moment when Bonaparte confronts a terrifying storm, aboard the frail bark whose makeshift sail is fashioned from his tricolored flag, the wind whipped up over Antibes. Menacing clouds gathered densely in the sky above, and the abruptly louder sound of waves crashing along the shore accompanied the images. As in a Magritte painting, with one canvas framed by a real sea and genuine storm clouds, each spectator had the Sensurround-style sensation of knowing what Bonaparte felt as he crossed the Mediterranean.

It was during the festival in Antibes that Henri conceived the idea for a new project, to be called "Memoirs of the World." Langlois, inspired by the nearby presence of so many great painters, wanted to incite these legendary creators to film their self-portraits. To this end, he gave them raw film stock to use as they pleased.

No business manager alive would have found it reasonable for a cinémathèque with limited resources to give away film to millionaire painters. Yet again, Henri had his sights set further than sensible management. For him, a gift of film stock made evident, from the start, the purity of his intentions and the utterly uncommerical aspect of the experiment he was inviting these artists to undertake. Neither Chagall nor Matisse nor Picasso would have accepted the kind of intrusion that would make mincemeat of his privacy with the jovial announcement, "Now, don't mind me. Just go on painting. Pretend I'm not here. You just go about your daily life, and I'll just set up my lights and my camera and I'll film you—but remember, I won't bother you!"

What Langlois was suggesting was altogether different. He was offering each artist the opportunity to present himself as he saw fit—to record the reflection staring back at him from his personal mirror. Since each artist would be the film's owner, director, and actor, he could satisfy his own desire to "exhibit" without the fear of being thrown to the lions for base commercial motives. That said, since even great artists could not do everything at once, Henri graciously put cameramen at their disposal.

The first to take Langlois up on his offer was Picasso. Shooting began that summer, with Frédéric Rossif and Jean Gonnet behind the camera. They filmed very few of his paintings, since Picasso preferred to be shown in the process of working. He created little scenes for the benefit of the camera and constructed a tiny arena in order to mime the various phases of bullfighting. *Picasso* would be incorporated into the 1980 film that Rossif made about the giant of twentieth-century art.

*Matisse* showed the artist in the process of directing an assistant as to the proper placement of elements to form a collage. If one looked closely, and had had the chance to see both men at work, there was a certain similarity between the special method whereby Matisse associated ideas and images and the way Langlois juxtaposed elements in his own programming.

Before shooting began on *Chagall*, Henri had several long conversations with the painter. He asked him about his life and pulled out elements of interest for the script. The film had to be in both black-and-white and in color, since Chagall wanted to film the landscapes and locations where he had worked. In certain cases, such as for Gordes and Vence, color was essential—particularly in Vence, where the colors of his ceramic work would burst forth in the middle of the scenery.

Henri envisioned three major themes in this film:

1. A theme by chronological order, whereby the paintings are grouped by periods and the periods don't mix. This is the only method by which to respect technique, but it's obvious that this need to maintain chronological order will dictate the script.
2. Against this visual background, in counterpoint, a second theme, being that of events, of life, characters, places, facts, general atmosphere for which Chagall has agreed to fill in certain gaps with paintings created especially for the film. This theme can be visual, integrated into the overall visual portion of the film or in the form of sound, indicated by commentaries.
3. Another theme: evolution of the work in relation to the man, which, logically, is just an additional subset of counterpoint 2.

"On top of these themes, which form the cement and the essential body of the film as well as its outlook, should float a fantastic plastic poetic theme stemming from the internal logic of the artist's works. This will establish the tone and the character as well as the originality of the grand portrait the film should be."

Marc Chagall loved to receive letters from Henri and constantly clamored to hear from him because he appreciated "his style, which was so affectionate." But the film shoot would be even better than letters—it would enable them to spend entire days together.

Langlois would dispatch cameramen or journey himself to the four corners of the globe in order to film Chagall's paintings where they hung. In Brussels, The Hague, Amsterdam, Vence, New York, Chicago, and all the way to Russia, cameraman Jean Gonnet and Henri went to capture the artist's canvases.

It was an enormous enterprise: 12 solid hours of footage had been shot, and the entire Cinémathèque staff found itself requisitioned in the name of the cause. Jean Gonnet spent a month in Vence, where he filmed Chagall in his workshop. Renée Lichtig, who helped edit the film, picked up and left off her work hundreds of times over a period of months. But it was Joris Ivens who did the most work on it. Finally, thanks to him, a black-and-white rough cut of the film, lasting 80 minutes, took form.

In the 1960s Langlois would return to the Soviet Union to shoot yet more sequences for *Chagall*. Throughout his trip, he discovered extraordinary landscapes that, give or take an upside-down fiddler or a purple cow, were the spitting image of the painter's canvases. One day Langlois spotted an ox with a yoke and gave the order to commence filming. Dovzhenko's wife, who was serving as Henri's guide, hastened to the scene. "It is forbidden to film that," she insisted. "That no longer exists in Russia."

But Chagall grew impatient with the long, slow cinematic process. In a letter dated 13 January 1954, Henri did his best to persuade him that whatever the delay, it was worth it: "As you can see, one musn't make sad remarks. Good films are like beautiful paintings; they take their course slowly, slowly but surely. And if in order to have an image that lasts one minute, or even one second, we have to film a painting 1,000 kilometers away from Paris, then we musn't hesitate, we must do it, because this film has to be *the* film and not just *a* film."

*Chagall* would undergo countless vicissitudes over the course of 15 years. Today a mystery remains: Do all those hours of film that were shot still exist? They may yet turn up in the uncataloged portion of the Cinémathèque's archives. In any case, whether by virtue of a desire to attain perfection or just because he was doing too much at the same time, Langlois would never manage to finish his grand *Chagall*, and this would remain a disappointment in his life.

The artists themselves could not remain indifferent to Langlois's cause in the face of so much effort. They helped out as best they could—and their best was very good indeed. Soon Renoirs, Cézannes, Chagalls, Matisses, and

Picassos were passing through the Cinémathèque's hands. There was so much artistic activity of a noncelluloid nature that Mary was beginning to look like something of a broker in impressionist, postimpressionist, and modern art. But every cent she made was for the Cinémathèque.

Mary not only spoke a half-dozen languages but knew exactly what to say in each one. She always managed to get her way when she had her mind set on something precious. "Leave this document at the Cinémathèque and you'll return to glory in your own country!" she might say, to entice a British subject. "You know, I saw the queen recently and . . ."

Jean Raine describes Mary's prospecting technique: "Mary had a method: say something leading in order to get someone to disclose something else. She'd use white lies to get at the truth. What Mary contributed to the Cinémathèque is nothing short of astonishing. And if she didn't go as far as Henri, that is because Henri's destiny was traced out in advance."

"I thought," said Langlois, "that the Bibliothèque nationale collected and preserved posters. I thought that there was no point in collecting photos. And then I realized that the National Library collected posters, but not *all* posters. The majority of film posters were not at the Arsenal Archive. I also realized that books are indispensable as a tool. As a result, we had to start buying up books."

Beginning in 1945, Henri asked William Novik to assemble the necessary material to constitute a library of cinema. Novik set off in search of old magazines from the silent era, such as *Pour vous, La Cinématographie française, La Revue du cinéma*, and the books of Canudo, Delluc, Marey, Moussinac, and so forth. They were still easy to find at that time. With the help of the set decorator Lucien Aguettand-Blanc, shelves were built on the ground floor at avenue de Messine, and in 1946 the library was all set to open.

Problems rapidly presented themselves, however. It was essential that two guards remain vigilant—seamlessly so—at all times. As soon as the librarian left for a moment to get a book, some people would take the opportunity to whip out their razor blades and slice entire pages out of other volumes. There were no photocopying machines in those days, and some boorish researchers wasted no time in making cubist Swiss cheese out of entire collections.

When William Novik left the Cinémathèque in 1948, Frédéric Rossif took over responsibility for the library during its afternoon opening hours: "Yes, the library was open, but we didn't actually want people to come and use it. [Laughter.] That's Langlois all over for you. He had all the qualities in the world and all the faults, at the same time. In any event, as far as the library's concerned, he was too afraid of thefts."

All the same, the collection grew from year to year to hold thousands of books and magazines, and until 1955 the public could come to consult its materials. Noted film scholars such as Mitry, Sadoul, and Bazin made use of its resources. Young foreigners with a budding interest in the cinema often made their way to the library. Langlois took them under his wing and helped them out.

The *photothèque*, which was not open to the general public for consultation, was initially run under the direction of Lotte Eisner, and then by Simone Cottance, sister of actor-writer Jacques B. Brunius. Beginning in 1947, the Press Department filled requests for cinema-related photos to illustrate books, magazines, and newspapers. Roger Vadim, among others, came from time to time to purchase photos for his articles.

Most of the photographs came from production companies, but many also originated in private collections. In 1948, for example, Jean Mitry sold the Cinémathèque a collection of 1,500 photos. In the course of 1952, according to Jean Grémillon, the *photothèque* increased its holdings to the tune of 3,000 stills related to films in current release and 1,000 photos concerning older movies. The poster collection received 800 new pieces, the most precious of which were mounted.

Langlois also oversaw the Committee for Historic Research on the Cinema, which he had created during the Occupation. Begun in 1943 under the direction of Joë Hamman and Jean Mitry, the committee gathered monthly at Germaine Dulac's apartment. Sessions were devoted to Sessue Hayakawa, Ferdinand Zecca, Louis Feuillade, Victor Jasset, Maurice Tourneur, Max Linder, Jean Durand, and Léonce Perret. The committee members interviewed old directors but also gathered information from cameramen, set decorators, and stuntmen. After Mitry's departure in 1946, Musidora, William Novik, and others took charge of the committee. Its members themselves set an example by sharing their own memories, as did Joë Hamman and Musidora. In order to better define the personalities under "investigation," people from outside the film world were also heard, be they friends or relatives. Madame Colson, Germaine Dulac's lifelong companion, provided a wealth of incidental information.

Between 1950 and 1952, the Committee for Historical Research, under the direction of Musidora, concentrated on 1918 through 1930, with particular emphasis on the works of Delluc, Gance, Epstein, Pudovkin, L'Herbier, Dulac, Baroncelli, and Renoir. The committee members visited film pioneers and questioned them systematically for hours on end. A woman who worked for Unifrance Film took everything down in shorthand. It was not yet possible to use a tape recorder or to film these lengthy sessions, because it would have been too costly.

It was believed, after Langlois's death, that the transcripts of these priceless sessions were gone for good. But as the result of a leak in the Cinémathèque's offices on rue de Courcelles, Marianne de Fleury came upon them concealed behind a fake wall. At least a portion of the committee's research still exists, and it makes for fascinating reading, since these documents were used extensively by Mitry and Sadoul in compiling their authoritative books on the cinema.

In view of the dazzling series of exhibits presented since 1945, the daily film screenings, the contacts maintained with other film archives worldwide, the library, and the *photothèque*, the Cinémathèque as it stood in 1954 would appear to have been humming along admirably. And yet ever since the Liberation, criticism had been leveled at Langlois for his management techniques or lack thereof. Beginning in 1946, a controversy had gotten under way in the profession, and Jean Mauclaire, former director of Studio 28 and then of *Le Film français*, published the following remarks in late 1948:

> It no longer seems possible to maintain at the head of a private organization someone who, through the clever selection of voting members and the machinations of proxy votes at the General Assembly meetings, is exercising—and has done so for far too long already—a direction almost completely without control.
>
> Too many disappearances and losses through negligence and disorganization, too many thefts of precious contributions, have already been recorded. These add up to a significant number of serious errors that the one person responsible still refuses to recognize . . .
>
> But there's worse to come: Answering the call of a higher authority, the Cinémathèque as it currently stands will become the private domain of its director. In effect, he no longer even bothers to observe the Cinémathèque's established form of voting; in sidestepping his customary sham vote, Monsieur Langlois drops his mask and openly dictates by himself, or via a select group.

According to Jean Painlevé, certain filmmakers had been complaining privately about Langlois's methods and the prevailing lack of order. Members of the Cinémathèque would also attempt to ask questions during meetings of the General Assembly or the board of directors only to get the runaround. What were the names of people who had donated or lent films or objects to the Cinémathèque? How many films were on deposit, and what condition were they in? Among those with pointed questions was, of course, Jean Painlevé:

> In general, when one asked Langlois a question he found annoying, he'd start off by telling you, "Yes, well, it's very simple. I'm going to tell you about it," and that would give him a little breathing space in order to think up some dopey reply that was neither here nor there. That enabled him to "legitimately" put things off until some archival document that would never be found could allegedly be consulted. That put off further discussion until the next meeting. . . . In the meantime, the questioner had forgotten his question or was no longer on the board. And then it took one, two, or three years until the next General Assembly, by which time everyone had *really* forgotten the question. . . . It's a classic strategy, and at every board meeting where there was someone irritating, that's how Langlois would behave.

Credit must go to Jean Painlevé for having protected the Cinémathèque Française during the brief period from 25 August 1944 until May 1945, when he was director of the CNC. It was Painlevé who increased the Cinémathèque's subsidy and who made it "official" with the agreement of the Cinema Liberation Committee:

> I always prevented the admirable finance inspector, an honest individual, Monsieur Jeauffre, from sticking his nose into Langlois's affairs. I covered for Langlois even if I knew that unbelievable things were going on at the Cinémathèque. For example, bills that were paid three times over—I knew all about it, but for 100,000 francs, *merde*. Langlois was doing important work; 100,000 francs isn't an awful lot of money. It was only much later, when Malraux really increased the subsidy at the end of the 1950s, that I openly objected to the way the Cinémathèque was being run. I didn't want to see Langlois bothered for an amount as ridiculously small as 100,000 old francs. When, however, it became 100 million old francs, I saw the usefulness of stricter control.

Henri had also developed an extraordinary talent for manipulating and then getting rid of the person with whom he was speaking. According to Pierre Kast: "If he was dealing with a minister, he had a special tactic. When he'd secured an hour-long appointment, he'd spend 58 minutes talking about things of no importance, either to him or the minister. And then he'd settle all his real business in the last two minutes. In fact, he'd pretend that they were in complete agreement on the unessential in order to obtain the essential. If you lose sight of the fact that Langlois was a fantastic tactician, you won't be able to understand a thing about him."

In much the same way that he didn't want to judge films, Langlois refused to align himself with any political party whatsoever. Ado Kyrou described Langlois's attitude well: "His relationships with people in the government were very much like a sort of cinematic game, and his relationships with the Communists, Malraux, the police, and a fair share of civil servants were just part of his own B-movie. How many times did I tell him, 'But Henri, don't talk nonsense! You know perfectly well I'm on the extreme left—don't tell me things like that.' And he'd reply, 'That doesn't matter one bit. Everybody has the right to speak nonsense.'"

Starting in 1954, Henri would have great need of his tactical gifts. According to the magazine *Objectif*, the Cinémathèque's accounting was far too imaginative. The magazine pointed out that the supervising minister had assigned Henri Durand as its government representative with responsibility for keeping an eye on the way things were being managed at the Cinémathèque:

> But Henri Durand had the door resoundingly slammed in his face. The Cinémathèque is quite amenable to receiving—and quickly—public funds, but will not tolerate the state asking for justification as to their use. . . . The

peculiar goings-on at the Cinémathèque must remain secret, and the money allotted to it by the state must not be subjected to the indignity of the slightest measure of control!

Meanwhile, the management of the Cinémathèque has been the object of investigations and complaints, of which, incidentally, the government is aware.

The magazine went on to repeat declarations made by Raymond Le Bourre, member of the board of the Conseil supérieur du cinéma, a sort of high court for the film industry:

I believe that the preceding minister ordered investigations and that Monsieur Jeauffre, government auditor, and Monsieur Durand, government commissioner, were to deliver a report aimed at reforming the board of directors of this singular association.

It is strange, in any case, that no action has been taken on any of the assorted reports resulting from the investigation. The authorities must at all costs be awakened from their sleep so that this establishment with its voracious appetite for public monies, is brought into line and compelled to account for itself . . .

If the supervising minister and the CNC plan to continue taking refuge in a complicitous silence, I am resolved to take this matter before the Conseil supérieur du cinéma, so that once and for all, public money ceases to be put at the total discretion of a little politico-commercial cabal.

When faced with this "attack within the rules," the government did take immediate action, but as *Objectif* angrily points out,

not remotely in the manner we were hoping for. Instead of taking those measures that reason and circumstances impose, instead of ordering that the board of directors of the Cinémathèque be dissolved, an additional civil servant has been assigned to the case, a new auditor to be added to the one who was previously assigned.

In effect, an order dated 11 October assigns the auditor, Monsieur Beau, to a six-month tour of duty with the Cinémathèque. Have people in high places really decided to clean up and reform this parasitic organization? Or do they simply want to create the illusion of doing something so as to calm Monsieur Le Bourre's worries and eliminate any motivation for *Objectif* to pursue its argument? We shall know in six months.

On 14 February 1955, Chief Auditor Beau submitted a detailed, 28-page report to the CNC. After a description of the essential tasks performed by the Cinémathèque, in accordance with its charter, and an outline, department by department, of the work being carried out by its employees, Monsieur Beau concludes:

I think, in consequence, that *if the goals and means of action as established in the charter are still looked upon as valid* [italics in the original], it is not possible to reduce the current personnel at the Cinémathèque. I am well aware that the administration may view as regrettable the financing of certain tasks it considers of secondary importance, but if this be the case, then the administration must indicate precisely which of those goals and means of action provided for in the charter it no longer wishes to underwrite.

I think I must add, in closing, that the working conditions and the "family-style" working methods of Cinémathèque personnel can be surprising to those accustomed to the rhythm of more conventional administrations, be they public or private. I think, however, that if overall these workers have been stamped in a special way by the habits peculiar to the profession of which they've long been a part, they do in reality form—however it may look—a united team passionately devoted to the organization of which they are a part.

The chief auditor's conclusions are therefore favorable. He points out elsewhere that, even before he was assigned to the case, the Cinémathèque had agreed that government officials who had expressed an interest in doing so were welcome to join the board of directors.

At the end of January 1955, the press announced the sale of the building at 7, avenue de Messine. The news was explosive—it meant that the Cinémathèque was being evicted, pure and simple.

For years running, requisition orders dating back to the time of the Liberation had enabled the Cinémathèque to remain where it was. Those days had now abruptly come to an end, and the Cinémathèque was nothing more than a squatter, without benefit of deed or lease. Learning from the newspapers of the Cinémathèque's imminent fate, several administrators were surprised not to have been informed sooner of the looming menace destined to affect them all. But since the situation had never looked particularly worrisome to Langlois or Grémillon, the late-January ruling took them completely by surprise.

The Cinémathèque did not have the kind of money required to buy the building, and the owner had arranged for the eviction to take effect in record time.

Langlois immediately orchestrated a press campaign. At Henri's suggestion, the young François Truffaut announced the news as a veritable scandal. In the magazine *Arts*, he wrote: "For the time being, Henri Langlois continues to occupy the premises. The three ritual screenings are held nightly at 6:30, 8:30, and 10:30 P.M. But a scandal *is* a scandal—this one is for real. A large space must be found—and quickly—that can contain exposition, equipment and archives, with a large projection room, at the entry to which one will no longer hear, "We're sold out. You have to get your tickets two weeks in advance." There have to be a beautiful screen, handsome projectors, and truly magical lanterns, and if there aren't any seats, well, then, we'll just plunk ourselves down on the floor!"

In a letter to Paolo Emilio Sales-Gomes of the Brazilian cinémathèque, Henri wrote:

> Just when the Cinémathèque was about to breathe easy and make some real progress, our landlord has us evicted. This is just to let you know what kind of problems and worries I'm up against. But you can help me out, if you get the newspapers talking about our eviction. For example, if it's said, "The sixtieth-anniversary year of the invention of cinema is off to a poor start. We learn from the French Press Agency that the Cinémathèque Française and the Paris Museum of Cinema, whose collections we greatly admire, and so on, must make way for a bank. This news cannot leave indifferent those enamored of both cinema and French culture, for it concerns a museum unique in all the world, which was a true home for international art. It strikes us as impossible that a nation such as France be deprived of such a treasure."
>
> That said, try to get a whole article going. It's important, because it will help me win the battle for a new location for the Cinémathèque—which is a question of time and money—by fattening the files of the civil servants who are fighting in order to turn this bad event into a good event for the Cinémathèque.

At the very same time the eviction notice arrived, Langlois got the go-ahead from the city of Paris to organize a large exhibition on the cinema at the Musée d'art moderne. Henri immediately contacted other film archives worldwide in order to assemble the objects needed to illustrate the show he would call "300 Years of Cinematography, 60 Years of Cinema." He decided to round up all the FIAF member archives in order to create an event he envisioned being "as successful as the 1900 world's fair."

That's how Langlois described the enterprise to his Brazilian colleague Sales-Gomes when asking him to send posters and other documents. And Henri had this valuable bit of advice: "Don't forget the current Brazilian cinema—it's an excellent opportunity for you to swipe some goodies from your directors and from your own productions."

Langlois contacted every filmmaker of stature he could. He wrote to Luis Buñuel, requesting the script from *L'Age d'or* and sketches for the sets in *El* and *Robinson Crusoe*, along with a costume or two. He got Carl Dreyer to provide scripts for *The Passion of Joan of Arc* and *Vampyr*. At Langlois's request, Marcel Carné offered storyboards from *Les Enfants du paradis* (*Children of Paradise*), and Jean-Louis Barrault complemented them with the actual costumes.

Every cinémathèque sent something for the show. Lotte came back from Denmark with an Edison Kinetoscope and one of Asta Nielsen's gowns. Henry Fonda dropped by at avenue de Messine and promised heaven and earth—or at least reasonable facsimiles—from Hollywood.

There are those who say that when the avenue de Messine headquarters shut down on 20 April 1955, the best years of the Cinémathèque Française had already come and gone. The Cinémathèque was scattered to the four winds, if only momentarily. It spent two months operating out of one room at 3, avenue de l'Opéra. The *photothèque* and the library found shelter in a café on rue Gazan, where the generous proprietor agreed to store thousands of books and photographs on the second floor of his establishment.

But Henri always found some miraculous way to stay on his feet during the kinds of crises that others might resolve with suicide notes. On 30 June 1955, at the sprawling Palais de Tokyo, Langlois inaugurated "300 Years of Cinematography, 60 Years of Cinema," his answer to the world's fair. One of the visitors was none other than the young critic François Truffaut, who took in "300 Years" on his way to *400 Blows*:

> I enter—all it takes is a trip down the five or six steps of the Palais de Tokyo. An inadvertent trip sends me hurtling into the arms of Marlene Dietrich, her "flesh" courtesy of Kodak and life-sized. This other lady on her way toward me is Françoise Rosay, whose outlook is rosy since escaping from a *Carnival in Flanders*. To the right and left, dresses without heads: Martine Carol in *Lucrecia Borgia* and Martine Carol in *Madame Dubarry*. Why headless? Because you can't be everywhere at once. There's also a full range of "scopes," and any monkey can give them a trial: the phantoscope, the pholioscope, the chorentoscope, the phenakisticope and the praxinoscope.
>
> On a giant billboard, Jean Dasté will wander for eternity on the bridge of *L'Atalante*, with Dita Parlo in his arms. The deserter Jean Gabin stands out against the background mist, hoping he hasn't missed Miss Michèle Morgan, who, in her see-through raincoat and tiny beret, will offer him a light on the damp paving stones.
>
> What else is there? A thousand things to see: manuscripts, autographs, sketches, and photos by the hundreds, gigantic or miniscule, carpet-size or postage stamp. There's the original editing room script from *La Bête humaine*, sketches from *The Divine Tragedy* and *Land of the Pharoahs*, doodles by Jacques Prévert in the margins of a first draft of *Children of Paradise*, and drawings by Fritz Lang for *Ministry of Fear*. I see a score belonging to Renzo Rossellini; an inscribed portrait photo of Maurice Burnan; Mr. Lincoln on his donkey; a copy of Frank Norris's *McTeague*, which was the basis for *Greed*, with Stroheim's own notes in the margins; 20 photographs of scenes that were censored from *Foolish Wives*; Zazu Pitts in bed with her one true love—gold; letters from Pudovkin to Eisenstein, and vice versa.

I learn that the arrival of the most famous costume in movie history is expected any minute. It consists of a pair of boots, a cane, and a bowler hat. You get the idea?

The time has come to go into the projection room, where the frenzied silhouettes of Greed—the most avidly "prospected" film of this permanent retrospective—are flickering on the screen. The tiny theater at avenue de Messine had 70 seats; here I count 240. Things have really changed since the days of fanatic viewers who were more likely to be lying down than seated, on the floor with their noses stuck to the screen, or mashed together against the half-open door or perched on the radiators. For the time being, there's room for everybody. Since those eternal malcontents, the critics, get in free with their press cards, they can now view or review the films they've so aptly referred to.

Three projections are held daily, each of a different film.

From 1 July through 30 September, one can see films by Ince, Griffith, Stroheim, Chaplin, Sjostrom, Murnau, Lang, Gance, Flaherty, Max Linder, Harold Lloyd, Renoir, and that whole crowd.

The summer heat is under way, along with the annual paucity of worthwhile films. The good movies are held for the fall, when everyone is back from vacation, and never have there been so few movies for active filmgoers to check off in their weekly program guides. That's why the reopening of the Cinémathèque comes at the perfect moment to enrich our evenings. For 1 franc—yes, exactly 20 sous—one may see nightly a Griffith, a Renoir, a Stroheim, or a Chaplin at the Musée d'art moderne.

The exhibition was so successful that Langlois extended it until 15 November. The show demonstrated, once and for all, the usefulness of the International Federation of Film Archives. Through the combined efforts of its members, thousands of visitors were able to admire the riches of the Cinémathèque Française as well as treasures from cinémathèques the world over. But the exhibition's very success engendered problems that Henri described in a letter to Ida Chagall:

The sly kick, pull a fast one, low-blow sort of thing. I never thought that the success of an exhibition could prove so annoying to the very people who should have been most thrilled by the fact that it's going well.

In brief, forced to move again, I had to get through an awful patch. And since, unfortunately, I don't have a phone at the Palais or at my place, I couldn't call you at a reasonable hour.

The last eight days before the show opened, I was sleeping two hours on a couch at the Palais every night. The last three days, I was convinced we wouldn't be ready in time, and actually, we weren't. It took us another 13 days to really finish up, and even then, when you were here Chaplin's costume wasn't in place.

Know that I still want to display Chagall's drawing and that I haven't been able to find a single second to call you up and ask for it. And yet, it's on the poster. Result: Since I didn't have it, I won't let myself hang the works by the other great painters that I wanted to put up with his. I have the portraits Léger and Picasso did of Chaplin, but I haven't exhibited them, because I don't have the one by Chagall.

At the same time that I was putting together the exhibition, I had to put out the catalog, do battle with my auditors—who wanted to see the accounts for the show before they were even done—draw up an additional budget, and find a new place to move to. And something that's going to strike you as very strange—I took advantage of the fact that Ivens was in town to do some work on the film.

Thank God, for once I realized how invaluable the help of a qualified assistant can be. Lichtig helped me show the film to Ivens, and it's thanks to her that the black-and-white copy of all the best shots has been printed.

My mother's become seriously ill, and I've been transformed into a nursemaid. I'm quasi-immobilized until 6 September, but fortunately, we'll be able to work on the film at my place, which means we'll have a sort of stuck-together version—just a general idea, really—to work on.

In another letter, this one to Marc Chagall, Langlois added: "My mother is very ill, and it's at her house that I'm working with the woman who's doing the editing. I hope that the doctors' ignorance means that the bad news they're giving me is the result of their incompetence and not because they know their business."

As Henri penned these lines, all hope was already gone. Annie Langlois, the loving mother who, whatever the evidence, always believed her son would do great things, died on 15 September.

## chapter 8

# REMEMBRANCE OF FILMS PAST (II)

Films are like Persian rugs: You keep them at their best by using them.

Henri Langlois

In October 1956, the Cinémathèque celebrated its twentieth anniversary. A new generation had grown up in the meantime, and it was to them that Langlois would address himself from then on. As Langlois noted in the commemorative brochure,

> In recounting the various stages of our development, it would be natural to sum up only our achievements, to explain the immense influence of the Cinémathèque Française abroad, the part it's played in the development and creation of cinémathèques throughout the world. But the retelling of what's been accomplished over these last 20 years would do nothing more than lull people's consciences into an even deeper sleep. Besides, in any event, an era came to an end when the Cinémathèque was evicted from its building on the avenue de Messine . . .
> One must always look forward. One stage ends, another begins. With that in mind, we must recall not what has been accomplished but what has not been accomplished, what should have been done and what remains to be done. . . . We are in the process of living a day-by-day repetition of the great fire of the Library of Alexandria—and with such indifference!
> This explains the profound solitude of film archives. They have to struggle not only against time, which each day renders the search for and rescue of 60 years of cinema more difficult, but against those who would just as soon ravage and pillage and wreck; against the distrust of an industry that

fears—and with reason—being dispossessed of its rights; against the machine's interests, which wants the cinema only to produce, even if it means feeding on itself; against the financial difficulties that all nonprofit organizations know only too well; against all these obstacles that hold back humane activity and prevent archives from falling into a routine that would be more ruinous still. . . .

True, the creation of film archives enabled some films to be saved. But it also left people's consciences falsely reassured, since, although archives exist, they've been left without the means to accomplish their task. In the United States, for example, museums have thousands of dollars to buy paintings, but cannot find a cent to save American cinematic art, which is the American art par excellence, the only art that has produced men of genius whose work compares to the European geniuses' in the domain of painting, sculpture, architecture.

Langlois goes on to describe the pressing need to prevent the destruction of original film negatives and the major stumbling block: a dim understanding of what it would take to rescue the world's films. He describes the ridiculously Sisyphean task all film archives face in their efforts to preserve something that most people, even as late as the 1950s, still took to be an ephemeral product:

We are at the eleventh hour. Never has the destruction of films been greater. . . . There is still so much to do—we must fight to do it. Help us, show us the strength, lend us the support of public indignation. Be it understood that nobody has the right to abandon to chemical-product factories the most significant, the most essential, the most constructive art of our time. Join with us to stop this crime against civilization that is the destruction of old film negatives. . . .

You must understand that everything is in your hands. You must help us to cross this desert, to overcome this wall of indifference. If we were able to save Versailles, then that is all the more reason for public opinion to rise and save our Versailles of the twentieth century: cinematic art.

To illustrate his appeal and make it hit home for all those who had been mere toddlers in 1939, Henri Langlois set out to educate this new generation on the historical and artistic value of the cinematic patrimony. If Henri had handed out a syllabus for the informal course to come, it might have read "Introduction to Film, Life, Art, and the Music of the Spheres 101." The years 1956 to 1960 are considered by many to be the most inventive period of film programming at the Cinémathèque Française. But before exploring them, it is best to return momentarily to 1946 and cover the years following the rebirth of the International Federation of Film Archives (FIAF), for the amazing retrospectives of 1956 to 1960 were in large part the result of Langlois's extraordinary efforts to rebuild and create other film archives through the FIAF.

In 1946, seven years had gone by since the last FIAF congress in New York. The MOMA Film Library and the British Film Institute recognized the important role played by the Cinémathèque Française's secretary-general. They entrusted to Henri Langlois, who had made the Cinémathèque the richest film haven in a war-torn Europe, the task of bringing the FIAF back to life. Langlois's personality and energy were at the center of countless dealings to come. He began by developing bilateral agreements to aid and assist other cinémathèques, taking care each time to insert a clause calling for their membership in the FIAF. After having reunited a certain number of delegates in Paris, Langlois obtained a consensus whereby the Cinémathèque Française would organize the third congress of the federation, to be held in July 1946. Eager to maintain FIAF international headquarters in Paris, Langlois orchestrated everything himself, attending to every detail, from the reception and lodging of the foreign members to the agenda for the work they would do in association with UNESCO, crowned as it was with the hope and glory of its then recent creation.

The congress, in return, would render a tribute to its founders. One speaker recalled that, during the hostilities, the FIAF, thanks to its founders, had played the role of a veritable international Red Cross for films. No one mistook his meaning, and the delegates rose to their feet, turned toward Langlois, and applauded long and hard. Each of them knew that it was Langlois's own experiences in occupied France that led him to propose to the congress a certain number of fundamental resolutions that were voted by the assembly. First of all, they refused to exclude the Reichfilmarchiv from its place as founding member. After its unconditional surrender, Germany in turn found itself under foreign occupation and cut into two separate political states, East and West. It was thus decided to reserve a place for the old German cinémathèque in anticipation of the day when it would be able to resume its activities.

Another resolution solemnly proclaimed that the cinematographic heritage of a given country not only was the privileged possession of that individual nation but belonged to humanity as a whole. The congress took the emphatic step of declaring that the protection of cinematic works must be ensured to the same extent as more universally recognized works of art are. They voiced the wish that those films that had been confiscated and were still detained by the victors be restituted to the diverse national film archives. It was merely a wish, but Henri would know how to use it as a potent weapon when the time came to launch a new campaign to save the Japanese cinema.

Henri Langlois made a proposal that the Soviet Union's film archive be voted the status of a FIAF founding member. This strategy did not stem from diplomatic respect alone. Owing to his encyclopedic knowledge of cinema, Langlois suspected that the Gosfilmofond contained film treasures that the

American, British, and French archives did not possess. The first task of each national archive was to track down its own film heritage; however, the only remaining print of an American film, for example, might be found in Czechoslovakia or Russia. Langlois's motion to place the Soviets in an equal position of power was readily accepted, and Moscow was voted in as a founding member.

Finally, it was necessary to reaffirm the noncommercial nature of the film archives, whose role was still contested by certain film producers.

Langlois would serve as secretary-general of the FIAF until 1960. He helped see to it that FIAF headquarters remained in Paris by offering office space at the Cinémathèque Française. He not only ran the Cinémathèque on a day-to-day basis but oversaw and controlled the FIAF as well.

Iris Barry was given the honorary title of founding president. In 1951 she resigned as director of the MOMA Film Library in New York because she had been diagnosed with cancer and was told that she did not have long to live. The doctors, however, were mistaken, and for the next 18 years she would enjoy a quiet retirement in Fayence, in the South of France, all the while remaining a faithful admirer of Langlois.

As for Ernest Lindgren, Miss Vaughan's successor at the BFI, although he would often fill the vice-presidency of the FIAF, he would also turn out to be Langlois's number-one adversary.

Jerzy Toeplitz, the Polish representative, was voted in as vice-president for one year, was promoted to president the following year, and would remain in that position for 25 years. His presence ensured the East-West balance and helped attract other Eastern Bloc archives not only to join the FIAF but to participate freely in film exchanges.

One of the first goals this newly re-formed "United Nations of film archives" set for itself was to avoid all political connotations in its work, the better to devote its members' energies to the pure if never simple task of saving films on an international level.

Year by year from 1946 to 1956, new film archives joined the FIAF. The original roster of 11 members in 1946 had grown to 34 a decade later. Henri Langlois was instrumental in that growth, and a certain number of archives owe him their very existence. Nevertheless, it would be wrong to say that Henri Langlois welcomed all new archives with equal ardor. He had a tendency to first sound out the archivists' motives and to test them on their love of cinema. Langlois would be reluctant to help anyone who was overtly dogmatic or bureaucratic. But if he had before him a passionate film lover with a creative spirit, he gave the person his entire confidence and limitless support. Langlois knew how to spot talent. He had no trouble recognizing men and women of faith and enthusiasm whom he helped to found film archives as lively as his own. The story of the birth of the Swiss film archive is a perfect example.

We must think back to the strong impression the "Images of French Cinema" exhibition produced in Lausanne in 1945, particularly upon a young student named Freddy Buache, who, leaving the screening of *Un Chien andalou* in a dizzy fog, collided right into Langlois, whom he did not know.

Langlois, however, knew a kindred spirit at first sight—or first clonk. He sensed in the young Buache that same passion and abandonment for the seventh art that had guided him as a youth in Paris. He quickly targeted Buache as the man to direct the future Cinémathèque Suisse.

But in order to reach that point, Langlois first had to contribute to the success of a ciné-club that could fulfill the same role in Lausanne as the Cercle du Cinéma played in Paris, eventually facilitating the creation of a full-fledged film archive. Langlois came to Buache's aid by lending him a series of precious films for his Swiss ciné-club screenings. The ciné-club soon blossomed into a source of cultural influence extending beyond the city limits.

The birth of the Swiss film archive was not, however, without complications. On 3 November 1948, an association named the Cinémathèque Suisse had been founded and its archives transported from Basel to Lausanne. But the General Assembly, held on 3 November 1950 at the Hotel de la Paix, produced little save disagreement. After many quarrelsome episodes, the Swiss archive's board of directors decided to invite Langlois to participate in a meeting at which the future of the organization would be decided. It was a question of finding a legal format that would permit the fledgling archive's members to put an end to the disputes and pursue their activities, or else give up for good.

Henri loved drawing up bylaws, but this affair was also going to give him the occasion to show off his diplomatic talents. The situation was doubly serious because the Swiss assocation of film distributors had asked its members to suspend all depositing of prints at the Cinémathèque Suisse. This was the recurring problem that had prompted Langlois to establish the principle of film archives as entirely noncommericial bodies in the first place. He developed a set of bylaws modeled closely on those for the Cinémathèque Française. Negotiating from his strong position as secretary-general of the FIAF, Langlois went on to Berne, where he elaborated on the bylaws' meaning for the secretary of the Swiss Chamber of Cinema. On 21 June 1952, the Cinémathèque Suisse's General Assembly convened in Lausanne and, their internal conflicts settled, passed the new bylaws prepared with Langlois's help.

A young American collector, James Card, had more than 800 films stashed in his garage in Rochester, New York. In 1947 one of Card's friends met Henri Langlois in Paris and told him about Card's private collection. Langlois wrote him a letter, and within a year the two men were exchanging films. Langlois sent prints of early French films—by Lumière, Méliès, and Zecca—while Card returned the favor with their American counterparts—films by Edison and Porter. Henri eventually sent Renoir's silent film *Nana* as the first in a long line of French feature films that at the time no longer existed in the United States. Within two years after their exchanges began, James Card's private collection served as the basis for a second major American film archive.

Officially chartered as a public educational institution in 1948, the George Eastman House Museum, situated in the historic mansion of the founder of the Eastman Kodak Company and until then serving exclusively as a museum of still photography, would, under the direction of General Oscar Solbert, welcome James Card's film treasures, along with Card himself, the following year.

Ricardo Vigan, a young, basically penniless Cuban, liked to sneak into Cinémathèque screenings. Instead of nabbing a gate-crasher, Langlois grabbed an opportunity. His sixth sense for detecting hard-core devotees of the seventh art told him that Vigan was special. The two men hit it off so well that Langlois found Vigan a job and a place to live. Before long, Vigan had a full-blown case of filmbug flu. He told Henri he was ready to go back to Havana to start his own film-preservation project. Henri suggested the by now tried-and-true method of starting with a ciné-club and building a following and a reputation from there. From 1949 to 1954, Langlois shipped several films a month to Cuba. With Langlois's long-distance assistance, the Cuban film archive was soon born. Ricardo Vigan's projections attracted a group of film buffs, several of whom would later become famous, such as filmmakers Tomas Gutierrez Alea and Nestor Almendros. After having made a film in Cuba, Almendros became the distinguished director of photography for Truffaut, Rohmer, and Terrence Malick, earning 1978's Oscar Award for Best Cinematography for the latter's *Days of Heaven*.

It was also thanks to Langlois that, after World War II, the Belgium film archive was able to resume its activities. Since the archive did not benefit from a state subsidy, it was to Henri that André Thirifays turned for a regular supply of films.

The prospect of founding an Iranian film archive might seem unrealistic—at least, that was Henri's initial reaction when Farrokh Gaffary, one of the more fervent disciples at Langlois's own screenings, revealed his plans to return to his native Iran and start a film archive:

> I'd written to friends in Iran telling them that we had to take advantage of the fact that there were already nitrate films there, most notably an entire collection of German films from the UFA Studios and American films that had survived, and that we should try to establish an archive.

Langlois was at first very distant when I told him my idea. Then suddenly, he became interested. He always had a passion for the Orient in general, and he had some imaginary view of Iran all his own, perhaps based on his memories of Smyrna. I never found out why Langlois was reticent at first. Perhaps it was because he was awfully shy, and each time someone approached him about something specific, he'd pretend to answer by saying, "Yes, we'll see about that. . . ."

Later, when he discovered that I wasn't the sort of man who wanted to organize a film archive along bureaucratic lines, he opened up and agreed to help. And from there we became friends. After the Cannes Festival in 1949, Henri took me with him to the FIAF congress in Rome and our ciné-mathèque was accepted as an "observer member."

I left for Iran that same year and didn't return to Paris until September 1951, whereupon I immediately contacted Langlois, who meanwhile had made that extraordinary first museum at the avenue de Messine. He wanted to know what had become of our archive. I explained how we'd collected some exceptional prints, notably *King of Jazz*, an original color print, *The Black Pirate*, and some UFA films from the 1920s and 1930s. Henri was ecstatic.

By 1948, the FIAF had agreed that Paris would remain its headquarters. With the cold war already in full swing (and destined to escalate during the late 1940s and 1950s), the fact that Paris was roughly equidistant between the poles of America and the Soviet Union provided a certain ideological freedom, especially with someone as intellectually strong and politically neutral as Langlois running the show. Also, beginning in 1948 Langlois was able to offer the FIAF a free office in the avenue de Messine building, which naturally reduced the FIAF's operating expenses.

Since FIAF's headquarters were in Paris and, moreover, at the Cinémathèque, it is no coincidence that Henri Langlois found himself at the center of FIAF activities until 1960. Langlois set a frantic work pace during a period already overloaded with activity. With the Executive Committee's approval, Langlois hired an executive secretary to handle the increasing volume of administrative work. From 1946 until 1951, Mademoiselle Z. de Malewsky-Malevitch took over and continued what had more or less been Georges Franju's job. When she left, Langlois faced the task of finding a replacement and turned to Gaffary on his return to Paris in late 1951.

Gaffary wanted to advance his university studies in Paris while still attending all the Cinémathèque's screenings. One day, Henri took him aside and told him that he was looking for a new executive secretary. "Who's better suited for the job than you?" asked Henri. As Gaffary recalls,

> I learned everything from my day-to-day contact with Langlois. He was not a teacher, but a master. Langlois's ideas about the cinema, his choice of films to project, and the extraordinary manner in which he presented them made him my mentor. I learned from him just by keeping my eyes open and

watching. Every day, new prints arrived from other archives, as did films belonging to the Cinémathèque. Langlois usually screened the silent films without their credits and title cards, and it became a game for him to identify them. I especially remember an occasion when he looked at just a few images of a film and said, "It's Danish, and it must have been made before 1914."

·And when I checked up on it, it *was* a Danish film from before World War I. I don't know how he guessed that—no doubt because he knew fashion inside out or was tipped off by the setting.

In addition to the annual congress, the International Federation of Film Archives's Executive Committee met three or four times a year in Paris. Each national archive compiled a list of its respective possessions in the hope of eventually tracking down lost films. In 1951 the congress was held in Cambridge, England. The General Assembly decided to publish an international catalog in French and English of all the films on deposit at the different archives; however, because of differing policies governing disclosure, the catalog would not see the light of day. Also proposed was a project to assemble an international library of film books.

The 1952 congress adopted most of Henri's suggestions, and his authority and thorough understanding of the problems facilitated a good working atmosphere. Archive delegates from countries as politically disparate as Argentina and Poland or Spain and the Soviet Union worked side by side. Langlois created the International Bureau of Cinematographic Historical Research (BIRHC). For Henri, this represented the extension of an idea that during the Occupation and immediately after the war had permitted him to gather documents and interviews of vital importance for the history of the cinema. The BIRHC met at various intervals and, by 1957, would ultimately bring together 120 delegates from 38 nations.

In the hope of fostering the spirit of solidarity that always guided him, Langlois proposed that the expense of printing copies be shared so as to help the less fortunate film archives in the group. This project, which was started up several times, would finally be nicknamed the "Pool." Providing copies of classic films in this way would permit the younger archives to have a core collection from the start. As one might expect, Paris once again was headquarters for the Pool. Yet difficulties would arise following the pirating of copies. This was a situation that Langlois would not accept and that would later prove to be a major source of discord and distrust, resulting in the rupture between the Cinémathèque Française and the FIAF.

If Henri encouraged national initiatives and exchanges, it was because he knew that all concerned would benefit, for although each archive was devoted to saving its national heritage first, a curious phenomenon had occurred whereby an archive frequently held a large quantity of foreign films.

By the end of World War I, the major American film companies had opened up branches not only in Europe but also in Africa, South America, and the Orient. Thus, it was not uncommon to find American films all over the world.

Iris Barry's successor at MOMA, Richard Griffith, remembered in particular the case of Ernst Lubitsch's *Forbidden Paradise*. The original negative had disintegrated in the Paramount vaults. In the hope of locating a copy elsewhere in the world, MOMA sent out a call by way of the FIAF, and remarkably enough, the Czechoslovakian film archive responded with news of a print. But this lone surviving print was in such poor condition that the archive was unable to make an internegative from it. Griffith accepted the film all the same and sent it to James Card at the George Eastman House, where, with Kodak's aid, Card succeeded in making a respectable print. The only remaining problem was that MOMA didn't have enough money to change the Czech title cards into English!

Sometimes all it took to find a lost film was the incentive to ask the right people if they had any old films lying around the house. Mary Pickford found a copy of D. W. Griffith's *Lady of the Pavements* and Gloria Swanson's *Sadie Thompson* in her own basement. But just locating a film was not enough.

Langlois recalled this never-ending search for *Cahiers du cinéma*:

> The problem is first to determine who's got the films, where they are (in what building, in what country), and whether there's a chance of being able to get at them. Then you have to convince the film owner to trust you—to tell you where the films are and to entrust them to you, even if that means promising the owner the seal of secrecy, so as to be in a position to safeguard them and ensure their survival. Finally, you have to look at the films, to know what they're worth, and secure the authorization to make copies and to project them.
>
> And when I think about films, I'm thinking not only of positive prints but of negatives as well, for only the survival of original negatives can ensure the survival, in all its original beauty, of the cinematographic work of art. To ensure that the original negative survives for as long as possible, to obtain it, to be able to watch over it—that is the most difficult of objectives and the most essential.
>
> Each case is special. Everything is a question of trust and mutual esteem between the producer and the film archivist. There is a slender thread that a mere trifle can break, a foolish mistake, an unfortunate remark. But after all, the results are there, and if the public authorities have never given a thought to safeguarding edited negatives from destruction, I never met a producer who destroyed a work with a light heart, unless he was obliged to do it. Most of the destruction has come about by chance, following bankruptcy, the disappearance of film production companies, forgetfulness—for in reality, unless a film is watched over constantly, it can disappear. So it is that most films lost in the United States died accidental deaths.

As if the stigma attached to movies as ephemeral entertainment were not bad enough, as the years progressed archivists discovered that merely collecting old movies was not sufficient to save them from destruction. All 35-millimeter films made before 1950 were printed on nitrate-based stock, a flexible backing that consists chiefly of nitrocellulose. According to a FIAF report, this base has good optical and physical properties, but the nitrogen compounds are very unstable. With the passage of time, the nitrate groups separate, and so, even under the most favorable conditions, nitrate film decomposes, slowly dissolving into a viscous goo. Like all substances of this group—which are closely related to the explosive nitrocellulose (guncotton)—the nitrate base is highly flammable. It ignites very easily (in the case of new nitrate film, at about 130 degrees Celsius [266 degrees Fahrenheit]; *old* nitrate has been known to spontaneously combust at temperatures as low as 40 degrees Celsius [104 degrees Fahrenheit]) and burns very quickly indeed—in large quantities, explosively: 20 tons of film (the equivalent of 8,000 reels of 1,000 feet each), can burn out within three minutes.

A collector who beat the odds triumphing over the specter of all-out destruction by indifferent film companies and the double whammy of two world wars, and who accepted physical flaws, including brittleness, ripped sprocket holes, and scratches, might find him- or herself in possession of a dangerous treasure. Archivists gradually realized that each nitrate film was a veritable time bomb, ticking away in keeping with its own chemical metabolism. The stock may begin to decompose from the first hours after its development. How long it will survive depends almost entirely on how thoroughly the film stock was washed after the images were chemically fixed. Consequently, there is no surefire method for determining, a priori, which films made before 1950 will endure and for how long.

Even archival professionals were slow to acknowledge the risk nitrate could entail. For half a century, nitrate films had circulated the world over without any special precautions. Like Henri Langlois and many others, Lotte Eisner traveled with cans of nitrate film at her side. Her sole concern was keeping smokers with lit cigarettes at a distance. Lotte recalled the time Gene Moskovitz of *Variety* dropped by her railway car puffing on a huge cigar. The diminuitive Lotte shoved the bulky Moskovitz back out into the corridor before he knew what hit him.

Henri Langlois remembered that when he founded the Cinémathèque in 1936, experts had warned him against conserving the Lumière negatives: "You're crazy, the chemical life of a film cannot go beyond 50 years." Yet 70 years after the films were made, Langlois pointed out they not only still existed but were in impressively good condition—a miracle due in part to the high-quality workmanship and chemical handling of the first films. Having kept the films despite the experts' pessimism, Langlois could profit from the improved techniques when the 1960s rolled around to make new copies of exceptional quality. Roughly 1,300 Lumière negatives, each lasting 50 seconds, still exist at the Cinémathèque. And in the Musée du Cinéma-Henri Langlois, one can even see Etienne–Jules Marey's filmstrips from 1888—seven years before the Lumières commercialized their ingenious filming device.

   There was also the problem of film piracy. On numerous occasions, Langlois brought up the subject with his closest associates in the FIAF, Freddy Buache and James Card. Essentially, Langlois claimed that other archives were using films for illegal purposes or that when he lent a film, it either would not be returned or would be copied during its absence.

One specific case spans almost 15 years. In 1951 the British Film Institute allegedly signed a contract promising to use the print of L'Age d'or lent to them by Langlois for a one-time-only showing. But in 1958 Langlois discovered that the BFI had indeed lent the film—without his knowledge or that of the actual owner—to someone in Israel and someone in Holland. In a letter to James Quinn, the ex-director of the BFI, Langlois claims that the BFI had continued its illegal deals and sent an illegal copy of L'Age d'or to Stockholm and to Warsaw and that almost all the film archives in the world now had copies to do with as they pleased, when in fact the film was supposed to remain a secret deposit at the Cinémathèque Française and the owner had made Langlois give his word not to allow other archives to duplicate the film. Langlois worried less about "illegal" possession by other archives than the eventual pirating of the film for commercial use.

There is no concrete proof of a pirating conspiracy, and even if Langlois was right, no one came forth to back him up, since doing so would mean the disintegration of the FIAF as a trustworthy organization. If it was all a game, Henri played it so convincingly that those accused of spying might very well have wilted under Langlois's accusations. The person he was speaking to, put on the defensive, needed to prove that he or she was not there to steal films or turn a profit. At one point or another, just about everyone connected with the Cinémathèque Française was accused of being a spy.

According to Langlois, Kenneth Anger was a CIA agent when he first arrived in Paris. James Card was a spy for McCarthy. William Novik worked for the French Intelligence Service, while Rossif was spying for the Vatican or possibly the Russians. Jay Leyda would later work for the FBI. And so on, depending on Henri's bent that particular day. Of course, as the saying goes, just because you're paranoid doesn't mean they're *not* out to get you.

Langlois sometimes had the feeling that there were conspiracies afoot aimed at stealing the Cinémathèque's possessions. As a result, those who worked at the Cinémathèque felt like they were living in a grade B spy–thriller-cum-detective film. Henri specialized in enigmatic statements, and, as François Truffaut noted, "Speaking with Langlois was like beginning a detective novel on page 84. It was impossible to know who X or Y was and consequently equally impossible to follow the action. Langlois always spoke to you like you were somehow in his head and would therefore be aware of everything. So when he'd meet you, he'd always start a conversation in the middle. It was very mysterious and frequently incomprehensible."

Farrokh Gaffary thought Langlois's approach was psychologically astute: "A woman arrives in Paris from a foreign country claiming she wants to create a cinémathèque. Two days later, because she's wearing such and such perfume, or saying such and such a phrase, she becomes suspect and we no longer know if she is the pope's spy or an operative for a South American dictator. But Langlois's suspicions took hold to such a degree that I'd end up telling the woman to stop calling me and coming to see me at the Cinémathèque, because Henri had chastised me, 'How could you possibly have let the wolf into the sheep's pen?'"

Langlois definitely felt persecuted. He saw conspiracies all around him, and these were just as likely to be on the national level as on the international level. Yet some of Langlois's mistrust was not entirely unfounded. As the Cinémathèque's treasures increased, so too were people's appetites whetted. By never giving those around him the complete picture, Langlois protected himself and the Cinémathèque from possible attack. What is extraordinary is that this climate was a double-edged blade. By accusing others, whether it be truth or fiction, Langlois convincingly transferred suspicion away from himself, and few began to notice that Langlois failed to return prints loaned to the Cinémathèque. The best defense is a good offense, and Henri Langlois may have been setting up a smoke screen to take the heat off his own illegal activities. Daniel Toscan du Plantier, former director of the Gaumont Company, witnessed this practice:

> One got used to the fact that Langlois did not return some of the films he borrowed, and finally it was common knowledge. But he was doing it for the common good. The Cinémathèque was created in opposition to the film industry in the first place, against the world film industry, because the people in charge were a bunch of crazies. But were they really crazy? More on the thieving side, it's said, but thank goodness! Because at that time, there were specific ideas in the cinema, and I say "at that time" with caution, because I dare not say the attitude has fundamentally changed: Use the movies and then throw them away. Langlois did not make money off those films. He never sold copies. But for him, it was necessary to remove the films from the hands of those who wanted to destroy them.

A polemic arose at the heart of the FIAF concerning the best method by which to determine the degree of nitrate deterioration in a film. One day at the avenue de Messine, the Cinémathèque's employees heard an unmistakably angry outburst from Langlois's office. Each one of his collaborators knew that for Langlois to get worked up into such a state, someone somewhere must have struck a blow at the sacred integrity of his films. The corpus delicti was resting on his table: a film had returned from London with holes punched out from the middle of its frames. After having vented his anger through screaming, Henri was completely depressed and, head in hands, repeated, "They've gone completely crazy. We must stop this massacre!"

Ernest Lindgren, director of the British Film Institute, had become the leader of those who believed that all nitrate films must be transferred to safety stock as soon as or sooner than humanly possible. Under his direction, the BFI developed a series of tests that involved punching a small sample from the nitrate film and testing it for instability. If the film had reached a certain level of chemical instability, it was thought to be urgent to immediately copy it to acetate stock and then destroy the original nitrate negative and print(s) for the safety of other nitrate films in the vicinity as well as the workers. This was the origin of the infamous holes that had set off Langlois's anger. He could not understand Lindgren's revulsion for old film stock when he himself felt a veritable veneration for the stuff.

The two men's temperaments differed totally. Langlois, whose silhouette was beginning to take on a slight chubbiness and who did not worry about personal appearance, loved the film stock itself nearly as much as he did the images fixed upon it. He was a collector for whom a simple reel of film was a rare object, one made much more precious precisely because it was fragile. Lindgren, always dressed to the nines, wore a determined, masklike expression and prided himself on his razor-thin, impeccably maintained, Hollywood-leading-man-style mustache. He was a textbook Anglo-Saxon, sure of himself, his empire, and the infallibility of his methods.

Not content to have destroyed the originals once he had copied them, Lindgren refused to even show the Lindgren-certified, safe-for-humanity results. He was the living antithesis of Henri Langlois, whom he detested all the more, since, within the British Film Institute itself, even the programming directors had begun asking the Cinémathèque Française if they might borrow the French copies of their own films because Lindgren obstinately refused to let them handle the ones on the premises.

James Card also believed that Lindgren was behaving in an utterly detestable manner. From Rochester, on behalf of the George Eastman House, he proclaimed that it was unthinkable that a director of an archive could carry out the destruction of original works:

> At the BFI in London, there was no way to see an original print. Nitrate originals were destroyed, including one of *our* originals, incidentally. It was an infuriating thing. *Old Heidelberg* (1915), Stroheim's first job as an assistant director, a beautiful original-release print, destroyed without asking us, simply because it was nitrate and the BFI had copied it—also without our permission.

The trouble really lies with the functionaries. They get to the point where they're more happy with their file cards than they are with the thing in itself. And they're the ones, as they run out of space, who'll say, "Well, get rid of the nitrate—it's dangerous, it's taking up space." The nitrate originals should be used when they're negatives to get the best possible prints; the original positives should be looked at as long as they can be put through projectors. Otherwise, you're talking not about films, but about facsimiles.

This idea of the intrinsic value of the original stock that went through the original camera, along with any prints struck from that original negative, is forcefully illustrated in an anecdote recounted by Georges Sadoul: "In 1947 the Prague film archive struck a print from a copy of *La Passion*, a hand-tinted Pathé film from 1903. The copy, which was made on Agfacolor film stock and fell far short of the original, has since self-destructed via a chemical reaction in its three layers of color emulsion. Fortunately, the original had been preserved. Must it now be destroyed because it's on nitrate and therefore flammable? But then, isn't that also the case for the piece of wood on which the *Mona Lisa* is painted? Must we toss it on the fire and replace it with a life-size reproduction on cement-backed asbestos?"

Sadoul's point is even more important when one considers the artistic nature of the object itself, for film is obviously both a chemical and an artistic substance. Beyond the elementary need to save movies from chemical destruction lies the even greater need for artistic restoration. Not only should film students, historians, and the general public be able to see what a film looked like in, say, 1922, but they should see a print that comes as close as possible to the filmmaker's original intent.

Film history is a battlefield littered with amputee victims. Be it *The Great Train Robbery*, *Greed*, *Potemkin*, *The Magnificent Ambersons*, the Zapruder 8-millimeter film of Kennedy's assassination, or, more recently, *Heaven's Gate*, the slightest editorial change can greatly alter interpretation. These "unkindest cuts of all," as Herman Weinberg calls them, were frequently the result of a filmmaker's struggle against a producer or the censor.

The Cinémathèque's role thus also entailed reuniting the different existing copies and even the outtakes needed to reconstruct a film in its integrality. It was with jealous care and sure-handed competence that Langlois transmitted his instructions, almost meter by meter, to Jean-Paul Boyer, who then ran off prints of the original films Langlois sent him. Henri had known Boyer since the days when he was still developing Lumière films in a simple washbasin. Having recognized his talent, Langlois helped Boyer found a laboratory in Redessan, near Nîmes. This laboratory, located in a small street called Georges Méliès, was to be the source of all of the Cinémathèque's Lumière prints, the enduring quality of which still warrants our admiration today.

Boyer, whose expertise matched his passion, took countless precautions to follow Langlois's instructions so as to arrive at a near-perfect copy while preserving the original. Henri wanted hand-crafted expertise, not mass production. Besides, he would never send a film to be restored without dozens of accompanying commentaries.

Beginning in 1953, Langlois would be aided in his mission to restore by Marie Epstein, who well understood the technical problems involved, since she had worked with Jean Benoît-Lévy and her own brother Jean on their films. Marie was put in charge of the Cinémathèque's relations with the laboratory and restored many old films:

> At first, I was very scared by my new tasks, and in particular, the possibility of making editorial mistakes. But Henri taught me a lot, and little by little, I learned how to do it. During the silent era, most films were tinted according to the scene. Purple was used for evening effects, blue for the night, pink for sunrises, yellow for the sun, and red for fire scenes. The negatives were not edited according to the script's continuity but instead were grouped by tinted color. Consequently, strips of film would be developed out of order, according to their color, and then a copy would be printed from the negative. The copy had to be broken down and reedited according to the chronological order of the shots, since a blue-tinted nighttime scene could be followed by an indoor shot of a completely different color.
>
> My work was to reedit those films as closely as their creators had intended. We wouldn't touch the original negative—too fragile—but an interneg-ative was made from a copy, and that would be our guide for editing. When the pieces of negative contained numbers, it was easy, by following them, to find the story line. But often they did not contain numbers, and then we had to guide ourselves by the continuity, because at that time there was a golden rule that no director would have transgressed: If an actress left a room to move into a garden, she had to arrive there wearing the same dress. Aside from that, editing is a question of instinct. It works or it doesn't. You feel it. I especially worked on films made by Louis Delluc, Marcel L'Herbier, Abel Gance, as well as all of my brother's films. Directors like L'Herbier and Gance were always coming to the Cinémathèque to take back their films in order to reedit them. Naturally, a director evolves over the years and in retrospect sees how to change a film. Henri Langlois always argued with these directors. He wanted to keep the film in its original version. For historical purposes, it would be a disaster to allow those directors to change the original film. When money was available, we would make another copy of their film and let them play with that.

Langlois had a sixth sense for discovering quality films. During the 1950s, James Card proposed that the film archive directors in the FIAF each choose an unsung film from their respective country. Henri Langlois loved the idea and told Card, "Fine, but I'm going to pick the American film for you."

He chose Maurice Tourneur and Clarence Brown's *Last of the Mohicans* (1920). Langlois had somehow obtained that silent film's original negative, either from Tourneur upon his return to France or maybe from the negative used in Paris for European distribution. Regardless, Langlois mailed the film to Card in Rochester.

Three or four years passed before one day, Card was reading an article in *Photoplay* magazine from 1920 that discussed *Last of the Mohicans*. There was also an article calling for the establishment of film archives, and in that article the author listed *Mohicans* as one film worthy of preservation. Card had been too preoccupied with more urgent preservation tasks than the idea of each archive showing an unsung film, and so, over three years after Langlois mailed the negative, Card made a fine-grain print from it and sat down to watch it for the first time:

> The film was extraordinarily beautiful and a breathtaking revelation to all who see it, and many now insist that it is unquestionably a masterpiece, among the finest American action films. It turned out to be one of the most beautiful prints in our collection. The whole film is so exquisitely done pictorially. You can see Tourneur and Brown just destroying themselves to get those magnificently framed shots. For me, it's one of the best silent films ever made—better than Griffith's work! So naturally, all of this was thanks to Henri, and when I told him that I was every bit as enthusiastic about the film as he was, his response was, "I never saw the film."

In a world where books *are* judged by their covers, Langlois had latched a gut instinct onto a title. Perhaps it was the *last* part that appealed to him. Whatever a Mohican was—good or bad—the last of 'em was surely worth saving.

Langlois's charmingly mystical approach to his job as secretary-general of both the Cinémathèque and the FIAF did not always please those who worked with him. The three-ring-circus atmosphere at the avenue de Messine must have seemed confusing to anyone but Langlois. Farrokh Gaffary eventually became disillusioned by Langlois's need to control everything. Since Gaffary sensed a growing hostility toward Langlois from certain members of the FIAF, and since he wanted to make a film, he preferred to resign from his post as executive secretary.

There were already power struggles in the works. For Jean Raine, for example, the Iranian film archive did not really exist. The Iranian film archive and Farrokh Gaffary were one and the same, and Gaffary, it so happened, was in Paris and not in Teheran. Jean Raine adds, "[A new archive] was very important for Langlois because it gave him another vote at the FIAF congress. He would have created a cinémathèque in the Sahara in order to have more representatives. . . . Stretching a screen between two camels in the middle of the Sahara and calling it a projection would not surprise me, coming from him. The Saharian film archive would then come and vote for Henri at the FIAF congress."

After Gaffary's departure, Langlois offered the post to Marion Michelle, an American living in Paris and married to a French painter. Michelle was a photographer, camerawoman, and scriptwriter who had worked with Joris Ivens. But she was not feeling much like a secretary, and besides, she got along too well with Mary and Henri to want to mix work with friendship, so she turned down the job. She did suggest that Henri contact her Australian friend Catherine Duncan, who was looking for part-time work to keep her in Paris. Catherine Duncan took the job and proved to be very efficient. She started the FIAF news bulletin. But even though she had married a Frenchman, it was he who found himself assigned to a post in Australia, and in view of this continental hopscotch, Catherine asked Marion to temporarily replace her—a "temporary" post that Marion Michelle would keep for 10 years.

Meanwhile, everyone recognized Henri's generosity toward the FIAF through his having offered it the nicest office space at the Cinémathèque. After leaving the avenue de Messine in 1955, the Cinémathèque found refuge, thanks to the producer Sacha Gordine, at 19, rue Spontini, near the Bois de Boulogne, in an old mansion constructed by the famous fashion designer Jacques Doucet. There one could admire doors painted by Watteau and remarkable woodwork. But it was the garden, hidden from neighbors' prying eyes by a thick wall, that gave the place its charm. It was a mysterious garden, filled with loose stones, rare plants, and fake grottoes worthy of a film set. Life there was organized in an informal way. The FIAF office was located in a passageway next to the garden. With limited space at his disposal, Langlois securely stored some of the most precious objects on the second floor. That left three or four large rooms on the main floor for the Cinémathèque's administration. The only dividing line between them was a giant curtain that, like a theater set, roughly defined each person's corner. Mary had her own, Lotte Eisner another, and so forth.

Every day was part of a season of experimental theater, and anyone who walked in the door was the unwitting recipient of box seats to the latest production. One long-running sketch might be entitled "The Mystery of the Missing Mail." Everyone, beginning with Mary Meerson, thought it her or his duty to insulate Langlois, swamped as he was by work. Sometimes the mail did not arrive at the FIAF desk, even though a special mailbox had been placed next to the one for the Cinémathèque. And for a simple reason: When the letter carrier handed the mail to Mary Meerson, Mary, so as not to lose it, would place it on her chair and sit on it. So all went out of their way to find a pretext to make Mary move, and it became a game. As soon as someone succeeded in making her leave her desk, another would swoop down to seize the letters and distribute them. Jean Raine remembers this game of hide-and-seek:

Mary hid everything she didn't want Henri to see. When I thought it was something of importance, I figured out a way to recover it and give it to him. Once I even spotted Mary burying papers in the garden. Then, with those fake Ali Baba caverns, I sometimes had to conduct incredible research and transform myself into a geologist. I should point out, however, that I was on Mary's side and to some degree her accomplice. I think she spared Henri many problems. He would have reacted very badly to certain letters that did not deserve an answer. Mary had an extraordinary sixth sense for that sort of thing. I often made my own selection and saw for myself what it was necessary to hide from Langlois. It also happened that I regretted giving him what Mary was right to throw away.

Since Langlois worked day and night, he saw no reason why his fellow workers should not do likewise. He could not be surrounded by people who expected to hew to a regular schedule, consulting their watches at a fixed hour. It was necessary to match his rhythm or give up.

For simplicity's sake, certain employees adopted the habit of no longer returning home. Raine, for example, stayed on eight days in a row. The technical service employees—the only union workers at the Cinémathèque—found they could not continue eating their sack lunches in the offices and demanded an employee lunchroom. Government officials complained that the Cinémathèque's restaurant bills were too high for its budget. The ministry's inspectors were mentally unprepared for the concept of working through lunch! One day, Jean Raine had the idea of installing a canteen with a real kitchen at the Cinémathèque. When he told Henri that they could prepare the food themselves, he thought it was a great idea. They installed a kitchen, equipped it, and finally figured out that it cost much more than the restaurant. Jean Raine humorously remembers this experiment:

> For one thing, we were even more numerous eating together, and for another, we had to allow for Langlois's special diet: thick steaks and raw vegetables in winter, which cost a lot. As for me, I love to cook dishes that call for a long preparation—Chinese-style—and I'd take an entire week to prepare a dish, which finally ended up meaning that I spent most of my time in the kitchen and had to enlist David Perlov and Tinto Brass to accompany me shopping. We made some fantastic meals. Everybody got fat during this period, which lasted for four or five months. But Langlois finally realized that I was in the kitchen morning, noon, and night.
>
> Everyone therefore returned to his own business and to the restaurants, where the Cinémathèque staff was always welcome. Our favorite was located on boulevard de Courcelles, across from the parc Monceau, but we also went very often to the Brasserie Lorraine. Nor have I forgotten Tachin, that delicious restaurant on the rue Spontini that gave us credit up to 500,000 francs!

Henri and Mary could not be absent for very long during the day or night. One of them stayed near the telephone, since, owing to the time change, calls could come in from around the world at any moment. For Mary and Henri, life was a battlefield, and leading the troops was more than a full-time job. Whether it was to find an enormous sum of money within a week or to face an apparently impossible task, such as putting up a new exhibition, they always managed to accomplish it.

Mary was as superstitious as Henri was. She never forgot to take the ritual precaution of slipping several pots of rock salt behind the partition or in the corners of a room to ward off evil spirits each time there was an inauguration of an exhibition or when she entered a new room. She believed in reincarnation and loved to repeat that she'd known Henri in ancient Egypt. Kenneth Anger dubbed them "the two pharoahs" and remembers that Langlois had written a script on Egypt and reincarnation. Mary believed herself to be Oscar Wilde reincarnated and, according to Anger, was also on hand to play *John the Baptist* as drawn by da Vinci. Insofar as Langlois had a volatile temperament, which caused people to continually fall in and out of favor according to his whims, Anger did not hesitate to call Langlois the Terrible Turk.

Traditional psychologists might contend that Langlois's lifelong dislike for being tidy was just an adult manifestation of his refusal to obey his father's command to clean up. But Kenneth Anger thinks the answer lies in the nature of art and creation:

> The subject of *désordre* once came up in conversation with Henri Langlois (I can't imagine why). Henri said that the passion for "too much order" leads ultimately to concentration camps: The road to Dachau is paved with obsessional neatness. The life process, Henri remarked, is inherently messy—try to clean it up too much and you'll kill it. (Henri loved paradox, but he had a point.)
>
> Who cares that Henri's shoelaces were sometimes undone, his filing hazy, and his accounting impressionistic? What counts is the creativity. The daring. The doggedness. Even the duplicity—always in pursuit of an idea. And in all circumstances, the perpetual *crise*, the pirouettes of wit. What a Scorpio!

Henri, like Mary, was born under the sign of Scorpio. And what textbook, chart-the-heavens, put-your-sign-on-the-dotted-line Scorpios they were! One way or another, we can better understand what unites the universe of Picasso, Malraux, Edgar Allan Poe, Camus, and Clouzot to the world of Langlois. Scorpio is a sign of extremes and excesses. Scorpios, it is said, are cut out to be assassins or saints. If Scorpios put their talents to work in the service of others, bring their power of reflection to bear in the service of research or an ideal, an art or an action, no one can go further than they. In fact, obstacles stimulate rather than discourage them, and since they cannot tolerate failure, they'll see to it that things work out their way.

Henri had not lost the habit of having his cards read. Lotte Eisner or Musidora were the fortune-tellers. A subtle game became established among them. Henri did not like to give the impression of taking advice, but by means of the cards, he could accept certain warnings. He was not taken in, but if what the cards foretold happened to agree with his own intuition, he did not have the slightest hesitation. In the evening, someone would bring him the newspapers. Before throwing himself into a cover-to-cover scrutiny of *Le Monde*, he never failed to glance at his horoscope in *France-Soir*. And if it did not suit his views, he would throw the paper away, screaming, "That woman doesn't know what she's talking about for tomorrow!" But if perchance Henri had a meeting the next day with the filmmaker Henri Storck and the *France-Soir* astrologer announced, "Beware of a man whose name begins with the letter S," Henri would immediately cancel the meeting.

Life at the rue Gazan apartment resembled a ménage à trois with Henri, Mary, and Lazare Meerson—or, rather, Lazare's ghost. Although the set designer had been dead since 1938, Meerson remained present, a component of all conversations. Certainly his ghost must have felt right at home in this studio that he had conceived and whose decor had never changed. It was hard not to think of him each time one climbed the stairway covered with the same white-on-white colored carpet that echoed Meerson's sets for the films of René Clair.

Mary entertained there lavishly. Her hospitality, in the great Russian tradition, was generous to a fault. She simmered delectable Italian and Russian dishes for hours on end. Her cooking was, by popular consensus, irresistible, and Langlois, who, accordingly, did nothing to resist, began growing fat. Mary's culinary artistry brought together both prominent businesspeople and simple workers from the Cinémathèque, such as Charlot Heimberger and Roger Tourret. Marion Michelle remembers one evening at Henri and Mary's place: "She prepared some extraordinary dishes for us. Mary bought some spit-roasted, free-range chicken and removed the breasts, which she reheated in a broth of meat and vegetables. The thighs were served separately on a bed of pistachios. It was both exotic and excellent. She was helped by her sister Helene; Mary was so nearsighted that one never knew if she was going to put the coffeepot cover in the sauce—but it always ended up fine."

Jean Raine and Mary suddenly got inspired to open a Russian restaurant in Paris. Everyone encouraged them. Jacques Prévert assured them that he and his friends would come there daily and organize poetry contests. Unfortunately, there was simply not enough time to run both a cinémathèque and a restaurant, and the project never became a reality.

If one was invited to Henri and Mary's place for dinner, it was for around 9:00 P.M. It was, however, unwise to arrive famished, since the meal usually did not begin before 1:00 A.M.! The conversation was so impassioned that guests lost all sense of time. Mesmerized, each person listened to Langlois as he spoke of a film and its historical considerations, delineating surprising parallels with current politics that one would never have imagined and that suddenly appeared obvious. When Henri held forth, he possessed the true gift of a snake charmer. His audience had no choice but to follow the seductive reasoning that led into the slippery coils of his intellect.

Those who had the chance to experience these moments at his side still have the feeling that Henri opened a door for them into an invisible parallel universe. Marion Michelle acknowledges that with her American sense of practicality, she attempted to mentally resist by thinking, "No, that's weird; what Henri says makes no sense." And then suddenly, she had the feeling that he had taken her by the hand and guided her into a new and unknown world: "It was as if I had crossed through a door and found myself on the other side with him. It was absolutely fascinating."

There remains at least one tangible image of this fascination-in-progress that Henri held over others who listened to him. It is a photo of Jean Riboud's living room, where one sees his wife, Krishna, and Mary side by side on a divan. They appear to listen, enchanted, to an invisible speaker. Henri is not in the photo. He was seated in front of the two women, and Cartier-Bresson, who was next to Henri, took advantage of this magical moment to snap the photo.

Although the exhibition "60 Years of Cinema" brought about a temporary solution to the loss of the avenue de Messine building, the Cinémathèque nonetheless continued to lack a projection room. Among the most fervent members of Henri's audience was Louis Cross, director of the Musée pédagogique, who brought Henri some unexpected help. After the almost claustrophobic screening room at the avenue de Messine, which seated barely 50 people, Cinémathèque regulars may well have suffered from temporary agoraphobia upon their first glance at the approximately 260-seat auditorium in the basement of the Musée pédagogique, placed at their disposal by Louis Cross. Located at 29 rue d'Ulm, a block away from the Ecole nationale des arts décoratifs and the Ecole normale supérieure, the theater was also close to boulevard Saint-Michel, the Ecole des mines, the Sorbonne, and the law school at Panthéon.

The Salle Jules Ferry had until then been used as a lecture hall. The room had a cold, ugly atmosphere and uncomfortably hard wooden seats. But its coldness was warmed by the joyous jostle of different student groups attracted to the quality, quantity, and unbeatable price of the Cinémathèque's screenings. These students would discover unexpected new horizons, and if the auditorium at the rue d'Ulm has remained famous as a model film school, it played no less of a role in the life of its other audience members. One finds today in every walk of life, from the arts to business and yes, even among civil servants, people who consider the hours they spent on those rock-hard benches to be the best memories of their youth.

Langlois kicked off the screenings on 1 December 1955 with a tribute to René Clair. Since this theater was at least five times as large as the avenue de Messine room, Langlois decided to show three different features nightly, at 6:30, 8:30, and 10:30. More often than not, these projections sold out. Tens of thousands of people crossed the threshold and had the privilege of learning to love the history of movies. During the first week in December, Langlois also paid tribute to Pabst, Buñuel, Renoir, Capra, Ivens, and Keaton. Then Henri began a series of national cinema retrospectives. The first, from 10 December 1955 to 20 January 1956, covered more than 75 feature films produced in the Soviet Union, followed by a retrospective, "60 Years of German cinema," with more than 110 films.

Langlois then tackled the Scandinavian cinema, with a major retrospective in April and May 1956. This undertaking included eight Ingmar Bergman films never before seen in France and served truly to reveal Bergman's genius to the French. In the space of a few days, the projection of *Fangelse*, *Gycklarns Afton*, and *Sommarlek* would render Bergman as famous in Paris as he was in Scandinavia. After having inspired the young critics and the public at the rue d'Ulm, Bergman would become the discovery of the year, thanks to *Smiles of a Summer Night*, which soon would be acclaimed at the Cannes Film Festival. In 1964 Henri would write:

> I still remember those evenings at the rue d'Ulm where everything seemed drab to us after having accompanied Stiller and Sjöström in their pure spaces. Then: *Himlaspelet* by Sjöberg and *Ordet* by Molander showed us new spaces, which led us to the baroque genius of Ingmar Bergman. . . .
>
> Bergman is a man of blood. Black or red, it runs in his films like a sacrifice, like at a clinic, like in a torture chamber, like in the bed of a delivering mother, like in first love—and that's why he is one of those rare artists who is supremely of our time.

The Scandinavian retrospective also introduced the extraordinary Danish cinema of the second decade of this century. Numerous articles in *Arts*, *Les Lettres françaises*, and diverse cinema reviews reflected the utility and significance of this cycle arranged by the Cinémathèque. Because the only publicity the Cinémathèque permitted itself was the publication of programs, its regular showings may have appeared divorced from current events, but in reality these series had a profound influence.

The Scandinavian retrospective did not follow a popular current of opinion but attempted to form one. It was an undertaking in which Henri played the role of a pioneer, convinced he would come up against considerable difficulties. The first of these was in procuring the films themselves. Although the Swedish film industry fully understood the noncommercial nature of the retrospective and did everything in its power to help, the Danish industry was much less understanding and made it extremely difficult for the French and Danish archives to select a program tracing the evolution of its production. Henri finally succeeded in overcoming that opposition, by obtaining the cooperation of the Nordisk Film Company.

A second difficulty was the accidental destruction, over the years, of a certain number of films that are—or would have been—an essential part of the history of the Swedish cinema. Thanks to the preparation of this retrospective, which necessitated searches through the vaults of the Swedish film industry to supply the films, Sjöström's lost masterpiece *Tosen Fran Stormyrtorpet*, which for a long time was believed to have disappeared completely, was brought to light. Although some crucial Swedish films had vanished, Denmark's film heritage had nearly been gutted. Obviously, a retrospective of the Danish silent era suffered terribly from the nonexistence of essential films.

The third difficulty lay in the fact that Swedish sound films were almost totally unknown abroad, particularly in France. The choice of films could therefore be only intuited by Henri Langlois, who had to depend on the critical opinion of the Swedish and Danish archivists. Even today, film enthusiasts who attend the programs of the Cinémathèque Française have a tendency to seek out films that are already known or at least cited in books on cinematographic art, and in the Scandinavian series, a substantial number of films were entirely unknown in France and had escaped mention in critical and historical works. There was an immense wall of prejudice to knock down, and Langlois feared that the Cinémathèque's faithful regulars would not follow the whole series. The retrospective represented a considerable risk that only the noncommercial character of the Cinémathèque made feasible. Finally, Henri was able to rejoice:

> Some stayed away from the first Sjöström films and deprived themselves of masterpieces out of blind solidarity to Griffith. But each day, it became clearer that facts were stronger than prejudice. The enthusiasm of those few who saw *Ingebord Holm* and *Terje Vigen* was so great that the projection of the two parts of *Jerusalem* was not only better attended but followed by an ovation. From then on, each new film of Sjöström or Stiller drew a larger audience, and on each occasion the films were applauded. After that, the battle was won, and the public followed the rest of the cycle with immense interest.

No sooner had the Scandinavian films faded to black than Langlois threaded the leader into the rue d'Ulm projectors for "60 Years of English Cinema." Approximately 70 British films were shown from 2 June to 12 July 1956, including 12 rare Hitchcock films never before seen in France. Shortly before his death, the avid Hitchcockophile François Truffaut remembered this as one of the best Cinémathèque Française retrospectives of all time.

Besides Hitchcock's British period, rue d'Ulm enthusiasts were treated to most of Anthony Asquith's films, and a smattering of works dating from 1896 to 1956, including films by Korda, David Lean, Powell and Pressburger, Cavalcanti, and Carol Reed. The season ended on 12 July with the screening of *Pandora and the Flying Dutchman*, *The Fox*, and Peter Brook's *The Beggar's Opera*. Since the rue d'Ulm theater was inside a state university and the building closed its doors for summer vacation, the Cinémathèque Française was obliged to halt its program until September.

Langlois shifted tactics after the national cinema retrospectives and opened the fall season with a series of tributes to great filmmakers. These lasted from 1 October 1956 until 31 March 1957 and helped celebrate the Cinémathèque Française's twentieth anniversary. Before beginning each tribute, which would vary from a single night's projection of three films to several days and 15 to 20 films, Langlois would hand out a mimeographed sheet with a few paragraphs he had written about each filmmaker. Since World War II, most French film enthusiasts had regarded the director as the true auteur of a film. Langlois did not like preconceived theories and showed that this "director-as-author" business did not always hold true. Certain producers were, for example, true creators, especially in the United States:

> Characters like Goldwyn, Zanuck, and Selznick directed huge film companies with enormous means of production and an entire bureaucracy behind them, but remained men of the trade. They knew how to dominate a situation and did their creating via producing—delegating responsibility. It comes down to a question of individual men. Warner without Goldwyn would never have become Warner, and when Fox died, there was another capable man who sensed the future, Zanuck, to take his place. A true producer must therefore be a creator. Besides, discovering is also a creative act, and for that you must know how to take colossal risks. That's how American producers have created some of the best Hollywood films. The producer has to be a visionary, able to look ahead. He's not only a businessman, but an artist who knows how to join forces with another artist who's ready to take every risk in the book.
>
> The tragic thing about the big French companies is that they never go broke anymore. Witness 1935—there were some bankruptcies that year, and it was a miracle for the French cinema. That was how, for three years running, there came to be the great cinema of Renoir, Duvivier, Carné, and others.

There have been and always will be great actors who do much more than simply play a role. The actor's share in the creation of a work can be preponderant. Langlois pointed out that the Cinémathèque Française and the George Eastman House represented two different tendencies and two distinct evolutions. Henri placed the accent on the director-as-author, while James

Card concentrated on actors, in keeping with the American concept that there are no great films without great stars. But Langlois also took into account the actors' influence on a film:

> Let's say that at the Cinémathèque we have auteurs emended by actors, whereas Eastman House has the actor through whom the auteur's emending is carried out. And that's the whole point. Why, for instance, do I have all of Dietrich's films but not all of Garbo's? Because Marlene, up to a point, means Sternberg. Whatever my admiration for Marlene, that admiration is bound up with my admiration for Sternberg. First there's Pygmalion, and then the actress. As a spectator, I may go to see Garbo or Marlene, but as curator of the Cinémathèque, I favor the creator.
>
> Nevertheless, actors can be creators. Consider, for instance, how Marlene obliged all her directors after Sternberg to do Marlene Dietrich— in other words, to do Sternberg—for although she was Marlene before Sternberg, she had not yet discovered herself. As far as we are concerned, she appeared out of nowhere, but in fact she had made films before *The Blue Angel* (1930). Fonda did not appear out of nowhere, but before Fritz Lang he performed variations in search of himself. He was a violin. Lang showed him he was a Stradivarius.

One screen actor whose presence rarely could be called the creative force in the film but whose meticulousness, once behind the camera, became his trademark and eventually caused his downfall was Erich von Stroheim. Langlois wasted little time in following a Zuckor-Lasky tribute with one to the original "man you love to hate." In addition to the seven truncated Hollywood films he directed, Stroheim appeared in numerous French and American films during the 1930s, 1940s, and 1950s. During the Cinémathèque retrospective, audiences saw such works as Cruze's *Le Grand Gabbo*, Chenal's *Alibi* and *L'Affaire Lafarge*, Renoir's *La Grande illusion*, and Wilder's *Sunset Boulevard*. All together, 17 films were shown, including the ultrarare *Queen Kelly* and *The Marriage of the Prince*, the second part to *The Wedding March*. Before the screenings, the enthusiasts could read this presentation of Stroheim by Langlois:

> Be it *The Merry Widow*, *Merry-Go-Round*, *Queen Kelly*, or *The Wedding March*, he puts us in touch with the truth. He shows in motion the crushing machine that was the society of the last of the divine-right monarchs. He shows us naked half-crazies, left to themselves by impunity and by the respect due to their rank by virtue of heredity. He spreads out before us the suffering victims, those who have abandoned hope, those who seek refuge in the artificial heaven of vice.
>
> He shows us in *Blind Husbands* and in *Foolish Wives* the true face of Don Juan, the one denounced by Molière, who knew what he was talking about when it came to absolute monarchs, something we seem since to have forgotten at the theater. And when one believes that he is turning away from

the cadaver, it is simply to better study it. In *Greed*, did he not bring all his skill to bear on an analysis of the little Germano-American world that believes it has escaped from hell but all the while carries hell within?

Unfortunately, America, which let him go about his business so long as it was a question of Central European monarchs, the antithesis of democracy, turned out to be much touchier as soon as it was a question of San Francisco and Death Valley. *Greed*, Stroheim's masterpiece of the American cinema, has, of all his works, been amputated the most.

Although all of Stroheim's silent films had been artlessly mangled by others, this did not prevent his acquiring a grand reputation in France. Langlois had projected his films for many years and dreamed of being able to restore them. When at the beginning of the 1950s, Erich von Stroheim returned to Europe and settled in a town near Paris, Henri invited him to the Cinémathèque to screen his early efforts, films Stroheim had not seen for 20 years. This marked the first time that the director was given a commercial-release print of *Greed* to see. At the end of the private screening, Stroheim, very depressed, took Langlois by the arm and told him with a sigh, "My dear Langlois, this copy is so mutilated that it no longer represents but a third of my original work." Henri was all the more sorry that it was the only commerical copy he could obtain.

In 1953 Henri and Lotte showed Stroheim *The Wedding March*. After several minutes, the director, who could no longer sit still, burst out in anger. He found the film boring and ordered them to stop the projection. Henri was outraged. How dare he say to those who admired him that his own master-pieces were boring! Then suddenly, Stroheim thought to ask what speed the film was being projected at.

"At the normal silent speed of 16 frames per second," responded Henri.

"You musn't!" Stroheim shot back. "I made the film at 24 frames per second—the speed of sound pictures. And to accompany it, I had music recorded on some records."

Langlois and Lotte were stunned by this revelation, since, in Europe, they had been aware only of the silent version. Straight away, Henri moved into action, obtaining an American copy of the film, thanks to Thomas Quinn Curtiss, a close friend of Stroheim who obtained it from the estate of Patrick Powers, a producer at Paramount. Then Russell Holman, who was in Paris, promised Langlois he would try to find the records in the United States. Holman made good on his promise, and Langlois, having brought together the neccessary elements, succeeded in making a sound print of *The Wedding March* with Stroheim's assistance.

Henri chose Renée Lichtig, Renoir's regular editor, to reconstruct the work at Stroheim's side. *The Wedding March*, made in 1926–27, had been released just when the talkies were beginning to catch on and had been accompanied by an original score with sound effects, recorded on huge 33-

rpm records. The appearance of each important actor was marked by a different musical motif.

Langlois first had the music recorded on a 6.35-millimeter magnetic band, which was transferred to magnetic 35-millimeter perforated stock. The fact that the film was already edited made it difficult to synchronize the sound and image, and these difficulties were accentuated by the fact that the film stock had shrunk with age. Renée Lichtig told *Cahiers du cinéma*:

> I can picture Erich von Stroheim seated in front of the little screen of the Morritonne. I usually let him have that spot because I had the impression that it made him happy to have, as we say in the business, the feel of the film. I noticed something very funny, because throughout our work, from start to finish, Erich, when speaking of the prince, never said "Nicky" but still identified himself as the character almost 20 years later by saying, for example, "I enter the room. I greet my father, and then I go find my mother. I ask her for some money, and we both leave the room," which gave me the extraordinary impression of reliving the film at the moment of the shooting. . . .
>
> Suddenly, Stroheim got angry while the military commanders passed in review: "That American editor knew nothing about military matters. He didn't edit it in the order of the commands!"

Langlois was burning with impatience, because he wanted to present the film at the Sao Paulo Festival. The restoration was finished just in time. On 9 February 1954 Henri and Lotte, this reconstructed musical version of *The Wedding March* in hand, boarded the airplane that would take them to Brazil. The film proved to be one of the great surprises as well as the highlight of the Sao Paulo Festival.

Henri Langlois was fearful that the Cinémathèque's move to the Latin Quarter would lead to a decline in habitual filmgoers. His fear turned out to be groundless, as the Left Bank simply replaced the Right Bank and the same group of film fanatics from the avenue de Messine jostled each other every night at the entrance to the auditorium on rue d'Ulm. Jean Rouch was among them. Then as now, he believed that the best way to see a film is to sit as close to the screen as possible:

> When you love movies a lot, you sit closer and closer to the screen. At the rue d'Ulm, the same bunch of us kept turning up in the front row. I didn't know who those guys were, but I overheard them talking nearby and we shared the same passion for consuming three films a night.
>
> Later, when I got to know them, I learned that their names were Godard, Truffaut, Rivette, Rohmer, Chabrol, and many others. I was slightly panic-stricken, because they knew everything. They were already film critics, and I was a little ignoramus. Yet we lived the same adventure. And

since I never went to a film school, if I ever learned anything, it was certainly there.

Today everyone knows the names it took Jean Rouch a while to discover. The New Wave—those filmmakers who gave a fresh strength to the French cinema at the end of the 1950s—was born from this daily attendance at Henri Langlois's programs. Langlois himself liked to say that he worked in the manner of a great couturier, hiding the stitches while weaving subtle connections into the fabric. As budding film buffs, they had already been fixtures at the avenue de Messine, where they had devoured the films of the past. They had naturally found a first vocation as critics, forming the group known as the "*Cahiers du cinéma* gang." One can speculate that Jean-Luc Godard, when writing, chose the pseudonym Hans Lucas so his initials would be H.L. In 1966 "H.L." paid tribute to Henri Langlois:

> Without Langlois's gigantic effort, today the history of cinema would be little more than that of Bardèche and Brasillach [authors of a French film history in 1935], that is to say, touristic postcards brought back from the land of movie theaters by two likable but not very serious public school teachers. One guesses immediately what a revolution this new vision of historicity might bring about in the aesthetic of the moving picture.
>
> Let's simply say that, thanks to Henri Langlois, we now know that ceilings do not date from *Citizen Kane* but from Griffith, of course, and from Gance; that cinéma-vérité dates not from Jean Rouch but from John Ford; the American comedy from a Ukranian filmmaker; and the photography of *Metropolis* from an anonymous French cameraman who was a contemporary of Bougereau. We also know henceforth that Alain Resnais or Otto Preminger has not made any progress compared to Lumière, Griffith, or Dreyer, no more so than Cézanne and Braque compared to David and Chardin: They've done something different.

The *Cahiers* group had found its calling, but the moviemaking establishment was ill inclined to answer the phone. Inspired by their long apprenticeship at rue d'Ulm, young people at the *Cahiers* would end up rattling the chains by which the French cinema found itself imprisoned. According to Alain Resnais, "The New Wave was more a new wave of spectators than of filmmakers. It was they who created the conditions that finally allowed new filmmakers to make films. We were in a completely blocked situation after the war. One could not hope to make a film before reaching the age of 40 or 50. It had been completely forgotten that directors such as Carné, Grémillon, Vigo, and Duvivier had begun at 20. It was implied that to become a director, there were so many secrets to unlock that you really had to spend 10 to 15 years as an assistant to begin to understand. Nonetheless, by watching films at the Cinémathèque I managed to get an idea about the film process."

Alain Resnais had first thought of becoming an actor and was part of a theater troupe that entertained the army. Like Jean Rouch, he was older than the group of film-loving kids of 1948 who, a decade later, as the New Wave, would turn the French film industry topsy-turvy as well as take the world by storm.

Henri Langlois would also play a less known but equally important role in certain dealings that would reinforce the projects of the *Cahiers* group. At that time, Roberto Rossellini resided in Paris and was living with Ingrid Bergman at the Hotel Raphaël. Rossellini did not know how to show his gratitude to Henri, who had been one of the first to make Paris aware of the importance of the director's neorealist films. The two men got along famously, since they shared certain character traits. Like Langlois, Rossellini could not live without agitation and was bored unless he was struggling against some obstacle. For Henri and Rossellini, life, like the cinema, was a raging battle.

Langlois organized private projections at the Cinémathèque's headquarters to enable Jean Rouch, François Reichenbach, and a few others to show Rossellini their short films. These meetings were the occasion for a lively debate on the essence and future of movies. It was there, around Henri and Mary, that Rossellini met several of these young critics who couldn't wait to make the leap and become full-fledged filmmakers themselves. Rossellini was a shining example of what it was possible to do. Hadn't he made *Open City* in the streets of Rome, without the proper authorization and the necessary capital? And yet the enormous international success of this unauthorized, underfinanced film had established Italian neorealism.

Jean Rouch, who took part in some of these meetings, looks upon Rossellini as a sort of spiritual father for the New Wave, stoking the young men's imaginations by sharing his own projects for independent productions. Thanks to the Cinémathèque and to Langlois, these meetings would eventually result in genuine contracts between Rossellini, as producer, and several critics from the *Cahiers du cinéma*, as film directors. François Truffaut figured among these talented young signatories:

> Rossellini had a sort of premonition for what would be called the French New Wave. That's indisputable. I saw a lot of Rossellini that year. He had chosen me to be his secretary, and I spent a lot of time taking dictation for two or three scripts. Rossellini wanted to become a producer. He told us that he had the funds and wanted to produce some films in 16-millimeter. Rivette and I signed a contract with him. Mine concerned a film that was supposed to be called *La Peur de Paris* but was never made. Our grandiose ideas about making low-budget fictional 16-millimeter films under Rossellini's auspices were abandoned when Rossellini took the opportunity to go to India. It seems to me that, upon his return, his admiration for Henri Langlois and Mary Meerson had only grown larger—he became a member of the Cinémathèque family.

George Braggiotti, Henri's American maternal grandfather, born in Charleston, South Carolina.

*G. Langlois Archives*

Count Delenda, Henri's great-uncle, began his diplomatic career at the French consulate in Port Said during the digging of the Suez Canal.

*G. Langlois Archives*

Annie Braggiotti, a young woman in Smyrna before her marriage to Gustave Langlois.

*G. Langlois Archives*

Gustave Langlois left for France in 1914 to fight in World War I. Pregnant with Henri, Annie Langlois remained in Smyrna during the war.

*G. Langlois Archives*

Smyrna (1914), the cosmopolitan city, hospitable to all races and religions, where Henri lived for his first seven years.

*G. Langlois Archives*

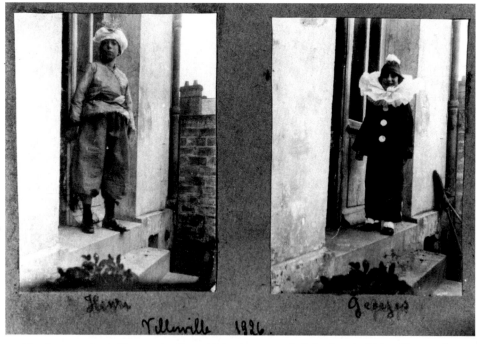

Henri on vacation in Normandy. For a children's costume ball, he disguised himself as a Turk; next to him is brother Georges as a Pierrot clown.

*G. Langlois Archives*

Henri dreams only of the cinema during his last year in high school.

*G. Langlois Archives*

Henri Langlois and Georges Franju in 1936 during the founding of the Cinémathèque Française.

*Courtesy of the Cinémathèque Française*

Henri used various strategies during the German occupation of France to transport films declared illegal by the Nazis. Here he plays the proud family man; the baby carriage contains films.

*Courtesy of Denise Bellon. Reproduction prohibited*

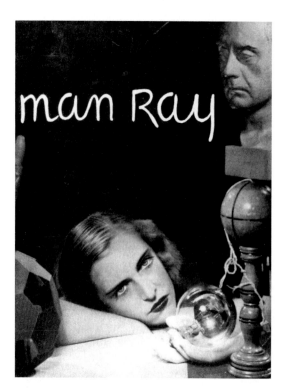

Mary Meerson?, 1934.

Langlois attracted to the Cinémathèque young film enthusiasts from around the world, such as Jean
Raine (left) and Kenneth Anger (right), 1950.

*Photo by Henri Storck. Courtesy of Sanky Raine*

Henri Langlois, 1952. This was William
Klein's first photo shoot, at the age of 24.

*Courtesy of William Klein*

Poster for the first film museum in 1948, at the avenue de Messine, with Marey's negative image of a man running, or *chronophotographique géométrique*.

Courtesy of the Cinémathèque Française

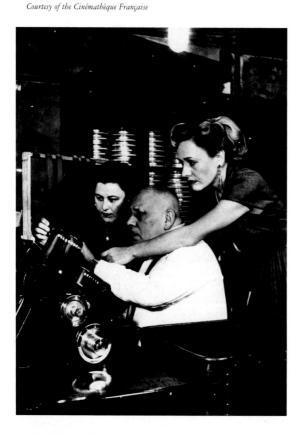

Restoration at the Cinémathèque Française of Stroheim's *The Wedding March*. From left: Renée Lichtig, Eric von Stroheim, and Denise Vernac (1953).

Courtesy of the Cinémathèque Française

Henri Langlois and Jean Cocteau at the Cinémathèque's offices, rue de Courcelles.

*Courtesy of the Cinémathèque Française*

Henri Langlois and André Malraux at the inauguration of the Charles Pathé Exhibition at the rue de Courcelles, 1959.

*Courtesy of the Cinémathèque Française*

The Langlois Affair, 9 February–22 April 1968. First spontaneous demonstration before the Cinémathèque's theater on the rue d'Ulm.

*Courtesy of France-Soir*

Meanwhile, Langlois asks the cards what the future holds.

*Courtesy of Paris-Match*

Reopening of the rue d'Ulm theater: "And now, on with the show!"
*Cahiers du cinéma*

Beginning in September 1968, Langlois gave a film course at Sir George Williams University in Montreal. The students nicknamed him "Jet Professor," owing to his transatlantic round trips. Here he attends a press conference with his friend Serge Losique.

Henri prepares a savory cocktail of Greek jams.

*Courtesy of the Cinémathèque Française*

With Iris Barry, former director of the MOMA Film Library in New York.

*Photo by Dimitri Fedotov, G. Langlois Archives*

With James Card under the Joan of Arc statue at the place de la République, Paris, 1974.

© 1974 by Pepe Diniz

Henri Langlois, portrait by Pepe Diniz, 1974.

© 1974 by Pepe Diniz

François Truffaut and Langlois during the filming of *The Wild Child*, 1969.
*Courtesy of Les Films du Carrosse*

Marie Epstein and Henri Langlois at the Cinémathèque, 1974.
Julien Quideau, © *L'Express*

Replica of *Metropolis* robot created for the museum in the 1960s by the film's art director, Schülze Mittendorf.

*Courtesy of Hugues Langlois*

Henri explains Eisenstein's theories of montage as applied to *The Battleship Potemkin*.

© by Guidotti/Courtesy of *Elle*

The "Cinémathèque under the Queensboro Bridge" project model interior by I. M. Pei.

*Courtesy of I. M. Pei & Partners Architects.  Photographer George Gabriel*

Jean Riboud, CEO of Schlumberger Ltd. and a friend and sponsor of the Cinémathèque.

Alfred Hitchcock offered Langlois a heady gift: Mrs. Bates from *Psycho*.

© Pierre Boulat—Cosmos

Hollywood triumphantly welcomes Henri Langlois as the "de Gaulle of Cinema," here between the producer Darryl F. Zanuck and the actress Gloria Swanson. Behind Henri is the director Otto Preminger.

*Courtesy of the Cinémathèque Française*

...enri receives a special Oscar from Gene Kelly, 1974.

*...rtesy of the Academy of Motion Picture Arts and Sciences. Photograph by ...edy and Long*

The Henri Langlois Cinema Museum is reinaugurated in 1980 by Minister of Culture Jean-Philippe Lecat. Next to Lecat is Mary Meerson.

© Hugues Langlois

Akira Kurosawa (here pictured next to Mary Meerson) in Paris in 1980 for the French release of his film *Kagemusha*, winner of that year's Palme d'or at the Cannes Film Festival. In his acceptance speech, the director dedicated his best picture prize to his late friend Henri Langlois.

*Hugues Langlois*

Henri Langlois monument, inaugurated 13 January 1991, Montparnasse Cemetery.

*Hugues Langlois*

Henri Langlois pays his respects to the reader.

*Courtesy of the Cinémathèque Française*

**Photo Research: Hugues Langlois**

Through his majestic knack for programming, Langlois seems to have succeeded at what he called "education by osmosis," programming that "must be subtle to serve creativity." Nonetheless, the film profession at that time still considered those who attended the Cinémathèque Française to be abnormal. Anyone who admitted to going there was classified among *les rats de la Cinémathèque*, degenerate losers who couldn't make films without stuffing their heads full of other films first. They forgot—or had never known—that Orson Welles had gone to MOMA to steep himself in the films of Stroheim and others before beginning *Citizen Kane*. Nicole Védrès had fun reminding us that "if one applied this same criteria to writers, it would be hilarious."

"Can one imagine," exclaimed Eric Rohmer, "a budding musician faced with the impossibility of listening to the works of Bach or Beethoven? In the name of what would one refuse the same rights to young filmmakers or critics?"

Despite the attempts Astruc, Malle, Melville, Vadim, and Varda made to break out of the system, in the 1950s the idea that one could not make a feature film before the age of 40 continued to prevail. That idea had to go. In 1958 François Truffaut was refused an invitation to the Cannes festival under the pretext that his articles were too virulent. At Cannes the following year, he had gone from unacceptably nasty critic to more than acceptably innovative filmmaker. At 27, Truffaut won the prize for best director for *Les 400 Coups*.

The same year, Alain Resnais showed his first feature, *Hiroshima, mon amour*. In recalling this success, Resnais points out that there was another preconceived notion, "the belief that if one made short films, one could not make features. At that time, people regarded these as two truly separate professions. Even so far as the union was concerned, there was a cameraman's card for short films and one for cameramen on feature films, as if they were two completely different jobs. Fortunately, the generation of Truffaut, Godard, Rivette, and Rohmer blasted away that taboo—which, thanks to Chabrol, finally allowed me to make *Hiroshima, mon amour* several months later. If Chabrol had not made *Le Beau serge*, I don't think a producer would ever have had the audacity to entrust me with a big film, since I had made only shorts before."

The movement was launched, and it was unquestionably a revolution for the French cinema. Like a relay team, as one set of critics put down their pens in order to grab cameras, another whole new set of critics took their place pushing pens, only to give birth in turn to new directors. If the most well known are Chabrol, Godard, Truffaut, Rohmer, and Rivette, one should not forget that the New Wave comprised no fewer than 30 young men and women who made their first feature film at that time. In 1976 Langlois, speaking in the language of the New World, modestly appraised his role in the birth of the New Wave:

People say that they came to the Cinémathèque and that this is the reason they became filmmakers. The New Wave claims they became inspired while watching films at the Cinémathèque. But they needed talent. At the same time, however, I know people who went each day to the Cinémathèque, French critics especially (I don't want to give you their names . . .); they came during five years every day for each show, and each time their reaction was so stupid that it became obviously a problem of what people have inside their heads and their hearts. The Cinémathèque is a place where you may go to see films and meet people. But if you are a sheep, if you are blind, you may see all the films and understand nothing.

I don't like people who take notes about a film. I like people who love the cinema. I wanted the Cinémathèque to be a place where one can be nourished by the cinema. When you eat and drink, you become stronger. To take notes while eating is stupid. Do you think the great painters went to museums to take notes? No, they went there to be fed. . . .

So for me, if you want to define the spirit of the Cinémathèque, it is antieducational. Because if you read the other film archives' introductions to films, they say this film is very good for this reason or that. The Cinémathèque shows films, but we never say whether they are good or bad. People come to see the films without prejudice. They discover for themselves what is bad or good. If we must explain to you what is good, you are only a monkey—you repeat what I say to you.

chapter 9

# THE DRAGON'S SECRET

A certain great and powerful king once asked a poet, "What can I give you of all that I have?" He wisely replied, "Anything, Sire, except your secret."

Opening quotation from Orson Welles's *Mr. Arkadin*

Although the Cinémathèque no longer had the space to set up a permanent museum or even temporary exhibitions, Henri Langlois continued to look for posters, costumes, sets, photos, and any other cinema-related objects he could get his hands on. In fact, it was during the 1950s that the Cinémathèque's collection of cinemabilia—objects apart from the films themselves—grew in nearly geometric progression. This was in large part owing to the indefatigable work of Lotte Eisner. Langlois knew how to choose co-workers as passionate and intuitive as he himself. When Eisner became the Cinémathèque's curator after Jean Mitry's departure in 1946, Henri told her, "Dear Lotte, we will never get any rest! We must find new objects for the museum before it's too late."

"Henri, at this pace, you're going to die way ahead of me," she sighed.

"The best way to get around dying is to be dead already!" Henri responded, laughing. "The next letter I send you, I'll sign it 'D.C.D.'" (These three initials, pronounced in French, sound like the French word for "deceased": *décédé*.)

Lotte loved Henri's jokes and could refuse him nothing. One day he interrupted her at her classification work: "Stop what you're doing. Go drop in on all the art directors in Paris and see what you can find. Begin with Max Douy, who's a friend. Do it quickly—one never knows."

Lotte rushed over to Douy's house and buried herself in his boxes full of sketches and renderings. She took out a number of film drawings, paused, and then took out still more. "But Lotte," protested Douy, "you're taking the most beautiful things!"

"I don't know why, but I believe I must take them today."

The next day, Lotte, continuing her rounds, went to see Jean d'Eaubonne, a disciple of Meerson and a former student of the sculptor Bourdelle. D'Eaubonne opened the door and greeted his visitor with these words: "Ah, poor Max!"

"What's wrong with Max?" she asked. "I was at his place yesterday, and he seemed fine."

"You don't know? There was a fire in his apartment, and all of his set designs burned."

"That's awful!" exclaimed Lotte. "Do you know where he is? I must call him at once."

When she reached Douy he had these words for her: "Thank you, dear Lotte. I give everything you took yesterday to the Cinémathèque as a gift, because you're the one who saved them."

To meet Langlois's demands, Lotte became a great traveler. She covered so much territory that Henri nicknamed her "My Lady of the Sleeping Cars"—an allusion to a famous French film from the early 1950s, *Ma madonne des sleepings*. On the occasion of the Berlin Festival, Lotte decided to return to the German capital she had fled 25 years earlier. Once there, she began looking for the great art directors she had known before the war. Robert Herlth, whose career spanned all of German cinema history, gave her many gifts for the Cinémathèque Française. Rohrig, an art director of the 1920s, was dead, but Lotte succeeded in finding his son and buying some of Rohrig's works from him. A quick sidetrip to East Berlin proved so fruitful that she returned weighed down with a cardboard suitcase so full that with each step Lotte feared it would burst open and scatter all her treasures. In order to catch her breath, she stopped at the German film archive. But when the solicitous director wanted at all costs to help her—"That suitcase is too heavy for you; let me take care of it"—Lotte was obliged to flee, leaving the poor man both emptyhanded and flabbergasted. Yet Lotte had feared that her bag might burst and reveal to the director the "local" goodies she was taking back to France.

Another time, Langlois told Lotte, "Thanks to you, we have many of Fritz Lang's things from *Die Niebelungen*, *Metropolis*, and *The Testament of Dr. Mabuse*. But we're missing stuff from Lubitsch's German films."

By a combination of circumstances, Lotte, while a guest of her sister-in-law in England, heard a Professor Stern mentioned. "But that was the set designer for Max Reinhardt and also Lubitsch," Lotte said. "Do you know if he's still alive?"

"No," answered the sister-in-law. "He's dead."

"Well, then, I'll have to find his widow!"

Like Miss Marple in an Agatha Christie novel, Lotte followed numerous leads. Her detective work paid off, and she succeeded in tracing the elderly woman in question to a hospital. Alas, Lotte was too late. Stern's widow was so sick that the doctors would not give Lotte permission to see her. Lotte, refusing to be discouraged, telephoned everyone under the sun, and managed to learn the whereabouts of a gentleman named Hopkins, who translated French books and whose wife was none other than Stern's daughter. As luck would have it, Mrs. Hopkins still had all of her father's theater and cinema sets and wanted to sell them for a reasonable price. From that same trip Lotte brought back not only a large number of set designs from Lubitsch films, but also a copy of *Waxworks* by Paul Leni. "My greatest reward," remembered Lotte, "was Henri's beaming face. He was as happy as can be."

Marion Michelle, executive secretary of the FIAF, also played an important role in this ongoing treasure hunt. In June 1957 she announced to Langlois that she planned to spend the month of July in Hollywood, visiting her father. Henri could barely conceal his glee. What better opportunity for the Cinémathèque than to have someone in Los Angeles for an entire month searching for cinemabilia? Langlois already saw himself in possession of costumes worn in the most famous American films. He need only convince Marion Michelle to be his ambassador in Hollywood. Langlois was a master of persuasion, and Marion Michelle soon found herself saying she'd be more than happy to oblige. What was supposed to be a one-month visit turned into a two-and-a-half-month sojourn that can only be deemed a major stroke of luck for Langlois and his future cinema museum.

Before her departure, Henri supplied Marion Michelle with numerous letters of introduction and gave her a seven-page list of all the objects he was looking for. Upon their arrival, in a whirlwind of activity Marion Michelle and her husband, Jean Guyard, contacted numerous movie celebrities. Walt Disney contributed original cells and backgrounds of his most famous cartoon characters and agreed to lend some of his films for an upcoming retrospective in Paris. King Vidor parted with scripts for *Hallelujah!* and *War and Peace*. Marion met with Jean Renoir, who was in Los Angeles at the time, and walked away with several scripts, plus a 35-millimeter print of *Swamp Water*. Dudley Nichols donated some of the scripts he wrote for John Ford films. Finally, Michelle even obtained Murnau's orginal script for *Sunrise*.

Although it is easy to rattle off these finds, let it not be assumed that these precious objects fell into the arms of Langlois's emissary like so much ripe fruit that need only be gathered up off the ground. From Paris, Langlois fired off daily telegrams and letters, full of astute pointers. His communiqués, which Michelle judiciously followed, reveal a man with a colossal store of film knowledge, as well as a diplomat's skill.

Henri loved costumes. But where to find them, and how to acquire them? Kenneth Anger, who was still in Paris, had told Langlois that the Western Costume Company in Hollywood frequently bought up used costumes from the studios in order to then rent them to the public. So one afternoon Michelle and her husband went to the company's office on Sunset Boulevard. Once they'd seen the size of the collection, they realized that one trip would not be enough. Much to their delight, during the days that followed they would find a Vivien Leigh dress from *Gone with the Wind*, a Douglas Fairbanks outfit from *The Black Pirate*, Rudolph Valentino's tunic from *The Son of the Sheik*, Mae West's serpent hat from *Going to Town*, and many other costumes.

But there was the problem of price. The Cinémathèque might not have the kind of money it would take to buy them, thought a worried Marion Michelle. Langlois stopped jumping up and down just long enough to wire back: "I received your telegrams this morning and confirm my telegram. First the costumes. How could I possibly pass up having a Fairbanks costume and one of Valentino's in the museum? I had never hoped for such a thing, and I cried my eyes out over this gap. Since you're there and you know better than I just how far we can lower our offer without losing the whole deal, I prefer that you set the price. Your price will be mine. . . . My dear Marion, every day I offer you with love 1,000 bouquets of flowers."

Michelle and Guyard quickly made an appointment with the director of the Western Costume Company to explain to him that they were looking for old film costumes in order to display them in a museum. Marion spoke of the Cinémathèque and of Langlois's determination to preserve the most prestigious souvenirs of American film. The director was at first interested only in the material aspect of the affair, but Michelle managed to convince him of the Cinémathèque's unselfish motive—so much so that he ended up inviting the couple to lunch, in the course of which he announced that, all things considered, he would make an outright gift to the Cinémathèque Française of several costumes.

Langlois, however, was insatiable. Buoyed by Marion Michelle's first achievements, he again wrote her:

Useless to tell you that for me, the costume is ideal when it combines the actor and a set element. That's why the Valentino and Blas costumes you refer to seem to me excellent. As far as women go, it's obviously Garbo, Marlene, and Mae West who take precedence. But for Garbo, I would prefer a costume either from the *Flesh and the Devil* period, 1920, or *Anna Karenina* style or *Camille*. For Marlene, we can always ask for a modern costume, for which the ideal would be *The Woman Is a Devil* [sic]. For Mae West, any costume, style 1900. For the silent stars, if you can have Louise Brooks's feather costume, I am fainting. If you can have the Nazimova big overcoat in *Salome*, I'm dying. If you can have a Lillian Gish costume,

Griffith type or Sjöström type, I'm enraptured. But if you can have a costume from the Babylon part of *Intolerance*, I'm going crazy. And if you can
have a Keaton costume or one from Chaplin (I doubt that he kept much of
anything since he left), you save our honor.

Among the other films, a man's costume, even something an extra wore
in Cukor's *Romeo and Juliet*, is worth the trouble. And I will not refuse you a
Bette Davis costume, the red dress from *Jezebel* or any one from *Elizabeth*.
There I go, I'm becoming greedy and lyrical. Let's come back down to
earth: Don't forget that I have Stroheim's costume and that consequently,
if the proposed costumes are too expensive, give up the battle.

Armed with letters of introduction from Langlois and from novelist
Romain Gary, who was the Los Angeles French consul, Marion Michelle and
Jean Guyard tried to organize a meeting with Cecil B. DeMille, who
Hollywood then considered to be God on Earth. DeMille, who had just finished *The Ten Commandments*, was an institution at Paramount and next to
impossible to meet. After two or three weeks of waiting, Marion Michelle
decided that something had to be done. She called Paramount and insisted
on obtaining an appointment that same day, saying that she represented the
Cinémathèque Française and that she and her husband had traveled all the
way from Paris solely to meet Cecil B. DeMille. Faced with her insistence,
the secretary finally gave in and told her to come by the studio.

And so the couple left for Paramount in a rented car. It was extremely hot
outside. They were obliged to wait a long time in a stifling hot office before
finally being guided into the gigantic air-conditioned office of Cecil B.
DeMille. Since Jean Guyard does not speak English, he did not say a word,
but DeMille addressed him and Jean had to pretend he understood, embar-
rassed at the idea that DeMille might ask him the slightest question.

Marion Michelle took charge and tried to explain the role the
Cinémathèque played in France. She hit upon a striking image in comparing
it to the Louvre—a sort of Louvre of the cinema. But DeMille seemed
strangely reserved. In fact, he did not think much of the Cinémathèque. It so
happened that Langlois's reputation in Hollywood was not all that positive.
Many producers at that time were suspicious that Langlois wanted to monop-
olize films for the Cinémathèque and had heard that he failed to return
loaned prints. Langlois, aware of these rumors, included a paragraph or two
in his letters to DeMille reassuring him that the Cinémathèque took great
care with the documents and films that were lent to it and reiterated the
strictly cultural and noncommercial nature of the Cinémathèque.

Langlois not only sent Marion Michelle a list of names of those she
should meet, but included a summation of the psychology of each celebrity
and the way he or she should be treated. Langlois had a psychoanalyst's
knack for intuiting the needs of directors he had never met. Thus, for
DeMille, he wrote:

Tell him how much we admire him, how much we would like to host a tribute to him in Paris. Remind him that we already wrote about him for the
sixtieth anniversary, remind him that he replied to us that he was busy
preparing *The Ten Commandments* but was prepared to lend us all the material for a grand exhibition about him, and ask him anyway, for the Paris
museum, for documents corresponding to the different steps in his marvelous career.

Flatter, flatter, flatter. He's a man who is so accustomed to flattery that
if by misfortune one doesn't flatter him enormously, he will imagine, like
Matisse, that one doesn't admire him.

Langlois's pointers did the trick, and DeMille soon agreed to donate some
photos and drawings and to lend several of his films for a Paris retrospective.
Langlois's letters show a man at the zenith of his career. Far from being disorganized, Langlois, when it came to programming, planned months and even
years in advance for the retrospectives he hoped to show the rue d'Ulm
crowds. Writes Langlois:

You cannot know, dear Marion, the joy I experience at the idea of putting
on this DeMille retrospective at a moment when the snobs find it fashionable to write him off as the symbol of commercial superproductions.

If we can pull off this program, it would be such a slap in the face to the
imbeciles and such a revelation to all those who are unaware of the
immense artistic importance of DeMille that I dance with joy and I sacrifice
to C. B. DeMille the dates I had reserved for Charlie Chaplin. We will
postpone his tribute until spring 1958, to make it coincide with the release
of his new film. But I find that it is more important for the Cinémathèque
Française to make the DeMille homage than to make an homage to
Chaplin, which is what everyone thinks we're supposed to do.

Despite all his efforts, Langlois was unable to obtain some of the films,
and, with the Cinémathèque's move from the rue Spontini to the rue de
Courcelles in January 1958, the exhibition did not take place. A much
smaller tribute to DeMille was eventually held in June 1959.

Upon her return to Paris, Marion Michelle wrote a report for Langlois
that describes in detail the welcome she received at various film organiza-
tions in the United States, including the Los Angeles County Museum, the
Academy of Motion Picture Arts and Sciences, and the Motion Picture
Association of America, as well as contacts with Universal, Columbia,
Warner, and MGM, all of whom were willing to eventually donate films to
the Cinémathèque. These contacts served as a strong base for further trips to
Hollywood by Lotte Eisner and Henri Langlois during the 1960s and 1970s.

In 1966 Henri would be welcomed in Japan as a king. In a country whose emperor is still considered to be a god, Langlois personified the god

of cinema. But such a greeting was not only a measure of gratitude for the efforts Langlois had begun in Antibes back in 1950 to make the Japanese cinema known. There was much more to the story than that. Everything began after the war, when Kashiko Kawakita came to Europe with her husband, hoping to establish contacts that might lead to the distribution of Japanese films. She had met Lotte Eisner at the Berlin Festival in 1953, and the two women had fast become friends. Two years later, Mrs. Kawakita was invited to Henri Langlois's great exhibition "60 Years of Cinema":

> My first impression of Langlois was of a man with great dignity, a true king. He had a faraway look like Louis XIV, very aristocratic. He impressed me a lot.
>
> From Paris I went to London, where I met Derek Prouse of the British Film Institute, who was preparing the plans for the exhibition that Langlois would next take on to London. Prouse asked me if I could obtain material about the Japanese cinema for the occasion. I then brought some photos and posters, and it was during the exhibition that I saw Langlois again. Prouse and he stopped by my house on Half Moon Street, unannounced. Rather shocked at their impromptu visit, I served them green Japanese tea. All of a sudden, Langlois suggested a great Franco-Japanese exchange of films. He offered me 150 French films in exchange for an equal quantity of Japanese films. That bothered me a lot, since the archives of the Tokyo Film Library only had roughly 20 films at the time. But Langlois's voice was so authoritative that I accepted out of obedience. I settled for telling him that I would do my best but that it would take me time to make the copies.

Mrs. Kawakita nonetheless succeeded in sending to Paris 15 films by Ozu and Kurosawa that could be projected at the Musée pédagogique. It did not take Langlois long to realize the poverty suffered by the National Film Library in Tokyo, but he had the tact to say nothing. During the 1950s, Japan was not yet the great industrial country whose cutting-edge technology would conquer the Western world. If the 1951 peace treaty had enabled the nation to keep its emperor, the country was still suffering from the aftermath of defeat. At the end of the fighting, the American authorities had clamped down on Japanese film production, and this action helped account for the lack of films in the Japanese film archive.

In January 1957, at the rue d'Ulm, Langlois showed *The Men Who Tread on the Tiger's Tail*, *No Regrets for Our Youth*, *Drunken Angel*, *Rashomon*, *Ikiru*, *The Idiot*, and *The Seven Samurai*. In the text he wrote about Kurosawa for the twentieth anniversary of the Cinémathèque, Langlois explains that he can only partly open a window on the cinematic art of Japan, since almost nothing remains: "The war and fire ravaged Japan, and its best films produced over 50 years are no longer in the hands of those who hoped to preserve them. It will require great devotion and much research for film archives around the world to help the Japanese cinémathèque to find some of its films and to reconstruct, at least partly, the heritage of Japanese cinematographic art."

Langlois himself would render this immense service following a string of extraordinary circumstances. Film historian Jay Leyda was working for a television station in London when he literally walked into Henri Langlois one day in 1955. They had not seen each other since their meeting in New York at the 1939 FIAF congress. After having worked with Eisenstein, Leyda was hired by the MOMA Film Library in New York. He told Langlois that, despite several years of intense work, he was beginning to have doubts whether he would ever finish his mammoth volume on Russian/Soviet cinema, eventually titled *Kino*. Langlois offered Leyda a part-time post at the Cinémathèque that would give him the time to finish his book. Leyda did not hide his interest but admitted that he still remained attracted by the possibilities offered in the United States. He would in fact work next for the Library of Congress in Washington and during the following two years assist Langlois by sending him catalogs and all sorts of information about the American cinema.

Then Langlois wrote Leyda that he could spend a year at the Cinémathèque as a researcher for the International Bureau of Cinematographic Historical Research (BIRC), as well as begin cataloging the collection of Pathé newsreels and films produced in Berlin and Moscow before World War I.

Langlois's letters to Leyda demonstrate yet again Henri's enthusiasm for and extraordinary knowledge of foreign movies. Jay Leyda responded with serious film research, including an astonishing discovery concerning Japanese and German movies:

Dear Henri,

On the way to you is a staggering list of all the German films confiscated (here and in Germany) by the U.S. authorities. This may explain why you and Lotte have difficulties in tracing certain German titles. Congress may return these to their owners (where they can be determined!) next year.

Here is also a similar Japanese list. The history of this confiscation has implications more nasty than I had ever realized—worse than what happened to your carefully preserved U.S. films in Paris. The only way to get anything [now] from either the German or Japanese list is through their foreign ministries, instructing their ambassadors in Washington to request [the films]. Because I had heard that Japan had extremely few of its wartime or prewar films, I thought that list might encourage a Japanese series *chez vous*. I did not then guess the connection between the list and the empty Japanese vaults—but it now seems a great service that you could do for Japanese films by taking some official action.

Henri immediately contacted the embassies concerned but also intervened in Washington, strengthened by his position as secretary-general of the International Federation of Film Archives. Henri bombarded the authorities with so many official procedures that the cultural treasures of Japanese cinema were finally restituted to their original country. Before sending them away, around 1958, the Library of Congress made 16-millimeter copies, whereupon the original 35-millimeter prints were returned. The National Film Library in Tokyo was soon on its way to becoming a major film archive.

Jay Leyda arrived at the Cinémathèque in September 1957. He did not have much luck, since his arrival coincided with the moment when the Cinémathèque was about to move once again and therefore most of the collections were in storage. He would never see the Pathé negatives on which he was supposed to work, but he did bring his own treasure with him. Jay Leyda had edited together a two-part, four-hour, 16-millimeter film of Eisenstein's *Que Viva Mexico!*—footage called "Eisenstein's Mexican Film: Episodes for Study." There has probably never been an adventure more complex in the history of cinema than that of Eisenstein and his Mexican film. An entire volume would not be sufficent to understand the problems between Eisenstein and his producer, Upton Sinclair. The director had launched himself into the most grandiose of projects. He had shot more than 60,000 meters of film in his determination to retrace the history of the entire Mexican civilization from before the discovery of the New World up until 1931. Sinclair accused him of having shot a film so complex and unwieldy that even Eisenstein himself could not make something out of it. And yet the great Russian director apparently *was* the only one who could turn the mass of film stock shot into the monumental work he had dreamed of. Eisenstein's departure for Moscow and his disagreement with Upton Sinclair and his wife were behind the edited versions called *Thunder over Mexico* and the *Kermesse Funèbre*; that left roughly 50,000 meters of unedited film stock, most of which would eventually find its way into the MOMA storage vaults in New York.

Langlois had insisted that Leyda bring his version to Paris. Leyda complied, and during his first month at the Cinémathèque, Langlois borrowed the films and then, much to Leyda's chagrin, made illegal copies of them without his or MOMA's permission. Then, without any warning, Langlois asked Leyda to resign from his post! To his dying day, Leyda was not sure why Langlois made such an irrational request. But since he had made plans to stay in Paris for the year to try to finish *Kino*, Leyda ended up ignoring Langlois's demand. He eventually helped Simone Cottance with the still photo collection.

One day during Leyda's beleaguered stay at the Cinémathèque, he was reading at a desk when Langlois burst into the room and, in a determined whisper, commanded: "Get under your desk immediately!" Leyda played along with Langlois's whim and positioned himself under the desk, whence he could see people only from the waist down. Langlois left the room and returned a minute later, talking to someone in broken English. From his low-level vantage point Leyda saw two shapely female legs saunter by. It was a memorable position and an unforgettable moment, since those legs belonged to Louise Brooks. Leyda assumes that Langlois made such a bizarre request so Brooks would not feel the urge to stop and speak to a fellow American.

Louise Brooks had come from the United States at Langlois's invitation in order to attend a special retrospective of films in which she had starred. After the projection of *Pandora's Box*, Langlois threw a large reception in her honor.

Today everybody thinks that Louise Brooks was always Langlois's favorite star; however, she only really entered into his life in 1953. At that time, she was long forgotten by the general public but, thanks to James Card, on the brink of dethroning the stars of Henri's youth. Card sets the record straight about the rediscovery of Louise Brooks:

> The article I wrote in *Sight and Sound*, beginning as it does with quotations of Henri's enthusiasm, gives the impression that he initiated the drive and always admired her. What really happened was that in 1953, during my first visit to the Cinémathèque, I asked to see both *Pandora's Box* and *Diary of a Lost Girl*. Henri refused: He then had no interest in either film and apparently knew nothing of Louise Brooks. It was Mary who talked him into showing them to me. "After all, Valeska Gert is worth watching in *Trois Pages*," she argued. So they showed me both films, and Henri watched with me. Fascinated, he fell in love at first sight. *Then* he started to learn about Louise.
>
> This rediscovery of *Pandora* at the Cinémathèque spurred me to renew the hunt. Back in the States, I searched high and low and finished by catching up with her in 1955. But not until I returned from Henri Langlois's astonishing exhibition in 1955 did it seem imperative to let Louise Brooks know that, after 25 years in limbo, Paris had restored her to stardom.

Langlois had hung a huge photo of Louise Brooks at the entrance to his exhibition at the Palais de Tokyo in 1955. Her arresting visage created surprise and considerable interest among visitors. To one critic who asked him why he had chosen an unknown, Langlois retorted, "Garbo does not exist; Dietrich does not exist. There is only Louise Brooks."

Meanwhile, James Card had persuaded the former actress to come up to Rochester so he could show her, at long last, the films she had appeared in but never wished to see. He wanted to convince her of her talent and perhaps even inspire her to step back onto the screen. That day, Louise Brooks fell in love not with her own talent but with the movies themselves. She had never taken a serious interest in films, but with these screenings she finally understood what her contribution had been. With Card's help, she began viewing hundreds of films at the George Eastman House and decided to write about the cinema. When Henri came to see her in Rochester, he was not in the least surprised to discover that Louise Brooks knew much of Proust by heart. "For Langlois," says Card, "Louise Brooks turned out to be not a whit more or less of an extraordinary being than he had expected."

In his program for the 1955 projections, Henri penned this portrait of Louise Brooks in the form of a declaration of love:

> Those who have seen her can never forget her. She is the modern actress par excellence because, like the statues of antiquity, she is outside of time.
>
> One need only look upon her to believe in beauty, in life, in the reality of human beings; she has the naturalness that only primitives retain before the lens. . . .
>
> She is the intelligence of the cinematographic process, she is the most perfect incarnation of *photogénie*, and she embodies in herself all that the cinema rediscovered in its last years of silence: complete naturalness and complete simplicity.
>
> Her art is so pure that it becomes invisible.

Langlois therefore helped to restore Louise Brooks to the history of movies. But she will always remain more famous in France than in the United States. When Brooks died in August 1985, her death was front-page news in the French press. Her photo stared out from the kiosks with the same undiminished power it had held 30 years before at the Palais de Tokyo. Lengthy articles attempted to elaborate what Langlois had so concisely said. In the United States, with a few rare exceptions, the death of "the most perfect incarnation of *photogénie*" was only briefly mentioned.

The Cinémathèque's offices at the rue Spontini were subleased from the producer Sacha Gordine. Gordine belonged to that brand of "take all risks" producers that Henri admired. His perseverance and love of his profession made him well liked by all. Yet Gordine was always on a financial tightrope. When he no longer had the means to hang on to his little jewel of real estate on the rue Spontini, Langlois once again found himself out on the street. This time Henri got mad—the Cinémathèque could not be condemned to wander eternally. Henri cajoled and badgered the public authorities into helping him obtain a headquarters worthy of the institution. After many administrative complications, the Cinémathèque moved to 82, rue de Courcelles, in the eighth arrondissement, just a block away from the parc Monceau.

Henri was ecstatic. This building was his to decorate, and he had elegant home improvements in mind. He set out to adorn the premises with eighteenth-century pillars, to frame the second-floor landing with Louis XV balusters, and, to accentuate the ceremonial effect, to add solid mahogany columns. He had Madame Pompadour's doors remounted on their rightful hinges in the salon on the second floor. Langlois took advantage of the large reception halls, where he positioned the rarest and most peculiar objects in his collection. The contrast between Old World elegance and newfangled invention was invigorating. Visitors to the rue de Courcelles entered a world of the marvelous, past and future. Here at last was a headquarters worthy of the Cinematheque Française. And so it would remain until Langlois's death.

General Charles de Gaulle had returned to power in June 1958 and shortly thereafter created France's Fifth Republic. André Malraux was named minister of culture. Malraux was both a member of the Cinémathèque and a long-standing admirer of Henri Langlois. Since the Liberation, the two men had met several times, and Malraux had always entrusted Langlois with the authority to vote in his name at the Cinémathèque's General Assemblies. The 1959 Cannes festival would be the occasion for the minister of culture to issue this promise: "I will make the Cinémathèque Française the richest and finest in the world." A little later, according to Lotte Eisner, Malraux turned to Henri Langlois and, gesturing toward his suitcoat, said, "You have nothing here."

Confused, Langlois at first thought, "Not again—I must have managed to get another stain on my jacket." Then he realized that Malraux was indicating that he had no Légion d'honneur ribbon in his lapel.

"You know," Langlois replied, "I would much rather have some money for the Cinémathèque. France lost out on the Cromer collection—which existed before the Cinémathèque—when the Americans bought it for the George Eastman House. Lotte can tell you that I sent her to see Madame Cromer, but it was already too late. It was a great loss for France, but we can make up for that. There is another collection I've had my eyes on for some time, and that's the precious English collection assembled by Will Day."

And Henri, like the connoisseur he was, proceeded to describe the rare and wondrous objects in the collection. Will Day had mostly preserved objects from the prehistory of cinema: Chinese shadow puppets, magic lanterns, hundreds of hand-painted glass slides. There were praxinoscopes, zoetropes and phénakisticope disks. Though their names were strange, their magic was accessible. These forgotten gizmos had entertained thousands in their day and could do so again if only Henri could get his hands on them. The collection also included Faraday's wheel, the first Edison Kinetoscope shown in London at the end of 1893, a Lumière *Cinématographe*, William Friese-Greene's films, and hundreds of documents, books, and magazines.

Malraux left Henri with these simple words: "Do what you think best. I will obtain the necessary funds."

Langlois did not waste a second and started negotiations with Will Day's sons. The price, after close negotiation, was set at 17 million old francs. Malraux kept his promise, and the contract was signed on 7 December 1959.

Today a major part of the collection is on display in the Henri Langlois Museum of Cinema.

As for the Légion d'honneur, in an intimate ceremony at the rue de Courcelles on 20 November 1959, Ambassador Yves Chataigneau took care of the "missing spot" on Langlois's suitcoat. Chataigneau reminded Langlois of their first meeting, in 1936, when young Henri and Georges Franju had come to ask for the Foreign Ministry's help for the newly founded Cinémathèque Française.

Although Langlois was pleased with the decoration, he almost never wore it. When he absolutely had to wear it for the visit of an official, someone had to sew it on his jacket at the last minute. The accompanying ribbon grew progressively narrower until it would have been simpler to put a red thread in its place.

Françoise Jaubert, the daughter of the composer Maurice Jaubert, came to Langlois in early 1958 to ask his advice about finding a job. Her children had grown up, and she had decided to go back to work. She spoke English and knew a little something about the cinema. She also knew how to type. Jaubert had come looking for advice, and Henri advised her to become his secretary. They got along very well, although they did have some peculiar fights. One day she pointed out to him, "You can't write that. Syntactically, it's not French."

He shot back, "Oh yes I can. Don't forget that I'm a Turk!"

What was the point of trying to contradict him? Like everyone else who ever worked with Langlois, Françoise Jaubert quickly understood that she was not working for just any boss or just any firm.

> Langlois had a certain notion of the cinema as a family. If you belonged, it was because you loved the cinema for the right reasons. This was very important to him. He loved the cinema. He loved it more than anything else on earth. As a result, Langlois observed everything that happened in the world in terms of what it meant for the Cinémathèque Française. One morning after the French government had changed hands once again, I asked him what he thought. He immediately launched into what was good or bad about it for the Cinémathèque. In a way, he might have been wrong to distill everything in terms of cinema, but I think that this dedication was what made the Cinémathèque such an extraordinary place. We had quite a few interns who, since then, have come a long way. We all found the work interesting, and sometimes we enjoyed ourselves a lot.

During the inauguration of the building at the rue de Courcelles, Henri, who had just put the final touches to an exhibition devoted to film producer Charles Pathé, wanted to help Françoise Jaubert. Malraux was expected any minute, and Françoise was trying to vacuum the floor. Henri grabbed the vacuum cleaner from her hands: "Listen," he said, "you're doing it all wrong." He then proceeded to push the vacuum into the handrail of the stairway with such force that the detachable end shot off like a cannonball and went careening over the edge. A few moments later and it would have landed on Malraux's head. Which would have been a painful illustration of "a cultural vacuum."

The date 24 June 1959 was an important one for Henri and for all lovers of cinema. All the newspapers spoke of the imminent inauguration. *France-Soir* pointed out to its readers that Henri Langlois had not slept for four weeks. Paintbrush and thumbtacks in hand, he had been preparing the tribute to Charles Pathé that Malraux would unveil. The newspaper also recalled that 82, rue de Courcelles had housed the first gambling club of the famous François Andé, casino master of Deauville and of Cannes.

André Malraux visited the exhibition under the guidance of Cinémathèque President Léon Mathot. The minister of culture was particularly attracted to the abstract paintings Henri had hung in honor of his illustrious visitor. When Léon Mathot asked him what at the Cinémathèque he had found to be the most admirable, Malraux, who had plans to establish cultural centers nationwide, replied, "It is to see what the Cinémathèque staff has done with nothing and 23 years of work. I hope that before another year has passed, the Cinémathèque Française's films will be projected in all French cities, and that within three years, it will be the leading archive in the world."

But Henri had no intention of waiting three years. In one way or another, each day was dedicated to a permanent enrichment of the collections. With Lotte Eisner as intermediary, Langlois had been in contact for some time with Fritz Lang, who had promised to give his scripts to the Cinémathèque Française. On 21 August 1958, while Lang was in Berlin making *Tiger of Bengal/Journey to the Lost City* (two films released as one film in the United States), Henri wrote to him:

> I renew our desire to organize a tribute to you, as we had agreed, with the equal hope that it will provide an opportunity to place in safekeeping certain of your films not yet preserved by other archives.
>
> Lotte Eisner will explain to you, on the one hand, what we already possess and, on the other hand, what we can hope to unearth here in Paris, and finally, the little extra push you might provide that, in our experience, would ensure the success of our own efforts.
>
> It would truly be a shame not to make this a complete tribute, even though an incomplete tribute is better than none at all!

Making reference to the feverish flu that had taken hold of him during a preceding trip, Langlois concluded, "In the hope that it will be possible for you to come to Paris, and that we will be able to welcome you and count you among our guests, permit me to thank you again, since I think you saved my life with those two little glasses of alcohol and those pills."

The tribute took place 11–26 June 1959. Langlois showed 22 Lang films, including his most recent, *Journey to the Lost City* and *Tiger of Bengal*. It was the first time that the Viennese filmmaker had been in Paris since his short stay in 1933, when he came to France to make *Liliom*. He was greeted at the Cinémathèque by thundering applause, which deeply moved him. As soon as he returned to Berlin, the man behind M wrote to Lotte with words of congratulation on both the inauguration of the rue de Courcelles exhibition and the speech Malraux had given there on the future of the Cinémathèque. Lang added that his first contact with the Cinémathèque Française, after too many long years in the United States and in Germany, had enabled him to renew his ideas about the cinema. In describing himself as a perpetual exile, Lang wrote that it was at the Cinémathèque that he had found his haven. His letter ended as follows:

> Your reception in my honor profoundly touched me, since it proved to me that the hard work that has characterized my entire life was not carried out in vain. You showed me that it was fruitful for the young and that it still represents something for them today.
>
> Maybe my attitude was "I don't care," but Mary and Langlois cured me of that. And for that, I am deeply in their debt.

On the morning of Friday, 10 July 1959, work began as usual at the rue de Courcelles. In the courtyard lay films ready for return to either the Cinémathèque's warehouse at Bois d'Arcy or the distribution companies whence they had come. It was a glorious day and was already unusually hot by late morning. Françoise Jaubert was in her sunny office when suddenly she had the strange impression that a cloud had dipped down to look in at her through the window. Looking up, she understood that the cloud was in reality smoke. She immediately called the fire department.

On the other side of the courtyard, between the rue de Courcelles building and the rue Alfred-de-Vigny entrance, stood two coach houses in which were kept films designated for shipment, along with the 16-millimeter films ordinarily cared for by Michel Zimbacca, who was not there that day. It was in these coach houses that the fire started.

The fire quickly spread. Thick smoke swept through the spiral staircase, which led up to the photo library on the third floor. The noxious smoke had already filled the second-floor landing when the firefighters finally arrived and swiftly got the blaze under control.

There was, however, a moment of complete hysteria when the captain of the fire brigade exclaimed, "Do something! There's a madman on the second floor who's breaking everything!"

The madman was Henri, who was smashing all the showcases in order to retrieve the Cinémathèque's precious belongings. Chief among these was a beautiful eighteenth-century table that also served as a display case. Henri had placed Eisenstein's writings beneath its protective slab of antique glass. In breaking it with his bare fist, Henri had cut his hand badly. He bore the scars of that rescue mission until his death.

Fortunately, what could have been tragic became rather comic. Lotte Eisner was plopped down on the sidewalk, sitting guard over all the kineto-scopes and magic lanterns that Henri had hastily placed there. Encircled by admiring onlookers, she very much resembled a saleswoman at a flea market. And, like any good flea marketeer, she did not budge but instead guarded her goods with an attentive eye meant to discourage any attempt at theft.

When the fire was finally extinguished, it seemed that little had been destroyed. Still, sadness prevailed. Like a chimney sweeps' convention, all the employees were covered with soot from head to toe; they stayed around Henri late into the night to sort things out.

The event made the front page of all the newspapers, accompanied by a photo showing that distinctive smoke that escaped from the building when the firefighters intervened.

Sonika Bo was in Venice at a children's film festival when she learned of the fire, through the press. The news was of more than passing interest, since she had left films in the courtyard of the building. She cut her trip short and rushed back to Paris, where she found the employees, under Mary Meerson's orders, loading a truck with debris from the fire. Sparks flew when the two women met. According to Sonika Bo, when she demanded some sort of explanation, Mary threw her out of the building. Sonika, naturally enough, wanted to know all about the fire, discover whether any of her films had been spared, and find out the name of the insurance company concerned.

Those were hard questions to ignore, but what response could Mary possi-bly have given? Henri and Mary had been in the office when the fire began and yes, all of Sonika Bo's films had indeed gone up in smoke. Mary was furi-ous with her for having left them in the courtyard after countless warnings from Henri. The films were not insured—not by Sonika Bo, not by the Cinémathèque, and not by the lab. What insurance company would have agreed to insure—and at what price!—flammable films. Had Henri been on hand when Sonika Bo arrived, matters probably would not have worsened to the extent they did (as we shall soon see), nor would they have set off so much controversy. But Sonika Bo was outraged.

Langlois believed that the fire had started when the sun's rays, concen-trated by a glass overhang, had set off the spontaneous combustion of several films sitting in the courtyard. Henri's opinion was in keeping with laboratory tests conducted in the United States in 1949, tests establishing that old nitrate films can spontaneously ignite at a temperature of 41 degrees Celsius (105 degrees Fahrenheit). In fact, the heat that summer of 1959 was exceptional. Henri's explanation was thus plausible, and everyone had accepted it except Sonika Bo's companion, Jean Painlevé, who had more or less become the opposition leader in the Cinémathèque's General Assemblies.

As a scientist and filmmaker, Painlevé was aware of the chemical nature of film stock and Langlois's report just did not seem right to him. For one thing, according to Painlevé, who was not present at the fire, "no matter how hot it was that day, and it was at least in the upper 90s, I've made several experiments using nitrate prints and if the film was inside the cans, it would not spontaneously combust. To set fire would require the glass roof to act as a magnifying glass and condense the sunlight into a more intense beam. On the other hand, the slightest exposed heat source, like a lit cigarette, could trigger a fire. I'd had a couple of small fires and they were always triggered by hot cigarette ashes—ashes that remained red-hot for some time. American cigarettes and Oriental tobacco are hotter than French tobacco."

We needn't search for an anonymous culprit who smokes Marlboros or some exotic Oriental brand, for an eyewitness seems to have solved the riddle. The fire started while most of the employees were out for lunch. Besides Henri Langlois, Mary Meerson, Françoise Jaubert, Lotte Eisner, and Simone Cottance, there were three visitors there that day: William Novik, Lewis Jacob's wife, and Georges Franju.

Franju had happened to stop by the Cinémathèque that morning and 20 years later tells a different account:

> The fire in 1959 is a mystery that's not really a mystery. I was there by chance. Not having set foot in the Cinémathèque for quite some time, I happened to be there that day and the fire didn't take place the way everyone said it did.
>
> I was in the courtyard with one of the Cinémathèque employees when, all of a sudden, he remembered that he'd left a burning cigarette in the pocket of his coat, hung up in the storage room. That's what started the fire. What followed was a lot of smoke and a very small fire. If the fire had been worse, as it would have been with a quantity of nitrate stock, then everything would have exploded.

In any case, Sonika Bo lodged a complaint and affirmed to the press that Henri Langlois was refusing to show her the insurance policy. Langlois responded that the Cinémathèque's policy was that of any film lab: that is, everyone knew that films deposited there were never insured. Henri was deeply wounded by the aftermath of this affair. Although the flames, such as they were, had been rapidly extinguished, certain parties were still determined to fan them. Sonika Bo, one of his dearest friends, was behaving like his worst enemy. How could a measly little fire have touched off so much ill will on the part of someone he still loved dearly? How could anyone have dreamed that he would attempt to profit from a fire by stealing his best friend's films and then claiming they'd burned or by trying to collect nonexistent insurance compensation for the Cinémathèque? That Sonika had reached the point where she was willing to sue him under the pretext of clarifying the fire's true circumstances, all the while meaning to verify whether her films had truly burned, profoundly affected Henri and caused him immense grief.

For her part, Sonika Bo asserted that she had written repeatedly to Langlois without receiving a response, but had her letters actually reached him? The true crux of the quarrel most likely stemmed from the animosity between two equally headstrong women who, each in her own way, loved Henri. Sonika had been Henri's early true believer, and Henri had been the first adult to attend, for his pleasure alone, Sonika's Cinderella Club projections. At the most tragic moment of the Occupation, it was at Henri's house that she had sought refuge, and later on it was Henri who had paved the way for her at the Venice Festival. But Sonika Bo could not stand Mary Meerson, and it is altogether likely that Mary tossed Sonika's letters to Henri into the wastebasket.

Thinking about Sonika's lost films from the "Cinderella" days and the memories they evoked, Henri could not hold back his tears. One night, unable to contain himself, he showed up at her main-floor apartment in Neuilly. Instead of ringing the doorbell—not wanting to find himself nose to nose with Painlevé—he knocked at the window. The shutters opened up, and Sonika Bo motioned to him to climb in over the windowsill. This romantic entrance accentuated Henri's emotion, and he swore to her, with tears in his eyes, that he had had nothing to do with the loss of her films. Sonika demanded that he break off with Mary Meerson. Langlois burst into sobs. "That is the one thing I cannot do," he told her. Regardless, Sonika withdrew her lawsuit months later when Langlois helped her to reconstruct some of her collection.

In reality, the fire at the Cinémathèque Française did not—at least, not directly—have consequences as catastrophic as fires that have broken out in comparable settings elsewhere in the world. Few archives have escaped this terrible menace. This would be the only fire suffered by the Cinémathèque Française during Langlois's lifetime. But for those who have a passion for the cinema, the loss of films—any films—resonates as an irreparable sorrow. Henri sadly noted in the months to come that several George Eastman House films were lost in the fire, including Street Scene by King Vidor and A Social Celebrity by Malcolm Saint-Clair, along with 10 films from the Cinémathèque Suisse, including a tinted copy of Jean Epstein's Finis Terrae. Several Brazilian films that had been temporarily stored in the courtyard while awaiting shipment back to Sao Paulo also perished. But the loss that caused Langlois the most anguish was the loss of the second part of Stroheim's The Wedding March, called The Marriage of the Prince. No other copy of this film exists. Finally, independent of Sonika Bo's collection and the strains that ensued, the loss of a certain number of films belonging to the Polish film archive would have much graver consequences. All together, roughly 5,000 reels, or 50 feature films, were destroyed.

In a letter to James Card in 1967, Langlois as much as admits to a fire coverup: "When I had my fire, Mary begged me to minimize the importance of the losses, saying to me that since they were reparable, it was worth it to cover it up." Shortly after receiving that letter, Card received a 16-millimeter replacement print of *Street Scene*. Other archives, however, were not so lucky and never received the slightest compensation for their loss. At the very least, the Cinémathèque Française could have notified the other archives concerned, and offered its condolences. Yet in the mystery climate forever surrounding Langlois and his Cinémathèque, either Langlois had no idea which films were actually destroyed (and, logically enough, could not send his apologies, because he couldn't be sure whom to apologize to) or, worse yet, he knew but chose not to say, thereby using the fire as a tactic for keeping certain films that did not belong to him. In many instances, there was no way of knowing a film was missing until weeks, months, or even years later, the owner asked for it. When it was nowhere to be found, Langlois concluded that it must have been lost in the fire.

It should be kept in mind that a fire is not the kind of thing an archive is proud to announce. Eyewitnesses to the rue de Courcelles fire claim that very few films were actually destroyed, and so a coverup, wherein the whole thing was played down for the press, would be understandable if those victimized had been properly notified. The fire department report says that the fire was extinguished in a half-hour. If the claim that 5,000 reels burned is true, especially if some of them were nitrate, the fire would probably have gone on for longer, and as Georges Franju and Jean Painlevé implied, destroyed a good part of the rue de Courcelles building. The question still remains, if relatively few films were actually destroyed, then why were so many films eventually announced as having been destroyed? It might make a peculiar kind of sense to inflate the figures if the Cinémathèque holdings had been heavily insured, but they were not insured at all.

In a Cinémathèque board of directors' meeting during the 1960s, Langlois said:

> The 1959 fire re-created an abnormal situation and prolonged it until the end of 1962, since we could no longer store films in the courtyard. It entirely disorganized the film service, which was forced to function in three different locations separated by a distance of several kilometers. One cannot know to what extent the fire was fatal. It intervened at the moment when everything had found its place again, when all that remained was to finish the collections' inventory, reopen the library, and return to the level of services available under one roof at the avenue de Messine in 1954.

> In particular, without the fire there would never have been the Sonika
> Bo affair and, consequently, no FIAF affair.

Langlois's statement about Sonika Bo is obviously true. But his implication that had the fire not occurred there would have been "no FIAF affair" is patently untrue.

Few foreign archives were informed about the fire before the Stockholm FIAF convention, held more than two months later, from 20 to 27 September 1959. At the news of the fire, Henri's true friends commiserated with him in his grief. It never would have occurred to Freddy Buache, James Card, the president of Paramount, or the director of the Japanese film archive to blame Langlois for a fire for which he was not responsible. The Polish film archive, however, was in no position to adopt the same sympathetic attitude—not when its director was reprimanded by the Polish government, which blamed him for the loss of those films sent to the Cinémathèque.

The circumstances in which the rupture occurred between the Cinémathèque Française and the FIAF have always been left somewhat vague. Maybe it was preferable to do that at the time, so as not to offend people's sensibilities. As a result, the break was mostly attributed to a sort of sudden whim by Langlois. Langlois was certainly capable of sudden whims, but they did not generally concern influential international organizations that he himself had struggled not once but twice to establish.

In the background was Langlois's obsessive fear of pirating. It was the trust of the film owners—who felt that Langlois respected their rights just as much as he believed in the nonprofit dissemination of films—that had engendered the Cinémathèque's success. We already know what happened with *L'Age d'or*, and unfortunately, the future would prove that Langlois was not wrong in his suspicions that the sanctity of archival deposits was not being fully respected throughout the FIAF. According to film collector Raymond Rohauer, even the director of the MOMA Film Library, Richard Griffith, was not above suspicion. Shortly before Langlois's break with the FIAF, Griffith, acting as a special adviser for a television series called "Silence Please," had made an agreement to lend several films from the New York archive to American television and supposedly accepted bribes for this service. In any case, the matter ended up in court in the 1960s, and Griffith was fired. When the producer of the television show was charged with having illegally used MOMA's films, he accused Griffith. Rohauer claims that Griffith started drinking and went for a walk, more or less drunk, on a country road, when an automobile struck and killed him. Strangely enough, per Rohauer, Griffith was struck dead the night before he was supposed to testify in court.

To understand Henri's state of mind at the time of the FIAF break, it is helpful to refer to this letter he wrote to James Card on 3 August 1967:

In reality, under Griffith, such things were going on in New York, in the black market, that if one believes the rumors, it is impossible not to take them into account. Now it is obvious that Griffith, on the one hand—and I have the proof in his letters—let himself be compromised with some trades-men and that, on the other hand—in my opinion, without his knowl-edge—there were some clandestine leaks. And that sort of thing can't go on without complicity. Van Dyke took up a very heavy heritage. He is cer-tainly the last to know of the gangrene that was not limited to Griffith.

I myself only knew of certain things because people knew in New York that I was not getting along with MOMA, that I no longer had any contact with them, and at the time they said to themselves that perhaps I'd be interested in benefiting from this secret network, from these human dregs whom collectors were profiting from.

The event just goes to show that these lower elements still exist, and finally, it is more worthwhile to have the courage to destroy them. . . .

But, you know, I have a certain instinct, and that's why I am truly sorry that someone did not undertake an investigation at the museum about the sources of certain copies on the black market and that only Griffith was the object of a decision for dismissal. In all friendship and in all trust,

Henri Langlois

This letter, written seven years after the fact, provides some insight into Langlois's reactions to his FIAF colleagues, even if, as we will see, he got car-ried away.

Ernest Lindgren was then vice-president of the FIAF, and his sensibilities differed greatly from Langlois's. Henri had never forgotten the incident in which the film he had lent Lindgren had been returned punched like a Métro ticket. At the 1953 FIAF congress in Vence, Lindgren had been expansively proud to present his grandiose project for an international filing system. Langlois reminded him that the urgency of the moment demanded the saving of films before placing them on note cards.

In other words, Langlois did not have only friends on the FIAF board. With the fire at the rue de Courcelles only two months before, the Cinémathèque Française found itself in a vulnerable position when James Card received what he called "a stupid, self-incriminating letter from Lindgren spelling out the whole campaign and inviting me to join the plot 'for the good of the FIAF.'" The plot, it seems, was hatched by FIAF President Toeplitz and Vice-President Lindgren, who hoped to organize a consensus among FIAF members that Langlois's sloppy recordkeeping and his negligence concerning films were sufficent cause to have him voted out of office.

Always ready to cross swords in the spirit of a Don Quixote, Henri would charge straight ahead. But instead of using Griffith as a target, he accused Jacques Ledoux of the Belgian film archive of illegal activities. According to

Card, when Ledoux approached Warner Brothers in the United States about obtaining some prints, he took it upon himself to inform the studio that the George Eastman House had certain Harry Langdon films. As a result, Warner—which had been unaware of those prints until Ledoux mentioned them—eventually pulled those prints out of the Eastman House's vaults. Ledoux also directly contacted UNESCO in Paris to obtain other films, a clear breach of the FIAF bylaws, which state that no foreign film archive has the right to enter into negotiations for films directly with the owner unless there is no FIAF representative in that country. Neither the George Eastman House, MOMA, nor the Cinémathèque Française (for UNESCO) had been contacted in order to act as an intermediary for the Cinémathèque royale de Belgique.

Jean Raine had been at Henri's side throughout the period when Langlois had diligently supported the fledgling Belgian archive. According to him, Langlois had never forgiven Ledoux for the manner in which he had treated André Thirifays, the original director of the archive. As Raine claims,

> Ledoux had too much ambition, and you could tell just how badly he wanted Thirifays's place. He was able to profit from Thirifays's alleged "bad management" of the Belgian cinémathèque to achieve his ends. Ledoux had become the bone of contention. He had nonetheless done his basic training at the FIAF next to Langlois and, in a certain way, resembled him. No doubt Henri was exaggerating his complaints. Mary Meerson, on the contrary, liked Ledoux a lot. She counterbalanced Henri's impulses. On the one hand, Langlois wrote to Toeplitz to explain to him that Ledoux was a Machiavelli, and on the other hand, Mary, knowing that Toeplitz would be sure to pass the letter on to Ledoux, would put an embargo on it and see that the letter was never sent.

Whatever the reason may be, at the 1959 FIAF congress in Stockholm 20–27 September, Henri Langlois made a formal verbal protest against Ledoux. If Langlois's accusations proved to be true, the FIAF was in danger of losing the trust and respect it required, since no film company or individual donor would thereafter have confidence in an organization that broke its own bylaws. Ledoux was not present, so Toeplitz called him in Brussels and asked him to catch the next plane to Stockholm to face the charges. Ledoux arrived the next day and denied any wrongdoing. He challenged Langlois to produce the slightest proof to support his accusation. Claiming that he had left the proof in Paris, Langlois could not make the charges stick and the Executive Committee dropped them. Langlois was reelected secretary-general of the FIAF. Then followed the election of the Executive Committee. Since Langlois could not support his accusations, the other members felt guilty for bothering Ledoux and so they voted him low man on the Executive Committee's totem pole. As soon as the results were announced, Langlois, furious, swept up his papers and stormed out of the meeting, shouting that it was impossible for him to work with "that person." Some claim they even heard him say he was resigning.

Since they went back to their hotel in the same cab, James Card tried to convince Toeplitz to talk to Langlois and bring him back to the congress. "It was then," remembers Card, "that Toeplitz turned to me and said, 'If it's the last thing I do, I'm going to get rid of Langlois.' He sneered at me in a twisted, grotesque face, similar to a ghoul's on Halloween."

Card tried to warn Langlois that Toeplitz was his mortal enemy. Henri refused to believe him. He had always fought to keep Toeplitz on as president. His entire policy as secretary-general had consisted of maintaining, come what may, a balance between West and East, especially at the worst moments of the cold war.

Lindgren is dead. Jerzy Toeplitz still lives in Poland and denies Card's interpretation. All we can be sure of is that when he boarded the train for Paris, Henri Langlois, reelected by the congress, was still secretary-general.

On 10 November 1959, Marion Michelle received a friendly letter from Langlois, notifying her that he no longer exercised the office of FIAF secretary-general and commenting, "I understand very well that the situation is extremely delicate for you." The same day, Michelle received a letter at her home address from Toeplitz in Poland. It seems he had written to her at the Cinémathèque's address on numerous occasions over the past month and she had never responded. Toeplitz suggested that Michelle set up a post office box in FIAF's name.

The next day, Marion Michelle went to the post office and began filling out the necessary forms for a postal box. One question requested the number under which the FIAF's bylaws were registered at the Prefecture of Police. She called the federation's lawyer, who told her that the bylaws had never been registered. Marion Michelle was shocked by this revelation.

But was it truly a secret? Upon his return from New York in 1939, Langlois had arrived in the middle of the mobilization. The FIAF was a foreign association, and Langlois had been wary of soliciting an authorization from a minister of the interior whom he did not know and reluctant to register the bylaws of a federation whose president was German and whose other members were English and American.

When Langlois learned of her attempt to find the FIAF's registration number, he became furious with Marion Michelle. She became the woman who knew too much. He pictured her conspiring with Toeplitz. All of a sudden, Langlois once again became secretary-general of the FIAF, and on 23 November 1959 he suspended Marion Michelle from her post, ordering her to leave the building immediately and never return.

Michelle could hardly believe her ears and at first thought it was a joke. Thirty years later, Michelle still remembers walking downstairs at the rue de Courcelles in a state of total confusion. At the bottom of the steps, she ran into Lotte Eisner, whom she told what had just happened.

"Oh, Henri," Eisner remarked. "He's fired me lots of times. Go to him on your hands and knees and beg his forgiveness. He'll surely take you back and forget about the incident tomorrow."

Marion Michelle refused to humble herself. As far as she was concerned, Langlois's condemnation was neither logical nor fair. She had done nothing wrong. Henri obviously thought otherwise. Since her return from California, he felt she had changed a great deal. Her stay in Hollywood and the welcome she had received from the most prominent names in the cinema had gone to her head. She had been his supreme ambassador, and now that she had accomplished her mission brilliantly, Henri imagined, she felt herself capable of taking on a larger role in the federation's administration.

From all this stemmed a problem of authority. Henri was secretary-general of the FIAF. He had been elected by the General Assembly, and it was he who had hired Marion Michelle as executive secretary. She was therefore under his orders. The other members of the FIAF board, however, thought that she could be fired only by a joint decision or specifically by the president.

On 5 December 1959, Michelle received a letter from Langlois stating, "I am sorry to tell you that I consider your presence in the *secrétariat générale* to be incompatible with mine. I ask you to consider yourself given notice as soon as you receive this letter." That was the straw that broke the camel's back. On 16 January 1960, the Executive Committee of the FIAF convened in Paris in the offices of the Cinémathèque Française. Everything revolved around one point: Did the secretary-general have the power to suspend the executive secretary, if the president wished him to retain her at her post?

Henri reminded them that he had been elected, and that no one doubted his ability to serve as secretary-general of the FIAF. Except perhaps Marion Michelle? The meeting ended in a stalemate, and the discussion was suspended until the following day. On Sunday, the seventeenth, the debate continued with little progress. Finally, Toeplitz put to a vote his resolution to allow Michelle back in the building and back in the FIAF. He tried to reason with Langlois along the line that everyone makes a mistake now and then. Seven members voted for, three against, and there was one abstention.

Then Toeplitz announced that inasmuch as the executive secretary was absent, they had better adjourn the meeting. But Henri stood up. He wanted to read his report, and he, for one, did not require Marion Michelle's presence. The discussion quickly grew bitter, and Toeplitz reminded Langlois that his vote was decisive in case of conflict within the administration. Nevertheless, despite being overruled by the committee, Langlois continued to insist that Marion Michelle would not enter the Cinémathèque building.

The meeting was postponed for the following day, at the Hotel Claridge. Langlois rebelled: "Meetings that are not held at the FIAF's headquarters are illegal."

The next day, the Executive Committee met at the Claridge on the Champs-Elysées. Marion Michelle was present; Langlois was not. When he thought he was right, Henri went all the way. He was unyielding, irrational, and stubborn. Shortly before his death, he gave this explanation: "When, in Stockholm, they voted to disavow me on a certain point, I resigned from my duties. That's it. I pulled out according to a good Third Republic custom. I'm going to make you laugh: Right there you have the entire problem of supra-nationality. I'd like to partake in a United Nations, but with the right to veto! That said, I abandoned the FIAF, but I did not declare war against it."

Langlois's actions, however, reveal just the opposite. During the months that followed, no explanations were forthcoming from Langlois about his accusations against Ledoux or Marion Michelle. Instead, a series of bizarre maneuvers by Langlois placed the FIAF in the rather embarrassing predicament of having no legal jurisdiction in France. At the following FIAF General Assembly in Amsterdam in June 1960, the motion to remove the FIAF headquarters from the Cinémathèque Française was passed by a vote of 41 to 3. Shortly thereafter, Toeplitz tried to appeal to Michel Fourré-Comeray and the CNC to either change Langlois's stance or at least remove the FIAF's documents from the rue de Courcelles offices and transfer them to Marion Michelle's home until another office could be found. To the amazement of all—as Toeplitz reveals in a letter to Fourré-Comeray on 22 July 1960—when they went to the Office of Associations at the Prefecture of Police to at last register the bylaws, they were told that there was already an association with that name and that it had been registered since 20 January 1960. In fact, on that date Langlois had filed bylaws for a "Féderation internationale des archives du film," signed by himself, Eisner, and Rossi, and thus usurping the organization that had physically existed since 1938.

Lindgren filed a deposition on behalf of Toeplitz as a private individual suing Langlois to gain the right to use the name FIAF, as well as to obtain FIAF documents, which had been confiscated by Langlois. Marion Michelle describes the situation as "an incredible hassle just trying to prove our legitimacy as an organization, despite the fact that we had existed for more than 20 years operating on an international level. It was like taking five steps backward for every step forward. And it wasted so much time and energy and for what purpose?"

Years would go by, and once the divorce was final, the passions would subside. But during the separation, there was nothing but heartbreak. One final absurdity—which can only be interpreted as an irrational act by Langlois against the FIAF—took place the following year, at the FIAF's congress in Budapest. Toeplitz invited Madame Madeleine Méliès to attend, since 1961 was the year of her grandfather's centenary and the FIAF planned to honor Georges Méliès with an enormous exhibition. What Madeleine interpreted as an international tribute to Georges Méliès, Langlois took to be the FIAF thumbing its nose at the Cinémathèque Française. When Madeleine mentioned to Henri that she was accepting the invitation, she was surprised by his reaction: He simply forbid her to go to Budapest! She told him that it was none of his business what went on between her and the FIAF but that what interested her was the tribute to Méliès, and so she left for Budapest. As she recalls:

> We arrived there and were received by the French ambassador. We ate lunch at the French embassy, and as we left, the ambassador said to me that he would be at the inauguration at 3:00 P.M. We had put together an enormous exhibition of blow-ups and original Méliès drawings, as well as a retrospective of his films. Thus, everything was set for the opening to take place before the Hungarian minister of culture, the FIAF members, and the French ambassador.
>
> At five minutes to three, an embassy chauffeur found me on the second floor, where the exhibition was, and asked me to come downstairs to the main floor of the Hungarian film archive. He handed me a letter from the ambassador that said he was sorry, but he had received a telegram from the minister of foreign affairs in Paris forbidding him to take part in the Méliès exhibition's inauguration.
>
> What happened was that Langlois, who was on very good terms with Malraux, had asked, through him, to have the foreign minister forbid the representative of France to participate in a tribute to a Frenchman, because at the time, the Cinémathèque was involved in a lawsuit with the FIAF. Langlois had placed his FIAF problems ahead of his friendship for me. If he had thought about me for a moment, he never would have made that maneuver, which finally served no purpose except to humiliate me and the other FIAF members. I must add that there was an official protest by the Hungarian government to the French government after this incident. After that, Langlois and I were no longer on speaking terms.

According to the minutes of a Cinémathèque Française board of directors' meeting in 1962, Langlois formally and categorically denies ever having called anyone in the foreign ministry. In any case, Langlois considered the FIAF congresses of Amsterdam and Budapest to be illegal. He had warned Toeplitz that should the Cinémathèque consider that the bylaws had been violated by the Executive Committee, the Cinémathèque would withdraw immediately, whereupon the headquarters of the FIAF could no longer be in France, since there would no longer be a French member.

The "headquarters" question was therefore central to the battle. Henri would be mollified only when the FIAF transferred its administrative seat elsewhere—as it eventually did, resettling in Brussels. In the meantime, Henri regarded the notifications he received as being worthless summonses to illegal meetings, and the other FIAF members grew impatient waiting for him to return. The Cinémathèque Française, not having paid its dues and having refused to acknowledge or attend meetings for more than two years, was suspended at the following congress, held in Rome in June 1962, by a unanimous vote except for four abstentions. The four abstentions were the Cinémathèque Française and its "three musketeers": Freddy Buache and the

Cinémathèque Suisse, James Card and the George Eastman House, and Mrs. Kawakita and the Japanese film archive.

The Cinémathèque Française pulled out with its faithful followers in tow. All that remained was for the FIAF to decide to eliminate the suspended archive completely, which it did, in Belgrade in 1963. Indefatigable, Langlois and the three other archives together formed another international film archive organization, called Union Mondiale des Musées du Cinéma. According to James Card, however, this organization never really became functional: "The Union Mondiale never got beyond the reams and reams of statutes and organization papers that Henri loved to draw up. He really should have been a statesman, or at the very least, a lawyer. He was one of the most brilliant speakers I have ever known and *loved* drawing up intricate rules and regulations. There was never any need for the Union Mondiale, as all of the resigned archives, in spite of the official boycott, found it possible through bilateral agreements with FIAF members to continue exchanging films."

That may have been true for the strong cinematheques. But Freddy Buache reminded Langlois that Lausanne was not Paris. If the Cinémathèque Française obtained everything it wanted, people still refused Buache films, reproaching him for not being a FIAF member. So Langlois gave Buache his benediction, and the Swiss film archive rejoined the FIAF. Henri was ultimately pleased by that development, since it meant that he would have a friendly observer in the ranks.

A situation that was no longer war had been established, and the Cinémathèque would profit by this separation. Henri was convinced that when an organization becomes too large, clans begin to form. The Union Mondiale des Musées du Cinéma would be a sort of club, a small group, tied together by the same passion for the cinema.

Why did Langlois refuse to reconcile with an organization he not only helped create but had spent 20 years shaping and leading? Françoise Jaubert, who became a FIAF Executive Committee member representing the Canadian archive in 1970, offers the most revealing explanation: "I think you can talk about many reasons why it occurred, but the main reason was that the FIAF was Henri's baby. There were two fathers and two mothers, but the true couple from whom it was born and who gave it its education were Henri Langlois and Iris Barry. All that took place between the founding in 1938 and the split in 1960 was that the baby had grown up and come of age. Some archives had grown in size and no longer wanted to listen to Daddy. Children separate from their parents when they outgrow them. Daddy resented it."

And perhaps "Daddy" could not help it. In Orson Welles's film *Mr. Arkadin* (also known as *Confidential Report*), during a masked ball in a Spanish castle Welles, as Gregory Arkadin, tells his captive audience a stinging tale about the nature of the scorpion:

A scorpion wanted to cross a river. So he asked a frog to carry him across on its back.

"No," said the frog. "No thanks. If I take you on my back, you will sting me and a scorpion's sting is deadly."

"But where is the logic in that?" asked the scorpion, trying to be logical. "If I sting you, you'll die, and if you die, I'll drown."

This made sense, and so the frog, convinced, allowed the scorpion to climb on his back. But when they were halfway across the river, suddenly the frog felt an awful piercing pain. As he lost control of his stiffening limbs, the frog understood that the scorpion had stung him after all.

"Logic?" cried the frog in agony. "There's no logic in that." Then he sank beneath the surface, carrying the scorpion with him.

"I know," said the scorpion, "but I can't help it; it's my character."

At this point in the film, Arkadin raises his glass and says, "Let's drink to character!"

True to his Scorpio nature, so long as Langlois could devote himself to a task—or to a cause, such as collecting films and presenting them—he was capable of prodigious efforts and rousing successes, for his passion was limitless. But as soon as someone questioned his leadership or doubted his word, Langlois behaved in an unpredictable and irrational fashion. No doubt that day in Stockholm he was tilting at windmills and ended up missing the target by a wide margin. But as Jean Raine points out, if Langlois did not have an enemy, he would have had to invent one. Henri required enemies. How else was he to exhaust his overabundance of energy?

It is also true that Henri could not put up with people who questioned his leadership acumen. With his unbending character, and more than a trace of the scorpion's logic, Langlois did not hesitate to risk the destruction of the FIAF's illustrious past and, with it, his proper image as founder.

"Every end is just another beginning," said Henri Langlois. The end of the Cinémathèque's involvement with the FIAF was definitely the end of a dream for the other FIAF members. They went on to make significant strides in film preservation without Langlois's participation. Yet according to Farrokh Gaffary, whose Iranian archive rejoined the FIAF in 1973, "I saw then that everyone still had a great amount of respect for Henri. Even Ledoux never said a single derogatory thing about Henri in public. On the contrary, he liked to mention Henri's name when he gave official speeches at FIAF meetings, making certain to add that, along with the Cinémathèque Française, Henri Langlois would always have his place in the federation."

When Françoise Jaubert met Jacques Ledoux in 1977 at Langlois's funeral, she would be moved by the presence of the man whose election had been the pretext that triggered the break in 1959. Moving in closer, he told her, "Henri Langlois was the father of us all—that's all that counts."

chapter 10

# CHAILLOT: CROSSROADS OF THE CINEMA

He who runs a cinémathèque is a kind of snake charmer. A Pied Piper of Hamelin. It's tough going.

Henri Langlois

In the spring of 1960, Langlois went to Moscow to meet with Pera Eisenstein, widow of the great Russian filmmaker. He was making a special trip to request her help in organizing a large-scale exhibition in Paris of Eisenstein's drawings. Like Méliès, Hitchcock, Kurosawa, Fellini, and other great directors, Eisenstein never began a film without first having worked out its imagery in hundreds of sketches and drawings.

In the 12 years following his death, Eisenstein's work had been almost completely forgotten, and Pera worried that it would remain so. She was therefore delighted to lend Henri some 300 of her late husband's drawings. In May 1960 the doors of the rue de Courcelles building swung open for the exhibition. The magazine *Arts* published photos of the show, accompanied by the following commentary by Paul Guimard, under the heading, "His Majesty Eisenstein Explained through his Drawings": "Thanks to the extraordinary erudition of Henri Langlois—who *is* the Cinémathèque Française—we are able to publish for your delectation the 'compared' images of preliminary sketches and film frames on these pages. This work represents hours of research in order to locate, in a print of the film, the shot that corresponds to a given drawing. Only Langlois could have undertaken such a task, and the earliest results exceed our wildest dreams."

The exhibition created such an impression that unprecedented crowds descended on the rue d'Ulm to see projections of Eisenstein's nine most important films. Public enthusiasm reached an all-time height when part 2 of *Ivan the Terrible*, with some sequences in color, was scheduled. The film had never before been shown in France, and, according to *Le Monde*, it took two police vans to channel the 5,000 people lined up all the way to the Panthéon. The crowd refused to disperse, and a second show had to be added at midnight. "This is a pinnacle," was the reporter's conclusion.

The initial atmosphere of reverent contemplation that characterized the rue d'Ulm facility had given way to wild enthusiasm. The old regulars didn't know whether to complain about it or congratulate themselves. The theater, larger than the one on avenue de Messine, was often overrun with people who just felt like seeing a movie and wished to do so as cheaply as possible, according to Jean Douchet, writing in *Arts*. But the faithful followers were still to be found seated in the first three rows, where the atmosphere was at its liveliest:

> The neophyte will quite possibly be surprised to find that this "Mecca of Culture" does not have the mothballed atmosphere of a museum. No, it's more like the Stock Exchange, since these noisy groups are engaged in constant quotation on the value of directors.
>
> As the Cinémathèque does not presume to judge, it leaves to each person the task of questioning the history of the cinema as he or she sees fit. It is the only place where one truly approaches the Cinema, with a capital C.

Immediately following the Eisenstein retrospective, Langlois launched into a look at Hitchcock, showing 26 of his films, silents and talkies alike. The Cinémathèque paused for summer vacation and, in the autumn, alternated classics with avant-garde films, all the while leaving space for moving tributes to Gérard Philipe, Jean Grémillon, and Jacques Becker, all of whom had died not long before. There were also retrospectives devoted to Joseph von Sternberg and, for the first time, producer Anatole Dauman and his company, Argos Films.

Apart from a handful of specialists and die-hard fans, the name and accomplishments of Buster Keaton had fallen into a crack between the past and oblivion. It had become nearly impossible to see his films. There were, however, individuals who, independent of any official film archive, had assembled film collections of their own in the hope that certain old films would one day fit back into the circuit of commercial distribution. This was the case for Raymond Rohauer, in California, who had begun to revive interest in Buster Keaton's films in the United States and, gradually, in Europe. Keaton had come to Rohauer in 1954. As Rohauer explains,

> His career was absolutely on the skids. He couldn't get roles anymore, and he needed money. He was almost completely forgotten. He had work prints of some of his features, but most of them were in terrible shape because he'd kept them stored in his garage. We had to find the missing titles, restore

them all, and work out the thorny matter of rights. Throughout this process, we were always partners.

When I started working with him, nobody wanted to see a single one of his films. You couldn't even give them away. Keaton himself had lost faith. It was a depressing situation.

In July 1960 Keaton and Rohauer went to Paris in the hope of showing *The General* there. Keaton and his wife had already been in town for four or five days when Rohauer in turn arrived. He joined them at the Hotel George V, where they were staying, and found Buster depressed about being there with nothing to do. Rohauer suggested that they have lunch together. But first he had a few phone calls to make, notably to Marion Michelle. Marion had a prior engagement with Jan de Vaal from the Dutch film archive, and Rohauer invited them both to lunch.

Buster, who was generally reserved in front of strangers, didn't say a word during the meal. Naturally, the conversation turned to movies. All of a sudden, Rohauer had an idea:

"Apropos," he said, "I've never seen the Cinémathèque Française. I'd like to take Buster there."

At which point Marion Michelle practically bit his head off. "You can't do that!" she exclaimed. "They're a bunch of gangsters and crooks—you'll never get out alive!"

"Whoever are you talking about?" asked Rohauer.

"The people at the Cinémathèque. They're horrible, terrible, unbearable. Don't set foot in there whatever you do."

This anecdote was told to Glenn Myrent by Raymond Rohauer. Marion Michelle says that Rohauer got carried away with hyperbole and that her remarks were not remotely that vehement: "What I said was, 'Watch out. If you're going to give films to the Cinémathèque, there's a strong possibility that those films will never again leave the abyss that is the Cinémathèque.'"

After Jan de Vaal and Marion Michelle had left, Raymond Rohauer and Keaton exchanged a wink. "Why not go there all the same?" they thought. "We'll judge for ourselves."

And so the two men hopped into a taxi to throw themselves into the lion's jaws. Whether the beast would turn out to be of the flat, MGM-logo variety or of the "Oh goody, Christians for lunch" variety remained to be seen. When Keaton and Rohauer arrived at rue de Courcelles they found a middle-aged man at the door who spoke a little English, and asked him to announce that visitors were there to see Mr. Langlois.

"Who shall I say sent you?"

"Just say that Buster Keaton is here."

Without revealing a hint of his suspicions or doubts, the man stepped back to use the phone, and Rohauer overheard him say, "There's a guy here who claims to be Buster Keaton."

Then the two Americans stood and waited in the courtyard. Suddenly, they heard the at-first-distant voice of a woman rushing down the staircase, screaming, "Buster! BUSTER!" It was Mary Meerson. Upon reaching street level, she ran up to Keaton and threw her arms around him, hugging him so tightly that she lifted him right off the ground!

Buster was momentarily dumbfounded and more than a little shocked to be welcomed in a hurricane of emotion by someone he'd never met. He had not forgotten Marion Michelle's words of warning and began to wonder if perhaps he *was* in danger of not "getting out alive." As for Mary—enthusiasm personified—she pushed the reluctant Keaton toward the elevator, all the while shouting, "My God, oh my God, Henri is going to be *so* happy to meet you. Come on—follow me!"

When Henri saw the great Buster Keaton walk into his fourth-floor office, preceded by Mary's clamoring, he poured on his own demonstrative welcome. Langlois then hastened to the telephone to ask one of his photographer friends to rush right over. Abel Gance also joined the crowd, and together they spent the remainder of the afternoon at the parc Monceau. While in the gardens, Buster entertained his newfound friends with an improvised show, including several gags performed with cigarettes as props. The camera captured it all.

That day, Henri not only met one of the greatest comedians the cinema had ever known, but also became acquainted with Raymond Rohauer, a remarkable businessman who would re-release many American classics of the silent screen and who would show an abiding interest in the films of Harry Langdon, Douglas Fairbanks, and the German expressionist period. Rohauer conducted business not like a simple independent distributor but like a passionate collector whose sensibilities were very close to Langlois's. The two men exchanged many films, and in the course of the 1960s and 1970s, Rohauer would deposit significant holdings with the Cinémathèque.

In February 1962 Langlois was finally able to program his homage to "the man who never laughs." Once again, the lines of people waiting to get in were so long that the films had to be shown and reshown several times—and still some would-be spectators were turned away.

On the evening of the premiere, Henri introduced Keaton to the public. Thunderous applause burst forth and proceeded to last for more than 20 minutes! Author and critic Robert Benayoun has every reason to vividly recall the emotion of that evening:

> I will never forget the moment he appeared. Petrified by 20 minutes' worth of clamor that made him himself again after so many hard knocks, he stood there on his short legs, hesitating, making graceful little side-stepping motions around a microphone. Little by little, the ovation died down into a silence as solid as marble. Buster, seized with panic at having to justify the enthusiastic welcome he barely understood himself, ended up asking, in a

voice choked with emotion, "Would anyone like to ask me a question?" The silence grew thicker. Nobody made a peep. So then Buster, who was lined up with the middle of the theater and standing there in front of the screen—in the middle of a frame he had so gladly shown affection for—looked straight ahead at the middle of the very front row and asked the person seated there, "Would *you* like to ask me a question?"

By a meaningless coincidence, that person was me, and I was confused by this close-up, this Keatonian glance that, for once, from in front of the screen, really was meant directly for me, without the subjective magic of illusion and with genuine urgency.

Keaton had unknowingly addressed one of the audience members most capable of asking him a question. Benayoun rose to the occasion and initiated a dialogue that, while not terribly long, saved Keaton from his customary fate when projected onto the screen as opposed to standing in front of it: playing the part of a lone statue, poised before a theater full of people who felt as warm as could be toward one nimble acrobat with a face of stone.

Thanks to Malraux, the Cinémathèque would have a new theater at the Palais de Chaillot. Naturally, in exchange the government requested a more important role in the internal affairs of the Cinémathèque, as well as the modification of its charter so that government representatives might serve in an active capacity on the board of directors.

For more than a year, board meetings revolved around the same question: What new form will the Cinémathèque Française take? Detailed proposals were drawn up, and on 27 May 1963, a special session of the General Assembly was called to vote on the proposed modifications. The result would be a reduction in the General Assembly's representation on the board so as to permit government delegates to serve thereon. In the future, only eight board members would be elected by the General Assembly, while eight more would be designated by the government, with a final group of eight to be co-opted by the initial 16.

Langlois's remarks were determinant:

> We must look at matters clearly—the Cinémathèque Française has nearly reached the end of its labors. We have collected

films—now we must archivally preserve them; we have collected docu-ments—now we must display them. And the problem is as follows: There was no point in doing the work we've done if the films continue to rot.

We have to look at what we're here for. We don't exist for the sake of existing; we didn't create the Cinémathèque out of vanity, or in order to be president or director or any other title—we made the Cinémathèque for the films. They must be saved, and since saving them requires money, we must unfortunately bow to circumstances.

I must tell you that the statutes being proposed to you today are the end result of lengthy and dreadful negotiations. What is essential emerges intact because the nonprofit association remains and the General Assembly retains its sovereignty. What possible difference will it make if three years from now the Cinémathèque has completed its task, if it has a museum, if everything is preserved and all the films collected, printed, stored? What difference will it make, then, if the government has veto power—for we will have finished our work.

One other fundamental change would also go into effect: The overall direction of the Cinémathèque would be divided between an artistic and technical director, on the one hand, and an administrative and financial director, on the other.

The Cinémathèque began functioning under its new bylaws in October 1964. Henri Langlois was the artistic and technical director; Claude Fabrizio was in charge of administration and finances. This change afforded the gov-ernment an opportunity to keep a closer check on daily management of the Cinémathèque. Langlois, for his part, thought there would be plenty of time to worry about overly strict supervision. He was looking to the future, and his priority was to find the financial support needed to build up a truly great Cinémathèque and its future museum in the Palais de Chaillot.

The attractive lines and still contemporary design of the Cinémathèque's movie theater in the Palais de Chaillot are yet again the result of Mary's extensive connections, for Mary knew Monsieur Carlu, the architect who had built the "new" Trocadéro palace in 1937.

Thanks to the funds allotted by Malraux, the former basement levels that, tucked into the hill, opened out onto the gardens and a splendid view of the Eiffel Tower, were remodeled under Henri's authority and in keeping with his conception. Langlois wanted the theater to be surrounded by hallways large enough to accommodate small temporary exhibits. The theater itself, boasting 400 seats, a huge screen suited to the full range of aspect ratios a projectionist might encounter, and thick green carpeting, was the most radi-ant extension of the Cinémathèque.

The new theater was inaugurated on 5 June 1963 with an homage to Charlie Chaplin, to be followed by a major retrospective of American films and, after that, an initiation into Japanese cinema. To top things off, Henri had transformed the hallways adjoining the theater into an exhibit on the work of the French inventor Etienne-Jules Marey. The public was made aware of this cinema pioneer who had conducted seminal experiments in the study of motion. His creation, in 1882, of the *fusil photographique* (photographic rifle) enabled him to capture and dissect the movements of a bird in flight. Langlois displayed not only this rifle, which was capable of "shooting" at intervals of one-tenth of a second, but also Marey's *chronophotographe à bande souple* (a frame-by-frame device loaded with a length of flexible film), which is, historically, the first motion picture camera. Henri never failed to add the personal touch that elevated each of his shows from the realm of mere exhibit to that of cultural event. In order to demonstrate the connection between the first motion studies and the work of the cubists and futurists, Langlois had persuaded artists such as Marcel Duchamp, Max Ernst, and Ginno Severini to contribute their paintings, drawings, and tapestries to this striking exhibit.

Henri now needed an assistant to help out with programming tasks. Langlois chose Bernard Martinand, who, with Bertrand Tavernier had co-founded Nickel-Odéon, a ciné-club devoted exclusively to American films. Henri had realized that Martinand was extremely knowledgeable about American cinema of the 1930s through the 1950s and could help him step up his programming now that the schedule called for 36 different films per week. And since Henri had not yet found the time to hire a cashier, it was Bernard Martinand who sold the very first ticket at Chaillot.

Langlois had realized that the launching of Chaillot had to be supported by impeccable programming if he hoped to continue to outdo the art houses of Paris. From October 1963 until October 1964, the Cinémathèque's efforts were concentrated on programming, publicity, and major events at Chaillot in order to increase the number of regular moviegoers. Between Chaillot and the rue d'Ulm, Langlois was soon showing a minimum of six or seven films daily. The people of Paris had an embarrassment of riches from which to choose. The films of George Cukor, John Ford, Joseph Mankiewicz, and Jules Dassin triumphed on the new screen.

Langlois and Martinand joined forces to present, for the first time, a series of retrospectives devoted to the great American studios. Between

1964 and 1967, and aided by Frederick Gronich, director of the Motion Picture Export Association of America, the Cinémathèque would pay tribute to Columbia Pictures, Warner Brothers, MGM, Paramount, and 20th Century-Fox. These companies lent Langlois prints of their films whenever he wanted them and frequently ended up leaving them on deposit with the Cinémathèque.

If Langlois celebrated the Hollywood "majors," he also introduced Parisian audiences to Brazil's Cinema Novo movement, followed by programs devoted to other national cinemas: those of the Third World, the Arab nations, and India. Jean Rouch recalls Henri's jubilation at a festival in Rio. Langlois was in seventh heaven—which was only fitting for a man who worshiped the seventh art—because what he experienced in Rio was his idea of cinema in action: people from Africa, Asia, and America, assembled together in front of the same screen, sharing the same experiences. Nor has Rouch lost sight of the fact that Langlois succeeded in making the Cinémathèque the center of the universe for young filmmakers:

> The avant-garde from all over the world came through the Cinémathèque: the first films of Kenneth Anger, Norman McLaren, the whole Quebec school, the first African films. I remember Henri's joy when he discovered a film made on a shoestring by a Nigerian. It was called Autour d'un aventurier, a sort of Western shot in Africa. And all of a sudden, the Cinémathèque went nuts over Africa. . . . Langlois's attitude was to take risks, and his goal was to show these people what those people were doing. For someone like Ousemane Sembene, who had just landed with his little films made in black-and-white for 1 million old francs, to see his films on a big screen was utterly fabulous.
>
> When Richard Leacock came to the Cinémathèque and his Primary, shot for television, was shown to an audience of 300 people, it was extraordinary. He'd never experienced anything like it in the United States. In other words, Langlois treated everyone in the same way and on the same screen. Whether it was John Ford or Sembene, Glauber Rocha or Rossellini, it made no difference.

Anyone at all, even a complete unknown, could show up at the Cinémathèque with a film in hand and propose it to Langlois. Mary was always nearby, and her generosity knew no bounds. She was eternally endeavoring to bring people together. This was true in the case of Curtis Harrington, before he had made any sort of name for himself. Mary spoke so highly of Harrington to Simone Signoret that she agreed, in 1966, to appear in his film Games. But the most important principle at work, according to Rouch, went beyond matchmaking and introductions: "It's that, at the same time, the Cinémathèque turned into a workshop of production and creativity. Films like the one Robriolle made were completely edited there. Langlois helped people out by giving them film stock. He was doing the work of a patron without the money. Mary would phone Truffaut and say, 'Would you happen to have an editing room to spare? Do you have 400 feet of film lying around? I have an African here—or an Eskimo—can you do anything to help these people out?' Langlois was doing all of this—and who else was at the time? Nobody—that's who."

Henri did not want Parisians alone to enjoy the privilege of Cinémathèque projections, and so he developed a program of decentralization. With the assistance of André Rieupeyrout, then director of the French Federation of Ciné-Clubs, Langlois launched the "Friends of the Cinémathèque" in order to show films from the collection in Bordeaux, Grenoble, La Rochelle, Lyon, Montpellier, Marseilles, Nice, and Toulouse. He also hoped to build a chain of friendship and solidarity clear across France. The "Friends" held their screenings in different settings, be it a cultural center, as in Grenoble, or a school, as in Marseilles, and also allowed for regional miniarchives to be established in key population centers around the country.

Thanks to the revenue from screenings, certain branches of the Friends of the Cinémathèque made enough of a profit to invest in a few films of their own. Other "franchises" were less prosperous, since, at about the same time, a network of art houses sprang up that, according to Monsieur Rieupeyrout, was given a great deal of government backing to be used in connection with film distribution.

The first effect of this decentralization project was the establishing of the Friends of the Cinémathèque Française of Toulouse in 1955. Two years later, a film storage depot was begun in a location donated by city hall. The key to this storage area was held by the Cinémathèque's correspondent in Toulouse, a Monsieur Tariol. A new experiment was under way, for this depot not only held films sent from Paris but also served as a place to warehouse any films the Cinémathèque might acquire in the South of France.

That same year, Raymond Borde, who had been assisting Monsieur Tariol, took his place as the Cinémathèque's contact in Toulouse. Henri quickly realized that Borde was applying all of the profits from the sale of admission tickets toward the purchase of films. At first he was quite pleased about this. But

Langlois subsequently noticed that Borde was buying up films and, as a consequence, was not contributing anything back into the system to help defray costs being shouldered in Paris.

Since the new statutes of the Cinémathèque called for teamwork and frugality, Langlois wrote to Borde in March 1964 to remind him of the rules as they applied to solidarity:

> I won't hide the fact that the administrator who will be working with me will, sooner or later, become much pickier than I am about this point and that I won't be able to defend the Friends of the Cinémathèque unless I can group all the branches together and prove that, taken as a group, they are covering their own expenses.
>
> For there are sections that, for the moment, are having a very hard time maintaining a balance: in Nancy, Bordeaux, Montpellier, Grenoble, Caen, almost all of these functioning in schools.
>
> I remind you of my wish that, in the future, any and all proceeds constituting profit be set aside unspent until the general situation in all the sections can be examined. In addition, quite a few titles have been added to our collection over the past three years and I don't want to end up with two copies of the same thing.
>
> In the hope that you understand, I send you my very best regards.

Borde would use this letter as a pretext at which to take offense. In reality, he had already made up his mind to found an independent cinémathèque. On 6 April 1964, Borde replied: "I just got back to Toulouse when I found your letter, and the very first move I'm making is to send it right back to you. You write to me using the tone of a boss speaking to an employee, and that, you must admit, is out of the question."

After indicating that he had sent 203 films to the Cinémathèque Française over the previous five years, Borde explained that the purchases he made for the 12 months of the 1963–64 season came to a grand total of 2,350 francs. He added: "We are living under the illusion that the Friends of Toulouse are comparable to the Friends of Nancy, Bordeaux, or Montpellier. That holds true for the screenings, but it is not true for the collection of films."

A collection for which, he pointed out, he worked under "obscenely poor, miserable, seat-of-the-pants, makeshift conditions . . . with, as sole budget, the problematic profits from the screenings." Borde concluded: "If these miserable profits must, in addition, serve to alleviate the deficits of other Friends in the provinces, I give up. I am not Christ."

That is quite possibly the capacity in which he differed from Langlois. Raymond Borde ended his missive in affirming, "You asked me to create a cinémathèque in Toulouse. It is done. The legal notification has already been published in the *Journal Officiel*. Voilà, there's the solution. Starting from there, it will be accorded an autonomous budget to make use of whenever a given company or collector doesn't want to deposit its films at the Cinémathèque Française."

Henri had never asked Borde to do any such thing. He wrote back immediately: "As for the solution you propose, consisting of giving an independent existence to our *filmothèque* in Toulouse, allow me to be slightly dumbstruck, as it seems to me impossible that this solution, in lieu of being a panacea, not evolve into—from fiction to fiction and misunderstanding to misunderstanding—a disastrous situation."

Overnight, the letterhead of the Cinémathèque Française–Toulouse Office became Cinémathèque of Toulouse. And from one day to the next, the vault containing the entire collection of the Cinémathèque Française's films being stored in Toulouse became the depot of the Cinémathèque of Toulouse.

Raymond Borde believed that Langlois, in the wake of his break with the FIAF, was all washed up, sick, and that he should step aside and let new blood take over. Borde had concluded that the Cinémathèque Française was no longer playing its natural role and that the Cinémathèque of Toulouse would eventually do so in its stead. This in no way altered the fact that Toulouse was harboring an important selection of films that their owners had put on deposit with the Cinémathèque Française. Langlois believed that the Cinémathèque had been fleeced of its stock and its property. Certain members of the board were prepared to lodge a formal complaint, but Langlois told them, "It is not theft when it is a son who takes something from his father."

What counted most for Langlois was that the Cinémathèque of Toulouse was born from the Cinémathèque Française. But Langlois's spirit of generosity would not be returned, because Raymond Borde declared himself Langlois's worst enemy and would spend a substantial portion of his life denigrating the man who had dared to speak to him as an "employee."

These battles did not prevent Langlois from tirelessly carrying on the crusade he had begun some 30 years earlier: the valiant struggle to preserve films. As Langlois wrote in a *Nouvel observateur* article of 22 April 1965, entitled "Films Put to Death":

The survival and preservation of a film present numerous problems, but little would be required to, at the very least, have the assurance that a film not be condemned to die. Ever since the Cinémathèque Française was created, I have been asking the authorities to vote a decree prohibiting the destruction of any complete edited negative. And for 30 years, such a decree, which would harm no one—*au contraire*—has been refused. And yet this very protection has just been voted in, in Algeria!

So long as no decree forbids wholesale destruction, nothing can prevent a female star from buying back all of her films in order to burn them because she finds her image in them ugly. Nothing will stop a rich Italian—it already happened once—from buying up dozens of films in order to make a montage, an "anthology," out of them, and subsequently destroying the originals so as to make certain that his film will become known because it's the only document remaining.

So long as no decree comes along to officially back us up, we will continue to bet on trust, to deplete our enthusiasm and our strength, and to waste our time in the hope of gaining this trust. And all this time the other great problems facing film conservation will not be solved. Yet they are going to grow increasingly urgent.

A film cannot be preserved indefinitely, even under the best conditions, without being taken care of, tended to, treated. At the Bibliothèque nationale, books are taken care of properly. We must be able to take care of films, and we will find a way.

The following year, at the Venice film festival, Langlois organized a colloquium devoted to "The Protection and Preservation of Works of Art on Nitrate Film," which brought together 100 filmmakers, critics, and scientific experts. Henri's distinctive style comes through loud and clear in the final resolution: "A prohibition upon striking prints, and the destruction of original works, would represent for cinematic art and for historians in all disciplines a catastrophe comparable to the destruction by barbarians of libraries and of works of art."

In order to celebrate the seventieth anniversary of the Lumière brothers' first public film projection, Henri organized an exceptional evening at Chaillot. Jean-Luc Godard, writing in *Le Nouvel observateur*, expresses the symbolic value of that screening:

I like to think that 70 years ago, just about the same number of people assembled together at the Grand Café [*sic*]. Our slight advantage is that at this very moment roughly 400 million of our brothers are doing the same thing, all around the world. Whether they be in airplanes, in front of television sets, in ciné-clubs, or in big-city movie theaters, what is it they're doing? They're drinking words. They are fascinated by images. In a word, like the Alice before the looking glass that Cocteau holds dear, they are in Wonderland.

> This possibility to be wonderstruck would be impossible—I'll come right out and say it, and the only real lesson of Lumière is that if a camera has lenses or *objectifs*, it's because the cinema is on the lookout for objectivity—without people like Henri Langlois.

In 1947 Louis Lumière had donated to the Cinémathèque nearly 2,000 films made before the turn of the century. Georges Sadoul went to Lyons to prepare an inventory of the tiny metal cans that had been stored in a shed for 30 or 40 years. When Sadoul opened the cans, he found negatives as gloriously intact as a book printed at that same time. The gelatin had not worked its way loose from its backing as old nitrate films were wont to do. It was from these exemplary original negatives that Langlois's friend Jean-Paul Boyer struck projectable prints of astonishing transparence and quality.

But simple renovation is not always possible. When a nitrate-base film is on the brink of decomposition, the best way to save it is to transfer it to more stable acetate stock. But this process requires money, and money, or the lack thereof, was an eternal story of major proportions. Lack of money created tragic problems for Langlois, who had to decide which film he would sacrifice in order to save another, when both could not be rescued. These dilemmas kept him up nights.

In a nation where at any given moment, many French workers were calculating the number of days until the next segment of their five annual weeks of paid vacation, Langlois never took a day off. He did not spend weekends in the country. He could barely survive being away from his films for long. Françoise Jaubert remembers the time some of the staff took a trip to the Boyer laboratory near Nîmes in southern France, an outing that gave the Cinémathèque's employees a wonderful opportunity to spend a half-day in utter relaxation: "Everybody was in a great mood, since we each felt like we were on vacation. We had a barbecue. We sunbathed. We forgot the meaning of the word *film* and could truly not have cared less about what might be going on in the world of cinema. All except Henri, who, as soon as he wasn't talking about the Cinémathèque and his work, felt out of place." Bernard Martinand shares that impression: "It was the only

time I ever saw him look lost. He wasn't in his element anymore. His life was the Cinémathèque. That day was a very beautiful day, and at one point he felt all alone. I can't remember ever having seen him like that. It made an impression on me. And that night, he went to consult the cards."

Before the Cinémathèque's theater at Chaillot, Langlois showed 900 films each year. With Chaillot, the figure topped 2,000. All at once, the Cinémathèque was showing more films in Paris, and taking part in more events throughout France and internationally than ever before. Between 1964 and 1967, Henri had accomplished a thing or two. There was a magnificent international exhibit at the Cultural Center of Bourges, a setting Malraux particularly liked, and there was an exhibit, "70 Years of World Cinema," that impressed everyone at Cannes during the festival in 1966. Henri's "History of French Cinema" at Expo '67 in Montreal was a major success. The international reputation of the Cinémathèque was such that when President Lyndon Johnson instituted the National Endowment for the Arts and Humanities, he asked the French ambassador in Washington to provide him with full documentation on the bylaws and functioning of the Cinémathèque Française.

Cinémathèque-held examples of the seventh art were also sailing the seven seas. Henri and Mary took it upon themselves to worry about the morale of crews in the French naval fleet. The result was a year-round program of film entertainment for sailors on long-haul journeys, including those aboard the cable-laying ships *Ampère* and *Marcel-Bayard* working off the icy coast of Newfoundland.

ORTF, the government-owned radio and television conglomerate, helped itself to elements from the Cinémathèque's collections without charge. As a result, the Cinémathèque's film viewer was being monopolized by television directors. The Cinémathèque had to assign one of its employees to help broadcasters full-time.

In the wake of the 1964 statutes, the financial control imposed by the government became increasingly severe. In 1965, at the request of the minister of finance, an inspector was assigned to draw up a full report on the activities of the Cinémathèque. The very manner in which the association was organized drew criticism, as did the absence of a thorough inventory. But the sternest reproaches centered on receptions, since the authorities did not consider lavish receptions to be a justifiable expenditure for an association whose goal was "the preservation of an artistic heritage and not public relations." This assessment points to a total lack of comprehension as to what a film archive must do in order to enrich its collections.

A primary example of this lack of understanding came to light in connection with Mary Pickford's visit to Paris, as a guest of the Cinémathèque, to be present for an homage to her career. Langlois chose the Ritz as a hotel befitting "America's Sweetheart," and Mary Meerson saw to it that the room was bedecked with thousands of francs' worth of fresh flowers. The civil servants in the Ministry of Finance could not accept this kind of extravagance. They were completely incapable of accepting that such "outlandish expenditures" ensured French prestige abroad and in turn attracted new riches. Mary Pickford's stay brought in far more than it had cost. Miss Pickford, duly impressed by the thoughtful and luxurious welcome she had received, permitted the Cinémathèque to make copies of 50 of her films that she had decided to destroy.

In this same report, the usefulness of Langlois's travels is questioned, and the notion of quibbling is taken to new heights:

> Finally, even when the reason for the journey is acceptable, certain expenditures are not accounted for with corresponding receipts: Document 398, Mr. Langlois's trip to Cannes. Out of a total of 443 francs, the following expenses are undocumented: 25 francs for taxis in Cannes, 17 francs for assorted tips, 23 francs at the hotel and assorted tips, 15 francs and 30 centimes for beverages with celebrities—making a total of 80 francs 30 centimes.
>
> Document 300: Mademoiselle Eisner's trip to Cannes. Out of a total expenditure of 203 francs, proper receipts are lacking for 17 francs in tips to personnel and 35 francs for Madame Ponsignon (who, according to Mademoiselle Eisner, is the secretary of Festival Director Favre Le Bret, to whom Mademoiselle Eisner offered flowers on behalf of Monsieur Langlois). The missing total comes to 137 francs 42 centimes.

Langlois was even criticized for his choice of film laboratory engaged to make projectable positive prints from the Lumière negatives. (It should also be noted that Boyer built a special device to enable the projection and transfer of Lumière's round-sprocket-holed, 35-millimeter film stock to the standard rectangular-shaped perforations found today.) Langlois dealt with Boyer, which charged 32 centimes per yard, whereas Kodak, it seemed, charged only 30! This particular criticism so annoyed Godard that he was moved to write, "One criticizes his choice of laboratory, whereas it would not occur to anyone to haggle with painters of *l'école de Paris* over their paints when they repaint the ceiling of the Opera House."

Langlois was also criticized for keeping his inventory secret. But as far back as the 1940s, the board of directors had voted a resolution whereby a film was or was not included in the Cinémathèque's catalog at the sole discretion of the depositor. Langlois made the reasoning behind this policy quite clear:

> Pirating—the fear of seeing a third party exploit for profit, through the means of purchase, films collected by the Cinémathèque in the form of deposits—brought the board of directors, and in turn the General Assembly, to consider the necessity of secrecy for deposits.
>
> Very quickly and parallel to this, the depositors themselves conveyed their wishes, for personal reasons, that third parties not be given access to the inventory of their deposits at the Cinémathèque Française, an exclusive right they reserve for themselves.
>
> Finally, secret deposits—that is, the noncommunication to third parties of the list of films on deposit, as well as the nonpublication of said list, except when authorized—is one of the obvious and fundamental bases facilitating and conditioning the depositing of films. This position on the part of the rights holders is in agreement with the film-preservation work of the Cinémathèque.

Therefore, it was none of Pathé's business what, if anything, Gaumont had confided to the Cinémathèque in the way of films, and vice versa. The film companies alone retained the exclusive right to reveal whether or not they were in possession of such and such a film. Langlois felt that the Cinémathèque should be something like a bank, since the vast majority of its films remained the property of those who had "deposited" them. This policy had never bothered the Cinémathèque. On the contrary, its strict application had created an atmosphere of confidence that enabled the Cinémathèque to diligently go about the business of safeguarding and collecting films. This system enabled the Cinémathèque to gain the confidence of the large American companies, as well as build up trust with independent producers.

This report to the Ministry of Finance marked the beginning of incessant harassment that would last until 1968. The government had certainly made an effort to invest in the Cinémathèque by according it Chaillot, but the operating budget was soon revealed to be inadequate in the face of so many film-related activities. "When you give someone a Rolls-Royce along with an order to keep it running," Langlois observed, "you must also give him enough money to buy gas."

Matters were not helped by the difficulties Langlois and Fabrizio experienced in attempting to work together. The division of powers provided for by the new bylaws was something of a two-headed beast—how were the two heads to collaborate? Naturally, at the Cinémathèque Henri's personality predominated, but personality or no personality, the other director held the all-important purse strings. After three years, Henri made this bitter assessment:

If I could have gone on driving alone, instead of being obligated to hand the wheel to someone who didn't know how to drive and had never driven in his life, the years 1965 and 1966 would have been quite different.

I was expecting an administrative director who would come to be my associate. What I got was a liquidator of all the values held by the Cinémathèque. We were expecting someone who would be the spokesman for our financial needs; they gave us a young finance director who couldn't make the distinction between a film and its negative and who set out to gut our staff by calling for the elimination of 20 people, including those who were doing the most to enrich the Cinémathèque.

When Henri hit the half-century mark, his face filled out to become the rounded countenance with which he would face the world until his death. His long hair was swept back off his high forehead, and two bags, one beneath each bright dark eye, already bore witness to hour upon hour of unflagging work.

The wild plans of his youth had become handsome realities. His exhibitions, his tributes, his brilliant retrospectives—all had restored films of yore to their former glory. Henri had renovated and renewed public taste. With the predicted expansion of television and its corresponding appetite for images, old films would take on commercial value anew.

But the myth that had grown up around Langlois—Cocteau, who had no choice but to sum things up as a poet would, had described him as "a dragon watching over his treasures," and that summary stuck—this and other factors contributed to the awakening of lusts and jealousies. And Henri, who by his very nature was leery of conspiracies, would find himself engulfed by an almost unimaginably perfidious plot.

Paradoxically, he was to be the victim of his heroic, meritorious efforts, dating back to before the war when, as a film-crazed youth of 24, he struggled to save the Eclair films that had been sold to a scrap dealer who intended to boil them down.

After the war, this same scrap dealer—who had finally given up and agreed to deposit the thousands of snippets of film with the Cinémathèque rather than feed them to the furnace— came to ask Langlois what had become of his films. As you will recall, in 1943 Langlois eventually retrieved most of the films that had been seized by the

Germans; however, an entire wagonload of films had been reduced to indecipherable goo by humidity after the Château de Coucy was extensively damaged by bombings that left its cellars exposed to the elements. Henri had asked the Germans for proof, and they had given him a smattering of unusable scraps. The Eclair collection that he had valued so was indeed destroyed.

Langlois therefore had no reason not to give the scrap dealer—a Jewish man, who had certainly had enough troubles during the war—a statement whereby he appraised the value of the pre-1914 Eclair negatives at 3 million old francs.

Fifteen years later, in 1961, the minister of construction, Monsieur Sudreau, was in a position to rule on an outlandishly steep claim concerning war damages to the Eclair film collection. This claim had grown by leaps and bounds as it passed through various hands, until, after two appraisals by experts, it had reached the astonishing sum of 800 million old francs! But since the same scrap dealer filing this claim had already attempted to collect reparations for a factory in Saint-Ouen-l'Aumône that had been demolished well before the war began, the minister had a right to be suspicious.

Monsieur Sudreau, who rejected the scrap dealer's claims, was shocked to discover that more than one highly placed individual had interceded to inflate the amount in exchange for a cut of the anticipated payoff. Therefore, on 24 November 1961, the minister lodged a complaint with the state prosecutor. Two months later, a press campaign was set off by Le Journal du parlement: "We will not stop calling for a commission of inquiry to clear up all the mysteries of the Cinémathèque. We have alerted André Malraux; we will inform all the parliamentarians: The longer we put off cleaning up this Augean mess, the greater the eventual scandal will be."

Henri had shrugged his shoulders, knowing full well that the very success of the Cinémathèque was enough to set off other people's ambitions. But he hadn't an inkling of the incredible machinations afoot of which he would be the victim. The examining judge's file cabinet held a file that was growing thicker by the minute. This dossier contained not only the signed statement that Henri had given the scrap dealer in 1947, but also a contract dated 19 February 1938 that appeared to make the two men business associates.

The preliminary investigation would, for the most part, be directed against Langlois and the Cinémathèque Française. The investigators first attempted to prove that the Eclair negatives had not actually been transferred from the Palais de Chaillot to the Château de Coucy when the war broke out, and even went so far as to imply that the films no longer existed as early as 1938. Witnesses had suddenly lost their memories—after all, they were being asked to remember things that had taken place 25 years earlier. And while these patient inquiries were under way, Langlois knew nothing of the shady dossier working its way through official channels.

The chief superintendent of the Criminal Investigation Department, Monsieur L.G., was a man of experience, often called upon to handle delicate cases. He had detected something resoundingly fishy about this particular dossier. Too many influential people had had a hand in this affair on its way to becoming a claim for the staggering sum set by the last expert of the Court of Appeals. And yet if Langlois had knowingly given the scrap dealer the documents that the chief superintendent now held in his briefcase, he was guilty. The whole affair would stop right there, with Langlois. There would be no need to look any further.

When told in September 1962 that a police superintendent wished to see him, Henri was a million miles away from suspecting what it might be about. "The matter for which I've come is very serious," the superintendent intoned. "It is in your own interest to answer my questions without beating around the bush. Why and on what basis have you, in the name of the Cinémathèque, requested, in conjunction with the X company, the considerable figure of more than 800 million francs?"

"I didn't request anything at all. What in the world are you talking about?"

"But you did provide Monsieur X with a written estimate."

"That's correct," said Henri, upon hearing the name. "You want to talk about the Eclair collection?"

"Yes, I do—if indeed it ever existed. I've been told you have a very active imagination."

"But of course it really existed!" Henri exclaimed. "It's mentioned in the minutes of the board meetings from that time. I'll find them for you. You can't possibly know how strongly I felt about those Eclair negatives. If you don't believe me, all you have to do is go to New York because I wrote to the Museum of Modern Art in the hope they'd help us save them."

Henri Langlois seemed so sincere and so sure of himself that the superintendent paused for a moment, pretending to take great interest in the poster on Henri's desk. And then, abruptly, he decided to put his trump card on the table:

"Well, then, I must show you a copy of this contract that is part of my dossier and that bears your signature. Do you deny that this is your signature?"

"That is my signature. I can't claim otherwise."

"Then you're guilty!"

"Allow me to read the text," said Henri, who proceeded to do so. "Yes, well—I would have had to have been completely out of my mind to sign this" was his assessment.

The contract stipulated that the scrap dealer was depositing his entire stock of pre-1914 films, valued at 40 francs per meter, and that he would remain sole proprietor until he had been paid. In the meantime, this collection of films was to be stored in the Trocadéro Theater. The end of the contract stipulated that Monsieur X and Monsieur Langlois "decide that copies struck from these negatives will be sold to any client making such a request and that the conditions of sale are to be settled as each individual deal arises. Representatives will be appointed in all countries so as to stimulate the clientele to order prints."

Henri, completely knocked for a loop, tried to think back. The signature was definitely his. And yet the text was insane: The films had never been worth 40 francs a meter—but more like 30 francs a kilo, and even that was a high estimate. When one took into account that a meter of film weighs 7 grams, the price had been inflated by a factor of 150. Aside from that, how could anyone believe that he could have turned into a merchant, selling copies, scaring up clients, appointing representatives? It was crazy, completely crazy.

As Henri went on reading, he came across other flagrant anomalies. This document dated 19 February 1938 had Langlois's address listed as 7, rue Troyon when in fact the number was 9. But beyond that, he wasn't living on rue Troyon at all at that time, because the Langlois family didn't leave the rue Laferrière apartment until October 1938. The final glaring aberration was that Henri was listed as representing "the Cinémathèque Française in the course of being established," whereas the Cinémathèque had been founded two years earlier, in 1936.

"This contract," Henri shouted, "is fake—a forgery. It's a complete fabrication."

The superintendent found himself all the more confused by the fact that to the attestation Langlois had signed in 1947 had been added, between the lines, "value calculated in 1939," which served to distort the meaning even more.

When the superintendent reported the results of this interrogation to the examining judge, he remained skeptical. It was not until 1964 that the judge reconsidered and decided to assign an expert from the Criminal Records Office, a Professor Ceccaldi, to determine if the documents in question were authentic.

At the time the documents had been submitted, photocopy machines were extremely rare and the Photostat method was used to reproduce a document. The Criminal Records Office photographed the Photostat and proceeded to enlarge it until one could make out the faint traces of an outline around the paraph, proving that the signature had indeed been cut out from another sheet of paper. The expert concluded that Langlois's apparently authentic signature, had been added "by photographic apposition of a signature figuring on another document, with the resulting combination subsequently rephotocopied." The expert would also prove that the phrase "value calculated in 1939," in darker type, had been typed in at some point after Langlois had given his original attestation to the scrap dealer.

As Georges Langlois recalls,

> We were each very busy with matters in our respective fields. But whenever Henri had a serious problem, he always came to me.
>
> "We have to unmask the people responsible for this!" Henri told me. "I want you to file my complaint immediately in association with the public prosecutor. Submit it to the most senior examining judge on the bench."
>
> The dossier revealed things that left us dumbstruck. The first expert, approved by the minister of construction and assigned to evaluate damages, had received the famous Photostat from the scrap dealer's own hands in 1955. The expert had stated at that time that the document was unquestionably very recent, whereas the scrap dealer claimed that the original had been confiscated by the Germans and had subsequently disappeared during the Occupation. The expert had therefore had serious doubts as to its authenticity but had made no effort to show the document to its alleged cosignatory, Henri Langlois.
>
> As for the document from which the "forged" signature had been lifted, it was safe and sound and easy to spot in one of the expert's other files. Who, then, had managed to remove it from the man's office to perpetrate the forgery? There was to be no answer to this question. The expert himself was dead, and everything conspired to make it look as if we'd never find the scrap dealer's true accomplices. And yet in this dossier, which ended up taking up an entire section of a judge's file cabinet, were a number of sealed documents. Upon opening them, we came across a hand-written list of names, and next to each one was noted the fees, payoffs, and percentages that had been promised to these people— intermediaries of all kinds

and in many different posts—all of whom had taken part in the operation in exchange for a piece of the eventual pie.

The scrap dealer's principal associate [whose name, even today, cannot be revealed], was no doubt an adroit bridge player. He was well connected at the private clubs and power circles of avenue Hoche and also counted an extremely high-up official among his close personal friends. With the help of an intermediary, he had obtained the cooperation of an attorney attached to another ministry, who agreed to present the dossier in a favorable light. We were to observe that the confrontations between these two individuals resulted in one denying what the other affirmed, and vice versa. What was certain was that at least one of them was lying. But which one? The entire affair left us with a lamentable impression as to the comportment of certain representatives in the sphere of public service.

These gentlemen were using their positions to perform private "services" in the hope of lining their own nicely tailored pockets. Among the documents were papers in which the scrap dealer had denounced Langlois as his worst enemy. His mythomania was so out of hand that he'd written that his wife had actually founded the Cinémathèque Française and that their children would succeed Henri Langlois!

The whole thing was incredible. And yet according to the law, it was necessary to wait until all those who played a role in the affair were either dead or beneficiaries of the statute of limitations until finally, in 1973, Henri, as a private party in connection with the public prosecutor, was able to demand and be awarded the symbolic sum of one franc in damages.

Langlois found himself face to face with a senile old man whose failing health would not even permit him to appear in court. For all that, the man was completely ruined and had ended up the victim of those who had sought to grow wealthier through this affair. As for Henri, the toll in mental aggravation had been enormous. He told his brother in 1967, "These people had a very close shave. They hate me and have the means to slander me with the administration."

In October 1967, in an unfortunate coincidence, and despite the fact that the investigation itself had been secret, the official magazine of police headquarters, Liaisons, published a photograph of the document that was in the dossier in the judge's file cabinet. The accompanying article, which discussed various methods for detecting manipulations and forgeries, was printed beside a photo of the portion of the document where the clearly legible signature of Henri Langlois was to be seen. Instead of taking the trouble to point out that this signature was itself an illegal reproduction, the caption said only, "The fluorescence of the document shown in figure 1 demonstrates that it is backdated, for it corresponds to a paper manufactured after 1952–53."

In other words, all the police department personnel and other important readers of this particular issue were left to draw the conclusion that Langlois had signed a backdated document.

It was in this empoisoned atmosphere that 1967 played itself out. Those who actually knew Henri, beginning with the members of the Cinémathèque, but also André Malraux and CNC Director André Holleaux, hadn't the slightest doubt as to Henri's integrity. Certain employees of the Ministry of Finance, however, were predisposed against Langlois, even though they had never laid eyes on him. This monumental error in collective judgment would lead to the events of February 1968.

In 1967 the operating subsidy for the Cinémathèque was transferred from the jurisdiction of the CNC directly to that of the government. The Ministry of Finance subsequently demanded a reorganization of the institution and blocked the subsidy until such time as the reorganization was carried out. Two important expiration dates fell due in 1967: (1) it was time to select new representatives to the board of directors, over which Marc Allégret had presided since the beginning of the year, and (2) the contracts of the two directors were up.

In October the minister of culture had suggested replacing Monsieur Fabrizio with a high-ranking civil servant who possessed all the necessary qualifications, Maxime Skimazi, with Langlois staying on as artistic and technical director. Henri, for his part, suggested Léonce Calvy. Since each man refused the other's suggestion, the situation was at an impasse.

Upon his return from a late screening, at an hour when others went to bed in search of a restorative sleep, Langlois wrote to the great Russian director Sergei Yutkevich to share his lassitude:

Tonight I return to the Cinémathèque at rue de Courcelles, bowled over from seeing a silent film, this cinema which is made out of heartbeats. Everything here is dying, everything is suffocating, everything falls silent, everything becomes more alone and solitary, everything is slowly turning into a desert for lack of the will to fight, for having been a mere handful to fight.

What remains? Just the facades of death that one washes and cleans like those cadavers to which one applies lipstick and rouge to give the illusion of life.

The General Assembly met on 19 December 1967. In order to show Henri the extent of his trust, André Malraux had sent Langlois his proxy vote. Henri thanked him in the following letter:

> I am that much more grateful to you, for this proxy vote takes on a special value for me in this time when the subsidy of the Cinémathèque is frozen and our government-appointed auditor has no qualms about announcing, without proof, that I habitually write rubber checks.
>
> I should like to thank you for all that you have done for this establishment and for all that you have tried to do.
>
> As for the rest, neither you nor I are to blame. For a year now, I've had the feeling that this house is condemned, no matter what, for reasons that the future alone may reveal.
>
> In thanking you once again for your friendship and your trust, I send to you, *Monsieur le Ministre*, this expression of my faith and respect.

In the course of this meeting of the General Assembly, Henri Langlois was reelected to the board of directors in the company of Yvonne Dornès, Louis Emile Galey, Alexandre Kamenka, Denise Lemaresquier, Pierre Prévert, Jean Riboud, and Hubert de Villez. Whether it was psychological wear and tear or a deliberate maneuver on his part, Henri had let it be understood that he could no longer be a candidate for the post of artistic and technical director. This was a surprising attitude when one knows that not long before, Henri, in speaking to André Malraux, had reached this conclusion: "I don't want to be the Pétain of the Cinémathèque after having been the de Gaulle. I've been tempted to go off and leave it in the hands of men who got themselves in, in order to destroy it. But that would be to desert and betray you. I refuse to do that."

Be it misunderstanding or a simple failure to truly appreciate the man in question, Malraux immediately gave the CNC director the green light to scout around for another candidate who could eventually replace Langlois. Pierre Barbin, director of the Festival of Short Films, held in Tours, was chosen.

François Truffaut would be one of those to fight most energetically in defense of Langlois. In January, Langlois asked Truffaut to attend a meeting. The director wrote to say he would not be in Paris on that day, but Henri was adamant: "It is essential that you come. The Cinémathèque is in danger. I'm counting on you."

Before the meeting, the two men had coffee together, and for the first time Henri revealed his plan with precision, explaining to Truffaut just what the board of directors was up against. This was the day the co-opted members of the board would be chosen, and if Truffaut would run, the government representatives wouldn't be able to turn him down. Once Truffaut was "in," he could help Langlois. The director, who had just shot *Farenheit 451* and *The Bride Wore Black*, had no free time to speak of, since he was preparing to make *Stolen Kisses*.

And yet he agreed to present his candidacy, and that is how, on 19 January 1968, François Truffaut found himself among the eight co-opted members of the board. The other seven were:

- Jacques Goultier de la Ferrière, head of the Office of Radio and Television at Cultural Affairs Headquarters
- André Laporte, one of the administrative directors at Pathé
- Claude Charpentier, representing the Ministry of Culture
- Léon Mathot, honorary president of the Cinémathèque
- Clovis Eyraud, director of Beaux-Arts for the city of Paris
- Jean-Albert Cartier, director of ATAC
- Ambroise Roux, vice-president of the National Council of French Employers (the French chamber of commerce)

The government representatives named to the new board were:

- Alain Trapenard, technical consultant, representing the Ministry of Culture
- Roger Malafosse, assistant budgetary director, representing the Ministry of Finance and Economic Affairs
- Pierre Moinot, writer and general director of Arts and Letters
- André Chamson, of the Académie Française, general director of the Archives of France
- Jean Chatelain, Director of the Museums of France
- Etienne Dennery, general administrator of the Bibliothèque nationale (represented by Head Librarian Jean Adhemar)
- Jean Basdevant, general director of the Ministry of Foreign Affairs
- Maxime Skimazi, assistant director, director of cultural and technical cooperation at the Ministry of Cooperation

Truffaut entered the boardroom to find men and women

whose personalities, when not a source of stupefaction, proved to be a source of amusement:

> These were very strange people. For example, there was a lady named Madame Lemaresquier. I think the only reason she was there was because she was Michel Debré's sister-in-law. It was certainly a clever move on Langlois's part to have the sister-in-law of the minister of finance on his side. But he didn't know that she was mad at her brother-in-law. And when anything bad was said about Michel Debré during a meeting, she'd shout "My brother-in-law has never understood the first thing about finance!"
>
> There was Pierre Prévert, who was absolutely charming—a true poet. And there was Ambroise Roux, a major figure in French employment. I thought it was strange that they were there. But the most solid presence, far and away, was Jean Riboud.

Riboud, general director of the multinational Schlumberger Corporation, was a great admirer of Langlois, and his wife, Krishna, was a good friend of Mary Meerson's. A journalist once asked Riboud what man had impressed him most by his intelligence, and the businessman replied, "Henri Langlois. He had a universal mind. He even gave me some very useful tips on how to run Schlumberger."

Riboud felt that matters had taken a turn for the worse when Minister of Finance Michel Debré had resolved to straighten out the Cinémathèque or else eliminate its funding. It was clear that the government wanted change, and several administrators believed there was room for improvement in the way things were being managed. Hubert de Villez and Jean Riboud had spent hours trying to convince Henri that a few of the government's ideas were not evil incarnate. But Henri, fearing that the Cinémathèque would become a "colony" of the government, would not listen.

The minister of finance brought increasing pressure to bear at the beginning of February. A few days before the board meeting scheduled for 9 February, André Malraux asked the representatives of the Cinémathèque to meet with him independent of Henri. Jean Riboud was chosen as spokesman for the group. Malraux arrived and began with a 10-minute speech. He did nothing but speak highly of Henri, showering praise on the man and his creation, the Cinémathèque Française, which had become unique in all the world and was therefore of extreme importance. He repeated several times that no one could have greater confidence than he in the future of the Cinémathèque. Nevertheless, one had to be realistic: The Cinémathèque needed to change because the Ministry of Culture was under terrible attack from the Ministry of Finance.

"It was a magnificent speech," Jean Riboud recalled. "In a word, what Malraux wanted us to do was to help him fight the Ministry of Finance. So, I said yes. One of the members of the board asked him if he intended to change Henri's job or responsibilities. Malraux replied that Henri had no greater champion and friend in all the world than he himself. . . . So, saying that under any other circumstances, I would have gotten down in writing what he'd just told us, but not doubting his word, I said that he could count on us to help him do battle with the minister of finance."

Then Malraux departed, leaving the group with his principal private secretary, whom Riboud asked to clarify what exactly Malraux wanted them to do. The secretary replied, "We want the government to hold a majority of votes in the board of directors of the Cinémathèque."

The administrators requested two hours in which to think it over. Given Malraux's verbal promise, they finally agreed to let the government have its majority. They were unaware—and Jean Riboud most of all—of the surprise awaiting them: "Practically the next day, they kicked out Langlois! What's always stuck in my mind is how Malraux made his speech, his solemn declaration, in front of all of us, and 48 hours later, Henri was out the door. It was quite some surprise! That Malraux could pull such a switch shocked me so much that I swore I'd devote myself to Henri's cause until the day he was reinstated as director of the Cinémathèque Française."

It was under these conditions that the historic meeting of the board of directors convened at 10:00 A.M. on 9 February 1968.

## chapter 11

# YOU ONLY LIVE TWICE: THE LANGLOIS AFFAIR

The whole story was pretty amusing for me—just like I was attending my own funeral. Imagine you're dead: Lots of people show up at the funeral to accompany you to the cemetery. There are those who liked you but also those who hated you. I never would have dreamed that so many people could like me so much. Maybe some of them didn't know me, but they liked the work I'd done. I've never wanted to talk about the "Langlois Affair." It's very simple—all you have to do is reread the newspapers. I don't want to go into the subject again as long as I live. Only after I'm dead. Then, if necessary, I'll come back as a ghost and I'll talk about it.

Henri Langlois

François Truffaut had already begun shooting *Stolen Kisses* when he attended the meeting of 9 February 1968. He arrived early enough to meet with Henri in a café near the rue de Courcelles: "I noticed that he'd managed to get a smudge of paint on one of the sleeves of his jacket. But it was too late to find something to clean it off with. Later, in the boardroom, I saw him standing there in front of 30 or so people, many of them civil servants who had never laid eyes on him before. And just from the looks on their faces, I could guess what they were thinking: 'Nah, you're not going to tell me *that's* Henri Langlois, the guy we've been giving money to all these years!'"

As in all meetings where the outcome has been arranged in advance, this particular meeting would be a shining example of unfaltering courtesy and ritual protocol. Alexandre Kamenka, as the oldest member in attendance, called the meeting to order. First, a successor to Marc Allegret had to be chosen as president, in addition to naming the other officers of the board. The first words spoken by the new president-elect, Pierre Moinot, were by way of reminding those assembled that the day's business included the designation of two directors for the Cinémathèque. Two candidates were present for the post of artistic and technical director: Henri Langlois and Pierre Barbin. The candidates for the post of administrative and financial director were Léonce Calvy and Raymond Maillet.

Monsieur Holleaux took the floor to announce that André Malraux's choices were Monsieur Barbin for artistic and technical director and Monsieur Maillet for administrative and financial director. He hastened to add that the minister had not lost sight of the fact that Henri Langlois's collaboration was absolutely essential to the life of the Cinémathèque. Since the statutes provided for only two directors, Monsieur Langlois's new function would be determined by the board later on.

Pierre Moinot specified that the first task for the new officeholders, presuming that Langlois did not figure among them, would be to propose a reform in the statutes whereby Langlois's new duties might be made clear.

Henri took the floor. He was quarreling not on the basis of personality conflict but as a matter of principle. He had decided to firmly present his candidacy after having learned that Pierre Barbin was the suggested candidate. He would have yielded had the post been entrusted to someone like Georges Sadoul, but Sadoul had died four months earlier.

François Truffaut spoke up to say that if Langlois was no longer good enough to head the Cinémathèque, it was out of the question to give him some other post. Hoping to soothe tempers and allay doubts, Monsieur Moinot in turn repeated that this was not a people problem but a financial problem. The government auditor could not approve the budget unless substantial reforms were made.

Alexandre Kamenka remarked with vigor that "the artisans of the Cinémathèque who have been pursuing their craft for 30 years are a hell of a lot more important than the government's money!"

J. A. Cartier, who had just been elected secretary over Madame Dornès, did his best to get Henri to say what he truly thought of Barbin: "Is it really 'a matter of principle,' as he claims, or is it outright hostility toward Monsieur Barbin?"

"I'm under no obligation to discuss this choice," Langlois replied. "But it's a question of standards. As for the way things are run, what has been called a certain eccentricity is in no way synonymous with abnormal management. If I dreamed one instant of resigning, it was after a complete disagreement over preservation methods. My technical competence cannot be faulted. As for being made a mere artistic consultant, I cannot possibly accept such a position. The blockhouse situation was not unknown to the government commissioner. I have always—with Marie Epstein's assistance—kept inventories. I agreed to share them with Monsieur Holleaux, but not with anyone and everyone."

A long discussion commenced. Should a vote be taken immediately, or should the board wait until Henri Langlois's new duties had been clearly spelled out? Truffaut protested the very idea of a vote that would impose a choice between two people whose respective qualifications were so disproportionate as he considered Barbin's and Langlois's to be: "I find it particularly unjust that Henri Langlois is being reproached for having character. As for Monsieur Barbin, I've never seen him at the Cinémathèque!"

The time came to vote. Truffaut got up and left, refusing to participate under the conditions offered. In his absence, the vote proceeded by secret ballot. Eight men—Kamenka, Roux, De Villez, Langlois, Riboud, Laporte, Prévert, and Galey—and two women—Lemaresquier and Dornès—refused to vote. Since the board comprised 24 members, 13 votes constituted an absolute majority. Twelve people voted for Barbin. There were 11 abstentions and one blank ballot. In an election this important, Barbin had not obtained a true majority. He was elected only because those who wished to express their categorical disagreement had refused to vote.

When it was time to conclude the meeting, Monsieur Basdevant paid tribute to Langlois and expressed his wish that all would go well. Henri only said briefly that he was sorry to see the Cinémathèque put in the hands of people he considered incompetent.

The meeting was adjourned. The matter seemed to be settled. The ninth of February was a Friday, and Monsieur Holleaux took off immediately to go skiing.

Pierre Barbin wanted to get going without further delay. The employees on hand at rue de Courcelles had the impression they were the victims of a commando raid. When the new team swept in, Henri had just left. Barbin declared to Marie Epstein, "I am the new director of the Cinémathèque. You understand that the bathtub era is over with. We're now in the Palais de Chaillot era."

Marie couldn't keep from asking, "And just who was it who led the Cinémathèque from the bathtub to Chaillot?"

"Uh, well," Barbin stammered, knowing full well who had, "uh, it was Langlois."

"Well, then, what are you doing here instead of him?"

And leaving Barbin to ponder that question, she returned to her work. The following day's newspapers would write that Barbin, having changed the locks, locked Marie Epstein in at rue de Courcelles overnight. Years later, she set the record straight: "Nobody locked me in. I locked myself in so as to put my files in order without being disturbed. And I wasn't alone—I had my cat with me, who, I might add, didn't understand what was going on and meowed the whole night through."

That same afternoon, Marie Epstein, Bernard Martinand, and all the other employees of the Cinémathèque received letters, dated 9 February, notifying them that they'd been fired.

These "We happily regret to inform you" forms bore the Cinémathèque letterhead but were on different paper from what the Cinémathèque normally used. Everything had been prepared, printed, and typed up before the actual voting had taken place. The eviction of Henri Langlois was therefore premeditated and carefully orchestrated.

The salaried employees were the first victims of the bid for power. It was clear that anyone who professed undying allegiance to Henri Langlois would pay dearly for his or her loyalty. Only those who renounced Langlois would be allowed to stay on. Preliminary interviews indicated how the staff felt about their former boss. Every last employee was loyal and true, but some were obliged to use trickery so as to hang on to their means of livelihood. Lotte Eisner, Marie Epstein, and many others wrote highly indignant letters and asked Georges Langlois to refer the case to the public mediator.

On Saturday, 10 February, the battle of the telephones and the jockeying for position began in earnest. There were already a few pointed articles in the press, prefiguring the bombardment of coverage to come. On the morning of 10 February, Henry Chapier opened fire in the left-wing paper *Combat*. The headline: "Scandal at the Cinémathèque: The Revolting Dismissal of Henri Langlois." Chapier concluded his article with a call to arms that would be widely repeated: "In the face of this measure that is sowing consternation and dread, after having rekindled a taste for conflagrations and barricades, the columns of this paper will be open to all filmmakers, writers, actors, and collectors who are stunned and distressed by the

fact that Henri Langlois has been forcibly removed from his work." *Combat* would unconditionally support and defend Henri throughout the affair.

Come late morning, the director's office at Arts and Letters, where Pierre Moinot was president, released the following communiqué:

> The evolution of the Cinémathèque Française—whose riches, accumulated bit by bit thanks to Henri Langlois, have made it an increasingly important organization—excludes from here on the cottage-industry-style management of its humble beginnings. This is what brought the government to make its granting of the subsidy that supports the Cinémathèque contingent upon indispensable improvements in the way in which the Cinémathèque is run. The duality of direction provided for in the current statutes enabled Henri Langlois to pursue a line of unbroken continuity in artistic direction but did not provide for the same in the case of administrative direction. The government, accordingly, asked the board of directors of the Cinémathèque, presided over by Pierre Moinot, to entrust the overall management of this organization to Pierre Barbin, leaving the board to decide in what sort of role Henri Langlois might best continue his work within the reorganized Cinémathèque Française.

By early afternoon, Jean de Baroncelli was riposting in *Le Monde*: "There is certainly no shortage of good accountants and good managers in France. But there is only *one* Henri Langlois. Are we going to accept his being taken from us?"

"No!" was the resounding reply throughout the profession—a response so swift, unanimous, and fierce that the government bureaucrats were stunned. In just a few hours, the cinema community was mobilized. Henri had cleverly left the impression that he was going to withdraw without a fuss. In reality, he was communicating with the entire world. The *Cahiers du cinéma* offices, which already bore a marked resemblance to a command post, had fired off more than 100 telegrams to the world's greatest living filmmakers, asking them to forbid the projection of their films as a sign of protest. Everyone was feverishly at work preparing communiqués urging critics, actors, directors, and writers to dissociate themselves from the arbitrary decision that had struck Langlois.

By the afternoon of the tenth, the first letter of protest, signed by some 40 filmmakers, had already appeared in *Le Monde*. Among its signers were Abel Gance, François Truffaut, Alain Resnais, Georges Franju, Jean-Luc Godard, Chris Marker, Jacques Rivette, Alexandre Astruc, Claude Chabrol, Pierre Kast, Claude Berri, Jacques Doniol-Valcroze, Jean Eustache, André Cayette, Eric Rohmer, Jean Rouch, Joris Ivens, and Robert Bresson.

Alexandre Astruc summed up perfectly the indignation of all creative types, while demonstrating why they recognized themselves in Langlois:

> At the very moment that Henri Langlois leaves the Cinémathèque Française, the Cinémathèque ceases to exist. Period. That's all, folks. This

is not, as one might believe, some official organism where, for reasons that can be talked over, one replaces one individual in charge by another individual; this is a private, personal, individual, unique work—the flesh and blood, mistress, wife and children, the property of Henri Langlois, private individual, who, for motives easily understood, one day felt the need to camouflage himself behind an official service.

I detest protestations, lists of more or less platonic signatures, and so on. As a film director, I believe exclusively in situations of force: A film is not the work of a director in the name of some immortal principle, but because, practically speaking, from the writing of the script straight through to the release print, not one foot of film can be exposed without him. The situation of the Cinémathèque Française without Langlois is exactly the same thing. Langlois, whoever his enemies may be, is invested by divine right from the very start with every power because he is the Museum of Cinema, the same way, for example, Gaston Gallimard is the NRF [Nouvelle revue française] or—if I may be excused for this example—in the eyes of the Gaullists, General de Gaulle is France. That is why, whatever the respect we may owe the French government and the rights it has over us, said government should not be surprised if, gradually, French film directors withdraw the films they gave to Langlois. They gave them to him and him alone, and not to X, Y, or Z. Because they knew that he would sooner see himself chopped up into little pieces than tamper with a single millimeter of film.

After the directors, the distributors will do the same thing, and the unfortunate fellow who thought he had permission to take Langlois's place is going to find himself presiding over papers, forms, dossiers, rubber stamps, empty corridors, exaggerated politeness, and so on. He'll only be missing two things: the films and the public.

That evening, it was as difficult as usual to find a free spot at La Coupole, the famous Montparnasse café-brasserie-restaurant. The arrival of a noisy group led by Henri, himself surrounded by several film directors, caused a mild sensation. As they cruised the mosaic-tiled aisles in search of a seat, they stopped often to accept handshakes and words of support and encouragement from other patrons. When they were finally seated, the atmosphere suddenly fell silent around their table: The neighboring diners were trying to pick up a few snatches of their conversation. At a nearby table, a young

lawyer who regularly attended Cinémathèque screenings listened fervently. When he came over to greet Henri, Langlois told him, "You've already heard enough. Since you know what's going on, see to it that my brother knows."

"And that is how," recounts Georges Langlois, "I was awakened at 2:00 A.M. by a phone call from my friend and colleague Jacques Saada." He continues:

> The next day, Sunday, Henri was nowhere to be found. I figured that we could all use our imaginations and take the initiative. Since I wanted to do something for Henri, I decided to go see what was happening at Chaillot. When I reached place du Trocadéro, I saw a newsdealer who had *Le Journal du dimanche*, the Sunday paper, on display. I saw photos of Henri and of Mary Pickford under huge headlines: "Henri Langlois Has Saved 73 Years of Cinema," and in smaller type, "His Eviction Raises a Tempest among Filmmakers."
>
> I bought every copy the guy had, and with this big stack of newspapers under my arm, I went around to the steps that lead down to the movie theater of the Cinémathèque. As usual, the steps were clogged with people waiting to get in. Obviously, nobody yet knew about what had happened. I started handing out papers to people on their way down the steps, and the reaction was like a scene in slow motion. People hesitated, stopped moving forward, read a bit, and then handed the paper on. All of a sudden, there was a backward surge toward the exit. The woman selling tickets realized something was going on. She came out, saw me, and embraced me, with tears running down her face. That night there wasn't a single spectator at Chaillot.

On Monday the twelfth, the first wave of articles unfolded in the Parisian press. In *Combat*, Philippe Tesson ran the headline, "The Malraux Myth Has Lasted Long Enough" and published an article by Truffaut entitled "L'Anti-mémoire courte," (literally, "In Objection to Short Memory," but also a pun on Malraux's experimental and autobiographical best-seller published the previous year, *Anti-Memoirs*) and a piece by Chabrol, entitled "Help!" Chapier decided not to let a day go by without talking about the affair. Things couldn't be allowed to get bogged down in monotony, and, as during the time of the Resistance, everyone began to keep track: first day of the occupation of the Cinémathèque, second day, third day, and so on, right up to the liberation.

In view of its tendency to side with the government, the daily paper *Le Figaro* said nothing more revealing than "The Reorganization of the Cinémathèque Causes a Stir." Pierre Barbin told the paper in a telephone interview, "Insofar as I've been on the job only since the day before yesterday, I have nothing to say. Check back with me a month from now. Those who have spoken of 'dismissal' are mistaken. This is merely a reorganization.

As for me, I most ardently hope that Henri Langlois will come to recognize that I am a man of goodwill."

Barbin's brief statement in *Le Figaro* would be his first and his last. André Malraux's office instructed him to remain silent thereafter.

That same Monday, 60 filmmakers decided to prohibit the projection of their films. Written protests also poured in from directors as famous as Joseph Losey, Vincente Minnelli, Robert Florey, Roberto Rossellini, Fritz Lang, and Nicholas Ray. Ray, who happened to be in Algiers, had immediately contacted Fred Zinnemann, former president of the Screen Directors Guild of America, and asked him to get the word out among American directors. Fritz Lang, in California, sent a telegram directly to the *Cahiers du cinéma* office: "Deeply outraged by scandalous and rude dismissal of Henri Langlois, who has consecrated his entire life to the Cinémathèque Française, whose magnificent accomplishments are unanimously recognized as unique by the entire world, thanks to his devoted work—Stop—This great institution he created will perish without him—Stop—In complete agreement with you, I ask you to include my signature in the letter of general protest—Stop—I also prohibit the projection of my films at the Cinémathèque Française until further notice."

The affair also took on broader political connotations when the Fédération nationale du spectacle, a branch of the CGT (Confédération générale du travail), one of the French entertainment trade unions, released the following statement: "This sanction confirms the current regime's intention to clamp down on activities in the domain of culture, just as it does in every other domain where it thinks that taking control might serve its own interests."

By six o'clock that night, 200 to 300 filmmakers, critics, film buffs, and actors had gathered together at rue d'Ulm without any organized plan of action. They formed a sort of picket line and began politely suggesting to would-be filmgoers that they refrain from attending Cinémathèque projections, since Langlois had been bounced. Slogans were hastily inked onto signboards: "We Want Langlois," "Boycott the Cinémathèque," "Langlois Oui, Barbin Non," "Reinstate Langlois"—and then hoisted above the door. Photographers and journalists, followed by a

number of police officers, were soon on the site. Only seven people bought tickets for the 6:30 P.M. screening.

By 8:00 P.M., Michel Simon and Claude Berri had showed up to join Godard, Rouch, Chabrol, and Kast. The crowd was thrilled to meet its heroes in the flesh. Simon, seated on a chair, gave an informal press conference: "It's monstrous. Langlois risked his life during the war to preserve the Cinémathèque's documents. Whatever we are we owe to him."

Jean-Luc Godard raged, "The government is bullying creators! They wanted to sic a cop on Langlois!"

"This is all-out war," affirmed Chabrol. "And we're certain to win it."

The first tracts also began to appear:

> Don't go to the Cinémathèque. Let it become an imaginary museum until Langlois's return.
>
> François Truffaut

A group of journalists from *Paris-Presse* were standing watch together when they spotted Henri having a drink at the corner café. They wrote, "As he walked past us, he nodded his head and, with a serious expression, murmured, 'There's still a slight chance to save the Cinémathèque.'"

On Tuesday, 13 February, when Jean Rouch's article entitled "Anger and Shame" appeared in *Combat* and Jacques-Arnaud Penet wrote of "Malraux; or, the Ministerial Condition," telegrams had in the meantime been sent and received. The tip of the telegraphic iceberg featured protests from Charlie Chaplin, Orson Welles, Luis Buñuel, Carl T. Dreyer, Elia Kazan, Otto Preminger, Arthur Penn, Samuel Fuller, Lindsay Anderson, Tony Richardson, and Albert Lewin.

That afternoon, Cinémathèque employees who had been fired demonstrated peacefully in front of Chaillot. That night, the authorities closed both theaters for "inventory and reorganization." The real reason, obviously, was because they could no longer guarantee the programming. At the National Assembly that day, the deputy from Nièvre and leader of the non-Communist left, a man by the name of François Mitterrand, submitted a question in writing to the minister of culture: "Would the minister be so good as to reveal the reasons that led him to evict—under particularly shocking conditions—the director of the Cinémathèque Française, to which the cinema owes so very much, as does our country, for it houses an artistic heritage of inestimable value."

On Wednesday, Saint Valentine's Day, the newspapers announced that a press conference was scheduled for six o'clock that evening, in front of the Cinémathèque. "Tonight, Everyone Goes to Chaillot!" was Chapier's war cry. Since a genuine "war council" was in place by then, Chapier predicted there would be violence. But how were Malraux and the police force going to react when faced with stars like Catherine Deneuve and Jeanne Moreau?

By late afternoon, 2,500 people had amassed on the Trocadéro esplanade between the Théâtre national de Paris and the Musée de l'homme. Starting at 3:00 P.M., 30 busloads of police and National Guardsmen had encircled the quarter, blocking entrance to the Cinémathèque by avenue Albert-de-Mun, a street running perpendicular to the Seine along the eastern border of the Trocadéro Gardens, uphill to the Palais de Chaillot. If the government-owned French television networks were conspicuously absent, all the foreign networks were on hand. Young people handed out a tract from the "Children of the Cinémathèque," which was read aloud by actor Jean-Pierre Kalfon:

> Using bureaucratic pretexts, the worst enemies of culture have recaptured this bastion of liberty.
> Don't stand there and let them get away with it. Freedom is taken, not received. All those who love the cinema, in France and throughout the world, are with you and with Henri Langlois.

The crowd surged into the landscaped area between the esplanade and the entrance to the theater, shouting for Barbin and Holleaux to resign. When they reached the first police cordon, the first blows were exchanged. Godard managed to break through the police line, but, breathless, found himself alone on the other side. The police decided he should be permitted to *vivre sa vie*, and let him go. The demonstrators backtracked to the esplanade and marched down avenue du Président Wilson, blocking traffic. When they'd covered the one long block to the intersection where Président-Wilson meets Albert-de-Mun, they hit a new police cordon, whereupon the police began to hit them. Billy clubs held high, the men in uniform struck more than their fair share of native talent. Godard and Truffaut were injured, and their wounds were tended to in the porchway of a building. According to *Cahiers du cinéma*, blood was streaming down Bertrand Tavernier's face, Anne-Marie Roy had a broken wrist, and Yves Boisset's wife fell to the ground, where she was beaten by the police. The crowd surged back toward Trocadéro, where, at 7:15, Godard gave the order to disperse.

The next day's headline in *Combat* was, "The Billy Clubs of André Malraux," whereas AFP, the French press agency, tried to play down the previous day's revolt, in which, in AFP's opinion, there were only "a few hundred demonstrators, rowdies daubed with Mercurochrome, like in the movies, to give the impression of wounded people."

*Le Monde* filed an objective report, but also tried to calm the prevailing agitation: "While the protest movement grows larger and louder, the Cinémathèque's board envisions conferring an important role upon Mr. Langlois. Certain decisions were made on Wednesday, during a meeting conducted by President Pierre Moinot. In particular, the board intends to confer upon Monsieur Langlois a special mission, apart from his realization of a Museum of Cinema and the conception of cinema-related exhibitions. This special mission will have as its goal the development of a center for cinematographic research and experimentation. Apparently, the direction of this center will be proposed to Monsieur Langlois in the future."

Was this alleged "future" truly foreseeable? It was flagrant, civil–servant-inspired errors that had started the whole affair in the first place. If the government had chosen Barbin, it was because they had no idea of Langlois's importance. And why had they refused Langlois the crucial element they were only too willing to accord the man who replaced him—namely, an administrative and financial director in whom he had confidence? Langlois had begged them to assign him an administrator who actually knew something about the Cinémathèque—Chief Auditor Léonce Calvy. And he had been turned down. What could be more absurd than wanting to "confer upon" him an artistic role when, up until the week before, he had performed precisely that in his position as artistic director? What's more, how could he logically be criticized for being a poor administrator when, in reality, his job description precluded all administrative functions? And why exactly had the government waited through six days of protests and near riots in order to announce via the press how very much it wanted to bestow these eminent duties upon Langlois? Was the government's sincerity to be believed?

In any case, it was now too late. The event had taken on the momentum of a revolt. The dispute had become a protest movement without precedent in the arts arena. People grabbed *Combat* off the stands on Friday, 16 February, in order to read Truffaut's article, "The Resistable Ascension of Pierre Barbin," and another, by Jean Dragon, entitled "For the Anti-Goering's Pleasure." The newspaper also announced a press conference, to be held that evening at 6:00 P.M., at the independent movie theater Studio Action on rue Buffault. Jean Anouilh added his name to the long petition in Henri's favor via telegram from Switzerland: "Request my name be added to theater list of protest against arbitrary dismissal of Henri Langlois—Stop—Personally vouch for signatures of Sophocles and Shakespeare so often invoked by culture ministry."

That night at Studio Action, five foreign television crews, 300 journalists, and 20 filmmakers gathered for the press conference. Jean-Luc Godard got things rolling:

> In my opinion, the cinema is at the same time both spectacle and research. Yesterday at Chaillot we did the spectacle; today we're doing the research. This will no doubt be less amusing but also more instructive. This affair presents a certain number of questions. . . . A comparison comes to mind. The director is not only a poet, he is a technician of poetry or a poet of technique. The two are absolutely inseparable. Well, for me, Henri Langlois was one of the greatest directors in France. . . . One might say that Henri Langlois was the director and scriptwriter for a film entitled *La Cinémathèque Française*, the production manager of this film being the Centre du Cinéma and the producer being the French government. The director, Henri Langlois, has always asked for an excellent production manager. And what did they send him? They sent him an enemy . . . Not only must he preserve films, not only must he know which films to print first in view of the meager funds he's got to work with, but he must also project them. Now, if Debré doesn't know how to handle all that, then it's his fault and not Langlois's.

"To take from us the Cinémathèque Française as it was with Langlois in charge," proclaimed Jacques Rivette, "is to take away our oxygen, force us to hold our breath, and now prevent us from even feeling like making films."

"This is a republic," added Jean-Paul Le Chanois. "And since the freedom to appeal to public opinion is guaranteed to us, we're making use of it. Under another republic, the Fourth Republic, another government made another error—the Blum-Burn agreement, which at the time literally sacrificed the French cinema. What happened then? The entire profession formed the Committee for the Defense of French Cinema, which grouped together the authors, technicians, directors, workers, and producers who, with support from distributors and theater owners, managed to bring about a reasonably happy resolution. Perhaps now would be the time to form a Committee for the Defense of the Cinémathèque Française."

Since Pierre Barbin knew that Frédéric Rossif had

not stayed on very good terms with Langlois after leaving the Cinémathèque in 1951 in order to work in television, Barbin asked Rossif to organize a televised debate. The projected date was 21 February, during a program called "Cinéma" produced by Michèle Manceaux and Rossif. The show was subsequently rescheduled for the twenty-ninth but would never actually come about. André Malraux, fearful of the consequences of such a broadcast, forbid it to take place. French television, controlled as it was by the government, did not cover any of the various events and in fact hardly spoke of the matter.

Malraux was furious over the role he'd been obliged to play. Moinot had been parachuted into the presidency of the Cinémathèque, an organization about which he knew next to nothing. But as he went along, he discovered just how important a figure—one with an international profile, no less—Henri Langlois was. Holleaux, being a public servant, had no choice but to stoically accept any and all blows directed his way. The higher-ups tried their best to discredit Langlois but were swept off like wisps of straw in the tempestuous outpouring of protest.

France was, of course, a Gaullist state, and yet the Cinémathèque found itself occupied. Naturally enough, it wanted to be liberated. Obviously, things were topsy-turvy.

But where was Langlois himself while all this was going on? He had retreated to his ivory tower and had made up his mind not to issue any statement. This wily decision proved to be wise indeed, for it completely disoriented the opposition. Henri positioned himself above the fracas. Since he had not spoken a single word against the government, the government could always call upon him as a last resort.

During the early weeks, Henri and Mary avoided journalists by staying on rue Tremoïlle with their friend Rose Lacau.

Meanwhile, back at the Cinémathèque, there was a secretary who, much as she thought the dismissal had been unjust, truly believed that it would be impossible for Henri to return. Since this was her sincere opinion, the new management concluded that she was not, in fact, one of Langlois's terminally loyal followers. As a result, she became one of the employees whose presence concerned them least. The woman in question, Jocelyn Abbondante, became the secret agent at the heart of operations. Each day, a woman would phone her to explain precisely which document, which set of minutes from which General Assembly or board of directors meeting Langlois needed. At lunchtime, she could hand the requested document to a young man who met her in the rue de Courcelles Métro station. The liaison would photocopy it and return it to her, and she would have it right back where it belonged in no time.

Lotte Eisner and Marie Epstein had decided to take advantage of the grace period before their dismissals took effect to stay on top of things within the Cinémathèque. They were too visible, of course, to make any strategic maneuvers, but they kept their eyes and ears open and were on-the-spot witnesses.

If the new administrators had been counting on the alleged disorder of Langlois, they had badly miscalculated. Henri and Mary both had exceptionally good memories. Although they had had to leave the Cinémathèque posthaste, without so much as a chance to grab their appointment books, one of them knew exactly where any given document or file card relating to a film on deposit could be found, and the other knew by heart the countless telephone numbers of their friends planetwide.

One week into the fray, Henri called his brother Georges: "We have to see where we're at. I'm having a copy of the most recent statutes and some reports and statements sent over to you. Examine them. Rendezvous tomorrow at 54, avenue de Breteuil. You'll see it's easy to find—it's on the ground floor, and they're shooting a film across the way. I'll be there."

"And he hung up," Georges Langlois recalls, "without even telling me where to go once I got there or whose place it was." He continues:

When I reached the esplanade, there were just a few film assistants left, packing up their gear. The shot was over with, and nobody could tell me where to go. There was nothing left to do but go into the building. I crossed a vestibule and came out in a courtyard planted with enough orange trees to bring Versailles to mind. I decided to ring the bell at the first door to catch my eye. The door opened, and what should I see but a huge fellow in a turban—he was practically a Bengal lancer, a sort of Hindu servant in a brocade costume. I managed to stammer that I had an appointment with my brother, Henri Langlois.

This guy bows down to his toes and makes a gesture for me to follow him. I'm more and more amazed at what I'm seeing. By then, I'm in a sort of small reception area. But whose place is this? It was just like Riri not to give me a clue. He probably hadn't wanted to name names over the telephone.

Just then, an exquisite woman wearing a silk sari came to tell me, "Please don't be impatient. We expect the master any moment now."

A few minutes went by, and I heard a young woman's distinctive laughter. It was Jeanne Moreau, in the company of François Truffaut. Mary Meerson and Henri were right behind them. The servant then showed me the way to the dining room, where the faithful were assembled. Behind each guest's chair stood a magnificent East Indian—half-warrior, half-servant—poised and at the ready. Their chief, who was acting as maître d'hôtel, commenced his duties. From snatches of conversation, I finally figured out that I was in the house of Jean and Krishna Riboud.

After we'd had our coffee, Henri, impenetrable as the Buddha, let us talk. I put forth my point of view. It was clear to me that, even with eight government representatives on the board of directors, the General Assembly of the Cinémathèque remained sovereign. The problem was that it was necessary, given the exceptional circumstances, to assemble the number of members needed to call for a special session of the General Assembly to be held.

Jean Riboud listened and leafed through the statutes. He agreed with me. At the same time, he already had an idea of his own: He wanted to create a "committee of wise men."

On Tuesday, 20 February, 400 demonstrators answered the call put out by Françoise Rosay, Jean Marais, and René Allio. The group that, by 6:00 P.M., had assembled at the Cinémathèque's offices on rue de Courcelles included students from all the film and drama schools in Paris and even a few from the suburbs. Loudly calling for Barbin's resignation, they circled the building, carrying slogan boards, and the tension mounted apace. A small group managed to get in through the ground-floor windows, and shortly thereafter, 60 people swarmed in to occupy the offices until police reinforcements arrived about a half-hour later. This time the police had been briefed to let the storm pass and to keep their cool. Most amusing of all was the badly timed footwork, whereby the demonstrators on the inside unlocked the door to let in a group intent on doing harm to Barbin. Barbin, it turned out, had been standing right there when the angry mob charged past in search of blood. Not a single demonstrator had recognized him!

That afternoon, the French press agency had sent the newspapers a communiqué announcing Pierre Barbin's forthcoming journey to the United States: "Monsieur Barbin's trip is officially motivated by the preparation of a decree regarding the legal deposit at the Cinémathèque of a print of each film, French or foreign, to be distributed in France, in accordance with the method utilized by the Bibliothèque nationale [which receives two copies of every book published in France]."

The following day, in *Combat*, Chapier responded by writing "Legal Deposit—Barbin's Suicide Weapon in the United States": "In no uncertain terms, this means that for the exquisite pleasure of releasing their new films in France, the American companies (Fox, Columbia, MGM, Universal, and United Artists) will have, as of next month, a special tithe to pay into Monsieur Barbin's coffers—for it so happens that a print of a color film represents the modest sum of one million old francs."

"Suicide weapon" was indeed the appropriate expression, since Frederick Gronich was about to join the war and, as president of the group of American companies known as the Motion Picture Export Association of America, had the green light from the majors to create general havoc through private means. Gronich put his cards on the table: If Langlois was not reinstated as the head of the Cinémathèque, then Gronich was fully empowered to withdraw all the American films on deposit there. New deposits had been suspended as soon as Langlois got the bum's rush, but this announcement of Barbin's forthcoming trip to the States to brandish the threat of mandatory deposit had the majors on the warpath. Gronich wrote to Monsieur Moinot, the new president of the Cinémathèque, to give him a taste of just how much fun being president could be:

> I have the honor of reminding you that I have entrusted the Cinémathèque Française with deposits, free of charge. By virtue of the present document and in view of the fact that said deposits are no longer entrusted to the guardianship of Henri Langlois, I am obliged to notify you of the following:
>
> 1. I intend to prohibit any and all use of the objects on deposit and notably their communication to the public, in any form whatsoever, either for remuneration or without charge.
> 2. I should be most grateful if you will make all the necessary preparations so that the aforementioned items on deposit may be returned to me within 24 hours upon simple request.

Two days later, the ministry backed down and announced that Barbin's trip had been canceled. As for the "legal deposit" issue, the ministry explained to *Paris-Presse* that "the project is currently undergoing study, but Monsieur Barbin is not authorized to talk about it." The authorities had been warned that the American companies intended to demonstrate when Barbin landed in New York and, if possible, keep him from getting off the plane.

On the afternoon of Friday, 23 February, Pierre Moinot organized a "guided tour" of the Bois d'Arcy blockhouse vaults for a select group of journalists and technicians, chosen by the Ministry of Culture so as to exclude all rabid partisans of Langlois. Paul Balta of *Paris-Presse* took down Moinot's words: "Had it not been for Langlois, this visit would not have taken place, insofar as there would have been nothing to see. But it is also due to Langlois, junk collector genius, that certain films are in deplorable condition."

"Why didn't the government do something sooner?" asked a journalist.

"First, we would have had to have known," Moinot calmly replied. "We were unable to enter these storage areas until a week ago. Langlois is obsessively secretive. Everything at the Cinémathèque is under lock and key. There's an enormous box full of keys back there, and the box itself is locked and carefully guarded."

Moinot wrapped up his remarks by emphasizing that the solution was to be found through moderation:

> In view of everything Malraux has done for artists and creators, it is absurd to accuse him of wanting Langlois's head. People are not at issue here; the future of the Cinémathèque is. Malraux is not out to devour geniuses—that much he's proved. But Langlois has to understand that what he cannot do others must do in his place. I believe I've persuaded him of that. I don't want to launch the war all over again, but certain things must be said. Because, when it comes to accountants and creative types, Malraux has always sided with the creators and he believed in Langlois. But it is also essential that the Cinémathèque truly be enabled to play its conservation role. Langlois had a runaway passion for collecting, along with its corollary, a jealousy that led him to sequestration. That's the source of the whole problem right there. This martyr is not a saint. The problem is to save Langlois from himself.

*Le Monde* on 27 February featured an article devoted to the "Mysteries of Bois d'Arcy": "On several occasions, Henri Langlois has saved from destruction large quantities of films destined for the scrapheap. For 10 years now, he has repeatedly denounced the insufficiency of Bois d'Arcy so far as the storage and the preservation of films are concerned. The newly completed blockhouse was constructed specifically at Langlois's request. Let us note, in this regard, that Langlois had made a priority request for the construction of a facility in which to store flammable films, whereas the just completed blockhouse is equipped only for films that are not flammable."

By Saturday, 24 February, André Malraux felt the time had come to counterattack. He set about replying to the written inquiries of Parliament representatives, starting with François Mitterrand. The minister's written reply, published in the *Journal officiel*, the French equivalent of the *Congressional Record*, was reprinted nearly in its entirety by *Le Monde* and excerpted in other papers.

Malraux began with a summing up in defense of the government's more recent efforts in relation to those in the past. From 1949 through 1958, the Cinémathèque had had at its disposal little more than the modest theater on rue d'Ulm and the blockhouses at the old Bois d'Arcy Fort, along with 400,000 old francs in subsidies over the course of 14 years. On the other hand, he indicated that as of 1959, the subsidies had increased by more than 50 percent, beginning with the year in which the Ministry of Culture was created. The government had built the theater at Chaillot and, most of all, had begun construction on ultramodern film storage facilities. One such building had been completed; another would be ready for operation within months. The result: 20 million francs spent in 10 years. The minister hastened to say that "if the Cinémathèque Française was born of the personal efforts of Henri Langlois, it has long since ceased to be a private enterprise and has become an institution responsible for providing a genuine public service."

In the second part of his reply, the minister reiterated his criticisms of Langlois. On the one hand, the CNC had never been able to find out the number of films held by the Cinémathèque or their titles or their legal status, and, on the other hand, Langlois persisted in viewing the administrative and financial director as a subordinate. To top things off, Malraux wrote that "of thousands of reels of film stored at Bois d'Arcy, many are in deplorable condition. . . . 1,500 copies of films have been made since 1963, and we don't know where they are."

Finally, Malraux concluded with a sentence that would gain some notoriety and would be echoed in newspaper headlines: "Monsieur Langlois has been of eminent service. What he likes to do he does well, and what he does not like to do he does less well."

Marie Epstein took offense at Malraux's insinuations and, on 27 February, fired off a scathing yet pertinent letter to Monsieur Moinot:

I learned in amazement, by reading Saturday's edition of *Paris-Presse*, that Monsieur Malraux did not know where to find the copies of films that have been made by the Cinémathèque Française, in accordance with its allocations for restoration work, since 1963.

You will permit me to express my surprise since, although I myself was in charge of the making of the copies in question, I did not have the pleasure of being interviewed by you on this subject.

I would have been only too happy to show you the order forms stamped by the CNC, the approvals signed prior to striking each print, the bills sent to the CNC requesting that payment be made directly to the lab, the receipts indicating delivery, and the notices indicating the films' entry into the blockhouses, and you certainly would have been able to find said copies with no difficulty whatsoever. In any event, I can tell you that a great many of them are right under your feet in the basement at 82, rue de Courcelles. Therefore, you won't have far to go to find them.

I fear, Mr. President, that you have not yet had the time to get to know the life of a film archive in general, and, in particular, the life of our Cinémathèque Française, into whose presidency you have recently stepped.

For, you see, it is by the hundreds that we brought rusty films in the state of deterioration that you are contemplating with such sadness in the photo that appeared in the same paper and that caused your guests to "break down in horror."

The only thing for which one may reproach Henri Langlois is that, gung-ho collector that he is, he never turns down a deposit. He welcomes all contributions, and, unable to inventory and classify them forthwith because of a lack of means and personnel, he "stocks" them, because that layer of rust might just be concealing a rare jewel.

That same day, the magazine *Cinémonde* published Henri Jeanson's article, "The Poet Assassinated": "They behaved so clumsily, so rudely, and so stupidly that the thing resounded like a thunderclap and the scandal took on cosmic proportions. Because from everywhere—from Hollywood and from Rome, Montevideo and Berlin, Stockholm and Tokyo—the world's most eminent filmmakers and most illustrious stars cabled their indignation. And in Paris, all the directors who previously wouldn't have dared to be seen together marched out into the street together to protest. A miracle of unity and one hell of a show!"

It certainly was a "miracle of unity," all the more so since it was pouring forth from newspapers across the political spectrum, from far right to far left. And yet Raymonde Borde was not afraid to buck prevailing opinion. In *Le Monde*, he wrote: "If I speak up today, it is less in order to give the opinion of the Cinémathèque de Toulouse then it is to elevate the debate. Now is the time to say that if Langlois cut himself off from his colleagues, if he stood tragically alone and his successor has been welcomed so favorably, it is due to the fact that for us, the best interests of the films go before those of people."

Langlois alone? Barbin welcomed favorably? The poor man is dreaming, for reality, quite the opposite, was to be found in the articles with bylines as prestigious as they come. It was with the crowds in the street, embodied in the telegrams from the four corners of the earth. Even the government was beginning to get the message.

The protests were not limited to France. There was plenty going on in Rome, Geneva, London, and, most of all, New York and Los Angeles. The director Pierre Rissient, then assistant to Fritz Lang, had taken the initiative to circulate petitions to American directors. In *Daily Variety*, in one among many articles covering the affair, more than 50 Hollywood directors called for Langlois to be reinstated. And if his post was not returned to him, then they were all set to create one for him in the United States, in Hollywood or perhaps in Washington.

The minister of culture would receive a petition signed by 278 American filmmakers, university professors, writers, and artists. Individual collectors also got into the act. Raymond Rohauer wrote to Malraux: "Thanks to the initiative and cooperation of Langlois, I've deposited more than 3,000 films at the Cinémathèque. I have very clear agreements with him concerning their security and conditions of deposit. I would prefer not to have to withdraw my films, in view of the fact that the activities of the Cinémathèque are unique in all the world and that those who are interested in the cinema have the exceptional opportunity to be able to see a vast variety of films there."

The Defense Committee had just been formed officially as a legal association. The honorary president was none other than Jean Renoir. The association's core of officers consisted of Alain Resnais, president; Henri Alekan and Jean-Luc Godard, vice-presidents; Pierre Kast and Jacques Rivette, secretaries; and Jacques Doniol-Valcroze and François Truffaut, treasurers. Other guiding lights included Alexandre Astruc, Roland Barthes, Robert Benayoun, Mag Bodard, Marcel Brion (of the Académie française); Marcel Carné, Claude Chabrol, Henry Chapier, Claude Mauriac, and Jean Rouch. All who wished to express their solidarity with Henri Langlois were invited to join the committee, located at 7, rue Roger-de-Lisle, as founding, supporting, or active members and to make a corresponding donation.

Meanwhile, behind the scenes Georges Langlois and company were still trying to come up with a solution that would enable the government to overcome this dilemma without losing too much face. The famous caricaturist Jacques Faizant had drawn a commentary of his own for *Le Figaro*. The panel shows a puny little Malraux perched on some elaborate scaffolding. Below him, he sees demonstrators carrying signboards that say "Vive Langlois!" A huge de Gaulle, with his back turned to the pathetic creature on the scaffolding, raises his arms heavenward and exclaims, "Great! Now we're going to have to *blanchir* Malraux!" The French verb *blanchir*, "to whiten, lighten, or whitewash," also means "to exonerate, absolve, or clear," as in "to clear one's name." The caption is a humorous reminder that one of André Malraux's first acts as minister of culture had been to order that all the monuments in Paris be sandblasted, cleaned, and restored. Faizant also put a third personality into his drawing: Georges Pompidou stands before a newsstand, clearly interested in what the papers have to say. The prime minister was an old habitué of the Cinémathèque, which he had frequented in its avenue de Messine days.

One morning, a meeting was being held at Yvonne Dornès's house, with François Truffaut in attendance. All of a sudden, he recalls, a woman ran in to announce, winded, "I've just been to see the prime minister, Georges Pompidou. Things can be worked out. Henri stays at the Cinémathèque. Mary has to go—she stays home."

Langlois grew spectacularly angry. Rising to his feet, in all the fury of his indignation he shouted, "I will not stand for any such thing! Mary remains at my side. Since that's the way it is, I'm going to call together all the administrators, all the members of the Cinémathèque, and have them vote on this proposition. Then we'll see!"

Was it at that very moment, as Truffaut liked to tell it, that General de Gaulle turned to his advisers and asked, "But who exactly *is* this Monsieur Langlois?" However appealing the anecdote, it is only an apocryphal story. Everyone remembered the general's journey to Canada in 1967 and his resounding pronouncement, "Vive le Québec libre!" ("Long live free Quebec!"), spoken from atop the Montreal city hall. That same evening, a grand reception had been given in his honor, at which Serge Losique found himself beside René Levesque, the future liberal prime minister of Quebec. When he was close enough to General de Gaulle to speak to him, Losique presented himself as follows: "I'm here because of Henri Langlois and his Cinémathèque Française. I'm their representative in Montreal."

To which de Gaulle replied, "Ah, yes, Henri Langlois! Of course. He's doing great things."

When Malraux and the CNC woke up to the fact that they were in a rotten position, it occurred to them that they'd do well to negotiate. Jean Riboud would serve as intermediary between Henri, the Cinémathèque, and the government. Following the advice of the lawyer Izard, Riboud thought of Professor Georges Videl, former dean of the Schools of Law and Economics of Paris, as the person most qualified to preside over a consulting committee that the public would dub the "Committee of Wise Men." Handily enough, the committee was formed at the request of the members of the board of directors, including those designated by the government. Riboud and Langlois's choices were ratified. Apart from its president, Georges Videl, the committee was made up of five personalities: producer Georges Lourau, filmmaker William Novik, high-ranking treasury official Du Pontavice, filmmaker Jacques Rivette, and producer Edmond Tenoudji.

The idea was for the "Wise Men" to conjure up suggestions enabling the government to institute a sort of "peace with honor" proposal that would restore sovereignty to the members of the association and enable the government to back out of its corner with a minimum of embarrassment. Yvonne Dornès asked Georges Langlois to summarize matters for President Moinot and to initiate the preliminaries required for calling a special session of the General Assembly.

In order to convoke such a session, it had to be officially requested by a specific percentage of the membership. And even if many of those members were at the ends of the earth, their duly signed request slips had to be in perfect order. The members of the Defense Committee, along with Mary Meerson and her magic telephone, would work wonders. The regulation request slips began pouring in from far and wide. A simple majority of the membership would have sufficed, but Henri felt that wasn't good enough. A race against the clock began.

The final days and the final hours were crucial. The atmosphere was supercharged as dozens and dozens of young people took off in all directions with stacks of request slips to be filled in and signed. Some of these young emissaries were bold enough to get celebrities out of their beds in the middle of the night. Georges Langlois recalls, "We were a bit apprehensive about the welcome they'd get with tactics like that. When they came back, they told us that not only had they gotten the job done but they'd been offered champagne!"

Finally, there were far more official requests than necessary, and the legal machinery was in place to notify Moinot to convoke a special session of the General Assembly for 22 April. Moinot was faced with hundreds of request slips, which together formed an intellectual autograph hunter's dream package. The list, which began, alphabetically, with the name of Marcel Achard of the Académie Française, also featured the following names: Henri Alekan, Yves Allégret, Jean-Michel Arnold, Georges Auric, Jean de Baroncelli, Madame Brassaï, Robert Bresson, Luis Buñuel, Marcel Carné, Henri Cartier-Bresson, Alberto Cavalcanti, André Cayette, Claude Chabrol, Christian-Jaque, René Clair, René Clément, Luigi Comencini, Louis Daquin, Jean Delannoy, Max Douy, Joris Ivens, Alexandre Kamenka, Nelly Kaplan, Pierre Kast, Joseph Kosma, Fritz Lang, Alberto Lattuada, Jean-Paul Le Chanois, Madame Lemaresquier, Albert Lewin, José Lichtig, Lucie Lichtig, Renée Lichtig, Norman McLaren, Jean-Pierre Melville, Jean Mitry, Noël-Noël, William Novik, Marcel Pagnol, Madame Gérard Philipe, Jacques and Pierre Prévert, Man Ray, Nicholas Ray, Satyajit Ray, Jean Renoir, Alain Resnais, Hans Richter, Jacques Rivette, Eric Rohmer, Françoise Rosay, Roberto Rossellini, Jean Rouch, Jacques Tati, Olwen Vaughan, King Vidor, Madame Vigo-Sand, Luchino Visconti, Joseph von Sternberg, André Thirifays, François Truffaut, Alexandre Trauner, Denise Tual, and Sergeï Yutkevich.

The papers announced the news on 6 March 1968, roughly a month after the affair had begun. *Le Monde* carried the headline "Toward a Solution to the Langlois Affair," and announced that a special session of the General Assembly had been called for 22 April, in a report that included the sentence "Pierre Moinot is taking over management of the Cinémathèque and himself suggests that Monsieur Barbin and Monsieur Maillet be removed."

For Jean Riboud, Moinot was a well-meaning man who had had no dealings with the cinema whatsoever before being named president of the Cinémathèque. Moinot, a writer and the director of the Academy of Arts and Letters, had been pitchforked into place by Malraux because he was an uncontested man of reason and accomplishment—that his accomplishments were in no way related to cinema was beside the point. Malraux saw Moinot not as a combatant but more as a peacemaker.

Just as the affair was allegedly on its way to being resolved, on 8 March, Pierre Barbin sent a registered letter to Lotte Eisner, the curator-in-chief of the Cinémathèque, indicating that she was hereby ordered to refrain from setting foot on the premises. On 14 March *Combat* published a communiqué from the Defense Committee announcing a new series of demonstrations in Paris and elsewhere throughout the country. The first of these demonstrations, which were to last until the General Assembly did convene, was called for 18 March at 6:30 P.M., in front of Cinémathèque headquarters.

Georges Langlois remembers these days

as an extraordinary time. Whenever an announcement was made, the general public came to our support. People who had absolutely nothing to do with the movies got all fired up in our defense. The Cinémathèque had become the symbol of entrepreneurial spirit up against state intervention. I was with Henri a fair amount. Henri's photo was in all the papers, and the press was pretty much in his favor. Since his picture was all over and since Henri's ample silhouette was easy to spot, he was constantly surrounded by strangers who would march up to say hello and cheer him on. When we'd get in a taxi to talk confidentially, the driver immediately knew who his passenger was. And when we got where we were going and it was time to pay, the driver would turn him down. He'd say, "No, no, Monsieur Langlois. I can't take your money. I'm only too happy to be able to help you out. Incidentally, my colleagues and I have all decided to drive you for free because what you're defending, in your field, is also a problem we cab drivers are up against. So please, do me a favor and put your money away."

In shops all over town, from the butcher's to the restaurants, it was the same. We'd keep hearing the same refrain: "Your problems are our problems. There has to be more freedom, fewer regulations, less state control." Everyone identified with our cause, because they felt it applied to them too. Onlookers and passersby would drop everything and join us—filmmakers, students, and the man in the street—all shouting, "We want Langlois!"

The eighteenth of March rolled around. It was 6:00 P.M. The National Guard stood watch, starting at avenue Hoche, carbines at the ready. Truffaut, Chabrol, Carné, Tissot, Lesaffre, Kast, Doniol-Valcroze, Lelouch, Frey, Léaud, and countless others were on hand, but many of them were blocked near the rue de Courcelles Métro station by another police line, made up of armed officers in helmets.

According to the *Figaro* reporter, the demonstrators— holding up enormous placards reading "No to the Barbinthèque," "Freedom of Expression," "Give Us Back Langlois," "Lynch Malraux," and "Films, Not Cops!"—began slowly to advance, shouting, "We want Langlois!" The authorities wanted to eliminate the most visible banners, and a clash ensued. The National Guard charged the crowd,

and one high school student was arrested. In order to free him, the demonstrators decided to sit down right there in the street on rue de Courcelles, while Jean-Pierre Léaud read a statement from the Defense Committee: "We miss the Cinémathèque. The suppression of cinematographic culture can no longer be endured. Give us back Langlois! Give us back a Cinémathèque worthy of the name. The government had hoped to pull off its dirty deed in secrecy. That's not the way things worked out. Today the government is jockeying for position. It thinks there's a truce. Yet Barbin is still in place. Each day that passes is a danger."

And Léaud finished his short harangue by shouting, as loudly as he could without a megaphone, "Barbin's Cinémathèque will never get off the ground!"

These defiant words sparked off an ovation, as all the demonstrators rose from the pavement, as if on cue, to shout, "No to Barbin! No to Barbin!"

In the meantime, according to *France-Soir*, Claude Chabrol had gone to see a police inspector in the hope of freeing the young demonstrator who had been arrested.

"Ah, Monsieur Chabrol!" said the police inspector, all sweetness and light. "I'm happy to see you. How are you? Say, Monsieur Godard isn't with you by any chance?" The inspector made no effort to conceal his pleasure at meeting such a big name in moviedom. And since the cop couldn't refuse a thing to his buddy Chabrol, the young man was able to head home safe and sound.

It was 9:00 P.M. before the crowd broke up, after one final oration by François Truffaut, reminding everyone to remain vigilant until 22 April, when the 780 members of the special session of the General Assembly were due to convene.

All this had gone on for far too long. The government, without an inkling of what it was getting itself into, had found itself faced with an all-out revolt that was growing increasingly political. On 21 March in Grenoble, ciné-clubs, college-level branches of the Socialist party, and the directors of university associations gathered together at the Rex Movie Theater, which was not quite large enough to accommodate the turnout. More than 1,000 people had come to the meeting. All of the members of the Defense Committee had traveled the 400 miles from Paris to attend. The meeting concluded with a long, prerecorded speech by Pierre Mendès France, legislator from Grenoble and former prime minister:

> Why has this wave arisen that today goes well beyond the realm of cinema and the borders of our country? Why have the great daily newspapers of 20 countries, including those most distant, in Asia, in South America, devoted full pages to the Langlois affair?
>
> Why are the very directors who cannot dream of making a single film without financial support from the CNC, that is, the state—and who know

that full well—ready to sacrifice their careers in order to defend Langlois and the institution he created?

Henri Langlois, whom I do not know but of whom I've long heard, is no doubt a likable character, brilliant and difficult, evoking, it seems, a Renaissance prince one day and a state-of-the-art hippie the next, capable, they say, of appreciating Louis XIV furnishings and the paintings of Chagall with the same taste and finesse he brings to Méliès or Griffith.

But beyond the man, or, more accurately, mixed up with him in a symbiosis that is likely to endure until his death, there is his work, the Cinémathèque. . . . Much has been made of unsophisticated, "hand-crafted" management. Langlois has been called a "junk collector genius," which, while recognizing his genius, seems to indicate that he is not particularly gifted for classic administration. He would probably not argue with that and would, in fact, with some insolence, put forth the idea that a cultural institution should not be a classic bureaucracy, pure and simple, but that something more is called for.

Let them be revealed, if indeed they exist, the worthy reasons that motivated the coup of 9 February. . . . A request such as this, legitimate though it may be, will not elicit an answer, for the Langlois affair is none other than an episode of open conflict between democracy and the administration technocracy.

Coming on the heels of the suppression of [the popular television program] "La Caméra explore le temps" and the banning of [Jacques Rivette's film] *La Réligieuse*, the decision of 9 February confirms the government's intention to apply a policy of infiltration and authority, of constraint and arbitrariness, directed against the cinema, against culture, against freedom of expression. . . . The ORTF, the French press agency, and the universities must not become servile instruments whereby the power of the state may better impose its ideas, its policies, and its law. . . .

The magnitude of reactions throughout the nation and the size of this demonstration show that we do not intend to lose the battle for French cultural freedom.

Mendès France waited for a reply that was never to come. Pierre Barbin and Raymond Maillet had in fact prepared a 20-page rebuttal to the Children of the Cinémathèque, but this document would never be distributed. Their document claimed to demonstrate that the seamless unity in Langlois's favor was not nearly so complete as the Defense Committee would lead one to believe.

Barbin, who clearly felt that he was no longer under the government's protective wing, established his own nonprofit organization, dedicated to "the revival of the Cinémathèque Française." This association was never heard from again.

Françoise Giroud analyzed the situation in the issue of *L'Express* covering the last week in March 1968:

> So it is that we have come to this paradoxical situation: For the most part, these are "left-leaning" people who want to wrest the Cinémathèque away from the state in order to turn it back into a private enterprise!
>
> We can see that this affair gets right to the heart of the problem of subsidies of a cultural nature. Whether a government leans to the left or to the right, the question is the same: Can there be compatibility between fertile, creative action and servility or allegience to the bureaucracy?
>
> The answer is no, in every country and under every regime. No work of the mind can develop without freedom, including the freedom to be mistaken.
>
> The Maecenas state that will protect artists, poets, and creators against the state itself remains to be invented.

Since the authorities prohibited a televised debate between Borde and Truffaut, Frédéric Rossif, who did not like being left in the lurch, videotaped two empty chairs! François Truffaut admits that there was a sort of intellectual terrorism inherent in the manner in which he and his comrades orchestrated the Langlois affair, but they had had no choice, given the almost hermetic seal the government placed on broadcast news. Despite the reams of articles and the demonstrations in the street, the French radio and television networks remained silent.

On one occasion, however, Truffaut did manage to get a pertinent word in edgewise on TV. On the evening of 16 April, the crew from the televised newsmagazine "Séance Tenante" had come to shoot a live segment of a debate about the future of the cinema. The debate was being held at the Studio Saint-Lambert Cinema, for the opening of a tribute to Henri Langlois. Between presenting Hitchcock's *Marnie* and his own *The Bride Wore Black*, Truffaut declared that the only important thing was to save the Cinémathèque—a topic on which the moderator permitted him to expound for five minutes.

The newspapers were beginning to tire of constantly passing along communiqués from the Defense Committee. In order to rekindle enthusiasm, Truffaut decided to hold another press conference and to do so on the Champs-Elysées this time around. It also seemed like a wise move to involve a new celebrity. Truffaut came up with director Henri-Georges Clouzot. Clouzot was ideal, except for the fact that he was almost completely unfamiliar with the Cinémathèque's problems. He took a crash course and subsequently agreed to preside over the conference.

The night before it was to take place, Clouzot phoned Truffaut to explain that the director of the meeting facilities on the Champs-Elysées had just called him to say he was afraid. The police had paid him a visit in order to intimidate him—they'd said he was renting space to excitable youths who would surely break windows and do other damage.

The conference went on according to schedule, and on 18 April Clouzot took the floor to describe the police pressure brought to bear in the hope of preventing the meeting.

The press was even more impressed than Truffaut could have hoped. The following day, L'Aurore made much of Clouzot as president, surrounded by Robert Bresson, Truffaut, Carné, Resnais, Godard, Lelouch, Rivette, Doniol-Valcroze, and the lawyer Kiejman. Truffaut and Clouzot enjoyed themselves thoroughly, as they took turns recounting, with wit and humor, the 69 days of resistance to date. They couldn't resist being a wee bit theatrical, because the affair was already tacitly settled. The pleasure of announcing Henri's imminent return was all theirs, although it was an announcement made with an emphasis on continued action: "If Langlois is not reinstated on the twenty-second, we will intensify our struggle, and notably, make use of the Cannes Film Festival in order to alert our friends abroad. If, on the other hand, he is reinstated, then the Defense Committee will assist the new Cinémathèque, remain vigilant against any new threat of attack, and study the reforms needed to conserve films."

On Monday, 22 April, hundreds of members of the Cinémathèque were spread out along the avenue d'Iéna en route to the Arts et Métiers meeting hall. A dozen patrol cars lined the avenue. Members of the CRS, the no-nonsense riot police, roamed the sidewalk in groups of four, now and then coming across people whose conversation was not entirely devoid of provocative boasting as they hurried to the meeting. Legion of Honor "boutonnieres" were in evidence, for these scurrying individuals were distinguished academicians, composers, members of the Institute, and celebrated filmmakers and producers, with a top-ranking rep-

resentative of the American studios and the dean of the French Law School tossed in for good measure.

Why was so much police manpower needed when the matter was settled and the lovely month of May 1968, with its promise of warmth and sunshine, was just eight days away?

The atmosphere in the auditorium suggested a forthcoming distribution of awards. In Moinot's absence, the presidency of the session was conferred upon Alexandre Kamenka, who immediately gave the floor over to Georges Vedel. Professor Vedel pointed out that the consulting committee's role had not been to arbitrate but to suggest paths that might lead to a reasonable solution. He explained that, after having heard from Monsieur Moinot, president of the board of directors, Monsieur Holleaux, general director of the CNC, and Monsieur Riboud, representative of the elected administrators, the committee gave its opinion only in those instances when feelings were unanimous or held by a firm majority of five out of six members. The following propositions had been unanimously approved:

> The Cinémathèque, an association constituted in accordance with the law of 1901 pertaining to nonprofit organizations, will be organized and managed as a private institution without government interference in its internal affairs. Consequently, its statutes must be modified in such a way that the direction and the management are exclusively dependent upon the General Assembly and the representatives it elects.
>
> The government envisions the creation of a public service devoted to the physical conservation of films. This service will receive deposits on a voluntary basis.
>
> The Cinémathèque will provide for the exhibition of films deposited with or lent to it. The public authorities will therefore, as in the past, place at its disposal, theaters suitable for projections and notably that at the Palais de Chaillot.
>
> Agreements to be drawn up between the public authorities and the Cinémathèque will determine, for the future, the rights and obligations of the public authorities and of the Cinémathèque in the matter of those films the Cinémathèque may deposit in blockhouses belonging to the public authority and the freedom the Cinémathèque will enjoy to use, withdraw, restore, and transmit its films . . . [as well as the] freedom to, at its sole discretion, make deposits, conserve films, and undertake any and all laboratory work.

Freedom, freedom, and more freedom—with a side order of liberty. It was on this theme that a beaming Henri, who was dressed for the occasion—if not exactly to the nines, then certainly to the eights—took the floor to speak, after so many days of silence:

If I am here among you today, if I did not permit myself to leave my colleagues who emerged from the most recent elections, it is because it occurred to me that I had no right to forget that, over the course of 30 years, it is you that I have approached to solicit the gracious deposits that were entrusted to this association, an association where you were at home and where you could leave your property as you would in your own home.

It was therefore indispensable that Monsieur Kurosawa—or Monsieur Rossellini, or all the rest of you—could benefit from all the facilities that had been promised to you and for which you had never lacked prior to 9 February. In order to bring this about, there was only one thing to do: The Cinémathèque Française had to be made itself again. And this was possible only through returning its sovereignty to the General Assembly. . . .

We also had to determine, in advance, a rough outline of the future relationship between the public authorities and the Cinémathèque in such a way that under no circumstances could the agreements subscribed to by third parties and depositors be put into question as they were on the morning of 9 February. . . . It was therefore essential that the Cinémathèque be assured of maintaining total freedom to use, withdraw, restore, and transmit any and every film, as well as to make deposits, conserve films, and undertake any laboratory work it deems appropriate, in keeping with its own resources.

We have paid for this freedom not only with the loss of our subsidy, but also with the corresponding loss of the financial leeway to pursue the unified assortment of activities we took to be fundamental to our mission.

We did not have the right to act in any other way vis-à-vis the members of our association, who believed themselves to be at home at the Cinémathèque and for whom the Cinémathèque was their home.

I should like to conclude by quoting a few words by Fritz Lang that accompanied his proxy vote and that express, far better than I could do, what the Cinémathèque Française has been and shall always be in the eyes of all those who know that the cinema is an art, and who love and respect it as such: "When I left Germany in 1933, I became forever after a cosmopolitan. Where could the hearth and home of a cosmopolitan possibly be? That is why,

deep down in my heart, my true, my only home was the Cinémathèque. But
if there is one thing in my life that I am completely certain of, it's that the
Cinémathèque Française will live on and prevail."

All of the propositions passed unanimously, and the meeting was
adjourned. Jean Riboud was assigned to handle questions from the reporters
who were impatiently waiting outside, while the board got together to elect
its new officers. Hubert de Villez was elected president, Jean Riboud and
François Truffaut, vice-presidents; Henri Langlois, secretary-general; Yvonne
Dornès, assistant secretary-general; and André Laporte, treasurer.

Two days later, Henri had an appointment with a government
emissary who proceeded to open the main door at 82, rue de Courcelles for
him. Upon entering his office, he discovered, in a large film can, the 68 keys
to the rooms, offices, drawers, file cabinets, and basement storage areas. They
had been placed there without any sort of note, and they weighed in at nearly five pounds.

The affair was over and done with, but those who experienced it firsthand
would not soon forget the giddy, inventive spirit of those days. *Les Cahiers du
cinéma* was a feverish launching pad for a movement run, fittingly enough, by
motion picture directors. Jean Rouch, for example, had been known to give
events a helping hand by announcing news that was not true—at least not
yet. Take the time he had *Le Monde* publish that Charlie Chaplin had wired
to inquire as to whether the Cinémathèque was planning to return his films
by plane or by boat. The telegram was, at the time, fake. But it was subsequently sent to Chaplin, who obliged by immediately returning it, properly
endorsed.

There was plenty of room for creative improvisation. When Malraux went
to Grenoble to attend an homage to Stendhal—who had been dead since
1842—someone on the committee came up with this telegram, which
appeared in the satiric weekly paper *Le Canard enchaîné* in February: "Having
recovered from my astonishment, I am obliged to protest most strongly
against the dismissal of Henri Langlois and to prohibit, until further notice,
(1) projections at the Cinémathèque of films based on my books, and (2) the
use of my name in ministerial speeches. Stendhal."

The solidarity that sprang up, from humorists to singing satirists, from
filmmakers to politicians, had been completely unexpected. Surprising
alliances had been forged between the New Wave and the Old Guard, as
well as between rival publications such as *Positif* and *Cahiers du cinéma*.

Those who refused to add their voices in protest were few, because,
beyond personal conflicts and apart from the controversy over nitrate stock
or hygrometry, one idea rose above the fray: Save the Cinémathèque as
Henri Langlois had conceived it.

He had meant it to be a laboratory of confrontation and research, a place where the private and workaday lives of cinematic art would be enriched and stimulated by the freewheeling interaction between films and the people who came to see them, in a realm free of censorship and free from bureaucratic interference. And this idea, born of the unexpected encounter between a praxinoscope and a bathtub, had made its way clear around the world.

Those who loved the cinema had fought as they had because they knew that there was only one Henri Langlois, a man who had gone on putting the cinema above his own comfort even after discovering that it was a fabulous deposit—a geologic find that could be mined until the celluloid cows came home. There was only one Henri Langlois to hold the deed to the gold mine of the silver screen and yet go right on wearing shoes with worn-out soles, completely uninterested in personal gain.

Why, then, had there been the Langlois affair? According to Jean Grundler of the Centre national du cinéma: "Langlois had annoyed and irritated. And despite the administration's immeasurable patience, at a given moment we just couldn't stand it anymore. Because we too had our responsibilities. In the end, it was a general misunderstanding. That sort of thing happens in family squabbles. And then, there was the amplification factor, resulting from the general tension and agitation that went along with that year. 1968 was a real double whammy of a year. There must have been sunspots riling the French at the time."

The theater on the rue d'Ulm was the first to reopen, on 2 May 1968. Prolonged applause greeted Langlois's return. Henri humbly directed the ovation toward François Truffaut. Forcing him to stand so that everyone could see him, Henri pointed to Truffaut and proclaimed, "Here is the man who saved the Cinémathèque!"

Addressing himself to all the faithful fans who had marched through the streets for him, Henri told them:

> If he were still alive, Eisenstein should have staged your demonstrations, because first you acted out the *Battleship Potemkin* on the steps of the Palais de Chaillot and then you did *October* at Courcelles. We are living

in bad times, and the cinema runs the risk of coming to a bad end if we let the Diocletian bureaucrats get their hands on it. . . . The demonstrations in the street were far from useless. In a way, they paid tribute to André Malraux, because they proved to him that he was right to have protected the Cinémathèque for eight years. Monsieur Luigi Charini has asked me to be a member of the jury for the next Venice film festival, which will be held at the end of August. In the meantime, and by special permission of Charlie Chaplin, tonight you're going to see the complete version of *The Kid*, along with Renoir's *A Day in the Country* and Stroheim's *The Wedding March*. And now, on with the show!

chapter 12

# JET PROFESSOR

The cinema is a means toward the acquisition of knowledge in the manner of Saint Thomas: by touch. Read all you like about love, but if you haven't made love, your idea of it will be totally false.

Henri Langlois

The Cinémathèque would experience freedom from now on, including the freedom to be poor. Between February and April 1968, the Defense Committee had attracted subscriptions from 2,776 members, whose contributions, tallied by Treasurer François Truffaut, totaled 71,800 francs. But the expense involved in printing flyers and a more detailed brochure, rental fees for the auditoriums where the press conferences were held, the colossal bills for telegrams, telephone calls, and postage, and the mobilization of hundreds of young committee members had left very little in the way of funds.

François Truffaut had emerged as the "Saint-Just of the Cinémathèque"—with the crucial exception of not going so far as to get himself guillotined. In one final effort to help the Cinémathèque, Truffaut set up a stand in the lobby of the Carlton Hotel during the Cannes Film Festival in May 1968 and appealed to festivalgoers in person: "In order to continue its work, the Cinémathèque needs financial support; that's why we need you to give, and to give generously."

But the vast majority of those milling through the lobby had already contributed to the cause. The source had run dry. Henri, of course, believed in miracles; otherwise, he wouldn't have believed in the Cinémathèque Française: "Each time it looks as if the Cinémathèque is going to fall apart, there's always a miracle," he was given to saying. "It can take the form of a minister, or people fighting in the streets, or some student deciding to hand over his inheritance. It doesn't matter where it comes from, since it always shows up when it's needed most."

This time, the miracle would originate from a fair number of time zones away. When Serge Losique first got word of Langlois's dismissal, he phoned Henri from Montreal. "So, they've kicked you out, huh?" observed Losique. "Listen, I'm going to arrange for you to teach a cinema course at the University of Montreal."

"You're nuts," Langlois had replied. "I'm completely self-taught. I don't even have a high school diploma, and you want me to be a college professor?"

But one month later, Langlois called back to say, "You know, I've been thinking—that idea of yours isn't so bad after all. Let's cook up a film history course."

The prediction Henri had made to his father had indeed come true: One *could* study film at the college level—universities were even handing out degrees in the stuff!

For Henri's first course, in September 1968, the 700-seat amphitheater of Montreal's Sir George Williams University was packed to the rafters. When Henri walked into the room, he could have sworn he'd stumbled into a giant aviary. Students were flitting about greeting one another, shouting across the room, and carrying on lively discussions while awaiting the exceptional man who had been chosen to pass along his wisdom. No fire inspector would have approved of the number of students blocking the aisles. The room was one big traffic jam at the intersection of culture and curiosity.

André Malraux was very well known in Canada. Henri was suddenly equally famous, and everybody wanted to see the guy who had stood up to Malraux and beat him at his own game. When Langlois reached the rostrum, the pupils of a thousand pupils looked back at him with a "Show me" stare. Losique began to introduce his learned friend: "Here, then, is the great Langlois, the man who—"

That was as far as Losique got. Henri grabbed the microphone away from him in order to enumerate his nonqualifications: "I don't know what I'm doing here. Losique wants me to be your professor, but I don't know how to profess. I don't know what cinema is. I don't know how to teach—I don't even know how to write! You're going to learn with me, and I'll learn with you. We'll see some images together, and I'll say a few words about them."

The students were delighted. Needless to say, no card-carrying, elbow-patched, pipe-smoking, dyed-in-the-tweed professor had ever come out and said anything like that to them. There was applause. Then the projector rolled, and Lumière films filled the screen.

"The problem," said Henri, speaking off the cuff, "is that Lumière was limited to a short length of film stock [lasting only one minute]. So, he set out to create scenes that are brief but composed." Langlois continued:

When you're watching a Lumière film, you tell yourself that everything you're seeing looks very spontaneous, that the film crew plunked the camera down in the street and let the street life stream by. But take a good look at *Workers Leaving the Factory*—the camera is placed so as to give an impression of movement. Everything was calculated and prearranged. This other film begins with a streetcar that enters the frame on the right and concludes with another streetcar that enters from the left. Do you think that was random luck? Not at all. The Lumière cameramen studied the movement on the street, deliberately chose the best angle to shoot from, and accomplished an extraordinary feat: In a matter of seconds, they managed to pack a maximum amount of action into the frame without actually moving the camera. You have close-ups, medium shots, and long shots, and you have the movement that holds it all together. Now that's not luck—that's science! Today we're beginning to discover that there were already tracking shots back in the days of Lumière. Even Fritz Lang told me that if he had seen these films in 1920, he would have been 20 years ahead. How is it that no history of cinema, and not one person alive at the time, ever said that the tracking shot, just like the panoramic shot and the moving camera, was invented by Louis Lumière? Well, quite simply, because they were blind. When they said, "Shot taken from a moving streetcar," they didn't realize that what they were really seeing was a tracking shot."

Henri paused a moment. The audience was fascinated.


You see, you have an element to work with, and that's the image. You can compare the image to a diamond. Now, the diamond in the rough, the stone of exceptional beauty—that's Lumière. Other people came along and learned how to polish this diamond. Griffith came along to sculpt and refine it, but that produced an overall unity of form, because the silent film is a single element. The talking picture consists of two elements: sound and image. Starting there, you've got something else. You've entered another realm. If you look at it in the absolute, it's alchemy. Let's take the easy-to-understand example of ceramics. There you have two elements: the raw clay and its glaze. You fire them together in a kiln and produce a new unified element—ceramics. The dramatic thing about the cinema is that very few people have managed to achieve that unity. Jean Vigo is no doubt the only one to have successfully made a homogeneous whole out of a talking picture. Vigo took sound, image, music and dialogue and fused them—and I mean *fused*, not just "mixed."

If we start with Griffith, we can find enrichment—pick up a few things. But if we start with Vigo, it's a mystery. We're stuck—we don't know. Even today we've been unable to figure out how they made the colors in certain ancient stained-glass windows; we haven't, for example, been able to unlock the secret of Chartres blue. That's precisely the case with Vigo. He made a blue, everyone tried to imitate it, everyone saw its beauty, everyone tried to follow it, but no one was able to duplicate that blue, because Vigo's secret has been lost. He took it with him, for he died too young. Like the stained-glass windows of the eighteenth-century, *L'Atalante* holds the key to the enigma, locked up within itself.


When the first class was over, the students swarmed around Serge Losique. "Mr. Langlois is wonderful," they said. "But with him, it's impossible to take notes. He starts off in one direction and ends up taking us in another."

To which Losique replied, "Well, that's the cinema for you. Langlois's thought process is like images streaming across the screen—subject to constant change. That's Langlois for you—that's how he operates."

When Henri came to the films of Fritz Lang, to the students' great amazement he suddenly called for the projectionist to cut the sound. Then Langlois explained:


You see, if we cut the sound to M, the image becomes flat. If we bring it up again, the image recovers its "volume" as well. This proves that M is a great sound picture. If you cut the sound to other films, you see people whose lips are moving but their eyes and their faces have no expression. You could say that they're pretending to talk. It was through conducting this sort of experiment that I realized that, without words to speak, Gabin goes out like a candle. Why? Because in view of the fact that the emphasis was on the dialogue, in order to give a natural impression he relied on naturalism. It's an astonishing observation because Gabin was, after all, the revelation of talkies.

Some years later, Langlois would declare in an interview for Le Monde that he refused to be considered a teacher: "I am not a teacher. Never in my life. I don't believe in courses—mine are anticourses. Is there a school for writers? All of this literature that's sprung up around the cinema horrifies me. You can't lie to people. They know what they want. I'm just trying to get them to look. No, I don't conduct a history of cinema. There was no art history before the mannerists, and yet da Vinci managed to exist, didn't he? The first time I heard about cinematic culture was in Italy, under Mussolini. In the name of culture, they persecuted the romantics, the naturalists, the impressionists."

The world's only anticourses for credit began in September 1968 and would continue for three years, during which time Langlois took the same airline between Paris and Montreal every two weeks. He would leave the Cinémathèque early on Thursday afternoon and make a mad dash for the airport, dragging along a suitcase stuffed with films. Langlois would arrive that same evening in Montreal, where Losique met him when he got off the plane. Henri gave his nonclasses on Friday, Saturday, and Sunday. Langlois, who on his own made up a scruffy subset of the jet set, already weighed upward of 220 pounds on his 5'9" frame. As a consequence, his ankles swelled up during each plane trip, since he suffered from circulation problems.

Henri traveled too far too often, but the Cinémathèque's financial needs were too pressing for him to think of letting up. The Cinémathèque received all of Henri's "full professor" salary. In Montreal, Losique forced Henri to see his physician, Dr. Laurier. Henri put his absolute trust in Dr. Laurier, whom he affectionately called "my country doctor." The doctor told Henri that his intercontinental to-ing and fro-ing, with its incessant changes of time zone, would eventually get the

better of his health. "If you keep going at this pace," said Dr. Laurier, "you have perhaps 10 years to live, no more."

He also put Henri on a strict diet of porridge, boiled chicken, and boiled leeks. This draconian menu produced a weight loss of nearly 25 pounds in just one month. Henri was swimming in his pants. He managed to keep up both the diet and his slacks for two or three months, but it was too much to ask of a man who zipped from airport to airport to limit himself to bland boiled foods and so, before too long, recidivism reared its famished head. His downfall was hastened by the fact that there was a Greek grocery right next to his hotel in Montreal. Every two weeks, Henri returned to Paris with jars of fig and rose petal and pistachio jam.

Langlois was always on the go, and depending on his destination, the vaccination requirements varied. Since there is no vaccination to prevent one from losing things, whenever Henri was vaccinated, more often than not he promptly lost the certificate of vaccination. That is how he came to be vaccinated against the same disease six times in the course of one year. In the frenzy of departure, he had also been known to forget his passport. One day, as a result of continuing to work on something while in a taxi, he even managed to lose his money between the Cinémathèque and Orly airport. One might be tempted to speculate that he did these things on purpose, just to see what would happen.

Henri traveled so much that the airline flight attendants ended up getting to know him. He was the "butterfly-pachyderm" who took up two seats on the plane. Langlois, of course, arrived with films to accompany his noncourses, and he had to show the Canadian customs officers all sorts of documents to go along with them.

On one occasion, Henri managed to get all the way to Montreal without so much as a passport. The very day he arrived, a gigantic separatist demonstration was being held and, to complicate matters, the radio had announced the presence of Turkish revolutionaries in Montreal. When the customs officials asked Henri to state his profession, he replied, "Secretary-general of the Cinémathèque Française." The customs officials were not impressed. They detained Langlois for an hour and a half and questioned him nonstop. When they asked him to empty his pockets, they turned up a crumpled French identity card from the 1930s. Noticing that their detainee had been born in Turkey, they wondered whether they'd gotten their hands on one of those notorious Turkish revolutionaries!

But Serge Losique, who was fairly well acquainted with the custom officers, came to the rescue. "Gentlemen," he proclaimed, "you have before you a man of considerable note—a great figure."

"That's all well and good," replied the customs officers. "But if he's such a great figure, why doesn't he have his papers with him?"

"But that's Henri Langlois!" exclaimed Losique. "I can give him any paper under the sun and he'll lose it. Listen, here's what I'll do. I'm going to go see your superiors. They'll tell you this: "Every two weeks, an important individual named Henri Langlois will be crossing the border. Let him through, whether he has his papers or not." And—most likely because no one except the genuine article would want to go to the trouble of disguising himself as Henri Langlois—this tactic actually worked. Henri had no further immigration problems throughout his three years of biweekly visits.

This did not, however, mark Henri's final run-in with customs officials. A few years later, Langlois called Losique from San Francisco to say, "I'm about to get on the plane. I'm stopping over to see you." After this visit, Losique accompanied Langlois to the airport to make certain he didn't miss his return flight. Henri was lugging a beat-up, overstuffed old suitcase that he'd reinforced with bits of rope and string. Langlois himself didn't look substantially better. He was less than clean-shaven and had knotted his tie backward. When he put his battered suitcase through the metal detector, it set off a series of warning beeps.

One of the customs officers approached Langlois and asked, "What have you got in there?"

"Nothing."

Another official opened the suitcase and brandished an object that appeared to be made of gold.

"And this? What do you call this?"

"That's an Oscar," replied Langlois.

An alarming silence fell over the personnel. It wasn't every day they discovered an Oscar in some bum's belongings. When the customs officials came to their senses, they crowded around to see just what an Academy Award really looked like up close. This one said, "Academy Honorary Award to Henri Langlois for his devotion to the art of film, his massive contributions in preserving its past, and his unswerving faith in its future."

When the "Langlois affair" had broken out, Henri became famous all over the world but especially in Canada and the United States. *Life* magazine and the *New York Times* had published numerous articles about him. What made Henri so appealing to Americans, Losique believes, is that he fit the unrelenting-hero mold to a tee. American romanticism favored the notion of the individual triumphing over all—

against evil, against the powers that be, against big business and the government itself, if need be. Langlois had goaded a Gordian knot to unravel in his
favor, and that was the stuff of celebrityhood in North America. In the wake
of 1968, every time the "Jet Professor" brought his updated Old World charm
to the New World, the papers announced his arrival.

In early 1969, the Smithsonian Institution invited Langlois to give a
series of lectures in Washington. That 28 January, Henri projected his montage of Lumière films at the Museum of Natural History. This 90-minute
compilation featuring *Workers Leaving a Factory*, *The Waterer Watered*, and *A
Train Coming into a Station*, along with dozens of scenes shot by Lumière
cameramen in their wide-ranging travels, was much acclaimed.

To present the program, Henri began by apologizing, in his irresistible
French accent: "I speak English like a dog you put in the water." While mim-
ing the breast stroke with his outstretched arms, he "swam" ahead, saying,
"America was discovered by the Vikings. But at school, you don't learn that.
When Columbus is in America, he thinks he discovers Asia. For me, Louis
Lumière is the Columbus of the cinema. Lumière didn't invent the appara-
tus, just as Columbus didn't really discover America, but he played a role of
like importance. . . . Without the cinema, you see paintings, you read
books—you see with the painters' and authors' eyes what it was. With the
cinema, you see with your own eyes what it was."

Langlois concluded with this pronouncement: "I am not nationalistic.
Cinema is my country!"

At the program's conclusion, one of the Smithsonian directors warmly
thanked Langlois, but as the applause continued, Henri got in the last word.
Turning to face the screen, he simply said, "Merci, Monsieur Lumière."

Henri was a hit in America. The *Washington Post* called him the
"Legendary Langlois." This portly living legend would go on to show his
Lumière montage at several college campuses, including Harvard.

A young American named Sheldon Renan was eager to create a film
archive in Berkeley. He had put together plans, but no existing American
museum, film institution, or archive would agree to help him. In 1968 he
ended up sharing his hopes with Langlois. Renan had little to show besides
a statement of goals on a piece of paper, but that was good enough for
Henri. Langlois showered Renan with advice, introduced him to several
directors and producers who would later give him grants, and finally
accompanied him to Berkeley with an architect's rendering of a film
archive in hand.

"And then Henri sent us films," remembers Renan. "Wonderful films—
*L'Age d'or*, *La Chienne*, unknown works by Méliès, things that had never been
seen here before, things that one can only show in an archive. Once Henri
recognized the Pacific Film Archive as an archive, we became an archive, a
cinémathèque with credentials. It gave us an enormous head start. I can't
begin to express how important it was, how much time it saved, how support-

ive it was for those years when all we had were a few films in an office, a file drawer, a borrowed auditorium, and some goals on a piece of paper."

In fact, Henri was making out so well in the New World that at least one post-Lumière luminary, Abel Gance, expressed his apprehensions about watching Langlois's brain get drained to the other side of the Atlantic: "I'm under the impression that the United States would like to see Langlois direct the Washington film archive, since the Americans come to fish out men of value from our troubled waters so as to spirit them away. This is a secret to no one. Are we going to let him go for good?"

Obviously, Henri did not intend to drop the Cinémathèque Française for the United States. But he did take advantage of his trips to Montreal to make brief excursions to New York, a city he appreciated all the more after his tangles with the French bureaucracy. Ever since his first trip to the United States in the summer of 1939, Langlois had greatly admired the most bustling of America's bustling metropolises, and it would be in New York, and not Washington, that new projects would take form.

Henri was a year-round pilgrim, and so it was fitting that he meet Tom Johnston and his wife, Mireille, over Thanksgiving dinner. Filmmaker Nell Cox thought Johnston and Langlois should make each other's acquaintance, and Henri was immediately won over by this enterprising individual who had worked closely with Robert Kennedy. He listened as Johnston spoke about the efforts he'd been involved in to clean up slum areas. But the assassination of Senator Kennedy had put an end to that project.

"I worked on this renovation program with one of my friends, the architect I. M. Pei," explained Johnston. "He's the one who drew up the design for me for the EYE Cinema."

"Do you want to create a cinémathèque?" asked Langlois, his interest piqued.

"No," replied Johnston. "My goal is a lot less ambitious than that, but it's very precise. I want to give short films the attention they deserve. I've found a terrific place to show them—right across the street from UN headquarters. There's an old Howard Johnson's there, practically falling apart. The Ford Foundation owns the property, and they're prepared to let us have it if we can renovate it. Pei has drawn plans for a series of small projection rooms ranging from 99 to 199 seats."

Johnston wanted to show the best short films from all over the world. He envisioned afternoon projections, in a continuous loop, totaling 90 minutes' worth of films that would be changed each week. The UN was one of New York's top tourist attractions, and this way, all that visitors would have to do would be to cross the street in order to see a film presentation that would fit right in with the international flavor of that day's sightseeing. Evenings would be programmed with an eye toward city residents and would feature the work of young filmmakers in emerging nations.

Nothing could have pleased Langlois more. He immediately promised to supply Johnston with films. But for some obscure reason, the Ford Foundation came up with plans of its own for the site and the EYE project was not to be. In the meantime, the city-subsidized New York City Center had asked Johnston to put together and promote film activities for it. When Johnston spoke to Langlois of this new prospect, Henri reacted by saying, "Maybe it's a good thing that EYE didn't work after all. We're going to create a cinémathèque in New York."

Conveniently enough, Jean Riboud happened to be in Manhattan. Henri immediately went off to tell him that City Center wanted to add a film component to its opera and ballet activities and that it was prepared to work in collaboration with the Cinémathèque Française. When Henri had stepped back into his rightful position at the Cinémathèque, he asked Riboud to be his vice-president. Riboud had promised to muster support from private industry, starting with a $10,000 annual cash donation from Riboud's own Schlumberger Ltd. He also convinced his brother, head of the Danone dairy-products empire, to contribute to the Cinémathèque's operating expenses.

Although the French tax advantages stemming from corporate sponsorship were not nearly as advantageous as similar arrangements in the United States, Riboud still suggested to all his business associates that they contribute to the Cinémathèque. He had also contacted John de Menil, who was affiliated with Schlumberger and supported the De Menil Foundation in Houston.

As of 1 July 1968, John de Menil informed Fritz Lang that he was creating an association called "The New Wave" in order to collect funds to help the Cinémathèque Française. He asked Lang, as well as Jean Renoir, John Ford, and King Vidor, to lend their personal sponsorship to the campaign. De Menil's goal was to collect additional donations from the 60 or so Hollywood producers and directors who had given Langlois their moral support when he was ousted. He hoped to come up with $120,000, which would cover roughly half of the now-rescinded government subsidy. Fritz Lang was a particularly generous donor, and, in all, Riboud's extended efforts produced nearly $100,000.

Henri enlisted Riboud to negotiate the financial arrangements between the Cinémathèque Française, Tom Johnston, and City Center's new director, Richard Clurman. Riboud recalls that Clurman was clearly fascinated by

Langlois and highly enthusiastic about the idea of creating a cinémathèque in New York. The eventual contract stipulated that City Center would pay the Cinémathèque Française $50,000 annually, in addition to all of Henri's travel expenses, for several years to come.

The City Center project was about to get off the ground. The architect, David Oppenheimer, had worked out plans for two 300-seat theaters and one 100-seat theater for the basement of the center's building on Fifty-fifth Street. The center was to be open from 10:00 A.M. to midnight, seven days a week. The program, under Artistic Director Henri Langlois and Director Eugene Stavis, would feature six to eight films daily.

Langlois and Stavis were so impatient to start that while waiting for the new theaters to be built, they decided to schedule a grand film retrospective from 29 July to 3 September 1970, at the Metropolitan Museum of Art, to be entitled "The Cinémathèque at the Metropolitan." With 70 films, Langlois set out to provide a glimpse of 75 years' worth of cinema, from its earliest beginnings to the latest work from Europe, Asia, and North and South America.

But this invasion of New York territory by Langlois was destined to create problems. Vincent Canby, writing in the *New York Times*, was of the opinion that the program at the Met and the proposed cinémathèque at City Center might leave the impression that MOMA was not doing its job when it came to showing the work it collected. MOMA in fact showed only two films per day, at 3:00 and 5:00 P.M. Some people felt that was insufficient, and others pointed out that most people were at work at those screening times.

In an article published on 26 July 1970, just a few days before "The Cinémathèque at the Metropolitan" opened, Canby wrote: "Trying to chart the maneuvering that is going on behind these plans is a little like attempting an analysis of some benevolent Mafia activity. Nobody wants to talk for attribution. It involves long-term strategy, short-range tactics, jealousies, personalities, a little bit of chauvinism and, most important, money."

Adversaries of the City Center project alleged that Henri would never have allowed a foreign archive to set up shop in Paris. That is not the opinion of Tom Johnston:

Langlois could be mean and vindictive if somebody got him mad, but I think that if someone else wanted to show a lot of films in Paris, he wouldn't have been against it, so long as the other guy didn't do anything to jeopardize Langlois's grant money. His impulses were generous and positive. He wanted everybody to be able to see as many films as possible. Langlois was like that. When he told me he'd help me out with EYE, he didn't know me from Adam. I think he just figured, "Here's a man who wants people to go out and see films." Langlois often helped people without stopping to think if there was something in it for him. He was an unselfish man, a real film nut. In comparison to him the others were pretty cold. In any event, we saw that in Paris the Cinémathèque was doing its job by projecting seven or eight films a day and that at the same time there were a lot of art houses. Whereas, in New York, there was nothing comparable.

Eugene Stavis had worked with Johnston since the EYE project in 1969. He thought it was inconceivable that a city the size of New York, with its multiple operas, ballets, and theaters, could not offer a greater number of films that had left the regular commercial distribution circuit. "Langlois and I," he recalls, "thought it would be nice to plant as many flowers as possible and that the city of New York could stand to watch several film centers bloom and grow."

But Willard Van Dyke, director of the MOMA Film Library, thought new blossoms should be cut off at the roots. He declared war, and his first hostile action was to ask all the distributors who were lending films for the Metropolitan retrospective to pull out certain titles at the last minute.

Henri had never dreamed he'd run up against such an odious offensive, but once again he was able to rely on the support of unwavering friends. Langlois called Raymond Rohauer and got him out of bed in the middle of the night to announce, "I've just been stabbed in the back by MOMA. It's trying to destroy our program. MOMA went to all the rights holders and asked them to withdraw their films. You're the only one who can help us with replacement copies."

And Rohauer came to the rescue with a print of *Birth of a Nation*, along with films featuring Keaton, Fairbanks, and Langdon. The show could go on. Rohauer recalls that on the evening of the gala reception in honor of Langlois, Miss Mancia of MOMA calmly showed up for the party. Henri, furious, marched right up to her and said, "You have a lot of nerve coming here!"

"Business is business," was her businesslike reply.

The retrospective, which lasted 35 days, featured two screenings per day, one at 6:00 P.M. and one at 9:00 P.M., and included a number of films that had never before been shown in the United States. The 70 movies were grouped under 11 general headings, including: "The Fantastic in Cinema,"

"Masters of Reality and Filmmakers of Our Time," "Comic Genius," and "The Western Saga."

The retrospective was not quite as successful as Langlois had expected. Late summer, with its punishing heat, was not the ideal season for such an undertaking, and the fact that it was vacation time meant that a potential student population missed out on the screenings. It must also be taken into account that American audiences were not accustomed to seeing unsung foreign films—particularly without English subtitles—as these occasionally were. As far as Johnston and Stavis were concerned, the retrospective was far from a failure and was doubly remarkable in that, despite opposition from MOMA, Langlois had accomplished the tour de force of projecting every film that had been announced.

It was nearly time for construction to begin on the three projection rooms when the directors of City Center changed their minds and suggested that the Beaumont Theater at Lincoln Center would be a perfect spot. According to Johnston, the director of Lincoln Center had gone to see his counterpart at City Center and asked for his help. He wanted to make the Beaumont profitable and saw a distinct possibility of doing so by transferring the City Center project there. Everyone thought it was an excellent idea except the principal parties concerned: Langlois, Stavis, and Johnston, who much preferred the basement level on Fifty-fifth Street. Johnston was categorical:

> We did not want to move to the Beaumont. One Sunday afternoon, I went to see the place with Langlois and Roberto Rossellini, and all three of us had the same reaction: It was a tomb. It was also a bad idea to use a space created for the legitimate theater by trying to convert it into a movie theater. Its very structure just wasn't what you'd picture for a cinema. So, right from the start, we were absolutely opposed to a cinémathèque at Lincoln Center.
>
> And yet the board of directors of City Center were adamant from that point on. In order for them to help us, we had to make up our minds to accept the Beaumont Theater. It was just then that the theater lovers got wind of the project, and they objected very strongly. They set off a whole

press campaign and proclaimed that it was just awful to want to convert a theater into a cinema, that there had already been quite enough of that as it was. If you read the papers from back then, you might get the impression that we were disappointed by the negative reaction, but we weren't, not at all. Langlois and I were very pleased that the theater enthusiasts put a stop to the plan for a cinémathèque at the Beaumont. But we hadn't spoken our last word."

While at the Dinard Festival in 1969, Jean Rouch told a journalist, "Langlois, who's been giving film courses in Montreal, is going to start teaching one at the university in Nanterre."

The journalist rushed off to a telephone to see if it was true. Nobody at Nanterre had heard about it, but if Rouch said so, it must be true. *L'Aurore* announced the news on 10 July under the headline "Cinema Chair for Langlois at Nanterre."

The idea of entrusting Henri Langlois with an experimental course in cinema and cinematic culture is the result of a meeting, several weeks ago, between the dean of Nanterre and the secretary-general of the Cinémathèque Française. The director of education had a dream. He thought that the creation of this chair might lead, within 10 years, to the teaching of cinema in French high schools.

It seems that this dream is on its way to becoming a reality. Monsieur Olivier Guichard, national minister of education, as well as a fervent film buff, has just put his stamp of approval on this project.

Therefore, beginning this fall Henri Langlois will become the recipient of the first chair in cinema in France.

In conjunction with a three-year cycle of film history classes, weekly film screenings will take place, both within the university and at a public auditorium in Nanterre so as to enable the general public to take part, to some extent, in campus life.

As soon as classes were back in session, Henri began teaching at Nanterre, a branch of the University of Paris in the western suburbs, and one with a reputation for residual student unrest. Langlois's first class took place in such a calm and attentive atmosphere that any fears the dean may have had were erased. As Henri left the classroom, he was greeted by a representative of the university at Vincennes, who wanted to know if he would also like to teach there, to the east of Paris. Langlois replied that he would have gladly accepted were it not for the fact that he already had more than enough to do, given his commitments in New York, Montreal, Nanterre, as well as at Chaillot.

For one thing, there was new talent to be discovered. Philippe Garrel would be one of Henri's last promising young discoveries. Since Garrel's films had no distributor, Langlois showed them at Chaillot and had nothing but praise for Garrel's work: "*La Cicatrice intérieure* is a chef d'oeuvre, a complete and utter masterpiece. I don't know how to explain it. . . . All of a sudden, all humanity, the entire Earth, speaks—the Earth without the antiquated implication of Mother. But it's not even exactly the Earth that speaks; it's the humus. . . . It's incredible—it's all right there."

Garrel has not forgotten Langlois:

> I really liked Langlois, because although he wasn't at all rich, he wanted to go beyond the Cinémathèque and create an institute of cinema. He was well aware of the fact that our lives have their highs and lows, and for all those moments in our existence when things are way off balance, he wanted there to be a place where you could go to work, with an editing table and cameras and all that. Whenever I finished a film, the sole person to whom I could go to show it—apart from the woman I'd made it for and four or five friends—was Langlois. He was the only one who treated us as artists. Langlois was an artist himself in the way he lived, and what he created never veered off toward the management machines. His relationship with artists had nothing to do with bourgeois morality. You were just as good a director to him whether you'd made a film that year or not. It's been said that the Cinémathèque was the Medusa's life raft. Well, thank goodness for that, because if it had been like all the other institutions, we wouldn't be where we are today.

No man is a prophet in his own land. The talents of the group of young German directors composed of Werner Schroeter, Volker Schlöndorff, Wim Wenders, Werner Herzog, and Rainer Werner Fassbinder were first recognized in Paris. Volker Schlöndorff had done an internship at the Cinémathèque—helping Langlois to subtitle German films—from 1960 to 1961. Wenders had spent several months watching films at Chaillot in 1965 and 1966, so as to broaden his base in film history. When Henri died in 1977, Wenders dedicated his film *The American Friend* to Langlois.

Werner Schroeter, a complete unknown in his native Germany, was made known by the Cinémathèque Française in 1970. Having seen Schroeter's *Eika Katappa* at Cannes, Langlois showed it immediately thereafter at the Cinémathèque in Paris (and later that summer at the Metropolitan in New York). Some spectators were confused; others were downright hostile. For the screening at Chaillot, it had been announced

that "the director will be present." Schroeter was seated beside Henri in the auditorium. Suddenly, a group of young men came up to Langlois and demanded to know, "Where's the asshole who made that? We're gonna smash in his face!"

"But Schroeter didn't show up," replied Langlois, without missing a beat.

The fond attachment these young German filmmakers felt for the Cinémathèque stemmed, of course, from the personalities of Henri and Mary. But Lotte Eisner, who served as a living bridge between the German expressionism of the 1920s and these young artists' own films, was also a crucial presence. In November 1974 Werner Herzog learned that his friend Lotte was seriously ill. Herzog, who is not known for doing things the easy way, vowed to walk from Munich to Lotte's bedside in order to save her from death's door. He strode off toward France in the middle of winter, cutting through fields and woods, with only a backpack and a compass. And sure enough, by the time the headstrong director had slogged from Munich to Paris, Lotte was on the road to recovery.

chapter 13

# HENRI LANGLOIS'S MUSEUM OF CINEMA

"Hey, listen—there's a treasure in the house next door."
"But there isn't a house next door."
"That's all right—we'll build one!"

The Marx Brothers

For the time being, the Museum of Cinema-to-be resembled nothing so much as it did the "Are we *still* pulling back?" sequence in *Citizen Kane* that shows thousands upon thousands of objets d'art and packing crates stacked up and splayed out at Xanadu like a high-flying bird's-eye view of an urban landscape. "When a guy's got that much stuff," the bird is thinking, "why'd he get so worked up over one little sled?"

In the post–May 1968 letdown, with his subsidy gone and in the wake of his vicissitudes vis-à-vis the government, Henri seemed doomed to leave the packing crates packed with the tens of thousands of documents, the original scripts and sketches and posters, the costumes, and

the various apparatuses that he and his colleagues had scouted up the world over.

The success of *Easy Rider* in 1969 sounded the death knell for the studio system of old Hollywood. *Easy Rider*, shot entirely on location for $380,000, brought in $9 million. Every time Dennis Hopper tacked another "Hey, man" onto the beginning, middle, or end of a sentence, more cash rolled into the till. Big-budget pictures had been losing money for a number of years. Part of the message of the French New Wave—that films could be made for less money with young actors and on location—had made its belated way to certain American producers.

One of the last of the noble dinosaurs, MGM, was on the verge of bankruptcy. In 1969 a businessman named Kirk Kerkorian, with interests in airlines, hotels, and Las Vegas casinos, bought up 33 percent of MGM's stock. Although this did not make him the majority shareholder, he still managed to have one of his associates, James T. Aubry, Jr., named as studio head. Aubry immediately decided to sell most of the land the studio occupied, keeping only 30 of MGM's 183 acres in Culver City. MGM's fabulous collection of costumes and props was ceded to the David Weisz Company, an international auction house, for $1.4 million. In April 1970 this company announced the forthcoming public auction of "an unprecedented inventory of the largest collection of motion picture memorabilia ever assembled." The MGM auction was scheduled to begin on 3 May on the Culver City lot.

In the space of three weeks, more than 150,000 costumes, furnishings, and props that had served in the making of some 2,200 films would be put on the block. Henri Langlois and Lotte Eisner were bowled over. For the first time, one of the most important studios was going to sell its treasures to the general public. Henri thought it absolutely essential that a representative of the Cinémathèque be within shouting distance of the auctioneer, but the expense of a three-week trip to Hollywood, plus a bankroll for acquisitions, was out of the question. Henri suddenly realized that Curtis Harrington lived in Los Angeles, and no sooner had he said this aloud than Mary picked up the phone: "Hello, Curtis dah-ling. You absolutely must go to the MGM auction for us—it's very important!"

Henri and Mary scraped together a few thousand dollars and sent it off, along with a list of the objects they most wanted, and especially which costumes. And voilà—Curtis Harrington was the eyes, ears, and wallet of the Cinémathèque Française in Los Angeles.

On Saturday, 2 May, workers emptied soundstage 27 and set up 3,000 wooden folding chairs. The sale began at 10:00 A.M. the following day. In order to give the crowd a better look at some of the more precious items up for sale, color transparencies of them had been shot. When the first of 11,855 slides appeared on the screen, the auctioneer launched into a series of "What-am-I-bids" and "Going-once, going-twices" that would last for three weeks up to the final "Sold!"

Curtis Harrington knew that Langlois was interested in anything and everything that had been worn by stars as famous as Marlene Dietrich, Greta Garbo, and Judy Garland. But it didn't take him long to realize that, in Debbie Reynolds, he had a bidding competitor every bit as rich as she was determined. Reynolds had in fact been collecting costumes since the 1950s in the hope of establishing a costume museum. Harrington remembers:

> I didn't know her then. The ironic twist was that a year later, she was the star of my film *What's the Matter with Helen?* I was too inexperienced in such matters to realize that when I saw the way the wind was blowing, that we were foolishly bidding for the same things, I should have struck some sort of an agreement with her. But I didn't know her, or enough about auctions to have the sense to go up to her, introduce myself, and say, "Couldn't we come to an agreement about some of these things? We seem to want the same stuff. Maybe you can have one and we can have the other," and so on, rather than bidding and making the price go up foolishly. So I was always bidding against her, and she had more money than I had from Henri—so, I did the best I could."

All the same, Harrington managed to walk off with a few trophies, including the dress Liz Taylor had worn in *Little Women*, Greta Garbo's dress from *Anna Karenina*, and Marlene Dietrich's three-piece black chiffon and gold-sequined getup from *Kismet*. Harrington fared especially well, if not altogether fairly, in acquiring Dietrich's duds. He noticed that one of his fellow daily visitors to the auction was none other than the owner of a Beverly Hills men's clothing store where Harrington had been a regular customer for years. Harrington struck up a conversation with the clothier, whereupon the director learned that the auctioneer was the store owner's father-in-law. Harrington, who had tired of being permanently outbid by Debbie Reynolds, mentioned to the auctioneer's son-in-law that he was representing Henri Langlois of the Cinémathèque Française and that Langlois absolutely had to have Dietrich's black and gold outfit. The fellow, sympathetic to Harrington's plight, suggested that an auctioneer could almost imperceptibly tip a sale in one bidder's favor by speeding up the conclusion of the procedure. And so it

was that an auctioneer in Southern California did his bit to make a corpulent *cinéphile* in far-off France one of the happiest men on the planet. When Harrington bid $500 for the Cinémathèque Française, Debbie Reynolds bid higher. When Harrington said $600, she said $700. But just as soon as Harrington gave the sign that he would pay $800, the auctioneer's "Going, going, gone" came and went in record time, and his gavel had closed the sale before the formerly unsinkable "Molly Brown" could make another bid.

Harrington's finest purchase may well have been Angela Lansbury's costume from *The Picture of Dorian Gray*. On the other hand, he failed to obtain Leslie Howard's costume from the 1936 George Cukor version of *Romeo and Juliet* with Norma Shearer. Henri was extremely disappointed. According to Harrington, Langlois had his heart set on this particular item, but he had no way of knowing that Norma Shearer would enlist Debbie Reynolds to buy for her all the costumes from her own films.

"I have the impression that Shearer told her," recalls Harrington, "I'll endow a Norma Shearer wing to the museum." "Debbie was absolutely determined to have that costume worn by Leslie Howard, and since Henri wanted it too, I continued to raise the bid. Finally, she won it—but that costume alone cost her $2,000!"

That was nearly the price paid for Charlton Heston's chariot from *Ben-Hur*, which was driven away—without harness or horses—for $2,600. But it was Judy Garland's ruby slippers from *The Wizard of Oz* that were purchased by someone (who no doubt had a controlling interest in a gold-brick road) for the modest sum of $15,000. According to Kenneth Anger, the pair in question was never actually used on the set.

Obviously, the Cinémathèque did not have enough money to compete with those prices. And yet Harrington acquired 20 or so more objects, among them, several Western costumes from *How the West Was Won* and the costumes worn by Wallace Beery and Robert Taylor in their respective versions of *Billy the Kid*. As for dresses, there were Katharine Hepburn's cream and brown dress from *Sea of Grass*, two dresses worn by Leslie Caron in *Gigi*, one of Ingrid Bergman's dresses from *Gaslight*, and one of Marilyn Monroe's costumes from *Let's Make Love*.

Visitors to the Musée du Cinéma-Henri Langlois often ask if there is a comparable museum in the United States, and the answer is still no. The American Museum of the Moving Image (AMOMI) in Astoria, New York, and the Hollywood Studio Museum, while a step in the right direction, are but two tiny drops in America's celluloid bucket. Debbie Reynolds's project has never come to fruition, partly through the fault of the city of Los Angeles and partly because of Hollywood infighting. There have been many discussions and fundraising galas, but there has apparently not been enough accompanying determination to succeed. There had been some talk of putting a museum on the Universal lot—which would have enabled it to be a companion piece to the famous Universal Studios tour—but everyone felt it would be unfair to put so much emphasis on Universal productions. As Curtis Harrington summed it up, with some feeling, "It's ABSOLUTELY APPALLING that we don't have a Hollywood Museum. It's a black mark on this most stupid city!"

At a given moment, producer Sol Lesser had even wanted to subsidize such a museum. After visiting Henri's momentous exhibit at the Palais de Tokyo in 1955, Lesser had approached Langlois to ask, "How much?" He wanted to buy the whole thing, just like that. It was not a simple task for Henri to explain that he had collected these treasures for the Cinémathèque Française and no one else.

"But I'm Sol Lesser, from Hollywood!" said Sol Lesser from Hollywood. More than once.

"Listen, Mr. Sol Lesser from Hollywood," Henri finally said. "Then make your own museum where you come from."

Lotte Eisner, who had overheard this exchange, took Henri aside. "You shouldn't have told him that," Lotte chided. "Because when you send me to Hollywood, he'll already have collected everything!"

When Lotte went to Hollywood for the first time, 10 years later, in 1965, and observed that Sol Lesser still had hopes of mounting a movie museum, she told him, "You were there to see what Langlois did at his exhibition. You should do what he did and come up with something extraordinary."

But even Sol Lesser no longer had the money it would take.

Ever since his adolescence, Henri had dreamed of creating the first and foremost museum of the cinema in the world. Even before the war, he had thought of installing it in Georges Méliès's former studio in Montreuil. But the owner of the property, a stubborn individual, did not want movie people on his land and had the glass and metal structure demol-ished in one night. After the war, Henri and Lotte had been the guests of Sacha Guitry in his private mansion near the Champs-de-Mars. The distinguished playwright-actor-filmmaker's home was lavishly decorated with the paintings, furnishings, and costumes from his films. This splendid residence, which would have been a magnificent setting for Henri's exhibitions, was demolished shortly after Guitry's death in 1957.

Langlois had ended up with more than one million photographs, 15,000 posters, 10,000 production sketches, and thousands of other objects, including costumes, sets, props, scripts, and original scores—in short, more than enough goodies from which to fashion a permanent exhibit on the cinema from its prehistory right up through the 1960s.

With the same perspicacity he had always applied to his work, Henri knew that his days were numbered. He had no intention of dying without first having accomplished his mission of giving life to a *grand musée du cinéma*. He knew, he felt down to the tips of the toes he could no longer make out over the horizon of his stomach, that at all costs it was up to him to demonstrate what a real museum of cinema should be. It was up to him to create the subtle relationship between object and viewer, plunging visitors into the phantasmagoric world of artistry that made the movies and, moreover, made them magical. He carried such a museum in his head and in his heart, and only his prodigious memory could hope to disentangle from their apparent shambles the thousands of objects he had collected, driven by an irresistible passion to acquire, preserve, and ultimately share. And finally, he had to put the Cinémathèque's holdings on display, in order to show that a museum should in itself be a work of art.

Since 1961, Henri had coveted the Palais de Chaillot as the setting for his museum, along with a conference room, an editing room, offices and workshops, a large library, a *photothèque*, and a documentation center. When, in 1967, Langlois learned that funds initially earmarked for the Cinémathèque had been withdrawn in favor of a school of architecture in Versailles, he had been terribly disappointed. When Edmond Michelet succeeded André Malraux, he could promise Langlois nothing more than the 21,000 square feet of basement space that had been freed up when the Museum of Popular Arts and Traditions was transferred to its new home in the Bois du Boulogne. Despite that promise, negotiations with the assorted administrations concerned were taking forever.

One day, Jacques Duhamel, who had inherited Michelet's post as minster of culture, took Langlois aside and whispered these words of advice: "Listen, I suggest you occupy the premises as a squatter. Put on an exhibition there and just stay on."

This was a risky proposition. After all, ministers came and went—the administration endured. But Henri decided to grab this unique opportunity.

The empty space in question was a long, abandoned tunnel. As Langlois explored it with Lotte Eisner, Lotte was openly taken aback by the endless series of gloomy roomlets. "But what in the world are you going to do with this?" she asked, bewildered.

"Something entirely different," replied Henri, who immediately set to work chalking in plans directly onto the floor.

Those who worked with Langlois were about to witness the sleep-deprived determination of a man who stayed up for nights on end to mold his construction site into "something entirely different." Langlois spliced his days together without any black leader in between, despite the fatigue that surely accumulated from carrying out his responsibilities in Montreal, at the Cinémathèque, and at Nanterre. When human-breaking-point exhaustion finally overtook him, he fell asleep on the spot, like a beast of the forest in the friendly confines of his kingdom. There is not a single partition in the expanse of the museum that was not built under Langlois's direct supervision. Entire nights were given over to thinking up colors and shades and tones. Langlois blended reddish-oranges and hit upon subtly dynamic blue-grays and mauves. For the room devoted to Lumière, he harmonized six different colors: yellow, straw brown, orange, reddish-orange, gray, and mauve. He chose fabrics, carpeting, and curtains that evoke the *salon indien* atmosphere of the Grand Café, where the first Lumière public motion picture projection took place in 1895. The room devoted to Pathé is shaded in blues, grays, and greens.

Langlois's astounding memory enabled him to pinpoint the location of a given object that would have been a needle-in-a-haystack chore for anyone else. "Go get me the preproduction sketch for *Tortilla Flat*. You'll find it in the sixth packing crate, to the left of the spilled coffee stain, marked with a cross." The staff would go to get it, and there, sure enough, it would be. In the meantime, Langlois would go on dipping his paintbrush with the gestures of a great chef dreaming up a sauce, accompanying his delicate preparation with a running commentary on the importance of color and whether a given shade should be opaque or transparent, depending on whether or not one wished the grain of the wood to show through.

From among the sets and props left over from the Jacques Charron film *A Flea in Her Ear*, Langlois had rescued two towering green caryatids in the sweeping art nouveau style of Hector Guimard. To *Le Monde* journalist Colette Godard, Langlois remarked, "You pass the very same ones on the way into Regine's [a famed night spot], but you don't see them, because they aren't displayed to their best advantage."

When another journalist from *Le Monde* asked Langlois about his working methods, how exactly he went about creating a museum from scratch, he replied: "On instinct. And with my subconscious. And with the cumulative benefit of 30 or 40 years' worth of cinematic history. I myself am surprised to have come up with such and such a color for a wall or an alcove when I had no precise idea starting out. . . . I work improvisationally, in disorder, by which I mean to say the apparent disorder inherent in life itself. A tree grows from one day to the next; it does not grow in keeping with some architect's schematic drawing. Taking the riches of the Cinémathèque into account, I had to eliminate instead of accumulate, to select carefully so as not to falsify the historical sweep of the cinema."

Guy Teisseire announced this masterwork in *L'Aurore*: "From the *Metropolis* robot to Scarlett O'Hara's dress, Paris will have its museum of cinema—it will be the world's most important."

Henri had hoped to inaugurate the museum on 28 December 1970, for the seventy-fifth anniversary of the first public screening of the Lumière films. But Langlois ran into technical problems as down to earth as plumbing, toilet facilities, and emergency exits. Langlois was not really fazed—in fact, he played up the advantages of the delay to *Le Monde*:

> It's all for the best. In two years I've been able to "mature" and "develop."
> In fact, I've been creating this museum since 1961. And even now, when
> I'm under the gun, when I'm not sure there won't be a document missing
> when the official inauguration rolls around on 14 June, I don't want any-
> thing to keep me from reflection. To reflect is to spend two hours in the
> same room asking yourself if something should be positioned to the left or
> to the right. It's having the color redone on the frame to an engraving. It's
> monopolizing workers for three whole hours—when they could be doing
> something else—in order to really set off a document with a very special
> setting. Of course, I could have just hung everything up any old way and
> left it like that, and maybe people wouldn't have noticed the difference.
> But I can't. This is the way I work, and I believe that the hanging of a show
> is a work of art in itself.

The delays created at least one good side effect: Pierre Bracquemond had the time to reconstruct a scale model of Emile Reynaud's *Théatre optique* (optical theater). Thanks to this ingenious device, more than 500,000 spectators had been able, before the turn of the century, to see animated cartoons at the famous waxworks museum, the Musée Grévin.

This first museum of world cinema, initially disguised as an exhibition entitled "Three-Quarters of a Century of World Cinema," was inaugurated on 14 June 1972, despite the fact that it was not entirely finished. Langlois had been promised a grand entryway that would permit visitors to enter via the place du Trocadéro, where the Métro station and bus stops were located. Throughout the period of construction, that entrance had been protected by a huge sheet of plywood. When everything was set, Langlois asked the workers to take down the protective barrier, whereupon he was astonished to find that the "entrance" was completely bricked up! He had arranged the entire museum, chronologically, beginning from the sealed entrance. Visitors were therefore obliged to enter through the exit and walk back through all 60 display rooms in order to reach the Chinese shadow puppets, where their tour was meant to begin. This monumental slip-up produced a trajectory reminiscent of the reverse-motion projections Henri had loved to create with his Pathé-Baby projector and his prized copy of *L'Assassinat du duc de Guise*: The people, who entered via the exit and were led on a winding hike toward the proper entrance, found the exhibition immense. But when they'd done their 75 years' worth, emerging in the 1960s, where they'd first come in, they inevitably told Henri, "You know, you're right—it's *not* big enough!"

Langlois had not set out to take people on a neatly segmented, rigidly chronological journey through film history. His achievement was more like a movie itself—a sequence of images that brought out the full resonating impact of the mythology of cinema through the use of color, lighting, costumes, sets, and props. Starting with the precinema, the cut-paper silhouettes, the magic lanterns and their hand-painted glass slides, the *pantomines lumineuses* of Emile Reynaud, and the first riveting experiments in capturing and decomposing motion as performed by Muybridge and Marey, a series of rooms lead up to the spaces devoted to Edison, Lumière, and Méliès. Then comes the birth of the French film industry, with the productions of Pathé and Gaumont and popular stars like Max Linder and Rigadin. The first art films segue into the Feuillade serials and the enduring myth of the suave caped avenger Fantomas. Then come the schools of Danish, Italian, and Swedish filmmaking; the birth of Hollywood and German expressionism, including sets from *The Cabinet of Dr. Caligari* and the robot from *Metropolis*; mementos of the French avant-garde; and the bold pictorial assault of Soviet imagery. Then, like a dissolve, talkies come to France and the musical comedy kick-steps forward in the splashy decor to *Broadway Melody*, the first musical to win an Academy Award for Best Picture, in 1929. Sometimes rooms partly overlap or backtrack to suggest a flashback, a widely repeated innovation, or a tangential discovery. Ideas surge forth in the heady confusion of cross-pollination. Stylistic influences ricochet from one country to another. Langlois enjoyed contrast and had no thematic qualms about placing a large photo of poverty-stricken Mexicans from *Que Viva Mexico* right beside Jeanette Mac-Donald's luxurious dress from *The Merry*

*Widow*, in the same display case. And what an unexpected pleasure it is to find Nosferatu stalking the set from *The Cabinet of Dr. Caligari*. Langlois loved to provoke visitors with unusual juxtapositions.

Having run out of space, Langlois was forced to condense the history of film from after World War II through the 1960s to fit into the last two rooms in the museum. What emerges is a collage that could serve as the coming-attractions trailer for the future museum he would construct the day more space was made available to him. As Langlois explained to *Le Monde*: "It was very complex to evoke the modern cinema, owing to the crampedness of the site. So, the exhibition spills out into the basement, into the entryway to the theater and the adjoining corridors. And then how can you best evoke the art of Godard, of Resnais, of Bresson, if not through the film itself? That's why the last room of the exhibition contains so many audiovisual images. Yes, at that spot we gave priority to living images—that is, to that which the cinema will once again become—whereas elsewhere we emphasized commercial exhibition, the posters, or the development of directing style."

This is also why the very last room at the end of the museum is a screening room—one that today is named in honor of Lotte Eisner, who died in November 1983, thereby, true to her prediction, outliving her hardworking friend Henri.

The Museum of Cinema is not the History of Movies. It would be futile to try to represent all films ever made. Comparing the cinema to the evolution of the automobile, Henri Langlois explained, "There are no new motors in the cinema since the arrival of sound. There have been differences in subject matter and style, but the form has remained the same." Langlois saw the cinema in terms of artists trying to create, and thus he championed film as art, be it the works of avant-gardists, documentarians, animators, or the makers of the most commercial feature-length films. From Méliès to Griffith, Stroheim to Welles, Cohl to Disney, Buñuel to Garrel, Flaherty to Rouch, or Ray to Guney, the museum attests to Langlois's firm belief in the unity of international cinema.

One day, the wife of a Russian film director paid him the loveliest compliment imaginable: "You guide people into a book that is no book. You have re-created an ambience that enables them, by plunging into it, to understand everything through a sort of osmosis." This was in reference to the Méliès exhibition at the Musée des arts décoratifs, but also totally true of Langlois's museum, about which he said:

> I would like the Musée du Cinéma to enlighten almost surreptitiously. I do not believe in education in the form that we call education. True education is osmosis. Latin, mathematics, and so on, are useful as mental gymnastics, but art is a subject that cannot be taught. It is learned through osmosis.

Among the Eskimos, all the games prepare the child for living. He plays, but in fact he is preparing himself for the hunt, for fishing. He imitates his father, and gradually, through his play, he learns. This is the opposite of a university education. . . .

For years, all exhibitions have been based on the idiotic system of education by explanation, because people like to learn what they should think. But art cannot be explained; it is felt. If there is to be a bond between art and man, we must re-create the umbilical cord.

Langlois wanted to transmit his own fervor to others through the medium of his museum. If loving the cinema—really and truly experiencing it, as opposed to just seeing it—could be spread to others through kindly contagion, then that was Langlois's goal.

The absence of explanatory labels disconcerted some people. But Langlois believed that when people go to museums, they tend to pay more attention to the identifying labels than to the works of art themselves. Even had that not been the case, Langlois didn't have a cent left to print anything, be it nametags or the catalog that he had in fact already put together. Museum visitors, left to their own devices, soaked up the magical atmosphere of the place and ended up wanting to find out more about the objects they had seen. Not every visitor, of course, had the good fortune to be guided through the collection by Langlois himself—as were Charlie Chaplin, George Cukor, Luis Buñuel, Akira Kurosawa, Nicholas Ray, King Vidor, Fritz Lang, Raoul Walsh, Joë Hamman, Joseph Losey, Mervyn LeRoy, Carlos Saura, Henry Hathaway, Vittorio De Sica, and others.

The inherent splendor of the collection would give rise to another problem. Lotte Eisner had been the first to point out to Henri, "We don't have enough money to put everything behind glass, but there are certain things you shouldn't leave out where people can touch them and maybe even steal them."

"Look, Lotte," Henri had replied. "It will be much more voluptuous if they're not locked up behind glass." It pleased him no end to display the magnificent cloak worn by Antinéa in *L'Atlantide* with nothing to come between coat and viewer.

Unfortunately, not everyone behaved in keeping with Henri's

idealism. Mere days after the exhibit opened, James Dean's jacket from *Rebel without a Cause* and the dress worn by Marilyn Monroe in *Let's Make Love* disappeared. Henri consoled himself as best he could. "After all," he reasoned, "whoever stole Marilyn's dress must really love her a lot. Fortunately, we have others in storage, and besides, if need be Cardin will make me a copy of the one that got stolen."

But deep down, he was profoundly saddened, and the fear of further theft forced him to close the museum to the general public in October 1972. Langlois had deliberately laid out his sinuous museum so that only a few rooms or select portions of rooms could be taken in by the eye at one time. This feature of carefully controlled sightlines, which meant that every turn held a new surprise, also made the premises practically impossible to guard. And so, until there was enough money to hire several people to patrol the museum, it would have to remain closed. It was nonetheless visited by film personalities from the world over and was open, by special arrangement, to student groups led by guide-lecturers or teachers. In reality, it was never completely shut down.

François Truffaut, who had been so active on the Defense Committee in 1968, couldn't understand why Langlois threw himself into building a museum:

> The post–May '68 atmosphere, when young people were trashing everything, stealing and breaking stuff, did not exactly favor the building of a museum. Henri wanted the museum to be based on the public's tacit agreement to respect it, but if people start helping themselves, stealing dresses, pulling things off the wall—obviously, it's not going to work that way. But it wasn't entirely his fault. When Henri returned to the Cinémathèque, he had become untouchable. The government was afraid of him. He had become "someone." So he collected some money, and these sums ended up being spent on the museum. It would have been better, in my opinion, to spend that money on transferring hundreds of films to safety stock.

But as far as Henri was concerned, the Cinémathèque without its museum would have been an unfinished work: "Yes, the Musée du Cinéma cost a fortune. I used funds for the museum to the detriment of other activities. It's a choice. There's nothing new about that. I've been told, 'You would have been better off striking copies.' I reply, 'No!' The film archives that don't understand that they must, first of all, be museums will be cupboards and nothing more. You know, the cinema is the huge screen of Lumière, not the pocket handkerchief of Edison. Ever since talkies, we've been in Edison's cinema, and the role of cinémathèques is to continue the Lumière era. They'll only be able to do that from the heart of a museum."

Moreover, Langlois had begun building the museum without actually having the necessary money. The Ministry of Culture had promised him 500,000 francs, but this sum would not be paid until two years after the museum was completed. Essentially, it had been built with Henri's personal resources and with the help of private enterprise. Mary Meerson had yet again made the rounds of her contacts. She arranged for the Mazda Company to donate lightbulbs and convinced other companies to contribute carpeting, paint, fabrics, curtains, and other basic decorating materials. But not everything was free, and the handiwork of countless craftsmen was required: masons, painters, electricians, interior decorators, architectural modelers, glaziers, and framers. Then there were the costly audiovisual fittings and fixtures: 16 cleverly concealed projectors that projected film loops onto the walls, along with the construction of a small projection room within the museum. All these expenditures created a permanent hole in the Cinémathèque's treasury, to the tune of two million francs. But as Jean Riboud pointed out, "If Langlois had left the financing of the museum up to the government, it would have been 10 times more expensive."

Jacques Duhamel was the first to be convinced of that. Victim of a prolonged and fatal illness that he faced with considerable courage, Duhamel confided that the creation of the museum was the greatest satisfaction of his late career. Each new minister, upon discovering the museum, immediately fell in love with it. The reinitiation of guided group visits under the direction of Alain Gabet in 1975 and the national celebration of L'Année du patrimoires (the Year of Heritage) in 1980 provided additional occasions for successive ministers of culture to have the satisfaction of inaugurating Langlois's dreamscape all over again. The Musée du Cinéma-Henri Langlois is no doubt the only French museum to have been inaugurated three times: on 14 June 1972 by Jacques Duhamel, on 22 March 1975 by Michel Guy, and on 19 February 1980 by Jean-Philippe Lecat. Since no government official would go out of his or her way to christen a sinking ship, surely this meant that the Cinémathèque Française and its museum would stay afloat.

chapter 14

# BREATHLESS

What else can I tell you?—Battle stations! Weapons and flying saucers! The Dragon will toady no more. He comes out of his den spitting fire, which will chase away the night, and the sun will rise on a new life.

A thousand kisses. A thousand flowers and confetti.

D.C.D. (The Deceased)

If in Paris the Cinémathèque's problems were a permanent source of worry for Langlois, his personal popularity in America had continued to rise. Between 17 and 31 October 1972, the George Eastman House paid tribute to him. After recalling all the American films Henri had saved, James Card presented Langlois with an engraved silver trophy cup.

This solemn gift was certainly nice, but Card knew what would truly make Henri happy and proceeded to give him a vintage 1913 Gaumont projector for the Cinémathèque Française. The American friend also took advantage of this sojourn in Rochester to force Langlois to slow down a bit:

Henri had been so busy those last 15 years, wheeling and dealing and running around, that he never—I won't say "never"—that he hardly ever looked at a movie in its entirety. Almost the only time that Henri sat down and looked at a film, from start to finish, in these last years was when he came to Rochester and we would plunk him down in the Dryden Theater. Out of politesse—he couldn't move away; he couldn't go to see anybody or greet anybody—he would look at a whole film. I think he saw more films

298

here than anywhere else because he was just absolutely into everything, try-ing to get films, get films, get films! And arrange to bring people to the Cinémathèque Française to do homages. But look at film? No. He no longer had the time.

The project to create a cinémathèque in New York had not been aban-doned. After the City Center project, then the Beaumont Theater, Eugene Stavis had continued looking for another location. In the company of Kathy St. John Feder, he visited more than 40 possible sites. They had pounded the pavements, reviewing all of Manhattan street by street, until one day they found themselves in front of the Queensboro Bridge on First Avenue between Fifty-ninth and Sixtieth streets. And there they stood, in a state of bedazzlement, like explorers face to face with an archeological find—they had just discovered a marvelous location!

Before it stretches out over the East River, the Queensboro Bridge is solidly anchored to the riverfront by a series of arches. In 1910, soon after the bridge was constructed, this long vaulted space served as an open-air market. Then in 1919, the area was closed off with glass partitions, and its 50,000 square feet served for more than 40 years as a storage depot for the police and highway departments. Over the course of a year and a half, Stavis and Johnston studied the possibilities offered by this space and evaluated the cost of its transformation into a fully equipped film center. After several rounds of paperwork, they succeeded in getting the green light from Mayor John Lindsay, state representatives, and Governor Nelson Rockefeller.

"Just the fact that we arrived at the starting line," remembers Tom Johnston, "already represents quite a feat. And we had gotten there." They received a $100,000 grant from the Ford Foundation and returned to see I. M. Pei, hiring him to make the blueprints and models of the future cinémathèque "under the bridge." Pei wanted to make a cathedral dedicated to the glory of the cinema. In the basement, under a dome would be a movie theater seating 500 people, and there would be two smaller screening rooms seating 250 and 150, respectively, under the bridge. He also envisioned a projection room with 50 seats for use by members of the ciné-mathèque and researchers. The other half of the site would be used for cinema exhibitions based

on those put on by the museum at Chaillot, along with a bookstore and a restaurant. A typical day's worth of screenings, from morning to evening, would include up to 14 films. With an admission price of $1.50 and a projected daily attendance of 3,000 to 5,000 people, they could hope to have more than one million visitors a year. According to Stavis, an attendance rate of around 47 percent of capacity would make the enterprise profitable.

The project was to remain secret until the day they had raised the $10 million necessary for its construction; however, as soon as the *New York Times* discovered that the city had decided to put the space under the bridge at the cinémathèque's disposal for the sum of $1 a year, the paper broke the news. The date was 13 April 1973, and $1 generally didn't go that far in New York City.

"They announced the project prematurely," says Stavis with regret. "Too many dreams, too much praise, too soon." Unfortunately, at this very time the New York stock market was plummeting. The project had attracted the interest of a number of foundations. Even so, in the space of several weeks they saw their profits drop by almost 30 percent. The Ford Foundation, for example, saw its capital gains drop from $6 billion to $4 billion, and the city of New York was on the brink of bankruptcy.

When Langlois, Johnston, and Stavis realized that the board of directors of MOMA, including the Rockefellers, were dead set against the cinémathèque under the bridge, they understood that their pet project had the same odds of succeeding as the proverbial snowball in hell. This strong and influential group, whose members would sooner have seen the planners jump off the bridge in question than let them turn the space below it into a hub of filmgoing activity, would exert pressure on the city to stop them from succeeding.

Langlois felt like he'd been betrayed by MOMA. "New York was gypped by some very shortsighted people," affirms Johnston. "MOMA wasn't doing its job. There, it was always the same few hundred films projected over and over, whereas all Langlois wanted to do was to give the people of New York a greater choice."

For Kenneth Anger and James Card, the "under the bridge" dream was too ambitious and, because of that, destined to fail. But Raymond Rohauer remained persuaded that they would finally have succeeded had Henri lived long enough: "It would have taken some time, but Langlois died. The cinémathèque-under-the-bridge project began in 1972–73, but in the archive world, three or four years is nothing. In the long run, Henri would have succeeded in creating his cinémathèque in New York."

Despite Langlois's death, many of the films he chose for a program entitled "Paris-New York" were projected in March 1977 at the Metropolitan Museum. It was, in a way, Henri's final adieu to the American public. Stavis would eventually direct an American cinémathèque from the basement of the Metropolitan for two or three years and would stage temporary film exhibitions in New York.

In September 1973, Charlie Chaplin came to the Cinémathèque to show *Monsieur Verdoux* before its re-release in commercial theaters in Paris. Despite his 84 years and declining health, Chaplin's insistence on showing the confidence and esteem in which he held the Cinémathèque by attending in person lent a very emotional tone to the screening. To see him with his white hair, leaning on a cane, supported by his wife, Oona, walking along side by side with Henri, filled with pride and joy, no one would have imagined that both men would soon be gone. After fulfilling its "photo opportunity" obligations and waving to the crowd, the tiny group slipped out of the auditorium as soon as the credits started to roll. The moment had arrived for Henri to show Chaplin his museum, through which they slowly proceeded, with a long pause in front of the posters lettered "Charlot."

Even though his Museum of Cinema was closed once again to the general public, Langlois was not in the least discouraged. The new Palais des Congrès, at the Porte Maillot, along the western border of Paris, was going to open its doors. Georges Cravenne, who was in charge of promotion for the hotel and convention center, invited Langlois to organize a major event to mark the opening of the Palais. Henri thought up a grandiose project, one the media would dub the "Cinémathèque's Crazy Day."

On Saturday, 2 March 1974, in the large, 3,700-seat auditorium and 20 smaller conference rooms in the Palais des Congrès, from 10:00 A.M. until 10:30 P.M., 400 films from 35 different countries were shown simultaneously. Some 15,000 visitors participated in what the press called "the cinema's longest and most concentrated day."

In honor of the occasion, Langlois devised an inspired and exhaustive film montage: "Paris through the Cinema, from Louis Lumière to Jean-Luc Godard." An enormous amount of preparation was involved: Henri screened hundreds of films in order to choose the excerpts that interested him. It was, of course, out of the question to snip sequences out of the prints. It was thus necessary to strike new copies of the desired sequences, which were then spliced together in the designated order. As Marie Epstein

recalls, "This remarkable montage constituted a synthesis of all films since the origin of the cinema to the present, illustrating Parisian life in a nonstop 12-hour projection."

The projection, which began in the morning, was held in the giant auditorium. But Henri kept thinking of other sequences to add, other inspirations to deploy, and around 6:00 P.M. the day was breaking only on Marcel Carné's *Le Jour se lève*. Michel Delain, journalist for *L'Express*, was able to slip into the projection booth and see Langlois in action, giving new meaning to the expression "creating under pressure":

> He had lost himself in the cans of film stock, which were delivered in a jiffy as he called for them and were piling up at his feet. At least, one would assume he was lost. But in a wink, he spotted *Nogent, Eldorado du dimanche,* or *La Journée d'une paire de jambes:* "Quick! Hand me *Chéri Bibi*! No, not that reel, that's *Crainqueville* with Féraudy. Give me the other one."
>
> He attached, detached, and reattached lengths of film, edited and unedited them, armed with only his memories and his scissors. A phone call distracts him. Too bad! for on the screen, later on, will appear the word *NIF* instead of *FIN*. "Shoot, it's backwards!"

The hostesses at the Palais tried to help the visitors by directing them to the 20 theaters. The public address system updates sounded like they belonged in a busy international airport: "It is 6:00 P.M. The Soviet Union has sold out its theater. . . . Your attention, please—there are no more seats available for Frank Capra's *Why We Fight.* . . . There are, however, still some seats available for the Canadian, Algerian, and Indian theaters."

Through his success in uniting so many films from foreign cinémathèques, Langlois proved once again that the Cinémathèque Française had no need for the FIAF's help. The "crazy day" was a big success, and many Parisian visitors, who up until then had known nothing of the Cinémathèque apart from what they'd heard, would soon make the trek to the Palais de Chaillot.

At the end of March, it was Gloria Swanson's turn to come to Paris to inaugurate a tribute organized in her behalf. Henri wanted the famous star to celebrate her seventy-fifth birthday at the Cinémathèque. He had prepared a special film montage for her, consisting of excerpts from her most famous films, ending with the final sequence in *Sunset Boulevard*. Gloria Swanson, while describing the party at a press conference, paid humorous tribute to Langlois's talents as a "director": "I'm thrilled with my stay in Paris. I'm very thankful to Henri Langlois and Mary Meerson, who have done their best to make this a marvelous birthday, with so much love and affection. . . . I hope to come back to France. But if I want to celebrate my eightieth birthday here, I don't know what I'm supposed to do for an encore! There were 75 cakes at the Cinémathèque with 75 candles—that's an incredible idea; I've never seen that in a film. It was marvelous, unimaginable! The next time, will I have to jump out of a cake or should I parachute out of the sky?"

Several days later, Langlois left for Los Angeles. He had won a special Oscar from the Academy of Motion Picture Arts and Sciences. Mary Meerson insisted that he needed a new suit for the occasion and persuaded Pierre Cardin (who had already made suits for Langlois in exchange for an occasional private screening) to make him a tuxedo. Henri, however, never got around to seeing Cardin, and when Cardin sent a tailor to measure him on the spot at the Cinémathèque, Langlois refused to get up from his chair so that the man could take his measurements. Cardin's cutter had to guess Henri's size, and when he insisted that Langlois stand up so he could verify his estimates, Langlois supposedly told him, "I will be more often seated in this tuxedo than upright. That's all you need to know."

The forty-sixth annual Academy Awards presentation took place on 2 April 1974. The show, televised to tens of millions of Americans, finally arrived at the moment where Jack Valenti, president of the Motion Picture Association of America, came on stage to introduce Langlois: "Tonight the Academy presents an award to someone who is not a maker of films but truly a savior of them. Films saved from destruction—ordered destroyed by producers who didn't like the way they turned out . . . , by political groups whose tyranny felt threatened by their existence . . . , films in the process of decay by simple neglect. This man stood guard when no one else was there, because he is committed to the belief that art cannot be explained—it is felt. Today as director of the French Cinémathèque, he has dedicated his life to see that *all* films live forever. I am proud to present this award to the curator, collector, and *conscience* of the cinema—Henri Langlois!"

Gene Kelly escorted Henri on to the stage. Jack Valenti gave him the Oscar, and then Henri expressed his thanks in French while Gene Kelly translated. Langlois spoke of the traditional passion of the French for American films and how much Jean Renoir, René Clair, and Abel Gance, among others up until the French New Wave, had unabashedly loved this cinema from which they had learned many lessons for their own works. Langlois ended his speech with the following sentence in English, which was greeted with generous applause: "This is the reason I like so much the film American, and nice to meet you."

Contrary to what one might expect of a man who never sought out honorary distinctions, Henri was quite proud of his Oscar. He was very moved to be the first film archive curator to be so honored. "When I arrived in Los Angeles," explained Langlois, "I thought that, for Americans, the Oscar was like our Legion of Honor. But it is much more important than the Legion of Honor, since everybody and his brother gets one of those eventually. An Oscar is truly very serious. I didn't realize it. It is comparable to being chosen as a master craftsman by one's fellows in the time of the guilds."

Eugene Stavis joined Langlois in Los Angeles. Together they visited Jean Renoir and other French filmmakers who lived in Hollywood, as well as several American friends, including Paul Ivano, a former director of photography for Valentino's films, the art director Ben Carré, actress Jennifer Jones, and directors such as King Vidor, Alan Dwan, George Stevens, and Robert Florey. They also had the occasion to have lunch at Chasen's with Groucho Marx, who had also just won a special Oscar.

But the high point of their stay was an invitation from Mae West. She greeted them at her house dressed in a pink and white nightgown. Lunch was served by a mulatto servant, and at dessert, Ms. West asked Stavis to place his hand on her breasts. She encouraged him by saying, "Touch the skin of an 85-year-old woman!" Which Stavis finally did. "Actually, it was unimaginable," he remembers. "It was not the chest of an 85-year-old woman. She was still receiving fan letters from 16-year-old boys."

Since their visit coincided with Easter Day, she gave each of them a magnificent bowtie as a memento.

François Truffaut was also in Los Angeles for the Academy Awards, winning that year's Best Foreign Film Oscar for *Day for Night*. He explained:

> It was the day Georges Pompidou died. When we learned the news of his death, I said to Henri, "I hope that François Mitterrand becomes president." And he answered me, "And I hope it will be Chaban-Delmas."
>
> Langlois identified himself so much with the Cinémathèque that, in politics, he looked for what would be the most beneficial for the Cinémathèque. And as he saw it, the best thing for the Cinémathèque was nonetheless the continuation of the regime. The thing that scared him the most was that the Cinémathèque would become nationalized and fall entirely into the hands of the state. So he had more confidence in Chaban-Delmas or Giscard.

Truffaut had resigned from the board of directors of the Cinémathèque more than a year earlier, on 20 February 1973:

> I told Henri in a letter, "I now travel too much. I am very often in America and can no longer participate in the meetings. Therefore, I quit." And Langlois took that as an attack. I became an enemy of the Cinémathèque, when in fact I was neither an enemy nor a friend. I was neutral. If there was anyone who did not need a board of directors, it was Langlois. Whenever we alluded to the fact that the Cinémathèque was not running well, he'd say, "Good. Don't worry—it's going to get better. I'll arrange it." And then finally, it got to be like a politician's hollow promise.
>
> I realized that it no longer served a purpose to be with him. We couldn't help him, and so I withdrew. The misunderstanding with him was that he thought I was against him. There was something de Gaullean in his attitude. There are famous phrases of de Gaulle: "One cannot be a Gaullist against de Gaulle," or, "If you are not with me, then you are against me." Langlois had all of those characteristics.

In March 1973, Léonce Calvy replaced Truffaut as vice-president. Filmmakers Pierre Kast and Jean Rouch became assistant secretaries. Jean-Pierre Rassam, a film producer, joined the crew as a financial administrator, accompanied by assistant treasurer William Novik and producer Anatole Dauman. But these changes in personnel changed nothing whatsoever concerning the blocked state subsidy. André Rieupeyrout assisted Langlois in the daily administrative tasks. The treasury was shrinking away. It was impossible to finance the building of additional storage vaults. It pained Henri to know that the films were disintegrating and there was nothing he could do about it. When the end of the month rolled around, it always brought the same diffi-culties for meeting the payroll and placating the creditors. Henri made out his list and Rieupeyrout made out his. They would sit down face to face, and Henri would take his large sheets of paper and say, "Okay, let's begin with the personnel." When that was finished, it was time for the suppliers:

"We can give this one a little something and that one, less."

"But Henri," reasoned Rieupeyrout, "that's it. We don't have another penny."

"That doesn't matter," replied Langlois, continuing with his list. Perhaps in his mind, working out the accounts, even with imaginary resources, was a more honest approach than simply not paying.

He had made out his budget based on 150,000 francs, but they needed twice as much. New discussions followed. It was red ink versus red ink, and the red ink was winning:

"No, Henri, I'm telling you," Rieupeyrout pleaded, "that one can wait. But this one—we have to settle up with him right away or he's going to pay us back in a nasty way."

Langlois then picked up all the piles of papers and went home to rue Gazan, where he'd start his computations all over again.

Jack Moseley, an American who worked as Langlois's personal assistant for a number of months, remembers one particular evening at rue Gazan, with the honor of the Cinémathèque's accounting at stake:

> Even at the medical school where I studied, I have honestly never seen a man work as hard as he did. He wore me out! Sometimes we'd begin at the end of the afternoon and not finish before dawn. We'd quickly eat something around midnight, while Mary stayed at Chaillot until the end of the last projection. I prepared something simple to eat, and then, as soon as we'd wolfed it down, we started in again working.
>
> I'd watch him—he'd start over 1,000 times, worrying about the last little fraction of a centime. We worked all night, and I'll never forget the face of the accountant the next day when he saw the pile of papers Langlois had filled out. He told him, "But you're crazy! It wasn't necessary to do all those calculations. No one expects you to do that."

A marginal, troublemaking element had gradually decided that the gardens surrounding the Chaillot fountains and reflecting pool were an advantageous place to hang out. The furtive shadows of drug pushers slid in and out among strung-out boys and girls, and to top this off, a group of greasers roamed the grounds, which they considered to be their turf. A stroll through the wooded area that abutted Chaillot was a risky proposition day or night. One of the Cinémathèque's employees had already been beaten up. Henri was worried about the safety of the personnel, who no longer dared leave work after the last screening. Each night, Langlois was obliged to order several taxis, which lined up in front of the stairway to take the cashier, the projectionist, and the ticket takers to their respective homes.

One evening, a group of ruffians forced their way into the theater without paying and helped themselves to seats on the main floor of the auditorium. A ticket taker followed them into the theater and demanded they pay what was, after all, the most reasonable admission fee in town. The next day, their leader decided on a punishment expedition, and a large group of toughs arrived at the Cinémathèque, their minds set on revenge. They roughed up anyone or anything that got in their way. When the projection began, they pulled out knives and began slashing the leather seats. Someone told Langlois. He had never backed down from brute force and wasn't about to start now. Langlois halted the projection, brought up the house lights, and walked up on stage to give the hooligans an indignant piece of his mind. The vandals made a savage lunge for the stage, pushed Langlois aside, and plunged their knives into the screen, leaving horrible long gashes.

For Henri, this was a tragedy of the first order. The Cinémathèque was strapped for cash. Replacing the now-tattered screen was an unaffordable luxury.

Several days later, he called his brother Georges around midnight. "We're stuck," he said in despair. "The employees are afraid. I called some taxis, but this time they're refusing to come. They claim that it's become too dangerous just to park in the garden alley. They suggested that I call the police station in the sixteenth arrondissement and that the police will know what to do."

The next day, Henri told Georges Langlois that they'd have to bring suit against the vandals. After all, there were witnesses to the laceration of the chairs and screen. They'd be sure to win and maybe collect some damages. Georges opened his penal-code book, only to discover that there was no law that anticipated this kind of destructive behavior. In fact, so far as the law was concerned, in France at that time someone could march into your house and carve up your favorite painting, and technically it wasn't a crime. (It was necessary to wait until something similar to the slashed-screen episode befell a judge in his own home, so that in 1981 this black hole in the French judicial system was finally filled in.) Georges Langlois explained this to Henri, who just couldn't believe his ears, and Georges added, "Wait a second. Were they in a group? If so, there is the *anti-casseur* law [French law that could be interpreted as an infringement of the right to assemble]."

Henri was really shook up: "No. I'm not going to be the one to hide behind that law. That's what they're hoping for, so they can accuse me of being a fascist."

Several days went by, and Langlois telephoned his brother once more to tell him that a group of young people who loved movies and who taught judo for a living were willing to help out at the Cinémathèque for a while as ticket takers.

The following evening, the hooligans returned. One of the

judo experts met them at the door, while another waited in the balcony. Instead of being faced by a pale, fear-struck employee, this time the assailants had met their match. Their leader groaned with his wrist twisted behind his back, menacing that he was going to sue them. Henri then appeared.

"Fine. Sue us," he told them. "Then we'll know who you are and where you live."

From that moment on, calm returned to the Cinémathèque, but the damage to the seats and the screen went unrepaired. The films and the auditorium were not at their physical best; fortunately, however, Langlois had other forms of consolation. He was excited over Paris's First International Film Festival, to be held between 17 and 24 November 1975 at the National Theater of Chaillot, which was generally used for legitimate stage productions. The festival opened with a gala soirée for which Henri prepared a film montage entitled: "80 Years of French Cinema." After it was shown, Langlois appeared on the stage. Before he even had time to open his mouth, the entire theater launched into a thunderous standing ovation. When he was finally able to make himself heard, Henri pointed to the empty screen and said, "But this is not for me. This is not for me! It is for them."

This festival was also the opportunity to hold some exceptional projections with full orchestral accompaniment. Henri Rabaud composed for *Le Miracle des loups* a score that 58 musicians performed under the direction of Adolphe Sybert. The same extravagant effect was obtained when an original score by Dimitri was played by a 25-piece orchestra under the direction of Marius Constant to accompany Gregory Kozintsev and Leonid Trauberg's *The New Babylon*. Eight years later, in New York, Francis Ford Coppola would take up this initiative by showing *The New Babylon* at Radio City Music Hall with live orchestral accompaniment. But the festival's most explosive event was Pier Paolo Pasolini's last film, *Salo: or the 120 Days of Sodom*.

To celebrate the U.S. Bicentennial, Henri whipped up a special exhibition for the Cultural Center in the Marais section of Paris, entitled "Hollywood in the Marais." From April to July 1976, the public could admire some 80 costumes worn by the greatest stars of American films. Each evening, thanks to Henri's programming, visitors to the exhibit could see these costumes come to life, worn on screen by such actresses as Joan Crawford, Norma Shearer, Vivien Leigh, Marilyn Monroe, Ava Gardner, and Grace Kelly.

The words *stop* and *relax* were not in Henri's vocabulary, and so on 3 July he inaugurated the new Cinémathèque Française theater in Nice, directed by Odile Chapelle. After a brief tribute to Dennis Hopper, with the honoree in attendance, Langlois presented an evening's worth of old movies starring Tom Mix. The week to follow featured a selection of films retracing the history of the American Western.

Upon his return to Paris, Langlois went to Lotte Eisner's place in Neuilly to help her celebrate her eightieth birthday. Since Lotte regretted the falling-out between François Truffaut and Henri, she invited both of them so they might reconcile.

This would be the last time François Truffaut would ever see Henri alive: "I spent a very enjoyable evening with Lotte, her nieces, Pierre Prévert and Langlois. Henri showed up out of breath and, for once, spoke to me not about the Cinémathèque's problems but about his bad health. On a rather light note, he told us how a dentist wanted to pull out all his teeth, a doctor wanted to send him off to the countryside for a cure, and a surgeon wanted him to have an operation. All of this bothered his friends more than it did him. He was not well. I could tell that he was very, very tired. But we had a grand evening, eating petits fours and drinking champagne."

In autumn 1976, Langlois traveled for the last time to the United States. He stopped off in Berkeley to see Tom Luddy at the Pacific Film Archive. Despite his state of health, Henri had lost none of his charm or his infallible flair for making new discoveries. Upon his arrival, Tom Luddy showed Henri a pile of film cans containing nitrate films that had been sitting there for some time.

"But you must look at them!" cried Langlois. "There might be something fantastic inside!"

Luddy hadn't touched them for two months. After having projected some of the films, he had concluded that they represented nothing of interest. He'd found only newsreel footage, some educational films, and documentaries, such as one made in 1924 by the marines on how to install toilets on a battleship.

Langlois grabbed the first film can, opened it, and, just like in the movies, unrolled it while holding it up to the light. He screamed, "But this is *La Tosca* with Francesca Bertini! I've been looking for this film for 20 years!"

"You're pulling my leg," responded Luddy. "You can't come here, pick up the first can, look at the film, and say it's *La Tosca* from 1919 with Francesca Bertini. That's not possible!"

"But it is, I assure you!"

And Langlois showed his friend the tinted blue film stock

where one could see a woman on a rooftop and the dome of a church in the background.

"You see—that's Saint Peter's in Rome, and that's Bertini in the last scene."

The two men cleaned the film and rushed into the projection room, where they realized that indeed it *was* the sixth reel from *La Tosca*. They spent the rest of the day screening other films. One of them dated from the 1920s. Henri glowed with enthusiasm: "That one is by a great director—it's a great film!"

Luddy recognized in it a minor actor named Tully Marshall, who had played in some of Erich von Stroheim's films. As soon as Henri laid his eyes on Tully Marshall's filmography, he pointed to a title and announced, "It must be *The Village Blacksmith*."

"Why that one, more than another?" asked a surprised Luddy.

"Because I think so."

They then looked over the plot summary of the film Langlois had picked. Sure enough, it corresponded to the picture they had screened. Luddy was thunderstruck: "Langlois had just found a film by John Ford. And in that pile of nitrate, we found other interesting films. For me, it was magic. I'm sure that if Langlois had not come, I would have looked at those films and found nothing. Langlois came, a tap of a magic wand, and the films were there."

This would be the last service Henri would pay to the Pacific Film Archive, which he had helped to found eight years earlier and which, thanks to him, had become a veritable cinémathèque.

Henri had gout and may well have had diabetes too. Mary had always refused to buy him mineral water or any other drink in plastic bottles, owing to her staunch belief that plastic is carcinogenic. She wanted to protect Henri from getting cancer but didn't stop to think that he might die from heart disease instead.

Jack Moseley remembers an occasion when, after a day of hard work at the rue Gazan, Langlois, after eating dinner, plopped down on a sofa to relax a bit. A light on the ceiling was shining directly into his face. To shield his eyes, he had astutely placed his tie over them. Mary, who had climbed up to the loggia, no longer heard Henri moving and cried out, "Henri! What are you doing? What are you doing, now?"

"I'm going into the lake," replied Langlois.

"But what do you mean by that? Where are you going?"

"*I'm going into the lake, Mary!*"

She became angry: "You're sick!"

Yes, Henri was assuredly sick, but physically, not mentally. His mind remained ultrasharp, but he was killing himself with work. After the period of grace that followed Langlois's return in 1968, the filmmakers who had fought for him were obliged to return to their own preoccupations, and

Henri was once again alone, fighting for his cause with the help of the Cinémathèque Française's administration and several other new administrators.

Among these was Léonce Calvy, a former government commissioner who threw himself into the battle heart and soul. Calvy phoned Georges Langlois every day so that they could work out solutions to the Cinémathèque's ever-increasing problems. Not unlike the Turks coveting the Smyrna of Henri's youth, someone was always salivating at the thought of conquering the Cinémathèque. Creditors, aware that Langlois was ill and that there were valuables to be seized, stepped up their lawsuits.

On 15 July 1976, Michel Guy, the minister of culture, addressed a letter to the Cinémathèque's President Hubert de Villez, telling him that he planned to accord one million francs to the Cinémathèque to help pay its debts. But the one million francs didn't come and would not arrive before Langlois's death.

This was a terrible period in Henri's life—one last battle in which he willed himself on, despite chronic exhaustion. One day, Léonce Calvy, who was concerned about Henri's health, told Georges Langlois, "You're the only one who can do something. You alone can tell your brother to stop knocking himself out so. Tell him he absolutely must see a doctor. I'm afraid for him!" But Georges realized that he was also the "only one" to know that when it came to Henri, it was impossible to tell him what to do.

In some respects, Langlois took care of his health. He didn't drink alcoholic beverages, and he had given up smoking. On the other hand, he still ate far too many sweets and had a veritable phobia about doctors. Jean Riboud wanted to place him in the hands of his cardiologist and had gone to great lengths to persuade Langlois to see this doctor. Finally, Henri agreed. While they were in Riboud's car, driving to the appointment, Henri asked, "Jean, what do you think he's going to do to me?"

"He's going to examine you, like all doctors do—take your blood pressure, give you an electrocardiogram, . . ."

"What?"

"An electrocardiogram."

"Never! Do you know, Jean, that an electrocardiogram can kill you?"

"He actually seemed to believe what he was saying," remembered Riboud, "so I turned around and drove him

home. I thought, 'My God, what's the use? It's over.' The next day, I came back and Henri told me the truth: 'I already know what the results will be, and they won't be good. So where's it going to get me? I can't change my life. Why do I need a doctor to tell me my days are numbered?'"

A short time later, Georges Langlois called Léonce Calvy to tell him about a lawsuit that had worked out particularly well in their favor. A woman's voice, choked with pain, answered the phone: "*Maitre*, my husband just died. He killed himself working for the Cinémathèque."

What was there to say to this unfortunate woman? Léonce Calvy had placed Henri's health before his own. He was not alone; President Hubert de Villez, the former adviser to the Revenue Court, who had accepted the presidency of the Cinémathèque out of friendship for Henri, had also died just a short time before. Henri Langlois had saved the "lives" of countless films, but from all appearances, a position working at the Cinémathèque was no boon to longevity.

In November 1976, while the Cinémathèque, beset with financial problems, was fighting for its life, Henri was invited to dinner at the Elysée Palace by President Giscard D'Estaing. Placing his Légion d'honneur rosette on the lapel of his suitcoat, Langlois thought back to the story of Malraux and his boutonniere, almost 20 years earlier. He would have preferred 1,000 times over that the Cinémathèque at last receive the promised subsidy that would get him out of the cash-flow hoosegow. But since the honor of this invitation reflected quite favorably on an allegedly sinking ship, captain Langlois went to the dinner with bitter satisfaction.

At Henri's side, in addition to Jean Riboud, was another man whose generosity should not be forgotten. Jean-Baptiste Goreguès, a well-to-do theatrical entrepreneur, had already given the Cinémathèque undulating veil costumes worn by innovative dancer Loïe Fuller; the nineteenth-century astronomer and publisher Camille Flammarion's glass plate photos of the heavens; posters, and numerous other objects from the 1910s and before. In 1968 he lent Henri two buildings he owned in the Paris suburb of Pontault-Combault so that Langlois might store his collections there before building the museum. In 1971 Goreguès wanted to free Henri from his financial difficulties by giving him the two buildings, then estimated at a value of two million francs. Henri turned down this generous offer, saying, "I want nothing for myself, and since the Cinémathèque does not have the right to accept gifts of real estate, I suggest you sell the property to us for a symbolic fee, equivalent to the cost of your most recent improvements."

Thus, a commitment to sell was drawn up whereby the Cinémathèque would purchase the two buildings in question for a total of 150,000 francs. More reasonable still, only 15,000 francs down had sealed the deal with the remainder to be paid in 11 quarterly installments.

These dates had come and gone when one morning, Georges Langlois received a legal cancellation notice, informing him that the deal between Monsieur Goreguès and the Cinémathèque had been rescinded. To put it mildly, this was not the sort of thing Langlois needed to hear. When, however, Georges Langlois called him for an explanation, Goreguès laughed and asked why Georges was worried. He simply intended to do what he had always wanted to do—he was taking back his buildings with the intention of giving them outright to Henri. They would, he explained, constitute Henri's personal donation to the foundation that would carry his name, thereby placing his work safely out of reach from those unscrupulous people whose ambitions ran toward overrunning the Cinémathèque. But Henri was stubborn and once again refused. Every bit as stubborn as he, Goreguès wanted to be reassured that if he consented to a new agreement with the Cinémathèque Française, his buildings would never be used for anything other than their original purpose of storing the Cinémathèque's treasures.

The Cinémathèque's board of directors held a meeting on 27 May 1975, during which it was voted that these buildings would belong to the Henri Langlois Foundation. A protocol agreement was signed. Goreguès withdrew his cancellation of the sales agreement and gave the Cinémathèque more time to make the remaining payments. Thus, thanks to Goreguès, for the first time the Cinémathèque owned some real estate of its very own. As a child, Henri had watched Douglas Fairbanks and his two fellow Musketeers proclaim their motto: "One for all and all for one." Once again, Henri had applied *his* motto: "Nothing for me, all for the Cinémathèque."

On 5 January 1977, Henri paid a visit to his brother. When he'd stepped in the door, he traced a line on his chest and told Georges's younger son, as if it was the most natural thing in the world to say, "Hugues, you see, I have water up to here and I'll die when it reaches my heart."

This was a rare breach of family etiquette. No alleged "health problems" could be acknowledged until the Cinémathèque's problems had first been settled. Georges and his brother were supposed to meet to discuss strategies to keep the Cinémathèque afloat. Until the festival to be held in the city of Tours toward the end of the month, the Cinémathèque needed to borrow money to make long-overdue social security payments to the government. When Georges told Henri about his most recent efforts to obtain an extension, Langlois replied, "If I must die so the Cinémathèque will live, well, then, so much the better."

Georges Langlois was in a deep sleep when, around 3:00 A.M., the sound of the telephone tore him away from his dreams. On the other end of the line, an emotionally charged voice announced that Henri had just died: "The telephone there isn't working. Mary Meerson asked me to call you. Come at once to rue Gazan!"

It was rainy and cold in the hours before dawn on 13 January 1977. Georges Langlois quickly drove through a deserted Paris, only to discover a small-scale traffic jam once he reached rue Gazan. Doors were being slammed, and automobiles were parked right on the sidewalk along the Montsouris Park. Other cars were double-parked in front of house number 21. In the early-morning obscurity, dark figures stood whispering in the shadows, not daring to raise their voices. The elevator was out of order, so Georges Langlois took the stairs, four at a time, up to the fourth floor. Two or three faithful friends were already there, but others arrived continuously.

Georges Langlois recalls:

> My grief on that drizzly morning has mixed up my memories. In my mind, I see only the convergence of heartfelt accolades, Mary's dignity in her pain, and the emotion felt by her friends. Was it that morning or in the hours that followed—well, anyway, I see it all again and it's like a dream: Rossellini kissing Mary in a long mournful embrace that expressed all the pain in the world, Jean-Pierre Rassam and his generosity, Henry Chapier, faithful as could be, and, of course, all their dearest old friends, Pierre Prévert, Marcel Carné, Roland Lesaffre, Michel Petitjean, Pierre Kast, Lotte Eisner, Marie Epstein, Renée Lichtig, Noël Simsolo, and many others. I can still picture Michel Lonsdale, in a strange outfit, with his beard and his cape, looking extratheatrical but sincere in his grief. And then there were all of those Cinémathèque employees whose struggles had only increased their loyalty to the Cinémathèque.
>
> I went to see Henri's body, which was lying in another room. I stayed near him a long time, struck by the expression on his face, which gave the impression that Henri was still fighting, even beyond death. The heart attack had happened while he was working.

The night before, Lotte Eisner, who was worried about Henri, went to rue Gazan to pay him a visit. As she was kissing him hello, he told her, "Lotte, I'm going to my death with serenity." She began to cry. Seeing her reaction, Henri quickly added, "Listen, it's no doubt much better this way, because

Nostradamus has predicted a terrible event for 1980. I prefer to die rather than to see what's going to happen."

On the night of 12 January, Henri was working away on the creation of a new Cinémathèque theater for the Pompidou Center. A spot in the impressive new arts center in the heart of town was another perfect occasion to move forward. He also placed the finishing touches on the program for the Tours Festival, which was set to begin on 21 January. Despite the late hour, he still needed to make some urgent phone calls. But the telephone had been cut off once again, thus obliging him to make a series of trips back and forth to his neighbor's apartment to use the phone.

It was 10:30 P.M. when he called Serge Losique in Montreal to settle some minor details for the Tours Festival. He was also preoccupied with the exhibition planned for the Metropolitan Museum and called New York. At 2:00 A.M., while climbing back up to his apartment, he was stricken with a terrible pain in his chest. Death did not take him by surprise, however; he most certainly never suspected how painful it would be. His body rebelled against the inevitable, and the pain was so overwhelming that he cried out to Mary, "I'm dying! I'm dying! My heart, my heart . . ."

His agony lasted almost three-quarters of an hour. There was a doctor in the building, and someone ran to wake him up. The physician did what he could, but it was too late, and when the medics arrived at last, they were unable to bring Langlois back to life.

       During the first televised newscast at 1:00 P.M. the next day, the newscaster announced Henri's death. However, neither that evening nor in the days that followed was any sort of TV documentary presented about Langlois's life and work. Perhaps the government-controlled television hierarchy thought it best to be prudent. On the other hand, the press had a respectful field day. French cinema was in mourning. Henri-Georges Clouzot had died the same day, and this double loss filled the newspapers. In the Parisian press, as in the regional and foreign press, articles brimming with praise poured forth. In flipping through them, one comes across any number of catchy potential titles for a book on Henri Langlois: "The Passion of Cinema," "A Passion for Films," "The Man of the Cinémathèque," "The Guardian of

the Temple," "The Memory of World Cinema," and, of course, "The Dragon Who Watches over Our Treasures."

Henri had been brought up in the Catholic religion, and although he wasn't a practicing follower, he had always shown a great respect for religious ceremonies. He counted among his friends a man of culture and faith, Father Jean Diard, who belonged to *La Compagnie de Jésus*. The parish for the rue Gazan was the Sainte-Anne de la Maison-Blanche Church. Although this was not Father Diard's jurisdiction, he obtained special permission from the priest to recite the funeral mass out of friendship for Henri.

On Tuesday, 18 January 1977, at 10:30 A.M., the church was packed. Next to Mary Meerson and Georges Langlois's family, Françoise Giroud, minister of culture, took a seat. When the first few notes of a Debussy flute solo broke the silence, those present understood that they were participating in a funeral a bit out of the ordinary. There was nothing more moving and yet not altogether sad than the sound of that flute. Jean Diard's eulogy also marked Henri's place in the spiritual sphere:

> Meeting Henri Langlois is one of those momentous and rare events that can change the course of one's life. And that is why his sudden departure is a serious loss not only for us, but for all the men and women living everywhere throughout the world. . . .
>
> Langlois was a human being in whom everything the world had to tell us resonated. A resonance that was established and amplified by an uninterrupted familiarity with the most voluble and most lively of the arts: that of the image and of the image become motion. . . .
>
> A man of his word, Henri Langlois held the secret of speech as action. You can ask yourself how Langlois managed to speak at length of the cinema without ever resorting to using a single word of that specialized vocabulary that annoyed him so. In that way, Langlois was the opposite of what is called a *cinéphile*. The movies drew out of him only concrete and sensitive words: "No, no, that's not it! Listen up, I'm going to tell you. . . ."
>
> In a world that has a tendency to withdraw into itself, the Cinémathèque is a fantastic oasis of space—a sensory advance for those who feel the need to live and to breathe. It was certainly very difficult to work with Langlois, because he was not easygoing; he would not put up with things. In order to remain with him, one had to understand that the disciple must also endure what the master suffers first, in order to accomplish his work. In order to work at the Cinémathèque, one needed and one will always need that passion in the heart, that absolute and selfless dedication, that spirit of poverty that molds beings in the white-hot crucible where the work is accomplished. . . .
>
> And so, in closing I return to the subject of the Cinémathèque's purpose. Since its soul has just departed, how, then, shall the Cinémathèque best survive? Its future cannot be projected by those lurking behind the screen or off in the wings. The torch that lights good works cannot easily be passed on if its flame was kindled in unselfishness, in unconditional love.

As for this torch, we know who holds it now, and those who keep watch
over it with her. I will not mention their names, for we all know who they
are.

As Father Diard quoted a Bible verse from the Book of Revelation, the
sound of the flute gave the impression of a soul rising to heaven. Mary,
wrapped from head to toe in a cape and with a black scarf hiding her face,
looked like a rock—a timeless figure of strength, like a character on loan
from Eisenstein's *Ivan the Terrible*. Once the ceremony had ended, after the
long cortege of condolences, there were many famous faces to be seen along
the peristyle: Jean and Krishna Riboud, Yves Montand and Simone Signoret,
Alain Resnais, Michel Lonsdale, Daniel Toscan de Plantier, Nicolas
Seydoux, Jacques Doniol-Valcroze, Paul Grimault, Pierre Braunberger,
Jacques Ledoux, Christiane de Rochefort, Roberto Rossellini, and Marcel
Carné, as well as Kenneth Anger and Tay Garnett, who had come from the
United States for Henri's funeral.

Georges Langlois remembers leaving with everyone for the Montparnasse
Cemetery, where Henri was buried beneath the pale light of a January sun.
Faced with the profusion of funeral wreaths sent from around the world, but
also from the major French production companies, the Ministry of Culture,
and the CNC, one could not help but think of the prevailing destitution of
Henri's last difficult days.

At Mary Meerson's apartment, telegrams continued to arrive, expressing
the condolences of foreign film archives, film festivals, and the governors of
the Academy of Motion Picture Arts and Sciences. But the most touching
were the personal tributes expressed by filmmakers and friends abroad, from
Renoir to Cukor, from Losey to Fassbinder, from Ingrid Bergman to Lillian
Gish to filmmakers in Mali,
Nigeria, and Mauritania.

Jean Renoir's telegram in
itself expressed everyone's
thoughts: "We have lost our
guide, and we suddenly feel
alone in the forest." All those
who had come close to Henri, to
that human volcano in eternal
eruption, forever on the move,
always ready to bring back to
life on the screen those silent
voices enclosed in metal cans,
all those who had experienced
the long game of hide-and-seek
he was forced to play with an
economic system only marginal-

ly inclined to grant him the financial means essential to his conservation work, missed him very much indeed.

"We will never thank him enough," wrote Abel Gance, "for having rummaged through those thousands of images, like an astronomer who brings back from the star fields those stars that had become invisible because of their distance."

Among the numerous articles written about Langlois after his death was one in *L'Aurore* by Guy Teisseire, addressing Henri himself: "What you have done, you have done well or badly but always with a passion that few people know how to keep up until their dying day. You have truly given your life to the cinema. If the seventh art had its god, you certainly would be canonized: the first saint of the cinema."

Henri a saint? Hardly. Serge Losique, who knew him better than most, had this to say:

> Langlois—you have to love him, that's all. You mustn't argue with him. When he says it's black, maybe at the same moment we see white, or vice versa—it makes no difference. That's why Langlois is the man who truly symbolizes the irrational essence of the cinema itself.
>
> Langlois was a builder of pyramids. He should have lived at the time of the pharaohs, because to be able to do what he wanted to accomplish would have required tens of thousands of slaves. In the twentieth century, this was impossible, or it would have cost him as many millions of dollars. Unfortunately, Langlois did not have millions of dollars at his command, and that was his personal tragedy. Henri was the only man I ever knew who never "tinkered" with the cinema, who never made the slightest concession, who never tried to use the cinema for personal gain. He could have become fabulously wealthy, but he never collected things for himself—it was always for others, for all the moviegoers in the world. That is why, for me, Henri Langlois will always remain the first citizen of cinema.

# EPILOGUE: WAS NOSTRADAMUS RIGHT?

"Tours . . . we must make a success of the Tours Festival!" These had been the last words spoken by Henri, and Georges Langlois was replaying them in his mind when Mary Meerson called to tell him some incredible news: the Cinémathèque's employees were locked out of the Cinémathèque. Official seals—ominous-looking government applied blobs of wax with ribbons protruding over the door frames—made it illegal to enter either Courcelles or Chaillot. The films that had come from around the world for the Tours Festival were stuck inside, the staff was stuck outside, and the festival's opening was at stake.

Mary Meerson next called Françoise Giroud. Ten minutes later, Georges understood the situation: the Ministry of Culture had taken this initiative to preserve Georges's "rights" as next of kin. No one had asked Georges Langlois's advice, and he was furious. His "rights" weren't doing anybody any good sealed up by fancy blobs of wax. The Cinémathèque's life was in jeopardy. To interrupt its daily functioning just after Langlois's death was, well, *deadly*.

Georges Langlois telephoned the ministry's lawyer to ask for

319

some explanations, demanding that the seals be removed at once. The lawyer told him he didn't have the time, and besides, Georges Langlois alone had the right to act on the matter. So Georges threw himself into a frenetic round of administrative errands between the magistrates' courts of the eighth and sixteenth arrondissements, the Cinémathèque's offices on rue de Courcelles, and the Palais de Chaillot.

The court clerks hastened to undo what needn't have been done in the first place, and the films were liberated in time for the festival's opening on 21 January. Georges Langlois, who had been invited to the closing-night dinner, joined Roland Lesaffre, Lionel Tardiff, Barbet Schroeder, René Silberman, Bulle Ogier, and a number of young filmmakers at the Moulin de Neuilly-le-Pierre. They pushed Georges forward, requesting a speech. Georges Langlois very simply pronounced: "Henri is near to us and we are near to him." As he later recalled, "It wasn't the most brilliant thing to say, but that's sincerely what I was thinking and the thought was shared by all present. Each one of us had the feeling that Henri was truly there."

As Georges crossed the city to attend the closing ceremony, he realized just how much the atmosphere was imbued with Henri's memory. Even the title of the festival had been modified. It was transformed into "The Henri Langlois International Meetings," and that was what the large banners proclaimed as they spanned the streets every 150 feet, rippling from one building to another high above the city's asphalt arteries.

On 19 February 1977, the French Academy Awards, Les Césars, took place. A special international tribute was paid to Henri Langlois, with live televised participation from Alfred Hitchcock in Hollywood, Simone Signoret in Aix-en-Provence, and Frederico Fellini in Rome.

During the first "post-Langlois" Cinémathèque board of directors' meeting, President Georges-Henri Rivière requested a minute of silence and then began a short declaration with these words: "Our genius is dead. We must now replace him with more order and method."

The Cinémathèque Française, for most of Langlois's life, was considered to be in the vanguard of film preservation and presentation. Inevitably, the ax fell after Langlois's death, and certainly by American standards, the Cinémathèque lagged for many years behind other modern film archives.

The Cinémathèque would go through a period as rough as anything in its past before catching its second wind. The reader will forgive us if we do not enter into the details here. Suffice it to say that recording them would entail a second volume. Henri, taking his cue from Nostradamus, had predicted a disaster for 1980. Curiously enough, on 3 August 1980, around 4:00 A.M., a violent fire broke out in one of the Cinémathèque's warehouses called Le Pontel, in Villiers-Saint-Frédéric near the town of Rambouillet. Despite the efforts of six fire brigades, the fire, throwing flames as high as 300 feet into the air, destroyed 21,000 square feet of warehouse space. Thousands of nitrate films burned in less than 15 minutes. The 4 August issue of *Le Figaro* contains a photo of the aftermath, showing the pell-mell remains of thousands of buckled and twisted metal film cans. According to Guy Lemaitre, who has been in charge of film traffic at the Cinémathèque for 30 years, more than 90,000 cans of film—corresponding to close to 20,000 titles—burned. Half the Cinémathèque's film collection was destroyed.

Three years after his death, neither order nor method could make up for what Langlois had most lacked and his successors had not yet obtained in sufficent amount: the enormous financial means prerequisite to film preservation.

The Pontel fire did, at least, prod the powers-that-be to allocate four million francs for the construction of new vaults at the Archives du film in Bois D'Arcy. The Cinémathèque would finally be able to store its remaining nitrate films in a custom-made building with all the necessary safety features.

And yet, during the night of 27 September 1985, a new fire broke out, this time in one of the ultramodern, constant-temperature, and hygrometrically controlled vaults, at the Archives du film in Bois d'Arcy. Another 1,000 reels of film were destroyed, among them some priceless negatives from the Albatros Company that had been part of the first collection given to Henri Langlois in 1936 by Alexander Kamenka.

Ideally, of course, all nitrate films would be transferred onto safety stock. But as we have already mentioned, Henri's triumph as well as his tragic dilemma was to have saved so many films—so many, in fact, that Hubert Astier, first director of the Cinémathèque after Langlois's death, when considering the number of films at the Cinémathèque and the government's annual financial subsidy earmarked for preservation, calculated that it would take *seven centuries* to complete the task of restoring them all.

Since 1 November 1984, several employees, under the direction of Claudine Kaufmann, have been working full-time to establish an inventory.

In 1980 the museum was officially declared the Musée du Cinéma-Henri Langlois at the initiative of Cinémathèque President Jacques Flaud. Cultural Minister Jean-Philippe Lecat made the necessary construction alterations so that the public might at last gain access as Langlois intended, by way of the main entrance to the Palais de Chaillot. The museum has since attracted each year around 30,000 visitors, who have enjoyed the collections in their correct chronological sequence without first having to tramp through from the opposite end of the building.

Word has it that the ghost of Henri Langlois haunts the museum. All those who knew him still find him playfully lurking about amid his handiwork, notes Françoise Jaubert: "I am still fascinated by this museum because it is exactly like Henri. Every time I walk through the museum, I feel Henri hiding behind each corner and I meet him once again." Haunted or not, the Henri Langlois Museum is most certainly a "spirited" piece of work and should be preserved like a true work of art.

In May 1981, François Mitterrand was elected president of France and named Jack Lang as his minister of culture. Mitterrand granted the Culture Ministry—which is traditionally underfinanced—an exceptional budget increase. The Cinémathèque quickly profited under President Costa-Gavras, as its annual government grant skyrocketed from 4 million to 10 million francs, then to 15 million, then to 20 million, and finally to 25 million francs—today, roughly $5 million. Henri Langlois never dared dream of such sums.

The seventh floor of the Palais de Chaillot, which the government had at first thought of reserving for Maurice Béjart's dance school, was vacant in 1982. This space allowed the library of the film school IDHEC and the Cinémathèque's library to share the same space while retaining their respective separate listings in the card catalog. Here too the work that needs to be done is monumental. Noëlle Giret, who curated this department from 1982 to 1993, estimated that it will take 10 to 15 years before all the documents Langlois accumulated can be classified. Among the holdings are numerous valuable works belonging to the old avenue de Messine library, including Marey's collection, the old Nadar Library, and rare eighteenth-century editions. Sadoul and Eisner left their private libraries and papers to the Cinémathèque, and these form part of the film-related riches to be rediscovered. There are thousands of books, posters, manuscripts, and filmscripts that are gradually being made available to students, historians, and researchers.

Bernard Martinand, who had been hired by Henri in 1963 to help him with the programming of Chaillot, returned to the Cinémathèque in 1982 and has been back at his old job, cooking up retrospectives ever since. In July 1982 Abel Gance's *Napoléon* returned to France for three shows at the Palais des Congrès, with an original score by Carl Davis, who directed the Colonne Concert Orchestra. It was a triumph for the Cinémathèque Française, attracting an audience of 10,000.

Hundreds of thousands of other viewers attend screenings at the Cinémathèque's movie theaters each year. Nevertheless, for Langlois it was essential that his projections inspire people to make films. These attendance figures, as impressive as they are, have not deterred some people from feeling nostalgia for the mood at the Cinémathèque while Henri was alive and actively pursuing his irrepressible desire to help young people make films.

On 30 August 1982, Yilmaz Guney premiered his film *Yol* at the Cinémathèque. Costa-Gavras introduced Guney, whose first words were in memory of Henri. Twelve years before, the Turkish filmmaker had been languishing in a jail in his country, imprisoned for political crimes. One day, forgotten by all and mired in despair, Guney saw a corpulent stranger enter his cell: "You don't know me," the stranger said. "My name is Henri Langlois, and I am the director of the film archive called the Cinémathèque Française. I saw your first two movies, *Agit* and *L'Espoir*, and I found them to be extraordinary. Well, I just came by to shake your hand and give you some encouragement. One day, you're going to leave this prison and make great films."

Guney never forgot those words. He thought often about what Langlois had said, and it gave him strength to know that someone cared and expected him to direct again. As for Henri, just as soon as he returned to Paris, he placed a photo of the imprisoned Turkish actor-director at the end of his museum as a sort of question mark pointed toward the cinema's future. Yet another of Henri's prophecies would be realized when Guney went on to share the top prize at the 1982 Cannes Festival, with Costa-Gavras's *Missing*, for *Yol*, which he wrote—and codirected—while in prison.

It has taken 91 employees to replace Langlois, and even this figure falls short of the number needed. Ninety-one employees who, for the most part, work regular hours. Even if someone as charismatic as Langlois were to come along today, it is unlikely that he or she would ever be able to assemble as tireless and devoted a team as Henri enjoyed in the persons of Lotte Eisner, Marie Epstein, Yvonne Dornès, and, of course, Mary Meerson. Although at times Henri had had close to 30 employees, it was these exceptional women, his "muses," who formed the backbone of the Cinémathèque.

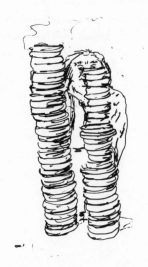

For more than 40 years Henri Langlois succeeded in preserving the Association's freedom to create, along with its status as an independent institution, while admitting that all cinémathèques have financial needs so great that they cannot assume all their tasks without help from the state. That help was not always forthcoming when it was most needed, but Henri managed nonetheless to collect and pass along an extraordinary treasure. His genius enabled him to find allies in all walks of life. He forged the Cinémathèque into one of the most productive hubs of French culture abroad.

What will be the future of the Cinémathèque Française? Its diverse services are to be brought together at the Palais de Tokyo. This close neighbor to the Palais de Chaillot is a majestic remnant of the 1937 World's Fair and former home to the art collections that are now to be found in the Pompidou Center and the Musée d'Orsay. The Cinémathèque's reserve collections, easily twice the number of objects on permanent display in the Musée du Cinéma-Henri Langlois, will be tapped for temporary exhibitions. And yet the Cinémathèque Française will not be cut from its historic roots. Its board of directors, while congratulating themselves on the possibilities offered by the new space at Tokyo, have affirmed their attachment to the theater and museum created by Henri Langlois in the Palais de Chaillot. The museum will be restored and its original audiovisual components will again be operational.

In 1995 the cinema will celebrate its hundredth anniversary. Are the penetration of electronic images into homes, schools, businesses, train stations, and airports, the success of VCRs, and the multiplication of cable and satellite channels sounding the death knell of cinema?

More than ever, the Cinémathèque will have its raison d'être, for should commercial moviegoing fall by the wayside, the Cinémathèque Française will then remain as one of the last public gathering spots where the entire cinematographic repertory will continue to weave its large-screen spell. Those who continue to observe the moviegoing ritual will carry on in the spirit of Henri Langlois, who wanted to use the cinema as a time machine not only for journeys to the past, but as a springboard toward the future.

## AFTERWORD: RETURN TO ABU SIMBEL

## by Glenn Myrent

This book was first published in French, in 1986, to coincide with the fiftieth anniversary of the Cinémathèque Française. During the yearlong celebration, French Minister of Culture Jack Lang strongly recommended that the Cinémathèque move all of its facilities, including the Henri Langlois Museum, to the Palais de Tokyo building, a few blocks away from the Palais de Chaillot. Lang wanted to create a Palais de l'Image, housing the Cinémathèque, the National Center for Photography, and the national film school, FEMIS, under one roof.

There would be more space for the Cinémathèque; close to 50,000 square feet for a new museum, temporary exhibitions, library, and three movie theaters. There was also, however, a real fear that if Langlois's museum was transferred as well, it would be dismantled and then, because of a change of government, lack of funds, or other reasons, never be reassembled.

World-class film producer Anatole Dauman, who was then a Cinémathèque vice-president,

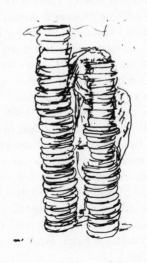

called the proposed transfer of the museum to the Palais de Tokyo another Abu Simbel, referring to the UN-protected Egyptian monuments that were dismantled stone by stone in the 1960s and then reassembled further up the Nile to avoid ending up at the bottom of the newly created Lake Nasser. Unlike the more than 125 miles of desert separating the former site of the Ramses II temples from the new Abu Simbel, the distance from Chaillot to Tokyo—2,000 feet—can be covered on foot in five minutes. The film museum, needless to say, remains in no physical danger of being flooded, even though the nearby Seine overflows its banks a bit each spring. For the record, Chaillot is on higher ground than Tokyo and attracts far more tourists, owing to its location on the Trocadéro esplanade, the ideal vantage from which to admire the Eiffel Tower directly across the river.

So why even think about moving it? The answer, in part, is linked to the lack of space at Chaillot to cover film history from the 1950s through the present. But also, the urge to merge—based on the philosophy that bigger is always better—has reared its unwieldy head. Simultaneous consolidation and expansion characterize several of the ambitious "great projects" of Mitterrand's presidency. The Palais d'Image was envisioned as a modest cousin to the expanded Louvre, the amply stocked Musée d'Orsay (which gobbled up other museums, including the well-proportioned impressionist collection that used to reside in the Jeu de paume), and the literally voluminous Bibliothèque de France (also known as "the TGB," or *très grande bibliothèque*).

Partisans of Langlois's museum believed that the battle to keep the museum intact in Chaillot was theoretically won, as stated in the previous chapter, in June 1986, when the Cinémathèque's board of directors voted as such, while still planning to build another museum in the space alloted to the Cinémathèque at Tokyo. This stance was reinforced on 25 May 1987, when the Cinémathèque's General Assembly, faced with an annual report from President Costa-Gavras and Director Bernard Latarjet condoning a complete shift to Tokyo, rejected the report and dismissed its authors.

Jean Rouch succeeded Costa-Gavras as president, and the board voted Pascal Leclercq into office as managing director. Much to everyone's surprise, the move to classify Langlois's museum as a historical monument was rejected by the government in 1988, despite Rouch's impassioned defense. Had the historical monument designation gone through, not only would the objects in the museum have been preserved, *but Langlois's museum design would also have been protected under French law*. Rumors circulated that the proposal was rejected because the Cinémathèque had refused to play ball with Culture Minister Lang and thus lost its real chance to be the dominant force in the still-on-the-drawing-board Palais de Tokyo.

This last statement is believed to be true by present Cinémathèque Director Dominique Païni. Formerly director of the audiovisual department of the Louvre, Païni came to the Cinémathèque in 1991 under the condition that he be granted a free hand in building another film museum in the Palais de Tokyo.

Although the film loops that Langlois artfully scattered through 16 locations in the Chaillot museum have been inoperative since 1985, and despite the absence of guards, restrooms, and adequate emergency-exit facilities, the Langlois museum continued to offer five guided tours daily. The most-cited excuse for not repairing the 16-millimeter projectors was that they emitted a gas that could not be properly ventilated. During his presidency (1987–91), Jean Rouch systematically refused, on aesthetic principles, to replace the film projections with video projections, be they cassette or laser disc-based. Consequently, for 10 years the approximately 300,000 visitors to the world's premier film museum passed through a space bereft of moving objects except themselves and the tour guide, spinning tales from inanimate objects.

If I may introduce myself into this story, for 11 years I conducted guided tours and lectured in the Langlois museum and saw every conceivable reaction to Langlois's legacy. The overall impression the museum leaves is one of palpable magic. It remains a unique place that galvanizes visitors, renewing their love for the art of film and inspiring them to seek out many of the films mentioned in the museum. At every turn of the labyrinth, it surprises. How, visitors often ask, did a dress from *Gone with the Wind*, or the robot from *Metropolis*, or Mrs. Bates from *Psycho*, end up in Paris?

The museum does have its detractors, especially those overly concerned with modernism (whatever that at any given moment may be) and the need for Cartesian explanations through captions. Henri Langlois held a theory that people visit museums and exhibitions only to read the captions first— "Ah, it says here that this is a Picasso from the Blue Period"—after which, nine times out of ten, they don't bother to *really* look at the painting. For this reason, Langlois deliberately omitted labels, allowing the objects in the museum to speak for themselves. Visitors often leave the premises with more questions than when they first entered. The museum has always been a place that can be revisited with pleasure rather than a "been there, done that" tourist attraction. Langlois's tacit communication, or education-via-osmosis, is a unique approach and—in contrast, perhaps, to

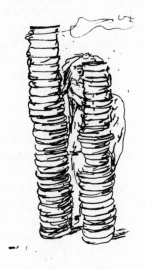

most other major museums—these vestiges of film history were placed in a specific setting by the one man who knew them best.

In May 1994 the museum was closed for one month during which time identifying labels were printed up and placed beside every object. Although this development is more in line with traditional museology, it runs counter to Langlois's views. The next time you go to an art museum, see if you can resist the temptation to "read about" a work until after you've *really* looked at it. It isn't easy!

If you had visited the Henri Langlois Museum between 1980 and April 1994, you would have seen the museum as Langlois built it. The museum reopened in June 1994 sporting new carpeting and a fresh coat of paint. But to give one example of the effect of these changes, in the Lumière room the colors are no longer those that Langlois chose to echo the *salon indien* where Lumière's films were first shown to the general public in December 1895. The lush burgundy curtains that evoked the original historic setting are gone for good. Three of the four walls have been painted utilitarian black.

More serious are the changes that deform film history. Langlois built a replica of the inside of Edison's Black Maria Studio that could be entered and in which Edison's films were shown on a small screen. That area has been walled off.

The small room dedicated to the European avant-garde of the 1920s, which included the bicyclist's distinctive wooden box from Buñuel's *Un chien andalou* along with still photos from that film and from Buñuel's *L'Age d'or*, the preserved starfish in a jar from Man Ray's experimental classic *L'Etoile de mer*, images from Vertov's *Man with a Camera* and from Diaghalev's *Ode*—the great choreographer's one attempt at an experimental film, which was projected on stage with live dancers in 1928—is completely walled off and now destined to be a storage area. Also absent from the new, labeled, and captioned museum are photos and posters celebrating Buster Keaton's *Go West*, Abel Gance's *Napoléon*, Raoul Grimoin-Sanson's spectacularly innovative 360-degree *Cinéorama* from the Paris Universal Exposition in 1900, and Pathé's *Dreyfus Affair*. Gone as well is the room-sized erector set–style metal replica of the very first film studio in France—Georges Méliès's glass-roofed workshop in suburban Paris.

As we have already stated, Langlois ran out of space way before he ran out of ideas. Although a guided tour of the museum requires some two hours, the reader will recall that Langlois was obliged to bring the collection to a more or less abrupt halt after the room devoted to the post–World War II Italian neorealist school. A nearby door led into a cozy alcove devoted to cartoony sketches by Eisenstein and props from his films, including the wool–imitating–chain mail costume and giant boots worn by the commanding Nikolai Cherkassav in the title role of *Ivan the Terrible*.

Down a small flight of stairs and around the corner, Langlois installed the papal vestments—complete with flashy film-frame trim—that Ringo Starr wore in Ken Russell's *Lizstomania*. In the large final chamber, Langlois mixed and matched choice morsels of cinemabilia, including annotated scripts from *Rebel without a Cause*, *West Side Story*, and *Cul de sac*; Zanuck's personal research volume for *The Longest Day*; Ken Adam's original production sketch for James Bond's gizmo-loaded Aston Martin; a swimsuit worn by Esther Williams; a Leslie Caron dress from *Gigi*; a slinky Cyd Charisse costume from *Singin' in the Rain*; and a gown worn by Marlene Dietrich in *Kismet*. Langlois saved one of the best specimens for last—a sweetly gory memento mori from the master of suspense: Mrs. Bates's shriveled head from Hitchcock's *Psycho*.

Readers wishing to see these artistic artifacts are out of luck. From nasty Ivan to Norman Bates's mummified mum, the exhibit space has been stripped of its contents and structurally altered to make way for a reception area that, as of this writing, has not been built. Whether or not individual objects eventually find a home in a prolongation of the museum, Langlois's judicious jumble is gone forever.

Several of the original movie posters, costumes, and scripts have been removed in favor of facsimiles. Visitors lose interest quickly if they discover that they are looking at a copy, and this raises very sticky questions about preservation versus presentation. Apart from its inspired design, one of the key assets of Langlois's museum has always been that visitors knew they were seeing all original objects. Many of the new film museums worldwide, including the Museum of the Moving Image in London, were inspired by Langlois's last will and testament. And since there are only so many originals to be had, other film museums must rely wholly or in part on replicas.

Since the appointment in 1993 of a new minister of culture, Jacques Toubon, and his cabinet member in charge of film, former Cinémathèque director Hubert Astier, the plans to build another film museum at Tokyo appear to be stalled. In April 1994 Astier granted 800,000 francs to "freshen up" the Langlois museum in the Palais de Chaillot. But in the next breath he also relaunched the idea of moving the museum to Tokyo. "The Langlois museum will be *translated* to the Palais de Tokyo," Astier, coining a term, told a reporter for *Le Monde*. "We will respect Langlois's *scénographie*. The Langlois museum will constitute the introduction to the Tokyo museum."

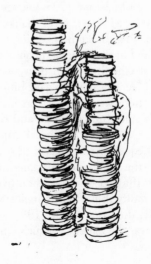

On 28 June 1994 the Cinémathèque's General Assembly was informed by its presi-

dent, Jean Saint-Geours, and the Centre national de la cinématographie's director, Dominique Wallon, that the Henri Langlois Museum will in fact be transferred to Tokyo in the next two years. An animated debate erupted, and as of this writing, the fate of the Chaillot museum remains unknown.

So, as the French are wont to say, the more things change, the more they stay the same. Abu Simbel, start packing your bricks, unless the next culture minister (coming up in 1995—after the presidential elections) decides to change once again.

To summarize: Either the museum stays in Chaillot with the government's blessing and is brought back to its original luster, including working audiovisual elements, or it stays in Chaillot, where Langlois's original intent has already been tampered with, and dies a slow death for lack of funds. Or the museum is moved to the Palais de Tokyo in its present form, with new elements added in order to bring up-to-date the history of film during the last 50 years. Or, after the transfer—unless written guarantees that Langlois's vision will be respected are secured—a new and different museum will be built. (In which case, the objects that Langlois and his dedicated associates lovingly obtained will be rescued, but Langlois's vision will perish.) Or, yet again, the Cinémathèque finds still another location in which to build another museum. So far, no official pronouncement on the subject can be taken to be the last word, since the verdict seems to change from one day to the next. Even the most objective observer would guess that the higher-ups are making it up as they go along. To date, no one has the dominant hand required to push through his or her plan. This circle game has been going on since 1984, when Lang first proposed the Palais de Tokyo for the Cinémathèque, and ever since, the museum has become a political yo-yo.

On 2 May 1993, Georges Langlois died of cancer. He was 73. I will always owe him a note of thanks for trusting me to tell his brother's story and for making the French edition come to pass. He truly believed in Henri Langlois and in the Cinémathèque's cause. The fight in 1992–93 to keep the museum at Chaillot, when many were determined to crate it up, certainly exhausted Georges but also gave him the will to live a little longer.

Then there was Mary Meerson, the nearsighted polyglot who was at Langlois's side through thick and thin—and who joined him in evolving from thin to thick. After Langlois's death, she remained at the Cinémathèque for three years in a mostly honorary capacity. In 1980 she retired to the rue Gazan apartment and, owing to poor health, rarely ventured out. If asked who would outlive us all, I would have nominated Mary for immortality. But Henri Langlois's modern-day Cardinal Richelieu to his Louis XIII died on 19 July 1993 at the unconfirmable age of 93. Mary Meerson was the Cinémathèque's éminence grise for 40 years, and her memory lives on.

Pierre Bracquemond, master technician and re-creator of Reynaud's *Théatre Optique*, died of cancer in 1992.

Marie Epstein (born in 1899), Yvonne Dornès, and Renée and Lucie Lichtig, although no longer present on a daily basis, are the surviving female guardians of the temple.

Georges Langlois and his son Hugues, in collaboration with filmmaker Jacques Richard, created the Henri Langlois Association in 1988 in order to raise funds to build a monument to Henri Langlois, to lobby to protect the museum, and to help young filmmakers make films. On 13 January 1991, 14 years to the day after his death, Henri Langlois's coffin was moved to its new resting place in the Montparnasse Cemetery. Sculptor Patrick Rimoux designed the glass and granite monument, which measures six and a half feet long by three and a quarter feet high by four and a half feet wide. Engraved on the front is Cocteau's phrase, "The dragon who watched over our treasures." The design echoes that of the double-winged form of the Palais de Chaillot. The upper part of the monument represents one second in Henri Langlois's life: 24 images from an imaginary film called *Henri Langlois*. Beneath, embedded in the sloping glass, is a 150-picture collage of stills from world film masterpieces that Henri Langlois championed. Both Mary Meerson and Georges Langlois are also interred under the monument. Cemetery-goers are attracted to the memorial's unusual design, and in turn, many people are prompted to visit the museum.

The date 13 January 1995 marks 18 years since Henri Langlois died. The post-Langlois Cinémathèque has reached the age when it can vote on its own. Langlois's image still permeates the institution he built. The flaws as well as its greatness stem from Langlois's character. Even so, an anecdote may prove instructive. One day at the Cinémathèque, I went to cast my ballot in an election to choose personnel representatives. Six employees were handing out ballots after verifying each prospective voter's identity on a preprinted eligibility list. On a lark, I gave my name as "Henri Langlois." To my utter shock and the hysteria of the other employees looking on, a

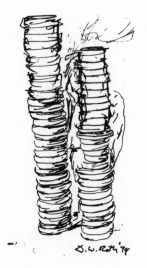

young poll watcher who had been working at the Cinémathèque for at least two years quite seriously went down a printed list of employee names in search of "Henri Langlois" and said "my" name wasn't on the list! I realize there is no law requiring employees to know the history of their company, but still, there should be limits to ignorance. Or perhaps it is simply a sign that the time has come for the institution that Langlois built to live on its own and stop incessantly referring to its past, even though film heritage is its raison d'être.

Just as there are no doubt hundreds if not thousands of films yet to be discovered at the Cinémathèque, there are still hundreds of large boxes containing thousands of documents waiting to be cataloged at the Cinémathèque's warehouse in Pantin. A company that is ignorant of its past is condemned to make the same mistakes, and so the future of the Cinémathèque remains unknown. Apropos, in the early 1970s the National Film Theater (NFT) in London asked Langlois for a loan of the Cinémathèque's print of Tod Browning's 1927 feature *The Unknown*. Langlois agreed. Months passed, and then suddenly, the print turned up in London. After thanking Langlois, the director of the NFT expressed surprise at the length of time it had taken to fill his request. Langlois's reply was, "Ah, but you see, we have so many cans of film marked 'Unknown' at the Cinémathèque."

# NOTES AND REFERENCES

All quotations by Georges Langlois not mentioned below are drawn from his personal experience, memories, or unpublished papers. All other quotations are taken from interviews conducted by the authors and the following written references.

## CHAPTER 1

pp.

1 – Henri Langlois (H.L.), unpublished journal, 1948.

2 – Mary Meerson, interview with Glenn Myrent (G.M.) and Jack Moseley (J.M.), 16 June 1979.

4–5 – *Smyrne, l'image de la Grèce*, introduction by Chapuisat, ed. (Geneva: Editions d'art, 1919).

6 – H.L., "The Seventh Heaven: Henri Langlois Talks to Rui Nogueira and Nicoletta Zalaffi," *Sight and Sound* (Autumn 1972): 182.

12 – Ibid.; Rui Nogueria, "Musée du Cinéma: Henri Langlois," ZOOM (June–July 1974): 84.

12 – Built in 1911, the Gaumont Palace was the showpiece of the neighborhood and in fact the world's largest movie theater at the time, with close to 6,000 seats.

13 – Denise Tual, *Le Temps dévoré* (Fayard, 1980), 80.

13 – H.L., quoted in Yves Kovacs, "Surréalisme et cinéma," *Etudes cinématographiques* (Spring 1965): 41.

15 – Georges Franju, interview with G.M., 13 July 1979.

16 – Thanks to Claudine Kaufmann, in charge of the film inventory at the Cinémathèque Française, *Le Métro* was found once again in 1985.

17 – H.L., interview with J.M. and G.M., "Vidéo in Paris," 19 March 1976.

17 – In the film journal *1895* (December 1992) film historian Claude Beylie notes that a young man named Henri Langlois showed his 9.5-millimeter-format film called *Entre deux ondes* at a screening for members of the Société française de photographie et de cinématographie (SFPC) in October 1935 (article in *Cinéma privé*, no. 24 [20 October 1935]). So either there was another Henri Langlois running around at this time, or he made another film, or this is *Le Métro* under another title.

## CHAPTER 2

pp.
18 – H.L., quoted in Rui Nogueira, "The Seventh Heaven," *Sight and Sound* (Autumn 1972): 182.

19 – Ricciotto Canudo, *Manifesto des Sept Arts* (Paris, 1911).

19–20 – Unpublished text by H.L., *L'Histoire du cinéma vue de France*.

20 – Louis Delluc, *Le Journal du ciné-club* (January 1920).

21 – Gilles Gressard and Michèle Levieux, "1928–1978: Le Studio 28 a 50 ans," program for "50 Ans de cinéma au Studio 28," 28 February 1978.

22–23 – H.L., brochure published for the Cinémathèque Française's twentieth anniversary in 1956.

23–24 – Sonika Bo, interview with G.M., Neuilly, 13 September 1980.

24 – H.L., "Classiques de l'ecran muet," *La Cinématographie française* (24 August 1935).

26 – Jean-George Auriol, "A la recherche des films classiques," *Pour vous* (12 September 1935).

26–27 – Jean Mitry, interview with G.M., 7 September 1979.

27–28 – H.L., interview with J.M. and G.M., "Vidéo in Paris," 19 March 1976.

28 – Madeleine Malthête-Méliès, *Méliès l'enchanteur* (Hachette, 1973), 422.

29 – H.L., Cinémathèque twentieth anniversary brochure, 1956.

30 – Ibid.

30 – Boleslas Matuszewski, *A New Source of History: The Creation of a Depository for Historical Cinematography* (Paris, 1898).

30–31 – Jean Mitry, interview with G.M., 7 September 1979.

31 – Lucienne Escoube, "Sauvons les films de répertoire," *Pour vous* (31 March 1932).

32 – H.L., "In Memoriam," *La Cinématographie française*, special issue, no. 2000 (Winter 1963): 7.

33 – Sonika Bo, interview with G.M., 13 September 1980.

34 – Iris Barry, "The Film Library," *Film Quarterly* (Summer 1969): 24.

35 – H.L., "La Cinémathèque de la Fondation Rockefeller de New York," *La Cinématographie française* (27 June 1936).

## CHAPTER 3

pp.
37 – H.L., quoted in Eric Rohmer and Michel Mardore, "Entretien avec Henri Langlois," *Cahiers du cinéma*, no. 135 (September 1962): 1.

37–38 – André Laporte, interview with G.M., Paris, 27 October 1982.

39 – Suzanne Borel (Bidault), interview with G.M., Paris, 27 April 1981.

40 – Georges Franju, interview with G.M., 8 April 1980; *L'Avant-Scène du cinéma* (15 June 1982).

44 – Adolf Hitler, quoted in William L. Shirer, *The Third Reich* (Paris: Stock, 1960), 267.

45 – H.L., "Aujourd'hui, la Cinémathèque Française est à la hauteur des cinémathèques des autres pays," *La Cinématographie française* (25 June 1937).

45 – Georges Duhamel, *Scènes de la vie future* (1930), 58.

46 – "Le Tout Paris rend hommage au cinéma d'hier," *Cinémonde* (15 July 1937).

46 – René Brest, "Le Grand succès du Gala des Fantômes," *Pour vous* (10 November 1937).

47 – Madeleine Malthête-Méliès, *Méliès l'enchanteur* (1973), 423.

47–48 – "Gala des Loufoques," *Pour vous* (9 February 1938).

48–49 – Jean Rouch, "Cinémappemonde," *Le Monde*, 9 April 1981, 17; interview with G.M., Paris, 14 June 1979.

51 – Alberto Cavalcanti, interview with G.M., Paris, 1 December 1981.

52 – Georges Franju, interview with G.M.; Georges Franju, "La Fédération internationale des cinémathèques est en formation," *La Cinématographie française* (15 July 1938).

53 – Arthur Knight, interview with G.M., Los Angeles, 20 April 1984.

53–54 – Jay Leyda, interview with G.M., New York, 25 February 1983.

54–61 – H.L.'s unpublished diary, recovered by Costa-Gavras at the Cinémathèque Française.

## CHAPTER 4

pp.

62 – Henri Amouroux, *Le Peuple du désastre* (Paris: Laffont, 1976).

64 – Alexandre Trauner, interview with G.M., Paris, 26 February 1985.

64–65 – Gianni Comencini, interview with Lisa Nesselson. Milan, 6 November 1984.

65 – Suzanne Bidault, *Souvenirs de guerre et d'Occupation* (La Table Ronde, 1973).

66 – E. Pichaud, "La Cinémathèque Française au service du pays," *La Cinématographie française* (30 March 1940): 6; "Brillant palmarès de la cinémathèque aux armées," *Cinématographie française* (18 May 1940): 2.

70–71 – Jean-Paul Le Chanois, interview with G.M., Paris, 12 March 1982.

72 – Suzanne Bidault, *Souvenirs de guerre et d'Occupation*, 12.

72 – Yvonne Dornès, interview with G.M., Paris, 22 May 1979.

73 – "Ordonnance concernant la saisie et la fabrication des négatifs de films du 17 oct. 1940," *Le Film* (15 November 1940).

73–74 – Georges Franju, interview with G.M., Paris, 8 April 1980.

75 – Max Douy, interview with G.M., Epiney Studios, Epiney, 9 February 1982.

75 – Jean-Paul Le Chanois, interview with G.M., Paris, 12 March 1982.

77 – Simone Signoret, *Cahiers du cinéma* (March 1968): 44.

77 – *Denise Tual*, Le Temps dévoré (1980): 199.

78–79 – Denise Tual, interview with G.M., Paris, 8 January 1982.

79–80 – Michel Rittener, interview with G.M., Paris, 19 July 1982.

80–81 – Marcel L'Herbier, *La Tête qui tourne* (Belfond, 1979), 288–89.

82–83 – Louis Emile Galey, interview with G.M., Paris, 28 September 1979. By 1944 the subsidy would increase to 120,000 francs per year.

83–84 – Confirmed by Pierre Riedinger in interview with G.M., Paris, 9 May 1980.

84 – Marie Epstein, interview with G.M., 12 February 1979.

85–86 – Lotte Eisner, *Films et documents* (October–December 1980); interview with G.M., 13 December 1978.

87 – Jean Mitry and Madeleine Malthête-Méliès, interview with G.M., 7 and 12 September 1979.

87–88 – Louis-Emile Galey, interview with G.M., 28 September 1979. The General Assembly meeting, where Grémillon was elected president, took place on Saturday, 19 February 1944.

## CHAPTER 5

pp.

90 – G. W. F. Hegel, quoted in P. Dupré, *Encyclopédie des citations* (Editions Trévise, 1959), 325.

91 – Jean Cocteau supposedly described Langlois as such at the Cannes Film Festival in 1953.

91 – Jean Cocteau, *Poésie critique* 1, 49f.

92 – Sonika Bo, interview with G.M., 13 September 1980.

91 – Malthête-Méliès, interview with G.M., 12 September 1979.

94–95 – Mary Meerson, interview with G.M. and J.M., 16 June 1979.

95–96 – Alberto Cavalcanti, interview with G.M., Paris, 1 December 1981.

99 – Denise Tual, interview with G.M., 8 January 1982.

99–100 – Henri Lartigue, interview with G.M., 17 February 1982.

101 – Goebbels, quoted in Georges Sadoul, *Histoire du cinéma mondial* (Flammarion, 1949), 287.

101–102 – André Laporte, interview with G.M., Paris, 27 October 1982.

104–105 – L. E. Galey, interview with G.M., 28 September 1979.

## CHAPTER 6

pp.

107 – H.L., brochure published for the Cinémathèque Française's twentieth anniversary in 1956.

108 – "L'Action par le film," *Film français* (8 December 1944): 10.

109 – *France-Soir*, 7 December 1944.

109 – William Novik, interview with G. M., Paris, 10 April 1982.

110 – Nicole Védrès, *L'Ecran français* (Christmas 1945).

110 – Charles Rochefort, "L'Activité de la cinémathèque," *Film français* (5 January 1945): 12.

110–112 – Charles (Charlot) Heimberger, interview with G.M., Paris, 23 August 1982.

113–114 – H.L., "Images du cinéma français," *Cinéma* 2; IDHEC courses and lectures (1945), 72–73.

115 – Farrokh Gaffary, interview with G.M., Paris, 13 May 1982.

115 – Jean-Charles Tacchella, postface to Dudley Andrew, *André Bazin* (Cahiers du Cinéma/Cinémathèque Française, 1983); interview with G.M., Versailles, 26 April 1982. Best-known beyond France as the writer-director of *Cousin, Cousine*, Tacchella would re-create the atmosphere of the postwar ciné-clubs and the Cinémathèque in his 1987 film *Travelling Avant*.

116–118 – Pierre Kast, interview with G.M., Paris, 20 November 1979.

119 – Charlot Heimberger, interview with G.M., Paris, 23 August 1982.

120 – Heimberger and Rittener, interview with G.M., 19 July 1982.

121 – Freddy Buache, "Entretien avec Freddy Buache," *Traveling* (November–December 1973): 19.

121 – "Nuits magnétiques," radio broadcast, "France-Culture," 5 June 1980.

121–122 – Pierre Robin, *Cinématographie française* (23 February 1946).

123–124 – Jean Raine, *Autothanatographie* (1972); interview with G.M., Rochetaillée-sur-Saone, 8–9 April 1985.


## CHAPTER 7

pp.

125 – H.L., *Cahiers du cinéma* (September 1962).

126–127 – André Bazin, "Un Musée des ombres: Magie blanche, magie noire," *L'Ecran français* (21 December 1948): 16.

127 – Frédéric Rossif, interview with G.M., Paris, 19 July 1979.

128 – François Truffaut, interview with G.M., Paris, 14 May 1979.

129 – Jean Raine, interview with G.M., 8–9 April 1985.

129 – Gérard Legrand, "Nuits magnétiques," "France-Culture, 6 June 1980.

131 – Jean Boullet, "Fireworks," *St. Cinéma des Prés*, no. 1 (1949).

131–132 – Kenneth Anger, interview with G.M., New York, 3 December 1980.

132–133 – Curtis Harrington, interview with G.M., Los Angeles, 2 June 1982.

133 – Jean Rouch, "Nuits magnétiques," "France-Culture," 6 June 1980.

137 – José Zendel, "Le Festival est bon enfant," *L'Ecran français* (18 September 1950): 6.

140 – Jean Raine, interview with G.M., 8 April 1985.

140 – H.L., excerpt from a film on Langlois by Jean Douchet for the TV program "Etoiles et toiles," 17 February 1986.

140 – Rossif, interview with G.M., 19 July 1979.

141 – Jean Grémillon, "L'Activité de la Cinémathèque Française," *La Cinématographie française* (5 July 1952): 11–12.

142 – Jean Mauclaire, whose letters appeared in *Le Film français* on 10 and 24 December 1948. Mauclaire had already written a letter voicing his opposition to Henri Langlois and his manner of directing the Cinémathèque as early as 29 March 1943.

142–143 – Jean Painlevé, interview with G.M., Paris, 4 April 1980.

143 – Pierre Kast, interview with G.M., 20 November 1979.

143 – Ado Kyrou, interview with G.M., Paris, 20 December 1978.

143–144 – "L'Affaire de la Cinémathèque," *Objectif* (October 1954).

144 – "La Cinémathèque est enfin sous contrôle," *Objectif* (November 1954).

145–146 – François Truffaut, "La Cinémathèque à la rue," *ARTS* (2–8 February 1955).

147–148 – François Truffaut, "Réouverture de la Cinémathèque au Musée d'art moderne," *ARTS* (13 July 1955).

148–149 – H.L., letter to Ida Chagall, 1955.

149 – H.L., letter to Marc Chagall.

## CHAPTER 8

pp.

150–151 – H.L., brochure published for the Cinémathèque Française's twentieth anniversary in 1956.

154 – "Entretien avec Freddy Buache," *Traveling* (November–December 1973).

154–155 – James Card, interview with G.M., Rochester, N.Y., 19 November 1980.

155 – Vigan story told by Nestor Almendros to G.M., Paris, 1980.

155–157 – Farrokh Gaffary, interview with G.M., 19 March 1985.

158 – "Entretien avec Richard Griffith," *Cahiers du cinéma* (October 1963).

158 – E. Rohmer and M. Mardore, "Entretien avec H.L.," *Cahiers du cinéma* (September 1962).

159 – Herbert Volkmann, *Film Preservation* (London: FIAF, l965), 6.

159 – H.L., "Nuits magnétiques," "France-Culture," June 1980.

160–161 – François Truffaut, interview with G.M., 23 September 1979.

161 – Farrokh Gaffary, interview with G.M., 19 March 1985.

161 – Daniel Toscan du Plantier, "France-Culture," 7 June 1980.

162–163– James Card, *Image*, no. 2 (June 1977).

163 – Georges Sadoul, "Le Cinéma, patrimoine culturel: Faut-il conserver ou détruire les anciens films inflammables?" *Le Monde*, 15 November 1966.

164 – Marie Epstein, *Films et documents* (October–December 1980).

165–167 – Jean Raine, interview with G.M., 9 April 1985.

168 – Kenneth Anger, *Film Comment* (March–April 1977): 32; interview with G.M., 3 December 1980.

169 – Henri Storck, interview with G.M., Paris, 26 November 1984.

169–170 – Marion Michelle, interview with G.M., 29 September 1982.

171 – H.L., "Ingmar Bergman et le génie de la Suède" (April–June 1964).

172 – H.L., *FIAF Bulletin* (June–July 1956).

173 – H.L., radio broadcast on "France-Culture," June 1980.

174 – H.L., ZOOM (June–July 1974): 85.

175–176 – Renée Lichtig, "En travaillant avec Stroheim," *Cahiers du cinéma* (July 1954): 18.

176–177 – Jean Rouch, interview with G.M., 14 June 1979.

177 – Jean-Luc Godard, "Grâce à Henri Langlois," *Le Nouvel observateur* (12 January 1966): 36–37.

177 – Alain Resnais, interview with G.M., Paris, 1 October 1985.

178 – François Truffaut, interview with G.M., 18 September 1979.
179 – Eric Rohmer, *Cahiers du cinéma* (September 1962).
180 – H.L., interview with J.M. and G.M. 19 March 1976.

## CHAPTER 9

pp.
181 – Orson Welles's quotation appears on screen at the beginning of *Monsieur Arkadin*, *L'Avant-scène du cinéma* (15 July 1982).
181–183 – Lotte Eisner, interview with G.M., Neuilly-sur-Seine, 13 December 1978.
183–184 – Marion Michelle, interview with G.M., 30 November 1982.
184–185 – H.L., letter to Marion Michelle, 7 August 1957.
185 – Ibid.
186 – Marion Michelle, interview with G.M., 30 November 1982.
186 – H.L., document supplied by Marion Michelle.
187 – Kawakita, interview with G.M., Paris, 29 July 1985.
187–188 – H.L., brochure published for the Cinémathèque Française's twentieth anniversary in 1956.
188 – Jay Leyda, interview with G.M., New York, 25 November 1980; and letter.
189–190 – Ibid.
188 – Jay Leyda papers, Special Collections, New York University Library.
190 – James Card, interview with G.M., 23 November 1980 and 17 February 1986.
191 – H.L., catalog for "300 Années du cinématographie, 60 ans du cinéma," 1955.
192 – André Malraux, *France-Soir*, 25 June 1959.
192 – Lotte Eisner, interview with G.M., 24 April 1979.
193 – Françoise Jaubert, interview with G.M., Paris, 30 September 1980.
194 – *France-Soir*, 25 June 1959.
195 – Fritz Lang, letter to Lotte Eisner, November 1959.
195 – Françoise Jaubert, interview with G.M., 30 September 1980.
195–196 – *France-Soir*, 11 July 1959; *Le Monde*, 12–13 July 1959; *Combat*, 11 July 1959; and *Le Figaro*, 11 July 1959.
196 – Volkmann, *Film Preservation*, (1965), 7.
197 – Jean Painlevé, interview with G.M., Paris, 4 April 1980.
197 – Georges Franju, interview with G.M., Paris, 8 April 1980.
198 – Sonika Bo, interview with G.M., 13 September 1980.
199 – H.L., letter to James Card, 3–4 August 1967.
199–200 – H.L., board of directors meeting notes, 23 March 1963.
200 – Raymond Rohauer, interview with G.M., 17 February 1983. According to Richard Koch, then director of administration at MOMA and Richard Griffith's boss, who was contacted for this edition (telephone conversation, 5 August 1994), if anyone was unscrupulous it was Rohauer, who was so clumsy in his "borrowing" of prints from MOMA's Circulating Film Department that he would tack on a "Raymond Rohauer presents" at the beginning of the borrowed film—and then forget to cut off the

MOMA identification at the end credits. Kock denies Rohauer's interpretation of Griffith's resignation and claims that Griffith was asked to resign for "ill health reasons," a euphemism for alcoholism. Griffith left MOMA in 1965 and, according to Ephraim Katz's *Film Encyclopedia*, was killed in an automobile accident in 1969. Koch claims no knowledge of a lawsuit involving Griffith, MOMA and the "Silence Please" producer.

201 – James Card, interview with G.M., Rochester, N.Y., 23 November 1980.
202 – Jean Raine, interview with G.M., 8 April 1985.
203 – James Card, interview with G.M., Rochester, N.Y., 17 February 1986.
203 – H.L., letter to Marion Michelle, 23 November 1959.
203–204 – Marion Michelle, interview with G.M., 15 March 1983.
204 – FIAF, board of directors report, 16–17 January 1960.
205 – H.L., *Le Monde*, 19 February 1976.
205 – Marion Michelle, interview with G.M., 15 March 1983.
207 – James Card, letter to G.M., 26 September 1979. The Union mondiale des musées du cinéma was created in Paris on 6 October 1960. Founding members present were Langlois (Paris), Maria Prolo (Turin), Agnes Bleier-Brody (Vienna), James Card (Rochester), and Freddy Buache (Lausanne).
207 – Françoise Jaubert, interview with G.M., 8 January 1981.
208 – Orson Welles, *Monsieur Arkadin, L'Avant-scène du cinéma* (15 July 1982).
208 – Farrokh Gaffary, interview with G.M., 13 May 1982.
208 – Françoise Jaubert, interview with G.M., 8 January 1981.

## CHAPTER 10

pp.
209 – H.L., *Cahiers du cinéma* (September 1962).
209 – Paul Guimard, "Sa majesté Eisenstein expliqué par ses dessins," *ARTS* (27 April–3 May 1960): 14.
210 – Yvonne Baby and Elvire de Brissac, "La Cinémathèque Française, notaire du cinéma," *Le Monde*, 23 August 1962, 9.
210 – Jean Douchet, "La Cinémathèque: Temple, musée, et bourse," *ARTS* (3 May 1960).
210–212 – Raymond Rohauer, interview with G.M., 28 November 1980 and 17 February 1983.
212–213 – Robert Benayoun, quoted in Serge Daney, "Le Regard du muet," *Libération* (2 July 1982): 24.
213 – Gérard Legrand, "France-Culture," June 1980.
213–214 – H.L., minutes of Cinémathèque's General Assembly, 27 May 1963.
215–216 – Bernard Martinand, interview with G.M., Paris, 21 March 1983.
216–217 – Jean Rouch, "Nuits magnétiques," "France-Culture," June 1980.
217 – André Rieupeyrout, interview with G.M., Paris, 2 January 1985.
218–219 – Borde, letter to H.L., 1964; H.L., letter to Borde, 1964.
220 – H.L., "Mise à mort des films," *Nouvel observateur* (22 April 1965).
220 – Georges Sadoul, "Le Cinéma, patrimoine culturel: Faut-il conserver ou détruire les anciens films inflammables?" *Le Monde*, 15 November 1966.

220–221 – Jean-Luc Godard, *Nouvel observateur* (12 January 1966).
221–222 – Françoise Jaubert, interview with G.M., 30 September 1980; Martinand, interview with G.M., 21 March 1983.
222 – Johnson's request reported by Jean Riboud to G.M. on 26 March 1980.
223 – *Dossier l'affaire Langlois*, no. 3 (18 May l968).
223 – Godard, *Nouvel observateur* (12 January 1966).
224–225 – H.L., report to board of directors, 1967.
226–227 – Cinémato, "La Déplorable gestion de la Cinémathèque Française," *Le Journal du parlement* (18 January 1962). In French legal proceedings, a person or group that cannot be called by name because that name is as yet unknown or for other reasons cannot be revealed, is designated X.
234 – François Truffaut, interview with G.M., 14 May 1979.
234–235 – Jean Riboud, interview with G.M., Paris, 26 March 1980.

## CHAPTER 11

pp.
236 – H.L., interview with G.M. and J.M., 19 March 1976.
236 – François Truffaut, interview with G.M., 18 September 1979.
237–238 – Cinémathèque Française board of directors' minutes, 9 February 1968.
238–239 – Marie Epstein, *Films et documents* (October–December 1980); interview with G.M., Paris, 3 January 1981.
240–241 – Alexandre Astruc, *Le Monde*, 10–11 February 1968.
243 – Jean-Louis Comolli, *Cahiers du cinéma* (March 1968).
244 – Ibid.
245 – Ibid.
246 – *Le Monde*, 16 February 1968.
247 – Press conference, published in *Cahiers du cinéma* (March 1968).
252 – Paul Balta, *Paris-Presse*, 24 February 1968.
254 – Raymond Borde, *Le Monde*, 4 March 1968.
256 – Yvonne Dornès, interview with G.M., 22 May 1979.
256 – Serge Losique, interview with G.M., Paris, 21 June 1985.
259 – *Le Figaro* (19 March 1968).
260 – *France-Soir* (19 March 1968).
262 – Françoise Giroud, "L'Affaire Langlois continue," *L'Express*, 25–31 March 1968, 89.
262–263 – François Truffaut, interview with G.M., 18 September 1979. In early April, the Cinémathèque's assistant Secretary-General, José Lichtig, traveled to Nancy with Pierre Kast and François Truffaut in order to convince the Federation Française des Ciné-Clubs—then holding its annual general assembly meeting, attended by representatives of hundreds of ciné-clubs in France—that they should support Langlois. Despite its previous difficulties with Langlois, and a tendency to support Barbin, the Federation was won over by the trio's arguments and issued a statement in favor of Langlois's return as director.
263 – *Le Figaro*, 19 April 1968.
264–266 – Cinémathèque Française board of directors' report, 22 April 1968.

266 – Jean Rouch, *Le Roman de François Truffaut*, special issue *Cahiers du cinéma* (December 1984): 126.

266 – Stendhal telegram, *Le Canard enchaîné* (21 February 1968).

267 – Jean Grundler, quoted in Alain Remond, "Parano à Chaillot: Le Roman de la Cinémathèque," *Les Nouvelles littéraires* (10–17 September 1981).

267–268 – *Le Monde*, 4 May 1968; *Rivarol*, 9 May; *L'Aurore*, 3 May 1968.


## CHAPTER 12

pp.

269 – H.L., ZOOM (June–July 1974): 88.

270 – H.L., "Etoiles et toiles," TV broadcast, 17 February 1986.

270–271 – Serge Losique, interview with G.M., Paris, 21 June 1985.

271 – H.L., *Lumière*, film by Eric Rohmer (1968).

272 – H.L., ZOOM (June–July 1974): 88.

272 – Losique, interview with G.M., Paris, 21 June 1985.

272–273 – H.L., *Sight and Sound* (Autumn 1972): 185.

273 – H.L., *Le Monde*, 15 June 1972.

273–275 – Losique, interview with G.M., 2 November 1985.

276 – Martin Levine, "The Legendary Langlois," *Washington Post*, 29 January 1969; Constance Holden, "A Turbulent and Living Tapestry," *Evening Star*, 29 January 1969.

276–277 – Sheldon Renan, *Film Comment* (March–April 1977).

277 – Abel Gance, "Un Coeur qui s'appelle Langlois," *Le Monde*, 21 February 1968.

277–278 – Tom Johnston, interview with G.M., Paris, 21 March 1985.

278–279 – Jean Riboud, interview with G.M., 26 March 1980.

279 – Vincent Canby, "Who Is the Films' Greatest Lover? Henri Langlois!" *New York Times*, 26 July 1970.

280 – Johnston, interview with G.M., 21 March 1985.

280 – Eugene Stavis, interview with G.M., 18 February 1983.

280 – Rohauer, interview with G.M., 17 February 1983.

281–282 – Johnston, interview with G.M., 21 March 1985.

282 – "Une Chaire de cinéma à Nanterre pour Langlois," *L'Aurore*, 10 July 1969.

282–283 – H.L., ZOOM (June–July 1974): 87.

283 – Philippe Garrel, "Dialogue en Apesanteur: Philippe Garrel rencontre Leos Carax," *Cahiers du cinéma* (November 1984): 39–40.

283 – Volker Schlöndorff, interview with G.M., 13 April 1983.

284 – Werner Schroeter, interview with G.M., Paris, 8 December 1985.


## CHAPTER 13

pp.

285 – Marx Brothers, quoted Louis Pauwels and Jacques Bergier, *Le Matin des magiciens* (1960), 25.

286 – J. H. Watkins, "Lion at Bay," *American West* (January 1971): 59; "Everything's on the Block," *Life* (22 May 1970), 42–48, and "Hollywood: Dreams for Sale" (4 May 1970): 36.

286–288 – Curtis Harrington, interview with G.M., Los Angeles, 2 June 1982.

288 – Kenneth Anger, interview with G.M., New York, 3 December 1980.

289 – Sol Lesser, quoted in Lotte Eisner, *Films et documents* (October–December 1980).

289 – Lotte Eisner, "Avant-propos," *Catalogue du Musée du Cinéma-Henri Langlois* (1984).

290 – Lotte Eisner, *Films et documents* (October–December 1980).

291 – H.L., quoted in Colette Godard, *Le Monde*, 15 June 1972.

291–292 – Yvonne Baby, "Un Voyage initiatique," *Le Monde*, 12 June 1972.

292 – Guy Teisseire, *L'Aurore*, 31 December 1970.

292–293 – H.L., "La Passion selon H.L.," quoted in Colette Godard, *Le Monde*, 12 June 1972.

294 – H.L., interview with J.M. and G.M., "Vidéo in Paris."

294–295 – H.L., *Sight and Sound* (Autumn 1972): 185.

295–296 – H.L., quoted by Lotte Eisner in interview with G.M., 24 April 1979.

296 – François Truffaut, interview with G.M., 14 May 1979.

296 – H.L., *Le Monde*, 19 February 1976.

297 – Jean Riboud, interview with G.M., 26 March 1980.

297 – Jacques Duhamel, interview with Georges Langlois, June 1972.

## CHAPTER 14

pp.

298 – "D.C.D.," H.L., letter to Lotte Eisner, 1 September 1956.

298–299 – Nicole Zand, "Un Nouveau héros américain," *Le Monde*, 2 November 1972.

299 – Eugene Stavis, interview with G.M., New York 24 November 1980.

299 – Mel Gussow, "Cinémathèque Planned uunder the Queensboro," and Ada Louise Huxtable, "Architecturally, a Promise in Use of 'Found Space,'" *New York Times*, 13 April 1973, 41.

300 – Johnston, interview with G.M., Paris, 21 March 1985.

300 – Rohauer, interview with G.M., 28 November 1980.

302 – Marie Epstein, interview with G.M., 3 January 1981.

302 – Michel Delain, *L'Express*, 11 March 1974; Jacques Siclier, "La Folle journée de la Cinémathèque," *Le Monde*, 5 March 1974.

302–303 – Gloria Swanson, *Cinéma 74* (May 1974): 86.

303–304 – Jack Valenti, letter to G.M., 7 January 1981, with transcript of seventy-fourth Academy Award presentation, 1974.

304 – H.L., "Etoiles et toiles," 17 February 1986.

304 – Eugene Stavis, interview with G.M., 29 November 1980.

304–305 – François Truffaut, interview with G.M., 18 September 1979.

305–306 – André Rieupeyrout, interview with G.M., 2 January 1985.

306 – Jack Moseley, interview with G.M., 4 May 1984.

308 – H.L., quoted by J.M., 4 May 1984.

309 – François Truffaut, interview with G.M., 18 September 1979.

309–310 – Serge Toubiana, "Entretien avec Tom Luddy," translated into French by Françoise Gloriod, *Cahiers du cinéma* (December 1978): 27 (translated back into English by Lisa Nesselson).

310 – J.M., interview with G.M., 4 May 1984.

311–312 – Riboud, interview with G.M., 26 March 1980.

314–315 – Lotte Eisner, interview with G.M., 24 April 1979.

318 – Abel Gance, *Le Monde*, 21 February 1968.

318 – Guy Teisseire, "Cher Henri Langlois," *L'Aurore*, 14 January 1977.

318 – Serge Losique, interview with Georges Langlois and G.M., 3 November 1985.

# EPILOGUE

pp.

320–321 – *Le Figaro*, 4 August 1980.

321 – Hubert Astier, interview with G.M., Paris, 3 January 1980.

321 – The Cinémathèque published catalogs of restored prints in 1986, 1987, 1988, and 1989, describing more than 400 of the Cinémathèque's films on deposit.

André Antoine's *L'Hirondelle et la mésange* is an exemplary case of restoration work. In 1920 Antoine shot the footage that would, 63 years later, become the dark yet lilting tale of a family smuggling jewels from Belgium to France. Antoine's work print was rejected at the time by the Pathé Company, whose employee in charge of distribution claimed it looked like newsreel footage of life on a barge. Antoine was forced to drop the project for lack of financing. The never-edited original negative—six hours of rushes—was discovered in the vaults of the Cinémathèque Française in 1982 and expertly assembled, according to Antoine's original script, by contemporary film editor and director Henri Colpi. Shot in 35-millimeter at 18 frames per second, with color-tinted scenes, it is a beautiful film and a unique restoration. Raymond Alessandrini composed an original score for the film, based in part on three musical themes by Maurice Jaubert. *L'Hirondelle et la mésange* is the missing masterwork in Antoine's careeer as a naturalistic filmmaker after revolutionizing French theater.

In 1993 Claudine Kaufmann and her crew discovered a print of G. W. Pabst's 1949 film *Geheimnisvolle Tiefe*. No other film archive had a print or the negative. The German film, found under the French title *Eternel mystère*, with French subtitles, was released in Alsace after World War II. Kaufmann and her staff also found Frank Capra's long-lost early silent film *The Matinee Idol* and four hours of rushes for Jean Renoir's *Partie de campagne*. All the Cinémathèque's nitrate prints are stored at the Archives du film in Bois d'Arcy. Close to 250 films per year are transferred and restored, but thousands of films still remain. Even if 15,000 titles remained in the Cinémathèque's catalog, at 250 films per year, that would take 60 *years*. Fortunately, not all of these films need restoration.

Some 2,000 new feature-length prints (720 titles) and short films (814) were deposited at the Cinémathèque in 1993. Sometimes 20 to 30 prints of the same film are donated after its commercial career is over. Bernard Martinand, the former Cinémathèque programmer, has successfully spent the last few years as director of acquisitions, persuading many film producers, especially American companies, to deposit films at the Cinémathèque.

322 – Françoise Jaubert, interview with G.M., Paris, 20 February 1981.

323 – Yilmaz Guney, interview with G.M., Paris, 30 August 1982.

324 – Death knell of the cinema? Although there were fewer commercial movie theaters in Paris in 1994 than in 1986, when this book was first published in French, there were more specialized settings than ever before. In 1988 the city of Paris opened the Vidéothèque de Paris. Collecting as many moving images pertaining to Paris as it can, the Vidéothèque sports three movie theaters that screen films six days a week, plus 30 easy-access TV monitor consoles with remote-robot-controlled videocassette players rapidly feeding one's choice of more than 5,000 films. Plans are in the works to connect homes by cable or satellite, permitting the use of home computers to call up a film instead of renting a cassette or seeing a film projection.

The Musée d'Orsay has a specialized film section that, since 1990, has programmed interesting retrospectives, mostly thematically centered on silent film artists. The Louvre also created special film-screening events, and the Pompidou Center has continued to show retrospectives in the Garance Theater on the main floor, in addition to having reopened the Cinémathèque's former fifth-floor screening room. In the city of Paris, close to 200 screens have been lost in seven years, but some 350 screens remain, so that Paris can still proudly claim to be the film-viewing capital of the world. And the Cinémathèque, despite all its problems, has remained an integral part of that world.

# AFTERWORD

pp.

325 – Jack Lang's plan for the Palais de l'Image: The Ministry of Culture is also merging the individual libraries maintained by the CNC, FEMIS (Fondation d'enseignements des métiers de l'image et du son—formerly the IDHEC), and the Cinémathèque Française into another nonprofit organization called the Bibliothèque/Filmothèque (BiFi). The proposed easy-access film library, where the public will be able to conduct research via magazines, books, scripts, and films on videocassette or laser disc, was supposed to open in the Palais de Tokyo for the centennial celebration of cinema's invention in 1995, but construction delays will postpone its opening until at least the fall of 1996.

326 – Dominique Païni, interview with G.M., Paris, 31 March 1994.

The Cinémathèque's theater and entrance hall at Chaillot were completely renovated and reopened, after a year of construction, in June 1992. A new, built-from-scratch theater in the Palais de Tokyo opened in 1990 but, to make way for massive structural renovations to the Palais, closed in the summer of 1993 and will remain closed until at least 1996. The Cinémathèque has leased in the interim the screen of an art house at the place de la République. Major retrospectives of films by Satyajit Ray, Frank Borzage, and Sacha Guitry, to name a few, have drawn sell-out crowds.

The "College of Cinematographic Art History" lecture series began in 1992, and these weekly colloquiums, programmed by film professor Jacques Aumont, have proved so successful that the classes have been obliged to shift from the 90-seat screening room named for Lotte Eisner to the main theater at Chaillot, which holds close to 400. Each week a different aspect of film history is explored by a guest lecturer, accompanied by excerpts from films. Attended by film students and professionals, the series, like the Louvre art lecture series, is open to the general public.

328 – There have been some thefts from the Henri Langlois Museum, but considering the total absence of guards and security measures, surprisingly few. Buster Keaton's hat was stolen from the museum in 1984. Shortly thereafter, a cryptic letter arrived at the Cinémathèque from a person who claimed he stole the hat hoping it would bring him good fortune as an actor and mime. He promised to return the hat if and when he succeeded. On 1 September 1993, I received a strange phone call at the Cinémathèque from a young man who wanted to know whether we still had Keaton's hat and whether we wanted the hat back. I said no, keep it (just kidding), and asked for his name and address. That didn't work, but the caller said he'd mail it to the Cinémathèque. We're still waiting. . . .

No such hope exists for the *Metropolis* poster, once situated behind the *Metropolis* robot replica, nor for the *Cabinet of Dr. Caligari* poster near the famous set from the same film. The *Metropolis* poster, if sold for its estimated worth of $200,000, could have financed the restoration of part of the museum or saved several dozen films. These were unique posters in excellent condition. Like closing the proverbial barn door after the horse has left, guards have been placed in the museum as of March 1993.

329 – Hubert Astier, quoted in Jean-Michel Frodon, "Images et mirages: La Transformation du Palais de Tokyo," *Le Monde*, 2 April 1994, 14. Astier used the word *translater*, which does not exist in the French language. *Translation* is the closest term, and he seems to mean that the museum will be transferred with as much respect as possible for Langlois's *scénographie* (design).

332 – H.L., quoted in David Overbey, "The Death of Henri Langlois and the Cinémathèque," *Paris Métro* (2 February 1977): 10–11.

# INDEX

# THE AUTHORS AND TRANSLATOR

Glenn Myrent, born in 1954 in Chicago, is a graduate of Northwestern University's radio, television, and film department. He worked as a production assistant, cameraman, and, finally, director of industrial films for Standard Oil of Indiana in Chicago before moving to France in 1978. He wrote and designed the catalog for the Henri Langlois Museum and has published articles on film in the *New York Times*, *Variety*, and the *International Herald-Tribune*. In addition to his 11 years as a full-time lecturer in Langlois's museum, he has toured American universities and cultural centers annually since 1987, presenting films restored by the Cinémathèque Française. He is presently writing a book on the Lumière brothers and their cameramen and teaches film history for Southern Methodist University in Paris.

Georges Langlois, Henri's younger brother, was born in Smyrna, Turkey, in 1920 and was the privileged spectator of his brother's childhood and adolescence. A participant in the Cercle du Cinéma and a firsthand observer of the birth of the Cinémathèque Française in 1936, Georges also helped Henri during the German occupation of France. A member of the French Resistance and an officer in the French Légion d'honneur, Georges Langlois ran a law practice in Paris for 50 years. He was elected to the Cinémathèque Française's board of directors, a post he held for 15 years, often handling legal matters for his brother and the Cinémathèque. He died in 1993.

Born in Cincinnati in 1956, Lisa Nesselson is *Variety*'s film critic in Paris, a post she has held since 1991. A graduate of Northwestern University's radio, television, and film department, she lent her voice to the commercial for Cartier's "Le Must" perfume and has written and anchored broadcasts for RFI (Radio France Internationale) and Radio Nova (Paris). Her previous book-length translations from French into English include biographies of Clint Eastwood and Simone de Beauvoir. Her feature writings on film have appeared in the *International Herald-Tribune*, *Harper's Bazaar*, and *Theater Crafts International*. She has sung professionally since the age of 15 and has performed her original comic songs in San Francisco, Chicago, and Paris.

Nosferatu, Glenn Myrent, Georges P. Langlois, at the Cinémathèque Française. © *Hugues Langlois*